# Jazz History Overview

Second Edition

Gordon Vernick

Geoffrey Haydon

*Georgia State University*

KENDALL/HUNT PUBLISHING COMPANY
4050 Westmark Drive Dubuque, Iowa 52002

Cover image © Liquid Library.



ISBN: 978-0-7575-3864-3



Printed in the United States of America
10 9 8 7 6 5 4 3 2 1

# CONTENTS

*About the Authors* v

1 **A Discussion of Jazz** 1

2 **Elements of Music** 7

3 **African Roots** 15

4 **African-American Music** 21

5 **New Orleans' Musical Tradition** 31

6 **"Harlem" Stride Piano** 43

7 **Two Great Soloists** 49

8 **Chicago** 57

9 **Early Big Band Swing** 61

10 **Duke Ellington** 67

11 **Kansas City, Bennie Moten, and Count Basie** 77

12 **The Swing Era, 1935 to 1945** 83

13 **The Decline of Big Band Swing and Rise of Bebop** 99

**14 Cool Style** 115

**15 Hard Bop** 129

**16 Jazz Singers** 143

**17 Miles Davis** 151

**18 Free Jazz** 161

**19 Bill Evans** 169

**20 John Coltrane** 173

**21 (Jazz-Rock) Fusion** 179

**22 The Future of Jazz** 191

*Bibliography* 199

*Index* 203

*Jazz History Overview Listening List* 219

# ABOUT THE AUTHORS

**Dr. Gordon Vernick** is an Associate Professor of Music and Coordinator of Jazz Studies at Georgia State University. He holds a Bachelor of Music from Ithaca College, Ithaca, NY; a Master of Music in Education from the University of Miami, and a Doctor of Arts in Trumpet Performance and Jazz Pedagogy from the University of Northern Colorado, Greeley.

As a professional trumpet player, he has performed in all musical mediums from symphony orchestra to jazz quartet and has freelanced in Miami, New York, Denver, Kansas City, and the Caribbean Islands. He is currently active in the Southeast United States as a clinician, an adjudicator, and as a freelance trumpet player.

As a jazz educator he is the past president of the Georgia Association of Jazz Educators, past chair of the International Association of Jazz Educators ***Curriculum Committee*** and was recently appointed as the Southeast Coordinator of that organization. He was the Director of the NARAS Georgia Grammy High School Jazz Band from 1994 to 1999. He is the co-editor of the book ***Teaching Jazz: A Course Of Study,*** published by MENC. He recently cowrote the college textbook, ***Jazz History Overview,*** published by Kendall-Hunt which has been adopted by numerous universities around the country.

He is director of the GSU Faculty Jazztet which performs regularly in Atlanta area schools and has appeared at the Atlanta Jazz Festival, the Brasstown Music Festival, Oxford University Music Series and many other venues in the southeast. He has performed with such world-renown jazz artists as Kenny Werner, Clare Fischer, John Hart, Kevin Hays, Conrad Herwig, Marc Copland, Randy Brecker, Paul McCandless, and many others. The Jazztet was twice invited to perform in San Jose, Costa Rica by the Centro Cultural Costarricense-Norteamericano. During the summer of 2001 the Jazztet performed in Moscow, Russia at the ***Tribute to Willis Conover Jazz Festival*** and in March 2003 performed at Capitol University in Beijing, China. The group was invited to perform in November 2004 at the Curso e Colegio Bardal in Florianopolis, Brazil. As a jazz clinician he served a residency at the Conservatory of San Juan, P.R. and the Taipei American School in Taiwan, and the Singapore American School this past March.

**Dr. Geoffrey Haydon** has successfully bridged both classical and jazz styles of performance. He has developed an impressive reputation as someone with a high level of expertise using technology in the areas of performance, composition, arranging, and pedagogy. Currently Dr. Haydon coordinates the piano faculty at Georgia State University where he teaches piano, piano literature, jazz history, and jazz theory. Known as a classical and jazz soloist, he is also a member of the Haydon/Parker Duo, and the Georgia State University Faculty Jazztet. He has given performances throughout the USA, in Europe, Russia, China, Japan, South America, and Central America with well-known jazz artists such as Eddie Daniels, Joe Henderson, Bill Watrous, Marvin Stamm, Nick Brignola, Randy Brecker, Indugu Chancler, Conrad Herwig, and Hal Crook. Dr. Haydon regularly performs with the Atlanta Ballet Orchestra and has performed with touring shows including The Phantom of the Opera, The King and I, The Producers, Hairspray, Sister Act, and Grease. In addition, Dr. Haydon is in demand as a clinician and adjudicator. He has numerous publications with Alfred Publishing, Warner Bros., Stipes Publishing and is co-author of Jazz History Overview, a textbook by Kendall Hunt Publishing. Dr. Haydon can be heard on Cabin Fever, a jazz CD by the McLean-Haydon Jazz Quartet, and My Foolish Heart, a jazz piano/vibraphone CD by the Haydon/Parker Duo. Both CD's are available on the ACA Digital label. Dr. Haydon received his Bachelor of Music degree from the University of Richmond and studied three summers at the Aspen Music Festival. He received his Master and Doctorate of Musical Arts degrees from the University of Texas at Austin.

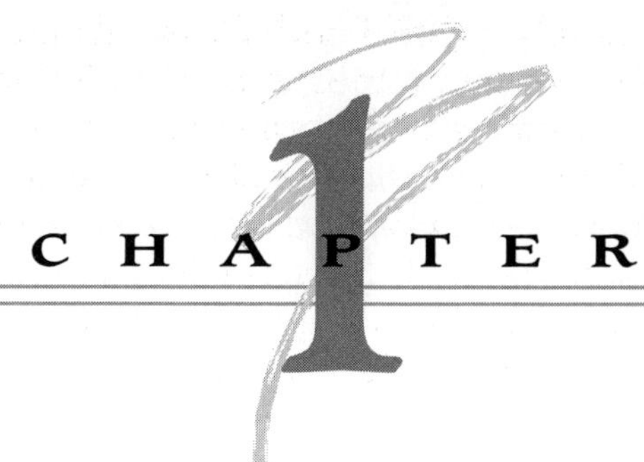

CHAPTER 1

# A Discussion of Jazz

- Jazz must be judged by separate, distinct standards and operates on two distinct aesthetic systems: African and European. Western music critics dealt effectively with the European aspects of jazz but often failed to grasp the African aesthetic.
- Music is comprised of sounds (notes) and rhythms assembled according to accepted cultural formulas for organizing these sounds. An example would be the music of nonwestern cultures containing sounds and rhythms organized in patterns or formulas that are unfamiliar to western ears. A small change in the musical/rhythmic formula could make the music sound more consonant or pleasant to ears not accustomed to such music. Music from different eras, genres, and cultures all have specific formulas. Music is constantly changing; consequently the formulas are also changing. Music tends to change from one generation to the next. Today changes *seem* to occur at a near blinding rate.
- Jazz from the early 1920s sounds vastly different from jazz of the mid 1940s, yet both are still jazz. How can one define something that is constantly changing, and still refer to it as the same thing? This paradox is one of the most confusing aspects of music and especially jazz.
- Jazz is a way to play music and has its own unique formula for organizing its sound. Country Western music has its own system of sound organization as does heavy metal and rap music. One is not necessarily better than another; just different. The way our ears are acclimated to certain sounds makes it easier or more difficult to understand different types of music.

- Jazz is the original **fusion music.** Many descriptive titles of the genres of jazz have been assigned by writers, critics, or other nonmusicians. The musicians themselves were rarely concerned with a descriptive title such as *bop* or *hard bop*. In jazz, plagiarism is regarded as the most sincere form of flattery. Jazz musicians freely borrow music from many different sources:
  - Musicians they admire and wish to emulate
  - Genres, such as European classical music
  - Modern twentieth-century compositional techniques
  - Music of different ethnic cultures used in different combinations to find new means of expression
- Therefore, jazz originally fused the African music tradition with the European music tradition. Early examples of this fusion of music traditions evolved into African-American music of the eighteenth and nineteenth centuries. Unfortunately no recordings exist, and existing reliable accounts of what the music sounded like are rare. The accounts were written by mostly white amateur musicians who did not understand what was technically occurring, but they were able to describe some of what they were hearing, such as the off-key pitches and the lazy manner in which the melodies were sung. Both of these observations refer to blue notes and the manner in which the melodies were sung or played slightly behind the beat.
- One of the most important aspects of jazz post-1900 is that it involves constant change. Once a style gains wide acceptance and commercialization, the musicians move on to something else. Jazz musicians are not concerned with being categorized as a *swing* or *cool* player. Although one might describe Chet Baker as the epitome of the cool style, he sometimes recorded with hard bop players. Baker was not thinking about a particular stylistic label, but rather he was interested in self-expression through his music.
- Jazz is associated with the release of social/urban tension. It is an expression of true feelings, especially in its simpler early forms. Changes in jazz have mirrored sociological and technological changes in the United States. Some technological advances that played a major role in the music of the twentieth century include the following:
  - Radio
  - Electric microphone (improved quality of sound recordings)
  - Advances in recording techniques
  - Development of tape recording
  - Stereo recording
  - Change of recording format (ten inch, 78-rpm disc; twelve-inch 33.3-LP disc; cassette tape; compact disc; MP3; and so on)
  - Multitrack recording
- Jazz can be reflective of the social climate of the time:
  - The carefree, lighthearted mood of New Orleans jazz reflects the libertarian spirit of the city.
  - Chicago-style jazz reflects the lucrative yet dangerous aura of that city during a time when gangsters and crooked politicians were in charge.

♪ The big-band swing style reflects a young generation of Americans who were feeling the effects of the Depression slowly dissipate.

- People may not be aware that **the jazz quality of a piece is determined by the manner in which it is played**—the title determines nothing.

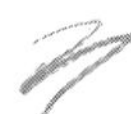

## MUSIC IN GENERAL: THE AESTHETIC EXPERIENCE

- Music is sound organized in some structural way to express feeling that cannot be expressed by any other means. It is almost always designed to elicit an emotional response and to provide listeners with an aesthetic experience. An aesthetic experience occurs when sounds are heard; then perhaps they are judged as beautiful, ugly, intriguing, and so on. A human emotion is then evoked in a manner that defies verbal explanation using any method of factual description.
- The slow progress in jazz analysis and research was probably due chiefly to the confusion of jazz with commercial popular music. Also, high-quality critical writings and research in jazz did not appear until the late 1950s. Earlier writings, while important, have significant limitations. Before the 1950s, jazz was not considered by scholars to be a serious art form worthy of study and research. Some European writers (Goffin, Delauney, Panassie) addressed jazz in writing in the mid-1930s. They were able to describe it (although often incorrectly) and pronounced some early jazz musicians geniuses.
- The word *jazz* has a variety of meanings—people have different concepts of jazz, particularly from one generation to another. In the process of evolving a satisfactory definition of jazz, writers seem to only agree that jazz is music. No universal definition has been reached, perhaps because jazz has proven itself to be constantly in a state of change.
- In the 1920s jazz or jazz-flavored music fast became popular. Chiefly because of "Tin Pan Alley" songs, increased record sales, and the 1920s being dubbed the Jazz Age, the music quickly became the appropriate backdrop for later depictions of that era. By reading early accounts of jazz and its effect on people, one can also ascertain that it was very popular. Early accounts of the effect of jazz on people were either virulently negative or more sympathetically and objectively positive.
- Once swing, as a popular movement, surged forward and Americans learned that other nations saw jazz as a threat to their way of life, many began to see jazz as a symbol of their own freedom. There was increasing support for jazz as an American idiom.
- Critics began to recognize the need for emphasizing proper jazz analysis and evaluation while de-emphasizing the social importance of jazz—apparently attempts to tie jazz in with sociology became less and less rewarding—until the 1960s and 1970s when jazz, as a social issue, became more relevant.

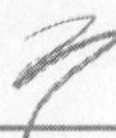

## DIFFERENCES BETWEEN JAZZ AND EUROPEAN MUSIC

- **Rhythm—**polyrhythms, an abundance of syncopation, and a tendency to place notes slightly behind the beat.
- **Harmony—**use of blue notes that cannot be notated according to the Western European harmonic system.
- European music is primarily based upon an accurate reproduction of the music from the page; it is a *composers' art,* and the performer is a secondary medium used to express the composer's wishes.
- Jazz is a performer's art because the performer utilizes improvisation and is therefore not expected to perform the music accurately as written on the page. In fact, performers are encouraged to use written music only as a guide, and they are free to change the original composer's conception to assert as much of their musical personality as possible.
- Jazz performers alter melody without necessarily obscuring beyond recognition its origins. However, jazz performers are also free to totally disregard the original melody (melodic variation versus free improvisation).
- Each jazz performance represents an event shaped by the understanding of each involved participant, including the audience who are also considered participants. There must be enough common understanding of the process for it to make sense. Sometimes in jazz, certain established conventions (rules) may be broken, but they must first be understood if this breaking is to make any sense—breaking a rule that no one knew as a rule in the first place is pointless.

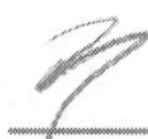

## SWING

- The term *swing* is often used to describe a particular aspect of jazz. Some experts consider the presence of swing to be necessary for the music to be defined as jazz. However, the definition of swing has always been vague and illusive. Even jazz musicians are hard-pressed to give an adequate response to inquiries about swing's true meaning. Louis Armstrong was once asked to define swing. His noncommittal reply was, "If you have to ask, you'll never know."
- *Swing* has at least two meanings:
  - ♪ The first is quite specific and is used as a shortened version referring to the big-band swing era in jazz history.
  - ♪ The second meaning is the elusive one just discussed. It refers to that easy quality of rhythmic propulsion that flows from relaxation and coordination of tempos within a jazz performance. Used as a noun, adjective, or verb, it still eludes clear definition. It is not only a rhythmic phenomenon, but it also involves experience; we experience swing, and for clarity we will think of it in these terms. If you find yourself wanting to move your body in some kind of way as a response to the music, then what you are hearing has a swinging feeling.

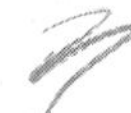 Some of the components of swing are easily observed, but others are very subtle. It can also be used to describe a mood. For example, "The joint was swinging" is sometimes used to describe an upbeat atmosphere.

## CHARACTERISTICS OF SWING

- Consistent tempo
- Melodies that are executed in the **swing eighth-note pattern** (pairs of eighth notes are arranged in long-short durations without altering the beat; the short note usually receives more emphasis—scat sing: doo-BA, doo-BA, etc.)
- Rhythmic lilt
- Animation or spirit
- Energy that makes a listener want to physically respond
- Use of syncopated rhythms
- Rhythms not placed directly on the beat, but slightly ahead or behind
- Cohesive group sound
- Tension and release
- Many different types of swing exhibited by different jazz artists and in different cultures

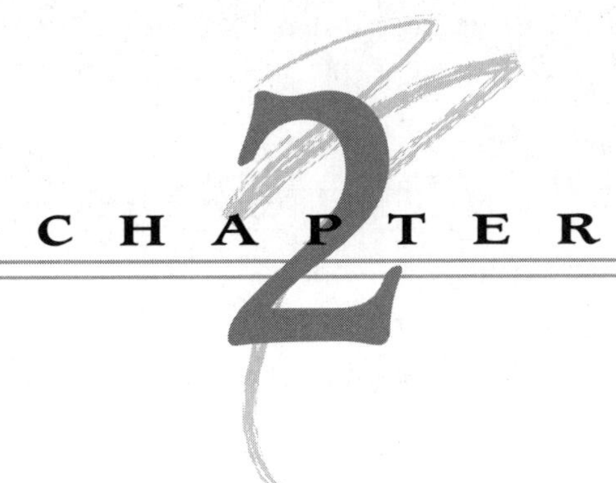


# Elements of Music

- **Melody**—a sequence of single notes arranged in time; generally what you sing is a melody. Music notation arranges melody notes horizontally from left to right. See example on page XX.
- **Scales**—a sequence of different notes arranged in ascending and/or descending order. Most Western European scales are seven different notes arranged a half or whole step apart. Most melodies are derived from scales; therefore they are the ABCs of **music**. See the following example:

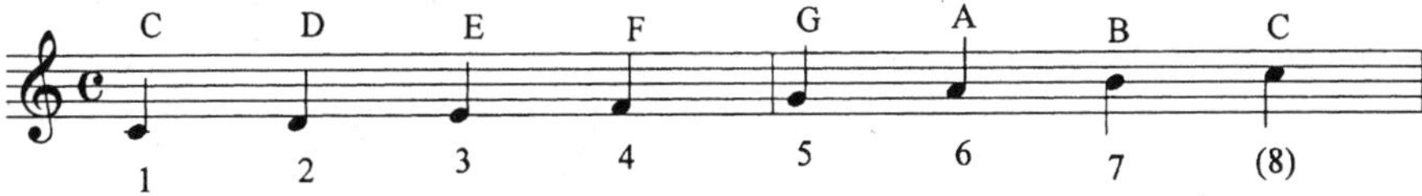


- **Harmony**—an arrangement of two or more notes that occur simultaneously. It is generally referred to as chords or harmonies; we are used to hearing the piano or guitar create two or more note sonorities. Music notation indicates chords (or harmonies) by stacking notes vertically. Most conventional chords are made up of the first, third, and fifth notes of a scale; thus each note in a chord can be referred to as the root (first note in the scale), third and fifth; and if the chord contains more than three notes (as is often the case in jazz), the designation can be expanded to include the seventh, ninth, eleventh, and thirteenth.

These harmonies are called seventh chords, ninth chords, and so on. See the following example:

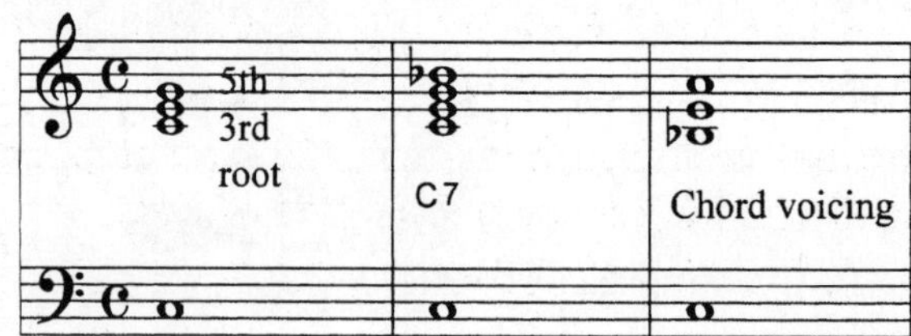


- **Voicing—**the way the notes of a chord are arranged on a piano, guitar, or perhaps in an ensemble of instrumentalists (see previous example). The way a chord is voiced contributes to its strength and timbre. For example, jazz pianists can often be distinguished one from another by their chord voicings.
- **Timbre—**the quality of sound. One's ability to discern the sound of a clarinet, trumpet, or violin would be based on one's ability to distinguish the timbre of these instruments. Each person's voice has a unique timbre, making it easily recognizable. Many significant jazz musicians have been sound innovators; they have become known for a specific unique timbre created on their instrument of choice.
- **Dynamics—**the intensity of sound. Generally, people perceive **music** to be soft (low intensity), loud (high intensity), or something in between. The change of intensity level is an important aspect of musical expression. In **music** notation, soft dzynamic levels are indicated with ***mp, p,*** or ***pp*** (for very soft) symbols, and progressively loud dynamic levels are indicated with ***mf, f,*** or ***ff*** symbols. Gradually building from soft to loud intensity levels is called a ***crescendo,*** and the opposite—gradually going from loud to soft intensity levels—is called a ***decrescendo.***
- **Rhythm—**events organized in time. In **music**, sounds are arranged to happen in a sequence at specific points in time. Rhythm encompasses beats, tempo, meter, and various time values assigned to events (notes or sounds).
- **Beat—**the basic pulse; usually your foot taps with the beat; often notated as quarter notes.
- **Tempo—**speed or rate at which beats occur; the rate at which your foot is tapping.
- **Meter—**arranging beats in groups of two (notated as 2/4), three (notated as 3/4), or four (notated as 4/4).
- **Measure—**also referred to as a **bar.** Each group of 4 beats in 4/4 time (also indicated with a C for common time), 3 beats in 3/4 time, or 2 beats in 2/4 time is arranged into one measure (bar) of **music.** In **music** notation, the measures are separated by bar lines, which explains why the term *bar* has come into common use. For example:

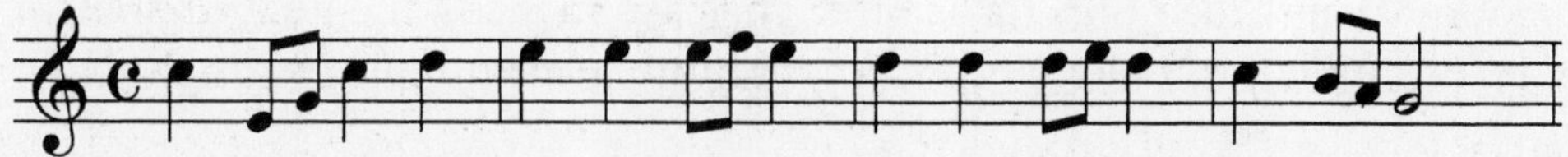

- **Syncopation—**intermittent events (notes) that happen between beats and/or sounds, which are stressed in unexpected ways.
- **Subdivision—**the division of each beat into equal or unequal parts. Music notation attempts to indicate beat subdivisions using whole, half, quarter, eighth, sixteenth, (and so on) notes.
- **Instrumentation—**the instruments used in a piece of **music.** Instruments can be grouped according to families:
  - ♪ **Brass—**trumpet, cornet, trombone, tuba, French horn, etc.

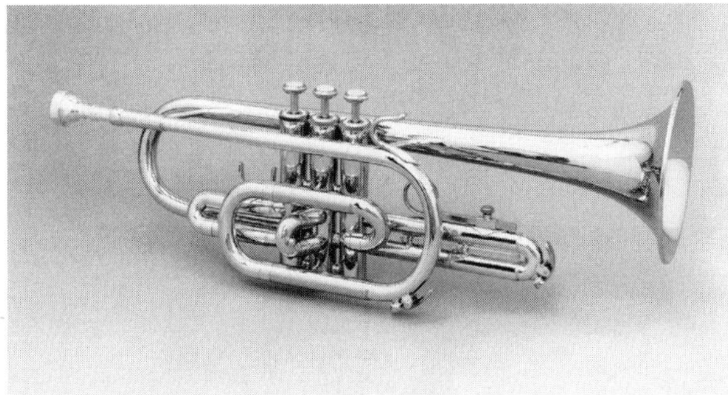

*Cornet. Courtesy of Vincent Bach division of the Selmer Company.*

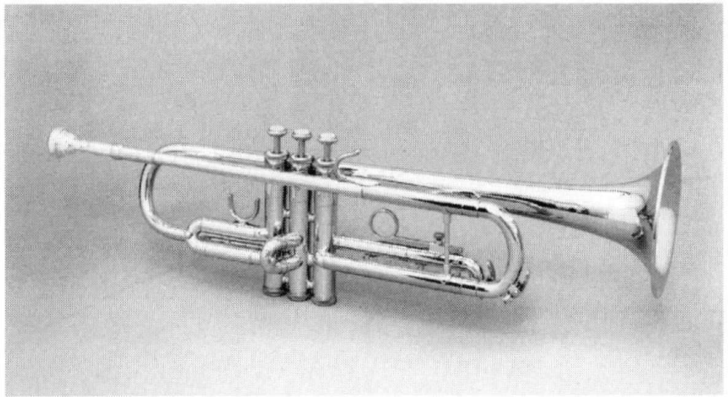

*Trumpet. Courtesy of Vincent Bach division of the Selmer Company.*

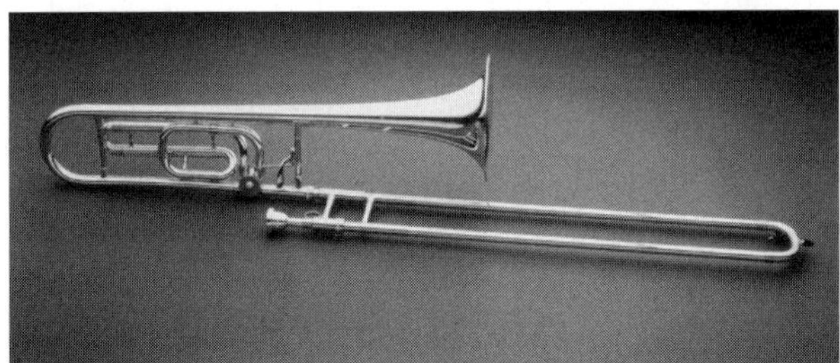

*Trombone. Courtesy of Vincent Bach division of the Selmer Company.*

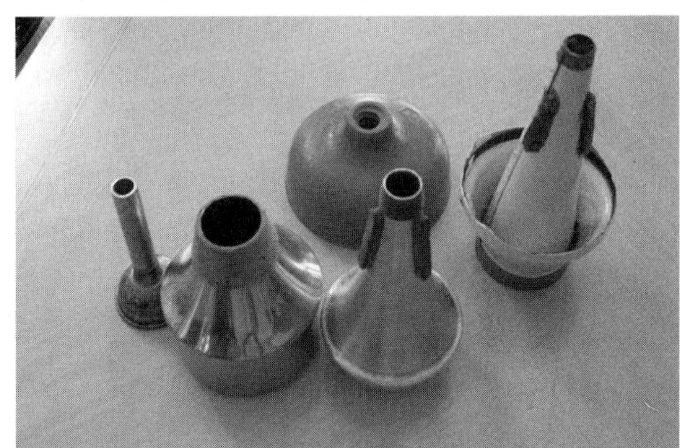

*Harmon stem and brass mutes. From left to right: Harmon, plunger, straight (metal), and cup.*

  - ♪ **Woodwind—**clarinet, flute, oboe, bassoon, and saxophone. There are several different kinds of saxophone ranging in size from small to large. The soprano, alto, tenor, and baritone saxophone are most commonly used in jazz. The tenor and alto are the most significant.

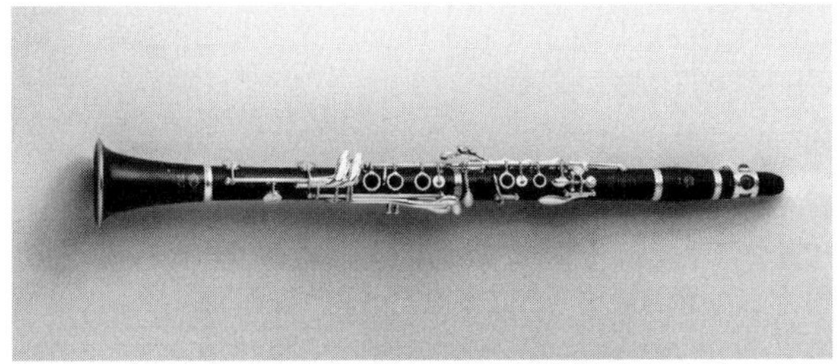

*Clarinet. Courtesy of the Selmer Company.*

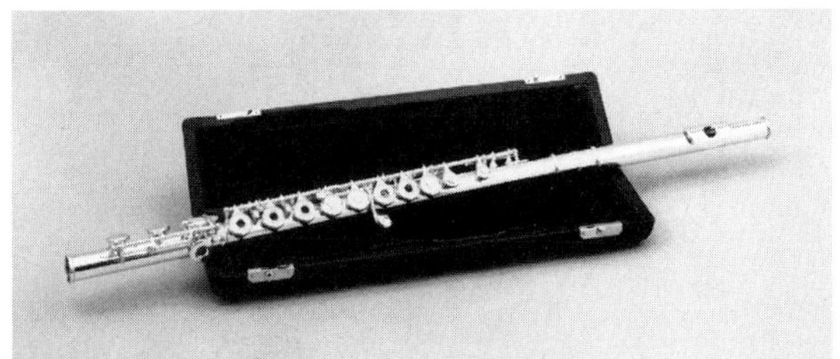

*Flute. Courtesy of the Selmer Company.*

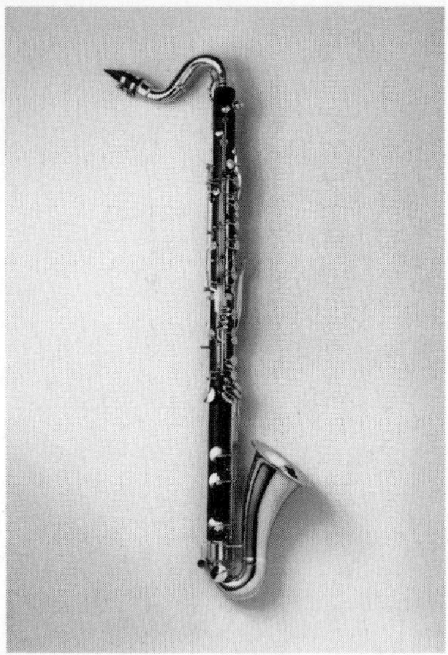

*Bass Clarinet. Courtesy of the Selmer Company.*

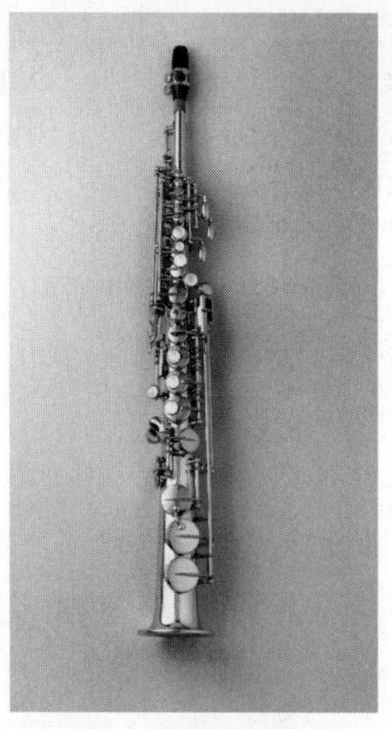

*Soprano Saxophone. Courtesy of the Selmer Company.*

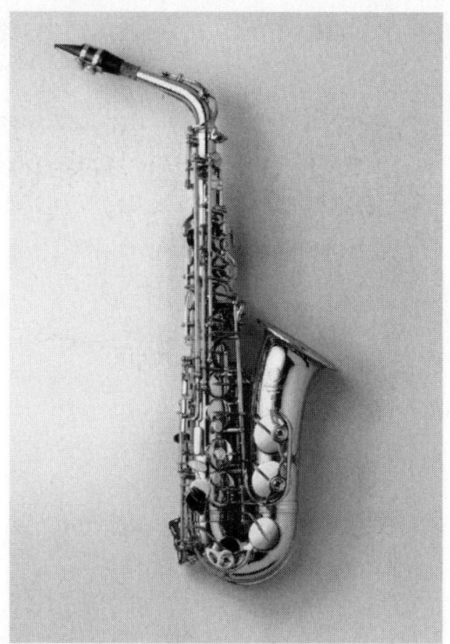

*Alto Saxophone. Courtesy of the Selmer Company.*

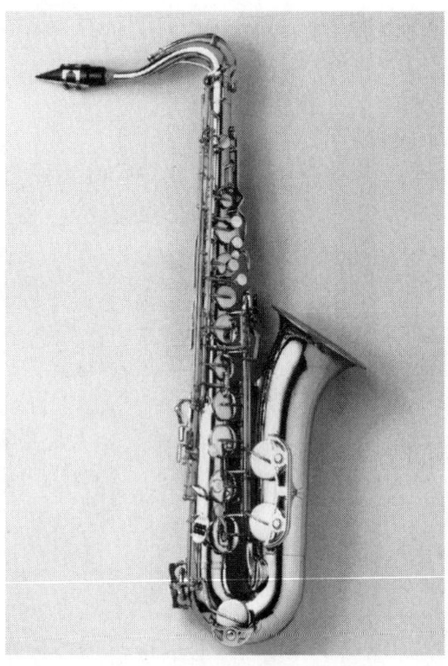

*Tenor Saxophone. Courtesy of the Selmer Company.*

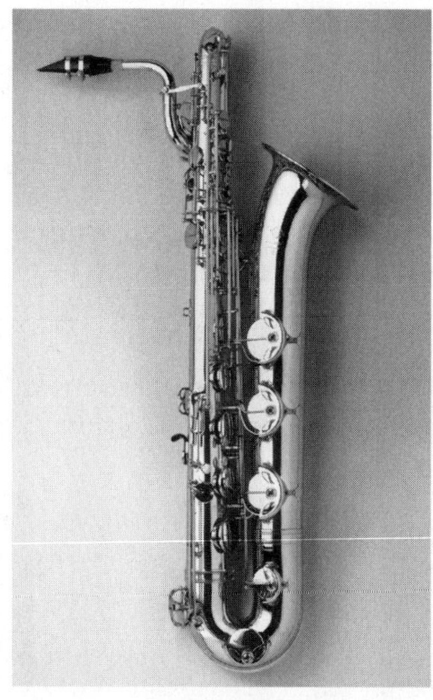

*Baritone Saxophone. Courtesy of the Selmer Company.*

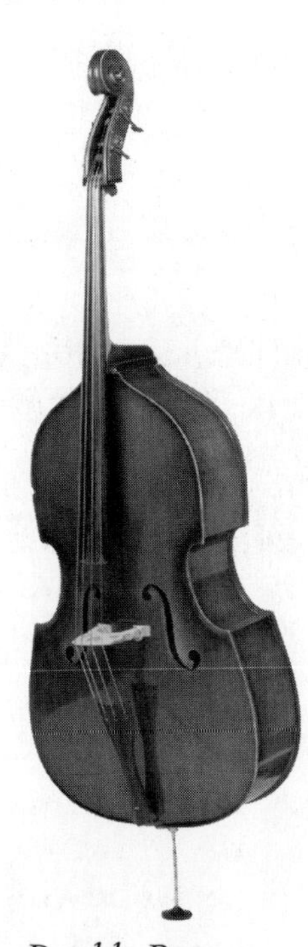

*Double Bass or Acoustic Bass.*

- **String**—violin, viola, cello, double bass (upright bass). The bass is the most important string instrument in jazz; however, there are important jazz violinists, and the cello and viola are sometimes found in jazz ensembles.
- **Percussion**—anything that is hit or struck to initiate the sound is considered a percussion instrument. Therefore, there are many possibilities; however, the most commonly found jazz percussion instruments include the drums, cymbals, congas, bongos, and the vibraphone.

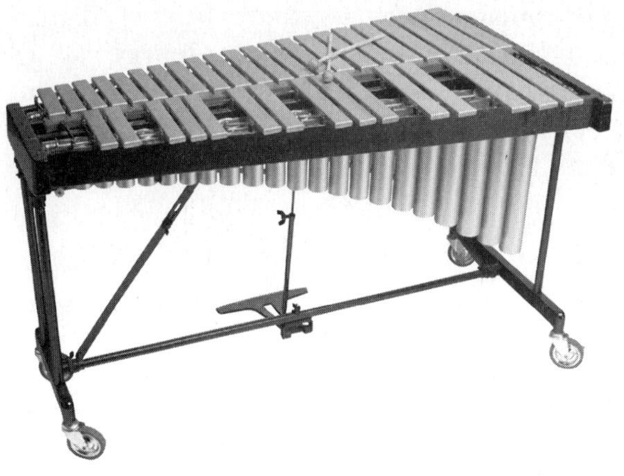

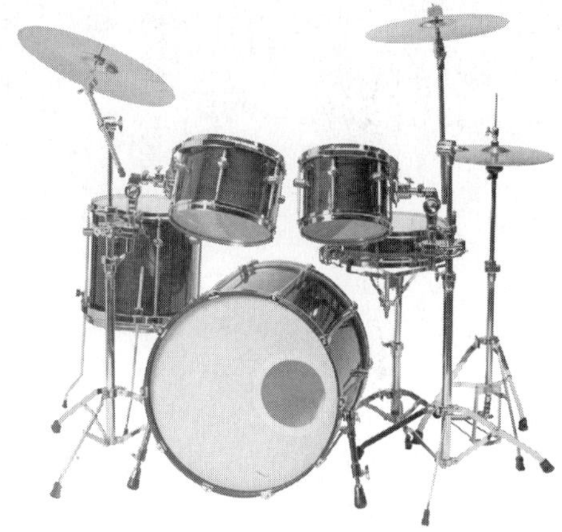

Before 1900, drums and cymbals were played by two or more players. The invention of the **trap set** of drums (later called **drum set**) made it possible for one player to play bass drum, snare drum, tom-tom drums, cymbals, and high hat cymbals.

- The piano and guitar belong to both the string and percussion families, since strings are generally struck to initiate sounds.

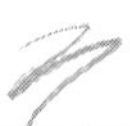

## THE JAZZ RHYTHM SECTION

The jazz rhythm section consists of piano, bass, drums, and guitar (optional). It is an essential core of any jazz ensemble, large or small. While any members can be omitted, it is unlikely they will all be absent. Even though each member has different functional roles, the rhythm section comes together to form a cohesive entity that defines the overall rhythmic feel of an ensemble. The following are contributions each rhythm section member makes to define the overall rhythmic feel:

- **Bass**—time keeper, plays bass notes at a consistent rate that outlines chords, creates rhythmic drive, helps to create rhythmic feel, in swing emphasizes beats two and four of each measure.
- **Piano**—provides harmonic framework by playing chords, improvises rhythms and chord voicings, and provides creative accompaniment for a soloist.
- **Guitar**—has the same function as the piano; therefore they are exchangeable. If both are present, then they must be sensitive to each other to provide one basic function and not duplicate each other's contribution.
- **Drums**—in conjunction with the bass, the drummer establishes the beat using the ride cymbal, high hat, snare, and/or bass drum. The drum set is also used to provide accents and color, and supplies excitement and drive. The drummer must know how to play many different styles and work closely with the bassist.
- **Form**—the content of any piece of **music** has one or more distinctive sections. Musicians usually label each section with a capital letter such as A (for the first section), B (for the second section), and so on. Many

jazz selections have sections that appear more than once; thus the form could be represented by repeating the letter. For example, George Gershwin's "I Got Rhythm" has the form AABA because the first section labeled A (eight bars long) happens twice; then a new section appears labeled B (also eight bars long and also called the bridge, since it connects the three A sections); then one more A section appears. Jazz musicians use their knowledge of a song's form to keep track of where they are while they are playing.

- **Chorus—**one complete revolution or cycle through a piece of **music** is called a **chorus.** Most of the time, jazz musicians cycle through a song more than once; in such a case, they would be playing more than one chorus. For example, four complete times through "I Got Rhythm" would be described as playing four choruses of "I Got Rhythm." Each chorus would probably have something different happen; yet everyone would still know that the selection being performed is "I Got Rhythm."

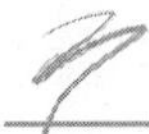

## JAZZ IMPROVISATION

- **Improvisation—**the spontaneous creation of something done in real time (at the moment). In the case of **music,** performers improvise by spontaneously creating **music** using a repository of ideas either arranged ahead of time or thought of at the moment.
- Improvisers spend time analyzing the output of other improvisers. Then they imitate such improvisers' output creating variations (emulation), eventually developing their own original ideas (innovation). Each era/style in jazz has its own distinctive musical idiosyncrasies. Improvising soloists make it a point to be knowledgeable about style; thus they are not completely free to spontaneously create anything. They are usually bound by stylistic criteria. See the following improvisational triangle.

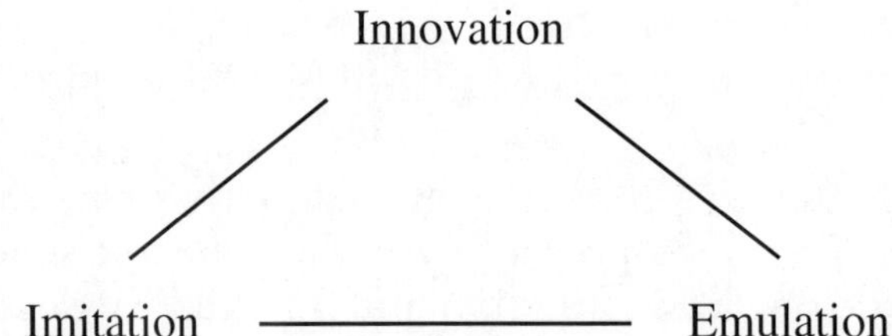


- Most improvisers remain at the imitate/emulate stage of development. It is the unique few who are able to reach the top of the pyramid where true innovation takes place. Some of the responsibilities of a good improviser include the following:
  - Know the musical language of the different jazz styles (e.g., Chicago, bebop, cool)
  - Remember chord progressions

- Listen to piano and/or bass for any variations on the given chord progression
- Create phrases compatible with the chord progression; stay within the harmonic structure
- Know and keep track of the form
- Respond to the supportive members of an ensemble
- Project sound and ideas in a convincing manner
- Possess an adequate technique; control intonation and tone quality
- Be familiar with "trading fours" where band members take turns improvising for four measures each through one or more choruses
- Create something original and perhaps personal
- Know introductions and endings to songs
- Possess the ability to discern harmony and melody on an advanced level
- Have the flexibility to react to band members

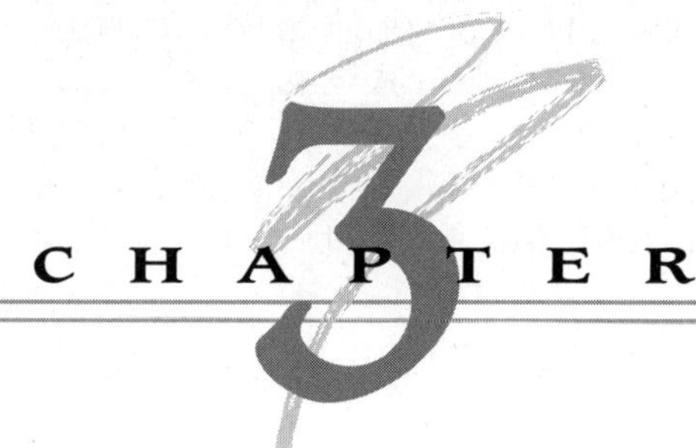

# CHAPTER 3

# African Roots

- The Africans of the seventeenth and eighteenth centuries were not likely to distinguish private life from public life. Events in the extended family or tribe were seen as group events. Birth, death, marriage, and reaching of puberty were seen as group matters.
- These Africans tended to receive musical training early in life as active participants rather than passive consumers. The music in West African culture was also strictly functional in nature; the concept "art" music did not exist. They began by imitating at an early age—the baby on its mother's back or a father standing over a child playing or singing a rhythm or melody.
- Music and dancing usually accompanied events. Music was also performed to inspire hunters or to pray for a bountiful harvest. Musical activity surrounded most secular (everyday events) as well as religious rituals. Each activity/ritual had its special songs and music.
- African music is endlessly varied; each type is appropriate to a certain activity. Work songs are important and constitute a large body of music. Each work song is rhythmically designed to accompany a specific task. Some songs are sung together, while others are sung in response to a leader.
- The drum dominates African instrumental music and comes in many sizes and variations. There are other percussive instruments such as bells, rattles, and shakers. Instruments on which melodies can be played are not sophisticated—mostly wooden flutes, animal tusks, homemade string instruments, and xylophones.

- African rhythm is complex and difficult for Europeans to understand. Cross-rhythm is central to African rhythm, which, put in simple terms, is the superimposition of duple over triple rhythms (two versus three). African music notably exhibits the simultaneous performance of several different rhythms; some of it is very slow and repetitive (dirge). Most of it is dependent upon the layering of several complicated rhythms. The central rhythm is usually established by the lead drummer, but can also be expressed by the rhythm of dancers or the clapping of hands.
- Once the central beat or rhythm is established, other different rhythms are superimposed atop the basic beat, creating a whirlwind of activity. The rhythms are performed by other drummers, dancers, vocalists, or instrumentalists according to specific formulas for the particular piece being performed. It creates a complex texture of polyrhythm that continually shifts with unending variations.
- The difficulty lies in keeping the parts independent. Some of the rhythms are only slightly different, while others completely different. They may be repeated for a long period of time until the master drummer or dancer directs a change to a different set of rhythms. The rhythmic patterns are based upon specific formulas that have been handed down for generations by rote. Much West African music defies analysis by European standards because of its rhythmic complexity.
- A coarse-sounding vocal timbre is common to African singing. African vocalists do not strive for purity of tone as singers in the European style. Africans are not so concerned with exactness of pitch. They will often slide between pitches. They will use a variety of techniques for thickening the tone. Modern blues singers use the same techniques when they growl or use a raspy sound when singing. This appears in jazz in the form of instrumental sounds that do not conform to European "standards"—evoking a more individual sound. It is also known as **tonal manipulation.**
- The existence of group participation in African music is one of its most important aspects. In jazz, rock, and gospel styles there has always been group participation in the form of singing, verbal exclamations, clapping, and dancing. This kind of group participation makes the audience a contributing member of the overall product before, during, and after a composition is performed. There is much more audience involvement in West African music, in stark contrast to Western European "art" music.

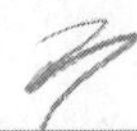

## PITCH INFLECTION—BLUE NOTES

- The melodic scales used by West Africans vary in range and number of notes from tribe to tribe. Many West African musical scales are based on pentatonic, or five-note, scales. They are commonly found in many different cultures. The fourth and seventh scale degrees are generally omitted, thus alleviating any half-step relationships. When slaves included these pitches in their work songs, they fell midway between the natural and flatted third, and it was the same with the flatted and natural seventh. The avoidance of the half steps in the scale came to be known as "blue notes."

- A characteristic of the field holler and the blues is the constant use of pitch bending also known as **pitch inflection.** As an integral part of the blues, most bending took place on the third and seventh scale degrees, as these tones did not exist in the African pentatonic scale. Originally vocally conceived, pitch inflection eventually came to be used by early jazz musicians.

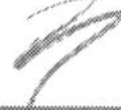

## IMPORTANT CHARACTERISTICS OF AFRICAN MUSIC

- Cross-rhythm
- Pitch inflection
- Steady tempo
- Tonal manipulation
- Repetition
- Call and response

### What Modern Jazz Has Borrowed from African Music

- Call and response patterns
- Cross-rhythm
- Greater dependence on syncopation
- Extensive use of percussive instruments
- Communal/collective participation
- Ostinato figures (repetition—rhythmic and melodic)

### Three Main Features of African-American Folk Music

1. The music performed **sounded slightly behind the beat** or sometimes rhythmically free of the main beat.
2. **Pitch Inflection**—black singers would bend (lower) the seventh and third scale degrees. By slightly lowering these pitches, the naturally occurring half steps are eliminated. These notes were known as *blue notes*.
3. **Tonal Manipulation**—coarsening or changing the timbre of the voice while singing, which later carried over into instrumental music. This gave the music more expressiveness and greater variety.

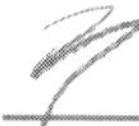

## SLAVE EXPERIENCE

- The slaves brought to New Orleans were from the Nigerian, Yoruba, and Dahomian tribes. They came from what is known today as Dahomey, Togo, Nigeria, and Ghana, or Western Africa.
- These slaves from diverse tribes were loaded onto ships and it was probably on these ships where the initial blending of various African cultures began. They turned to their music as a common mode of

expression and communication. Their mutual plight enabled them to transcend ancient intertribal hatred and competition.

- When the surviving slaves of the "middle passage" (the crossing of the Atlantic to the Western hemisphere) reached the Caribbean, they were sent to camps to "season" them (break their will). During this period the blending of the music of various tribes intensified. The witchcraft-practicing Arada and Yoruba tribe from Dahomey and Nigeria dominated the integration and influenced the music of Ibos, Sengalese, and Congos. The interaction of these groups with European music formed a common African base, which undoubtedly led to developments such as jazz in New Orleans, steel bands in the Caribbean (calypso), and the samba in Brazil.
- The Yoruba and Dahomey belief in witchcraft (voodoo) and the accompanying ceremonies, helped keep much of the African music tradition alive. Some form of religion has always existed in African culture it was a way to explain the unknown or attempt to control unpredictable forces that affect life. When different religions come into contact with each other, an accommodation and synthesis of values called **syncretism** takes place. Christian saints and symbols have found their counterparts in African religion.
- It was the Arada and Yoruba tribes with their gods and music that had a dominant influence on the spread of witchcraft throughout the Caribbean, New Orleans, and Brazil. The voodoo, or witchcraft, was aided by the parallels between Catholic saints and African deities. In New Orleans the witchcraft of the Arada tribe made contributions to the development of vodun secret societies, which eventually led to the establishment of fraternities and clubs that had their own brass bands.
- The rote imitation technique of learning music in Africa probably had a great deal of influence and contributed to the development of jazz improvisation by early New Orleans musicians.

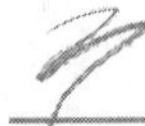

## THE AMERICAN EXPERIENCE

### New Orleans

- In New Orleans, because of its French and Spanish heritage, and its large Catholic population, slaves and former slaves found elements of voodoo that helped them to identify with Catholicism. This encouraged syncretism—the hierarchy of saints, missing in Protestantism, offered parallels with specialized African deities. This includes the sacred statues (idols), medals (charms), call and response of Gregorian chants, use of ornamentation, clerical dress, and regal titles. Africans were able to identify certain familiar elements that facilitated the assimilation of Christianity in their beliefs.
- Until the mid-1850s, slaves and free blacks were permitted to sing and dance publicly once a week in **Congo Square.** Accounts of the music played in Congo Square speak of spasm bands (musicians playing

together on mostly homemade instruments such as the jew's harp, washtub basin, washboard, kazoo, etc) performing a peculiar brand of music to accompany festive activities. Here, as it had been in Africa, the slaves dealt with dance, music, folklore, and costumes as a completely integrated entity involved in all phases of life.

- Many New Orleans black funerals employed bands to add dignity to the occasion in tribute to the deceased. While traveling to the cemetery located outside the city, bands would play slow, serious funeral dirges. After the burial, the band would usually break into a more spirited rendition of a dirge or other appropriate tune while marching back to the city. It was during these moments that the first jazz improvisation probably took place. These bands became so popular that they were also hired to play for other functions such as picnics, weddings, and parades. Their repertoire consisted of marches, blues, rags, hymns, and other popular songs of the day. They developed a musical practice of their own, borrowing from both the European and African musical traditions.

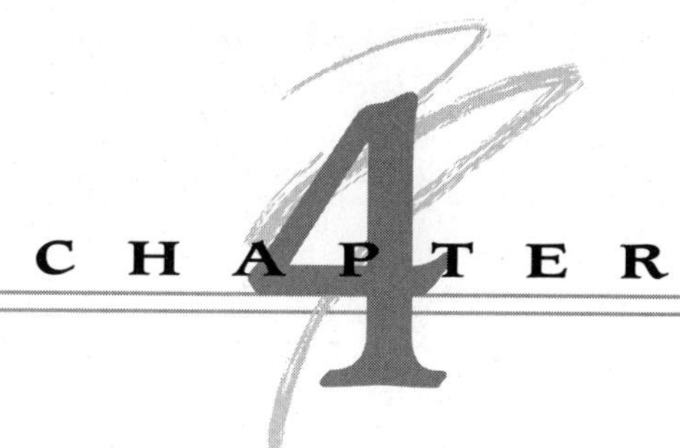

CHAPTER 4

# African-American Music

- The music of many nineteenth-century African Americans, like African music, was essentially functional; it was associated with an activity such as work, dance, or church. The main function of the lyrics was to express an attitude reflective of some aspect of life.
- Transplanted Africans created a new musical tradition not totally European based, which had more than a few African embellishments. It was an expressive music from which work songs, the blues, and spirituals evolved.
- Because dancing was popular, musicians were in demand, and both slaves and free blacks were pressured to learn to play dance music. By the beginning of the nineteenth century, there was a class of professional black musicians. They were familiar with European music as well as the performance practices of work songs, the blues, and spirituals.

## MINSTREL SHOW

- The minstrel show first evolved in the 1840s and quickly became a popular form of entertainment. At first, the performers were white and the material consisted of songs, dances, and comedy sketches that caricatured plantation slave life.
- Eventually the first black minstrel troupe was formed in 1855, and black minstrel troupes soon came to dominate the field. The wave of black minstrels created a new group of professional black

entertainers. They became singers, comics, and dancers. Many nineteenth-century American popular songs were written for minstrel shows.

- **Stephen Foster** (1826–1864), born in Pennsylvania, was an important white popular songwriter who understood that the minstrel show was where an audience for his songs could be developed. His hit "Oh! Susanna" was performed by the Christy Minstrels in 1848. Even though he was white and from the North, Foster's songs were simple in nature and the lyrics effectively captured African-American slave life. Other well-known songs he wrote include "Old Folks at Home" (1851), "My Old Kentucky Home," "Good Night" (1853), "Camptown Races," and "Jeanie with the Light Brown Hair" (1854).
- Another important nineteenth-century songwriter was **James Bland** (1854–1911). He performed with the Georgia Minstrels, an all-black minstrel troupe founded in 1865. Some of Bland's most popular songs include "Carry Me Back to Old Virginny," "Oh, Dem Golden Slippers," and "In the Evening by the Moonlight."
- In the early twentieth century, the minstrel tradition eventually gave way to two important forms of American entertainment: vaudeville and the circus. However, many important early twentieth-century black performers including W. C. Handy, Ma Rainy, Bessie Smith, and even tenor saxophonist Lester Young, spent time performing with minstrel shows.

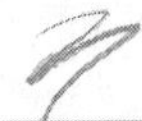

## WORK SONGS

- The majority of black music was the work song. As in African music, it was functional. Europeans never had a strong tradition of work songs except for sea chanteys. Slaveholders approved of work songs; blacks insisted that singing made the work easier. The work song was the principal medium through which the black musical tradition survived until the early twentieth century.
- Work songs were also a means of communication under the watchful eye of slave masters. The *double entendre*, or double meaning of phrases or words, is a practice still in use today.
- Work songs were varied. The tempo was always steady and based upon the type of work being done. Many times there would be a leader, and the group would answer in call-and-response fashion. Oftentimes lyrics were related to the job or anything the singer/leader felt like singing about.
- Work songs, prison songs, and spirituals are all very closely related. The main difference is that in spirituals, the text is taken from biblical or sacred sources, while work songs are secular in content.
- Work songs contained syncopation, call and response, melodies performed slightly behind the beat, blue notes (flat third and flat seventh scale degrees), and tonal manipulation.

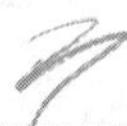

## THE BLUES

- Blues evolved from the work song, prison song, and street cry. The performance practice has much in common with work songs and spirituals, but blues developed a more strict form. The subject matter of blues closely resembles that of the work song, but more often had something to do with *personal* relationships.
- The blues and the **sound** of the blues most likely developed in the nineteenth century. It is possible that it began to evolve as a separate entity in the late nineteenth century. Early blues were sung a cappella (unaccompanied) with no formal harmonic sequence and could vary in length and structure, but by about 1910, it conformed to the more common twelve-measure structure.
- The twelve measures are divided into three equal parts, each containing a line of text; usually the second line is exactly the same as the first. The third line of the blues is usually a reaction to or commentary on what is stated in the first two lines. We label the blues form using capital letters that follow the three lines of text: AAB. With the appearance of the first published blues compositions in 1912, the norm was established to let each section be four bars long. Therefore, an entire chorus of blues is twelve measures long. Often the text fills only about two measures of each four-measure section, leaving room for a short instrumental fill or response (usually done on guitar, harmonica, horn, etc.).

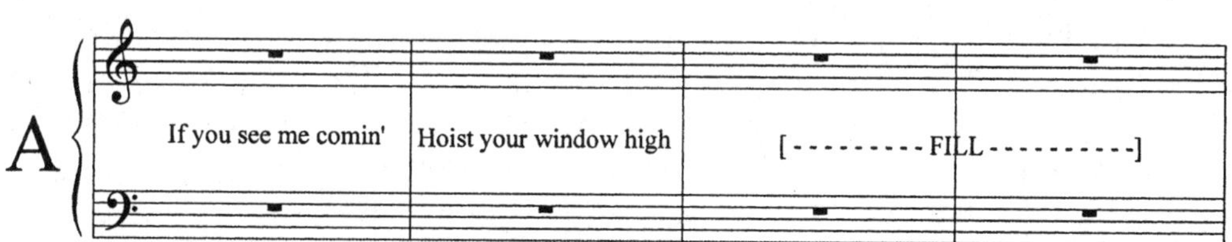


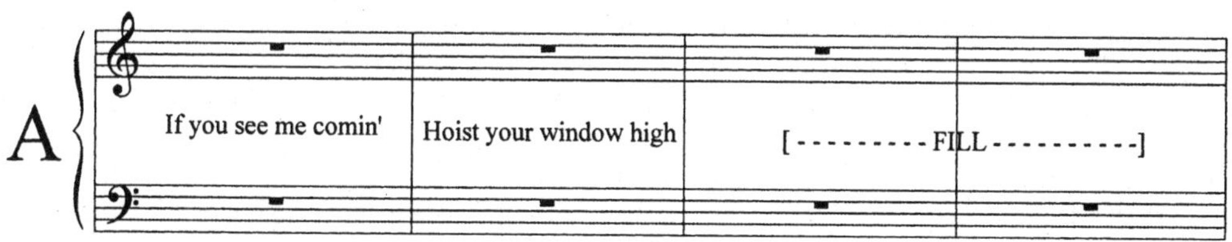


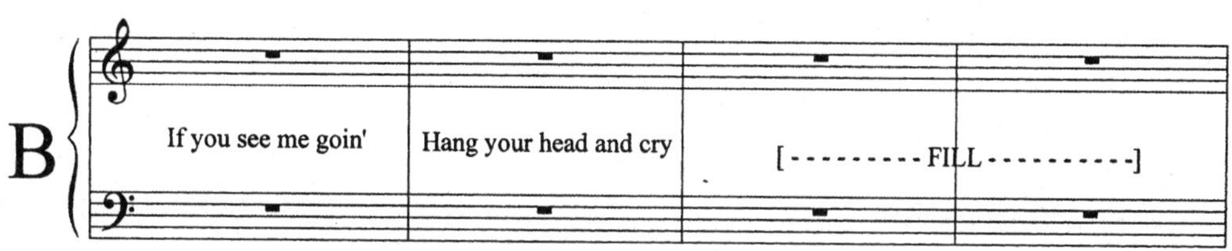


- Another important characteristic is the way blues singers approached the flat third and seventh scale degrees often referred to as blue notes. Blues melodies concentrate on these two notes. The existence of tonal manipulation, sliding between notes, performing rhythms slightly behind the beat, and the secular nature of the lyrics make the blues or other African-derived types of music easy to identify.

- The term *blues* first appeared in the titles of W. C. Handy's 1912 compositions "Memphis Blues" and "Dallas Blues" by Hart Wand and Lloyd Garrett.
- The older style of blues, country or primitive blues, varied widely in structure and chord progression. This style was still being performed in the 1930s by musicians not necessarily influenced by current musical trends. In the 1920s, 1930s, and 1940s, blues performers such as **Blind Lemon Jefferson, Charlie Patton,** and **Huddie Ledbetter** gave us a representation of this early blues style by performing it just as they had learned from their mentors and idols. Their playing and overall lifestyle is representative of a tradition that goes back an indefinite and unknown number of years.
- **Blind Lemon Jefferson** (1897–1929) was born near Wortham, Texas. He learned to play the guitar and became an itinerant musician, working in east Texas towns and eventually settling in Dallas around 1917. In the 1920s he played in mostly southern states. Between 1925 and 1929 he made recordings mostly for the Paramount label. He died in Chicago under mysterious circumstances.
- **Huddie Ledbetter ("Leadbelly")** (1885–1949) was born on the Jeter plantation near Mooringsport, Louisiana. By age twenty-one, Leadbelly was traveling in Texas and Louisiana, playing guitar and singing. At one point, he served as an assistant to Blind Lemon Jefferson, from whom he learned the blues tradition. Leadbelly spent several periods of time in jail—first in Texas for assault; then in Huntsville, Texas, for murder after killing a man in a fight; then in the Louisiana State Penitentiary. In 1933, John Lomax and his son Alan discovered Leadbelly while researching unwritten ballads and folk songs for the Library of Congress. The Lomaxes knew that southern prisons were a good place to find folk music. Apparently, Alan Lomax convinced Governor Allen of Louisiana to pardon Leadbelly. In 1935, Leadbelly traveled to northern cities, where his music became a sensation. He made recordings in the 1930s and 1940s. As a minor celebrity he eventually toured Europe.

## Early Male Blues Performers

| | |
|---|---|
| Huddie Ledbetter ("Leadbelly") | Robert Johnson |
| Blind Lemon Jefferson | Big Bill Broonzy |
| Charley Patton | Son House |

- **William Christoper (W. C.) Handy** (1873–1958), known as the **Father of the Blues,** grew up in Florence, Alabama, where he was exposed to music by his family and the church. At a young age, through a method known as *solfege* still taught today in music conservatories, he was able to catalog the songs of birds and nearby riverboat whistles. From the late 1880s until 1909, Handy traveled extensively performing with bands and minstrel shows. He also secured teaching positions for a short period of time until he became disenchanted with the teaching profession. In 1909, Handy moved to Memphis, Tennessee, where in 1912 he published the first blues composition, "Memphis Blues." His most famous composition, "St. Louis Blues," was published in 1914. Eventually his success led to the creation of his own publishing company, which was active in the 1920s and 1930s. His biography, *Father of the Blues*, was published in 1941. Handy stated many times he was not the first blues musician, but he was the first person to write down blues he heard many traveling musicians perform while growing up in the South.

- The 1920s saw a proliferation of blues recordings, most of which were made by black female vocalists accompanied by small ensembles. These blues recordings showed influences of current musical trends because most ensemble members were jazz musicians. Thus a new style of blues emerged which has been labeled "urban blues."
- **Ma Rainy** (1886–1939), known as the **Mother of the Blues,** was born Gertrude Pridgett in Columbus, Georgia. She began performing in traveling shows in 1900. In 1904, she married Will "Pa" Rainy, and they teamed up to be "Ma and Pa Rainy, the Assassinators of the Blues," performing as part of the Rabbit Foot Minstrels. In 1914, Ma Rainy became an important mentor for Bessie Smith who was a performer with the Rabbit Foot Minstrels. Not known for her beauty, Rainy used glittering outfits and gold jewelry as part of her costume. She became a big name performer for the Theater Booking Owners' Association (TOBA). Before her recording debut in 1923, she was known only in the South. From 1923 to 1928, Rainy made ninety-two recordings for the Paramount label. Musicians who accompanied her included Kid Ory, Johnny Dodds, Joe Smith, Louis Armstrong, Buster Bailey, Fletcher Henderson, and Coleman Hawkins. Some of her most successful recordings were "Weepin' Woman Blues," "Hustlin' Blues," "Stormy Sea Blues," and "Jelly Bean Blues." In 1933, Ma Rainy retired to Columbus, Georgia, where she died six years later of a heart attack.
- **Bessie Smith** (1894–1937), known as the **Empress of the Blues,** was born in Chattanooga, Tennessee. Her mother and father both died while she was young. She was encouraged by her brother Clarence to sing and dance. Clarence arranged for Bessie to join a traveling show in 1912. Eventually, she came into contact with Ma Rainy while performing with the Rabbit Foot Minstrels in 1914. Bessie went on to become a huge TOBA star. In 1923, she made her first blues recordings, "Gulf Coast Blues" and "Down Hearted Blues" for Columbia Records, selling more than 750,000 copies that year. As a result, Bessie achieved a national reputation with both black and white audiences. Over the next ten years she made over 160 recordings for Columbia, including "Mama's Got the Blues," "Careless Love Blues," and W. C. Handy's "St. Louis Blues." In addition, she composed and recorded "Back Water Blues" and "Poor Man's Blues." Notable musicians who recorded with Bessie were Louis Armstrong, Fletcher Henderson, James P. Johnson, Coleman Hawkins, Don Redman, Buster Bailey, Jack Teagarden, and Benny Goodman. She also appeared in the 1929 movie *St. Louis Blues*. In the 1930s Bessie's career declined, as did all the careers of the black female vocalists who emerged in the 1920s. Her last recordings were made in 1933. She experienced an enthusiastic reception at the Apollo Theater in 1935 while with a touring show—a reason for optimism regarding a career

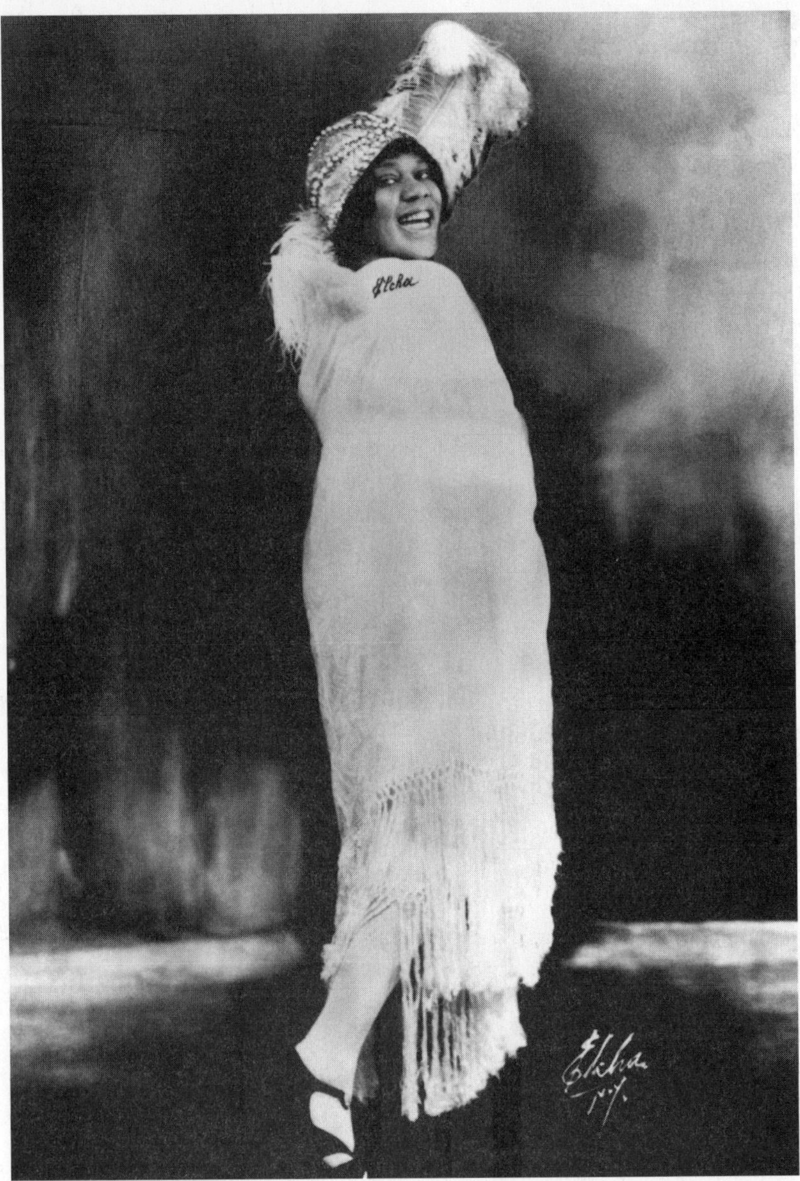

*Bessie Smith. © Bettmann/CORBIS*

turnaround. However, in 1937 she was killed in an automobile accident while traveling through Clarksdale, Mississippi.

- Bessie Smith suffered from personal problems with alcohol and broken relationships. Her mastery of the blues vocal style enabled her to express her frustrations through her singing in a way unparalleled by her contemporaries. This fact, coupled with her unequaled voice, has made her the most significant black female vocalist of the 1920s. The following are some other important urban blues vocalists:

## Urban Blues

| | |
|---|---|
| "Ma" Rainy (Mother of the Blues) | Bessie Smith (Empress of the Blues) |
| Mamie Smith | Ethel Waters |
| Trixie Smith | Ida Cox |

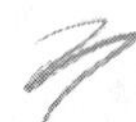

## SPIRITUALS

- Many churches were integrated in the eighteenth century. It was customary for the leader or minister to perform in a call-and-response manner, with the congregation giving the responses in spoken prayer and music. As separate black churches were established in the early nineteenth century, they, too, needed music. They adopted the Methodist hymns, but performed them in a style that represented the performance practices found in work songs. Many spirituals are based on biblical passages.
- In the revivalist "second awakening" of the 1830s, emotional religious experience came to the forefront of white churches. The revival meetings might go on for days, and many blacks recognized the similarities to African rituals. This tradition remained steadfast in black churches (sanctified or fundamentalist) long after most white churches abandoned it.

## FIELD HOLLER

- Church songs and work songs constituted the largest part of slave music, but there was more. The field holler or cry has been written about, but its function is not clear; possibly used as a call-and-answer signal. Musically it consisted of a series of notes of indeterminate pitch sung in free time. Another similar genre is the street cry—a method of advertising a street vendor's product. Vendors sung about their merchandise as they traveled the streets of small towns and cities in America. The concession salespeople we see moving about the stands at baseball games are a carryover of such a tradition.

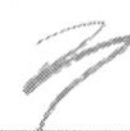

## RAGTIME

While blues, spirituals, and minstrel songs are important to the development of jazz, the ragtime style also plays a significant role. It is primarily a pianistic idiom that became established in the mid-1890s and remained popular until about 1918 when the first jazz recordings pushed it aside. Its creation was most likely due to piano players' efforts to improvise versions of brass band marches in the absence of an actual brass band. However, African-American piano players began to syncopate (rag) march melodies. The existence of syncopation, most likely an African influence, is what makes ragtime compositions different from marches. Ragtime compositions were written down and often published. They were also available on player piano rolls, which could be put inside player pianos (pianos capable of mechanically producing music without a human performer) to create the music. Therefore, little if any improvisation was present in ragtime. Ragtime has the following characteristics:

- The left hand goes back and forth, alternating bass notes or octaves with midregister chords, creating the "oompah" rhythm of a brass band.
- The right hand plays melodies syncopated against the regular left-hand rhythm.

- The form of most rags closely resembles brass band march form (e.g., marches by John Philip Sousa). Marches generally have a sixteen-bar A section (in 2/4 time) that repeats, followed by another sixteen-bar B section that repeats, followed by another sixteen-bar C section that repeats, and so on. Each section is called a strain. See the following example:

### March Form

- Most rags are similar, but a nonrepeating A section is inserted between the B and C sections. See the following example:

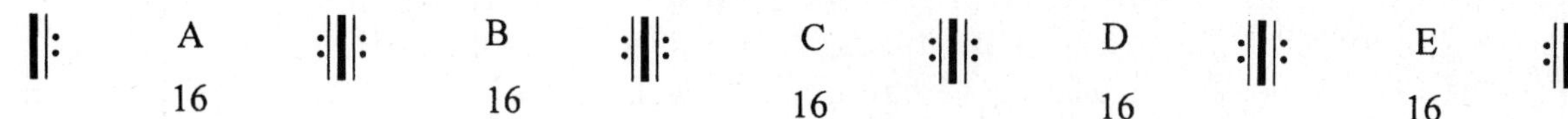


### Ragtime Form

A 16 | B 16 | A 16 | C 16 | D 16

- "Ragtime Baby," composed by Fred Stone in 1893, was the first composition to use the word *ragtime*. Published in 1897, **Tom Turpin's** "Harlem Rag" was the first ragtime composition to be published by an African American. Tom Turpin published only three more ragtime compositions. His father was the owner of the Silver Dollar Saloon in St. Louis, and Tom Turpin eventually opened the Rosebud Café in St. Louis. Both establishments were famous for ragtime entertainment. However, ragtime's most prolific and significant composer was Scott Joplin, who at one time frequented both the Silver Dollar Saloon and the Rosebud Café.
- **Scott Joplin** (1868–1917) was born in Texas and raised in Texarakana. As a boy he showed obvious signs of exceptional musical talent. A local German piano teacher was so impressed that he gave Joplin lessons free of charge. Joplin learned to read and write music, becoming knowledgeable about European classical composers. In his teenage years he was an itinerant musician, mostly in the Midwest. At some point in the 1880s he settled in St. Louis, but he also lived in nearby Sedalia, where he attended the George Smith College for Negroes. While attending the Chicago Exposition of 1889, Joplin became aware of and interested in a newly developing piano style that would eventually evolve into ragtime.
- Joplin's first ragtime composition, "Original Rags," was published in 1899. Later that same year, he met a white publisher in Sedalia who offered to publish what would become his most successful and popular composition, "Maple Leaf Rag." John Stark was an exceptional businessman who cared little about race, creed, or color. He is now perceived as a champion of ragtime music who helped talented composers and performers, white and black, become successful.

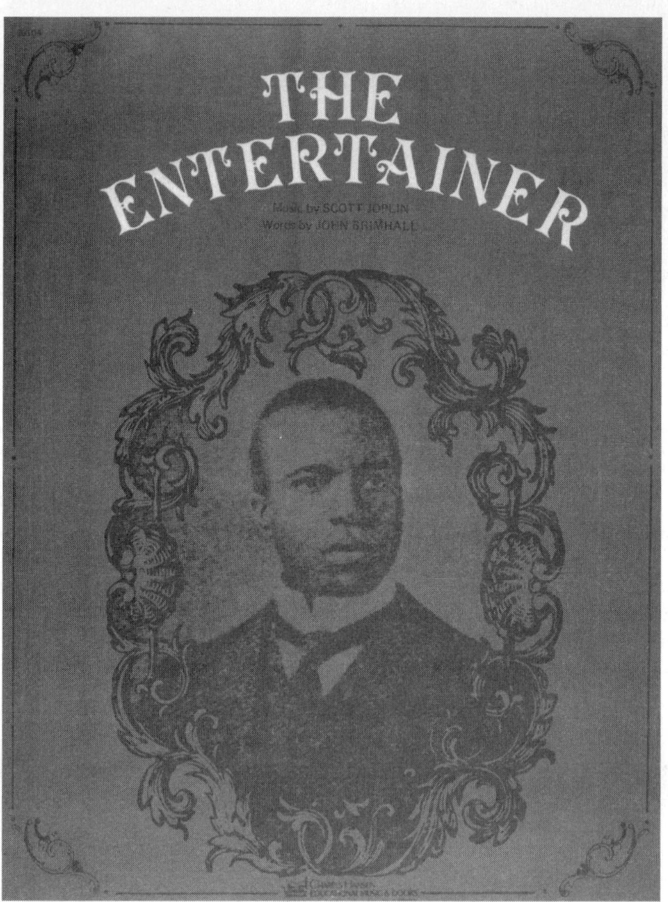


*Scott Joplin. © Bettmann/CORBIS*

He published many of Joplin's rags. Stark's success made it possible for him to eventually move his publishing business to New York City.

- In 1903, Joplin composed and produced his first ragtime opera, *A Guest of Honor*. Very little is known about the opera, and the score has been lost. Joplin was attempting to elevate the status of ragtime and solicit public acceptance by composing a ragtime opera.
- Joplin moved to New York City in 1906. He lived in Harlem, where he also gave piano lessons. Joplin wrote several ragtime methods that clearly articulate how to become a ragtime performer.
- In 1911, he composed and produced *Treemonisha*, his last ragtime opera. Few people, however, were ready to take a ragtime opera seriously. Even John Stark was not willing to publish it. Since Joplin was not able to afford an orchestra, the opera was performed with two pianists and minimal stage props. The opera was not a success, and Joplin suffered until his death from the effects of its failure.
- Joplin died in New York in 1917, leaving behind thirty-three rags, six method books, a ragtime ballet, two ragtime operas, and numerous songs and waltzes. His music was rediscovered in the 1970s, and in 1977 *Treemonisha* was finally be performed as Joplin originally intended (by the Houston Opera).
- Other ragtime composers include **James Scott, Joseph Lamb,** and **Scott Hayden.**

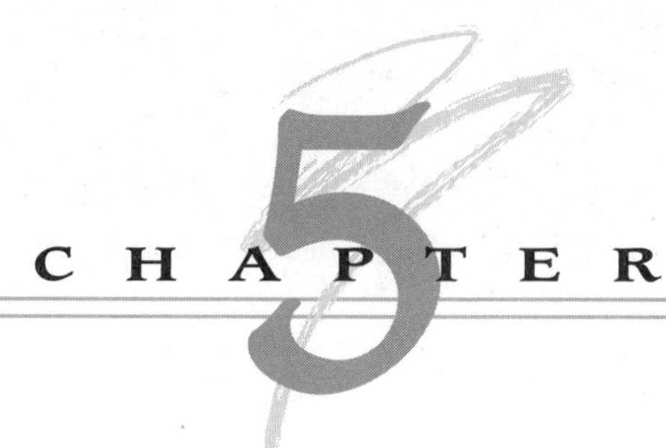

CHAPTER 5

# New Orleans' Musical Tradition

- The beginnings of jazz dates back to the late nineteenth century, and the acknowledged birthplace is New Orleans. While it cannot be proven that the true genesis of jazz took place in one city and it is more likely there were contributions to the beginnings of jazz from other locales, the unique atmosphere of New Orleans, more than anything else, lent itself to the creation of a new and exciting music. In fact, it is quite possible that jazz would never have been created had it not been for the existence of a city like New Orleans.
- New Orleans has always had a liberal attitude towards pleasure and self-indulgence. It had a very strong musical tradition, with many orchestras, brass bands, and opera companies. Even though it is geographically located in the South, it was more racially tolerant, relatively speaking, and offered black musicians many opportunities for musical expression.
- From 1897 to 1917, New Orleans had a unique red light district where prostitution and gambling were legal. The district was quickly set up by businessmen to cater to sailors. The legislation that made such a place possible was initiated by a politician named Harry Story. The district was therefore nicknamed **Storyville.** Many of the buildings that housed the brothels can still be found today in the French Quarter. Many early jazz musicians found employment in Storyville, often playing from sundown to sunup. More upscale houses could afford bands, while others had only piano players (some of whom were called "professors"). By 1910, there were over 200 cabarets, honky-tonks, and dance halls. In 1917,

the U.S. Navy closed Storyville because alert, healthy, focused sailors were needed to fight during World War I. Many musicians left New Orleans around this time to seek work elsewhere, some ending up in Chicago.

- Musicians also played at establishments located on nearby Lake Pontchartrain, at picnics, weddings, funerals, or on riverboats traveling the Mississippi River.

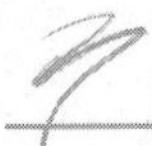

## CREOLES

- Originally, "Creole" was the designation given to whites who were descendants of mixed French and Spanish heritage. At first they occupied important positions of power and influence in society. As more Americans came into the area after 1803, Creoles felt their culture being threatened. As a result they made great efforts to isolate themselves. They clung to their European-based culture by continuing to speak a French patois and maintaining a more "continental" attitude.
- Many Creole men kept mistresses of mixed heritage (black and white), resulting in offspring that were given European education, culture, and values. As a result, a subclass of black Creoles of mixed race emerged who adhered to the Creole customs and often were considered a part of the white class.
- Creoles always took pleasure in their relationship with music. To be versed in European music showed a certain refinement. Creole children studied music by taking lessons in the European tradition and attending musical performances. Creole musicians were taught to read music, rejecting musicians who could not read and those who played the blues. They had little use for work songs, spirituals, hollers, and ring shouts. Being primarily Catholic, they did not attend churches where this type of music was performed.
- Jim Crow laws of the late nineteenth century suddenly defined Creoles with any African blood relation as "Negro," denying them the right to occupy important positions of power and influence in society and forcing them to live and merge with the lower-class African-American society. Therefore, as these Creoles, with their tradition of owning good instruments and the ability to read music, mixed with other black musicians in the late nineteenth century, a transference of style and technique emerged.
- In general, Creoles stayed away from the blues in favor of more formal European-based music, while black musicians were more likely to play the blues and other styles of music learned aurally with more ragged rhythms.

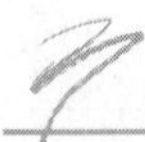

## EARLY NEW ORLEANS JAZZ

- By the late nineteenth century there emerged a group of musicians, black and Creole, who could play rags, blues, marches, popular songs, and so on. Both black and Creole musicians began to develop a different kind of music that would eventually become known throughout America and the rest of the world. Today we refer to this style of jazz as early New Orleans style (sometimes called Dixieland–a Northern term applied to anything south of the Mason-Dixon Line).

- It wasn't so much what they played, but how they played it. The marches, rags, work songs, blues, and popular songs took the form of the European-African hybrid that would come to be known as jazz.
- Instead of playing music with two beats in a measure, as in typical march music, many of these musicians superimposed four quick beats in the same time span (twice the speed). At the same time all the beats were not enunciated with equal force. Sometimes beats one and three were enunciated, but later it came to be beats two and especially the fourth beat. Jelly Roll Morton claims to have invented swing rhythm with this lilt to the notes.
- The typical instrumentation of the early New Orleans jazz ensemble grew out of the brass band tradition. The **front line** consisted of cornet, clarinet, and trombone. The rhythm section consisted of a tuba or upright bass; drums, cymbals, and other optional percussion instruments; and piano, banjo, and/or guitar. Any combination of these instruments make up what we know to be the traditional early New Orleans style jazz ensemble.
- However, it is important to remember that not all early New Orleans music was played using the previous brass band-derived instrumentation. Many of the groups were "salon" groups. The salon groups were better suited for more intimate settings because they also had string instruments such as the guitar, string bass, and violin.
- Early New Orleans jazz was built around "hot" bands playing their interpretations of marches, rags, polkas, blues, quadrilles, and popular tunes. Early jazz musicians were not improvising the way today's jazz musicians do; they were simply embellishing and ornamenting familiar melodies. They were syncopating (ragging) these melodies and often creating a coarse tone by using mutes and sometimes growling into their instruments. They also added blue notes.
- Unlike today's jazz, early New Orleans jazz featured "collective improvisation" where several players were improvising at once. The overall group effect took precedence over the importance of any one player at any given time. The cornet, trombone, and clarinet all play different melodies at the same time, yet they are able to avoid chaos because of their advanced knowledge of individual roles and their sensitivity to each other. Occasionally there are instrumental "breaks" where the band stops and one player is featured in a short solo improvisation, but these breaks seem to be more the exception than the rule. In many marches by American composers, the last section, or "dogfight," usually contains much interplay, with two or more melodies being played simultaneously. This interplay influenced the New Orleans musicians in their approach to collective improvisation.

## Review of the Characteristics of Early New Orleans Jazz

- Collective improvisation
- Brass/military band tradition and instrumentation
- The use of string instruments in salon bands
- Ragtime and blues influence
- Use of blue notes, growls, loosening of melody line, ornamentation/embellishment, combined with rudimentary improvisation

- Ungirding of the 2/2 beat with an underlying 4/4 beat
- Uneven playing of eighth notes (long-short)

***European influences***

- Melodies—French/Prussian marches, Spanish rhythms and melodies, etc.
- Harmony—European diatonic system and notation
- European instruments and technique
- Counterpoint—collective improvisation
- Brass band tradition
- British folk songs and hymns

***African influences***

- Rhythm and time feel
- Cross-rhythm
- Overlapping call and response
- Tonal manipulation
- Pitch inflection
- Melodies subservient to rhythm
- Instruments played as an extension of the voice

***Differences between ragtime and jazz***

- Jazz was mostly improvised—ragtime was not.
- The jazz rhythmic feel was much looser and relaxed whereas ragtime had a more strict rhythmic feel.
- Collective improvisation was of primary importance in jazz and was a very complex interweaving of instruments, each with a specific and well-established role.
- Jazz had more vitality and variety.

## Performance Characteristics

- The cornet (or trumpet) player played the main melody. It was often altered melodically and rhythmically, but it could still be recognized.
- The clarinet had a dual role, serving a harmonic function above the melody (embellished filigree) and was used to create momentum and excitement with its natural flexibility.
- The trombone played a "tailgate" style, often creating "smears" or trombone glissandi as the trombonist outlined harmony and made it recognizable to the others.
- The tuba or string bass played the bass notes or chord roots as it does in marches, usually in 2/2 time.
- The drums (snare, bass drum, cymbals) and banjo (or guitar or piano) were the rhythm section where the banjo plays chords rhythmically and the drummer(s) played in a rudimentary march style.
- The standard format of arrangements tended to be as follows:
  - ♪ Ensemble chorus

- ♪ Collective improvisation (later solo improvisation)
- ♪ Stop time breaks (where band stops and one player has a short solo)
- ♪ Ensemble melody
- ♪ Short musical tag at the end

- Collective improvisation was responsible for the rhythmic variety, texture, and interest, causing the constant shift of accents among the three front line instruments. Each player knew his role and how to fit in with the others to complement the ensemble.

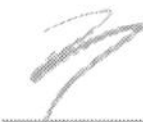

## EARLY NEW ORLEANS JAZZ MUSICIANS

- **Buddy Bolden** (1877–1931) is given credit for being the **first "jazz" musician.** A somewhat mythical figure, he is remembered by New Orleans musicians as being one of the best cornet players from about 1895 to 1906, when he began to show signs of mental illness. The next year he was committed to an institution where he spent the rest of his life. After 1900, many bands in New Orleans were playing in the collective improvisational style reminiscent of Buddy Bolden's band. Of the same generation are drummer D. D. Chandler, trombonist Willie Cornish, cornetist King Oliver, and members of the clarinet-playing Tio family.

### Cornet

- **Joe "King" Oliver** (1885–1938) was one of the most popular and best-known New Orleans cornetists. He was a mentor to young Louis Armstrong. Oliver played with many successful bands in New Orleans

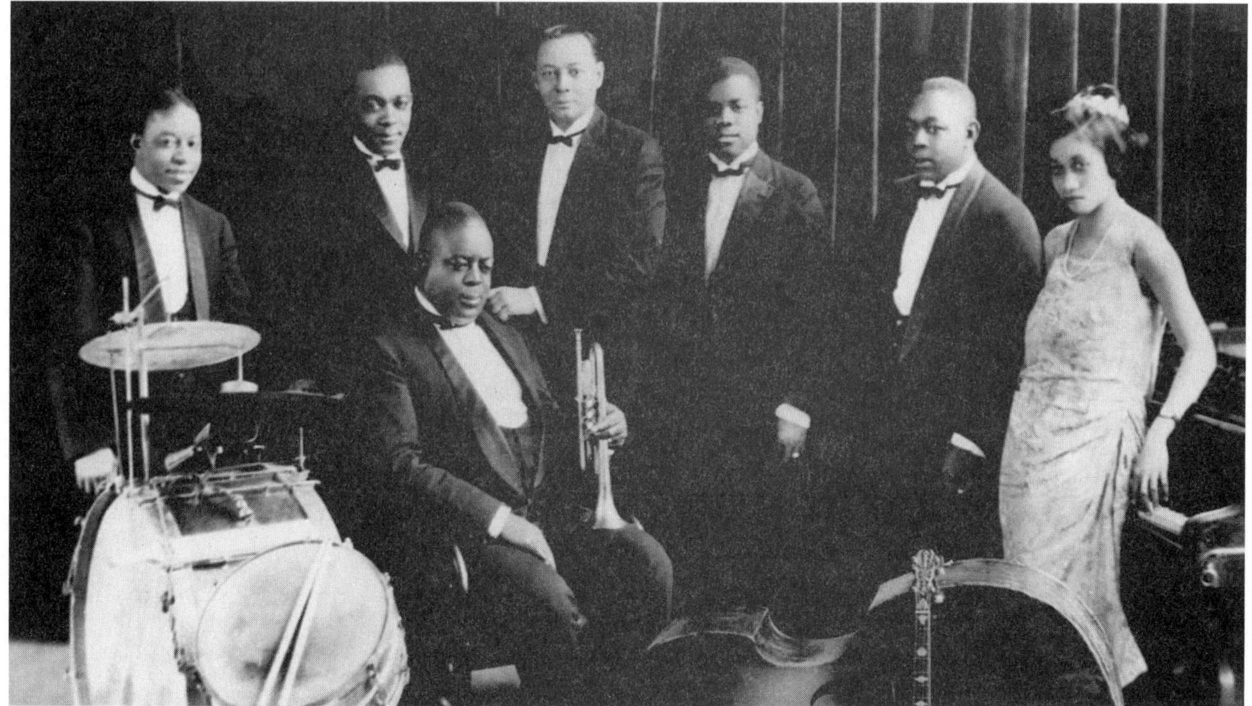

*Joe "King" Oliver and his Creole Jazz Band. © CORBIS*

before moving to Chicago in 1918. He excelled at the collective improvisational style. He was also a master of tonal manipulation and the use of mutes. His **Creole Jazz Band** was one of the most popular bands in Chicago and boasted a collection of the finest New Orleans musicians. The Creole Jazz Band made important recordings in 1923 that featured his protégé, Louis Armstrong.

- **Bunk Johnson** (1889–1949) was active in New Orleans until 1914 when he traveled extensively, playing with minstrel shows, theater orchestras, and circus bands. Around 1931, he lost his teeth, which temporarily ended his career. In the late 1930s, Johnson was discovered in New Iberia, Louisiana, by a group of jazz historians who arranged for Johnson's teeth to be fixed, allowing him to play again. In the 1940s as New Orleans-style jazz enjoyed a revival, he made several recordings.
- **Buddy Petit** (1895–1931) was revered by New Orleans musicians as one of the greatest New Orleans cornet players. He led many bands in New Orleans but was never recorded. In 1917 he played with Jelly Roll Morton's band in Los Angeles but was not happy. He returned to New Orleans and never left the area again.
- **Freddie Keppard** (1890–1933) was a top player in New Orleans. According to Jelly Roll Morton, Keppard was given an opportunity to make the first instrumental jazz recording ahead of the Original Dixieland Jazz Band, but declined the offer on the grounds that he might "give away his tricks." He eventually moved to Chicago in 1920, making recordings with Doc Cook's Dreamland Orchestra and Erskine Tate's Orchestra.
- **Paul Mares** (1900–1949) was a white cornetist who made influential recordings with the New Orleans Rhythm Kings in 1922 and 1923.
- **Nick LaRocca** (1889–1961) helped form the Original Dixieland Jazz Band (ODJB) in New Orleans in 1914. Through the ODJB's recordings in 1917, LaRocca became a significant influence on jazz musicians active in the 1920s.
- **Manual Perez** (1873–1946) was famous for his work in New Orleans brass bands. Before 1900 he played with the Onward Brass Band, then he formed his Imperial Orchestra. In the mid–1920s he made his only recordings with Elgar's Creole Orchestra.
- **George Mitchell** (1899–1972) performed on many of Jelly Roll Morton's Red Hot Pepper recordings.

## Clarinet

- More common in early jazz than sax, it usually played countermelodies around the cornet.

Some important clarinetists:

- **Johnny Dodds** (1892–1940) was a leading second generation New Orleans player who moved to Chicago. He had an edgy tone with fast vibrato, and he played wonderful countermelodies. He could also bend pitches with strong effect.
- **Jimmie Noone** (1895–1944) was a more polished player than Dodds, with a dark, warm sound more characteristic of the New Orleans Creoles.
- **Sidney Bechet** (1897–1959) played clarinet and soprano sax. He was one of the most highly regarded musicians in early jazz and one of the

first important soloists to appear. Had a big sound with a wide vibrato and played with imagination and authority. Known primarily as a soloist, he hated to relinquish the spotlight to others. His carefully chosen and bent or scooped notes had tremendous impact in solos. Bechet influenced Johnny Hodges and John Coltrane.

More early jazz clarinetists:

- **Barney Bigard** (1906–1980)
- **George Lewis** (1900–1968)
- **Omer Simeon** (1902–1959)
- **Leon Roppolo** (1902–1943)
- **Buster Bailey**(1902–1967)
- **Larry Shields** (1893–1953)

### Trombone

- **Kid Ory** (1886–1973) was a great trombone player active in New Orleans before 1920. From 1912 to 1919, he led one of the most successful bands in New Orleans. King Oliver, Louis Armstrong, Johnny Dodds, Sidney Bechet, and Jimmie Noone played in Ory's band at one time or another. He was the originator of the "tailgate" trombone style. He was also a composer and appeared on recordings made in the 1920s with Louis Armstrong's Hot Five and Seven groups, and with Jelly Roll Morton. Kid Ory also toured and recorded during the 1940s Dixieland revival.
- **Honore Dutrey** (1894–1935) began his career in 1910 playing in New Orleans bands. In the early 1920s he played with King Oliver's Creole Jazz Band in Chicago.
- **George Brunies** (1902–1974) played in New Orleans bands until 1919 when he moved to Chicago eventually playing with the New Orleans Rhythm Kings (NORK).

### Drums

- **Baby Dodds** (1898–1959) was an important New Orleans drummer. He played in Kid Ory's Band before joining Fate Marable's riverboat bands in 1918. He recorded in the 1920s with Joe "King" Oliver's Creole Jazz Band, Jelly Roll Morton's Red Hot Peppers, and Louis Armstrong's Hot Five and Seven groups.
- **Zutty Singleton** (1898–1975), along with Baby Dodds, came from the military style of rudimental drumming. Zutty pioneered the use of brushes, was one of the first to use the "sock" cymbal (high hat), and play ride rhythms on cymbals. He is an important transitional figure from the older New Orleans style to the 1930s swing style.
- **Paul Barbarin** (1899–1969) had a long and distinguished career performing with many legendary New Orleans jazz musicians including Louis Armstrong, Joe "King" Oliver, Sidney Bechet, Buddy Petit, Freddie Keppard, Jimmie Noone, and Luis Russell.
- **Papa Jack Laine** (1873–1966) formed the Reliance Brass Band in the 1890s. Many important white New Orleans musicians played in his groups over the years.

### Guitar/Banjo

- **Johnny St. Cyr** (1890–1966) was playing in New Orleans beginning in 1905 with the Superior, Olympia, and Tuxedo Brass Bands. He also played in Fate Marable's riverboat bands. He made recordings in the 1920s with King Oliver, Jelly Roll Morton, and Louis Armstrong's Hot Five and Seven groups.
- **Lonnie Johnson** (1899–1970) began playing in New Orleans establishments and in Fate Marable's riverboat bands. He traveled Europe in 1917 playing in revues and with Will Marion Cook's Southern Syncopated Orchestra. In the 1920s he recorded with guitarist Eddie Lang, Louis Armstrong's Hot Five, and Duke Ellington's Orchestra.

### Brass Bands

- Onward Brass Band
- Olympia Brass Band
- Excelsior Brass Band
- Tuxedo Brass Band
- Reliance Brass Band
- Superior Brass Band

### Jelly Roll Morton

- **Jelly Roll Morton** was born around 1890, leaving New Orleans in 1907, and traveled to California, then Chicago, before settling in New York. Jelly Roll was a pianist (see Chapter 6), composer, and arranger. He is

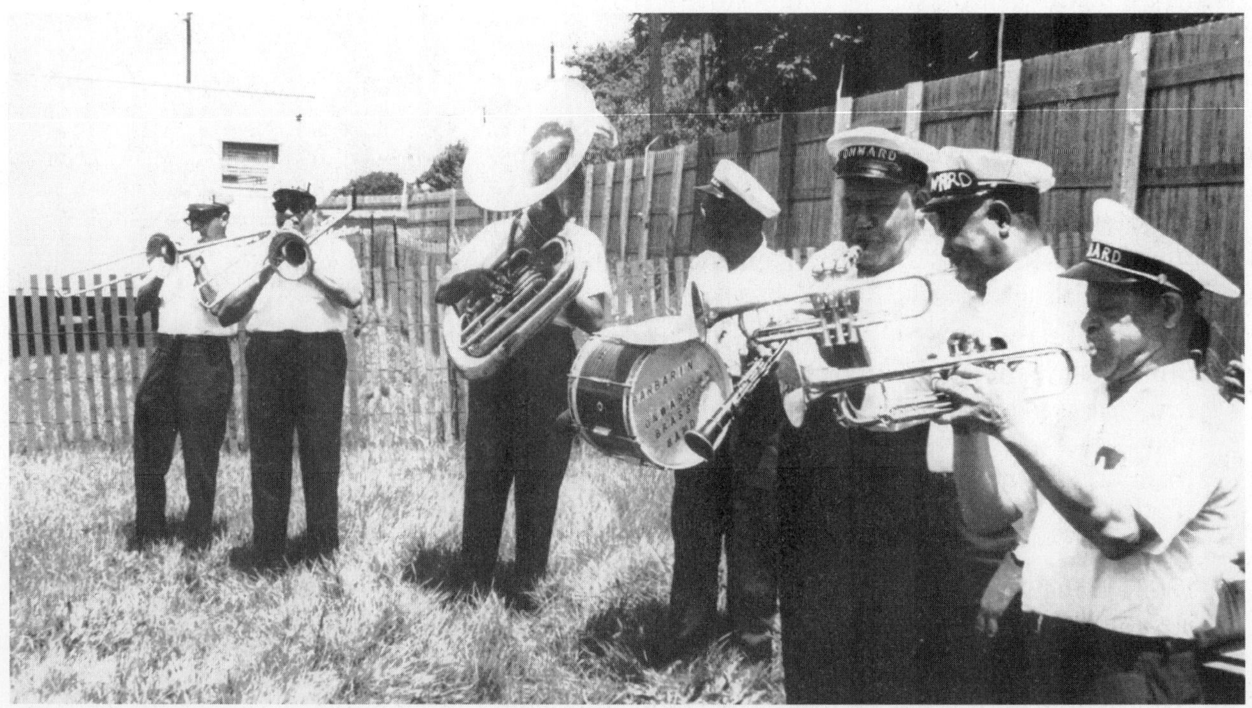


*Onward Brass Band. Courtesty Rutgers Institute of Jazz Studies.*

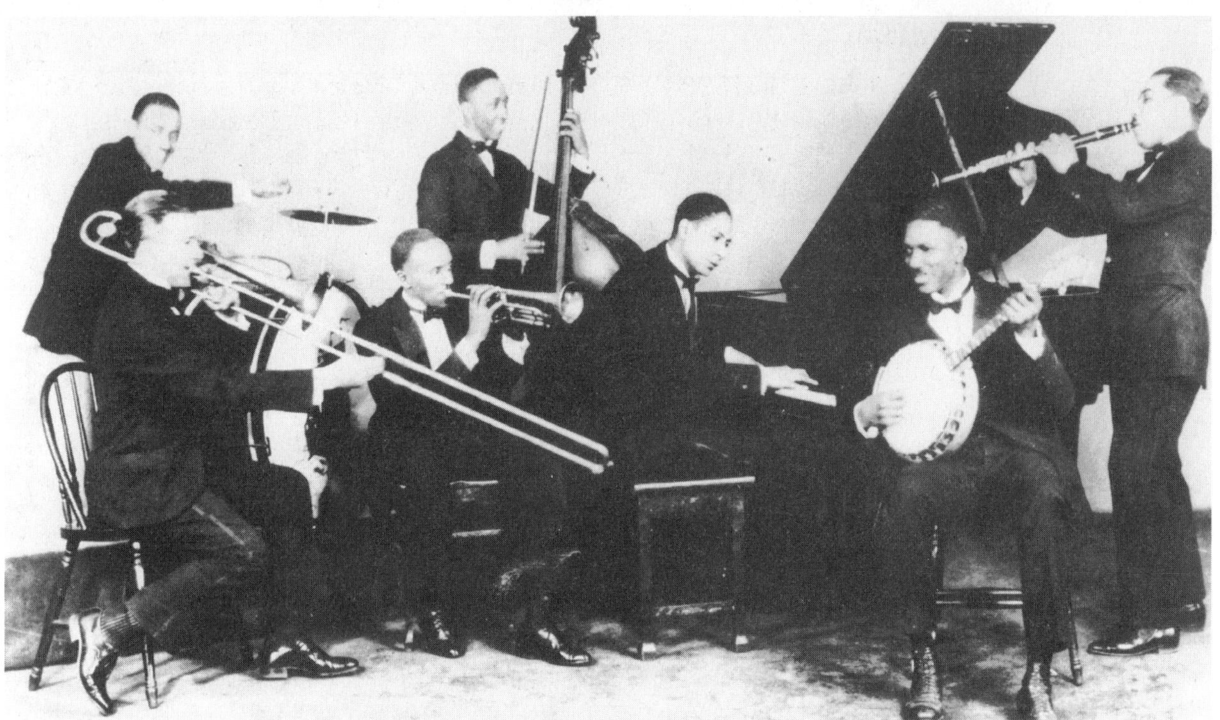

*Jeilly Roll Morton and the Red Hot Peppers. From left to right: Andrew Hilaire (drums), Kid Ory (trombone), George Mitchell (comet), John Lindsay (bass), Jelly Roll Morton (piano), Johnny St. Cyr (banjo), Omer Simeon (clarinet). Courtesty Rutgers institute of Jazz Studies.*

generally given credit for being the first jazz composer/arranger. He perfected rhythmic techniques that evolved into the *swing eighth-note* style. His most famous band was the **Red Hot Peppers.** His music offers a polished, well-rehearsed performance and mixes ragtime with blues flavored New Orleans style. Morton was a perfectionist who is known for the following:

- Was the first jazz composer/arranger
- Composed a large body of original jazz compositions
- Was an excellent improviser, playing solos that were well executed
- Establishing basic jazz arranging practices
- Blended composition with improvisation in a good balance, predating Duke Ellington and Charles Mingus
- Helped alleviate the stiffness of ragtime rhythm by playing with a more loose rhythmic feel and playing eighth notes in a long-short manner

## WHITE NEW ORLEANS JAZZ BANDS

- White New Orleans musicians developed a style that borrowed from the jazz played by black bands. Black bands were rhythmically looser, closer to the blues, and characteristically played with a more ecstatic feeling. White-European musical practice was based on an accurate reproduction of a composition; black musicians saw music more as a

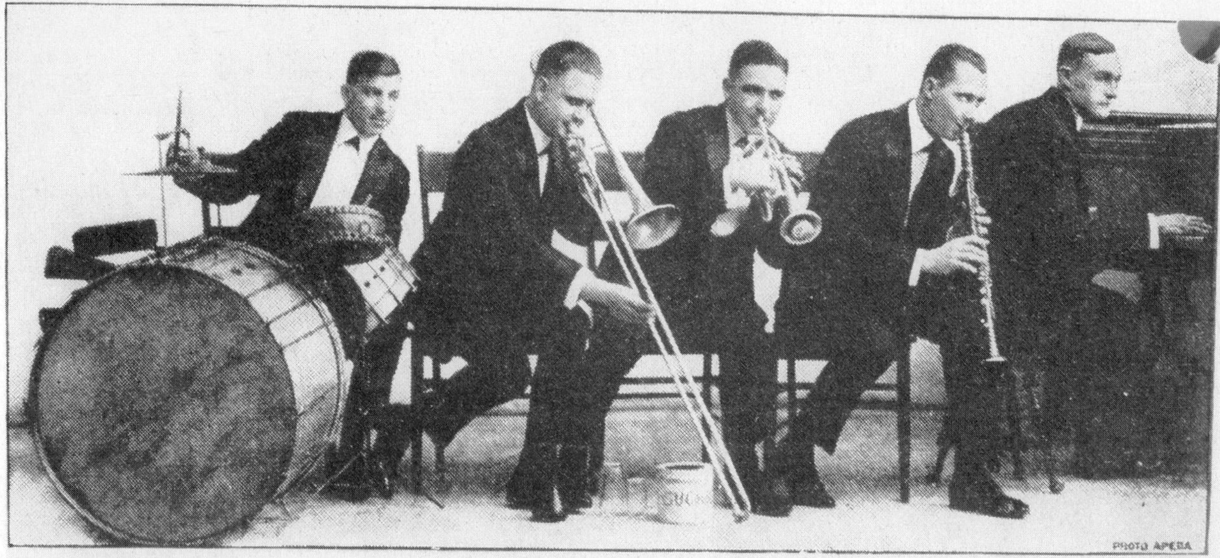


The Original Dixieland "Jass" Band

*Courtesy Rutgers Institute of Jazz Studies.*

means of personal expression. By 1915, there was a growing audience of mostly young white people who viewed jazz as an exciting new music worthy of their respect and attention.

- The **Original Dixieland Jazz Band** (ODJB) was a band of white New Orleans musicians led by cornetist Nick LaRocca. They learned to play jazz by imitating black New Orleans musicians active in the first part of the twentieth century (although LaRocca denied this for years). In 1915, a group that would soon become the ODJB, performed in Chicago, where they were an immediate success. They were in New York by 1917, performing at one of the Reisenweber Cafes, where they were also a great success. Their recordings of "Livery Stable Blues" and "Original Dixie Jazz Band One-Step" from 1917 are considered to be the first instrumental jazz recordings. They sold over one million copies and attracted national as well as international attention to this new music. The group enjoyed tremendous success but was thought of primarily as a novelty act. As jazz became more popular in the 1920s, musicians all over the country were attracted to it; they began to assemble bands using the Original Dixieland Jazz Band, King Oliver's Creole Jazz Band, and the New Orleans Rhythm Kings as models.
- Another successful white band from New Orleans was the New Orleans Rhythm Kings (NORK). This band eventually settled in Chicago in the early 1920s and enjoyed great success there.

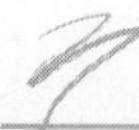

## CHANGE IN AMERICAN ATTITUDES

- A social upheaval shook American culture between 1890 and 1920; the American ethic of hard work and emotional constraint was replaced by a new ideal that emphasized pleasure and self- expression as acceptable modes of behavior. The result of this change in attitude was the appearance of dance halls, opulent restaurants, cabarets, and theaters. There was also rising interest in black entertainment in the early 1920s.

- **Prohibition**: Intellectuals and young people, in general, saw prohibition against alcohol as an outdated remnant of old Victorian society. The illegal speakeasies and cabarets of the Prohibition years were regarded as exciting and romantic. Jazz became the perfect musical backdrop for these establishments. Jazz became a symbol of rebellion. F. Scott Fitzgerald dubbed the 1920s as "the Jazz Age."
- There was more interest in social dancing; consequently dance halls and cabarets were everywhere and were socially acceptable. Jazz began to spread from New Orleans with the rise of the dance boom. The first authentic New Orleans jazz band to leave was organized by Bill Johnson in 1908 and went to California. His band, the Original Creole Band toured the vaudeville circuit and made it to New York City by 1915. Jelly Roll Morton was also in California by 1917. Trombonist and bandleader Kid Ory was in California by 1919, and Joe "King" Oliver was in Chicago by 1918.

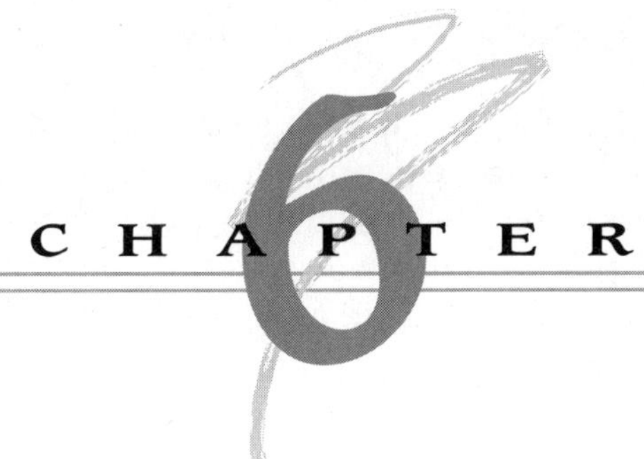

# CHAPTER 6

# "Harlem" Stride Piano

- The stride piano style has its roots in the ragtime style. Many stride pianists first learned to play ragtime compositions by composers such as Scott Joplin. Early stride piano styles evolved from ragtime where players were able to improvise rags and/or embellish preexisting ones. Influences of early New Orleans jazz gradually crept into the stride piano style. Elements of the ragtime style were also retained, such as the left hand going back and forth imitating the two-beat style of a brass band march and an "oom-pah" effect. The left hand sometimes incorporated tenths (instead of octaves) and/or walking tenths into the two-beat accompaniment.
- The right hand also featured syncopated melodies. However, the new elements in the stride piano style featured the following:
  - ♪ A right hand that used a familiar melody as its basis for an improvisation. Therefore, the right hand was likely to be different from one performance to the next.
  - ♪ The presence of swing eighth notes as a general part of the rhythmic feel. Unlike the ragtime rhythmic feel, which used an even-eighth (military) rhythmic feel, stride pianists arranged pairs of eighth notes in long-short durations.
- To discern the difference between the ragtime style and the stride style, listen for the following elements:
  - ♪ The improvised nature of the right-hand material
  - ♪ The swing eighth-note rhythmic feel
  - ♪ The existence of tenths or walking tenths in the left hand

- Sometimes stride piano is referred to as "Harlem" stride piano, since many of its practitioners were active in the Harlem district of New York City. These players often played from sundown to sunup at saloons, dance halls, cabarets, and even rent parties. The rent parties, given to help friends with financial burdens, often developed into informal and friendly piano contests as players would take turns showing their various talents as stride pianists. In this way, players exchanged ideas and information about piano technique, harmony, improvisation, rhythm, and other various elements of the stride style.

Some important stride pianists include:

- **James P. Johnson** (1894–1955) Born in New Brunswick, New Jersey. In his early life, Johnson was interested in classical and ragtime piano styles. By his teenage years, he was working in dance halls, rent parties, and cabarets. In the 1920s he made piano rolls and recordings of popular songs, some composed by himself, including "The Charleston," "Snowy Morning Blues," and "Carolina Shout," a mandatory stride piano standard even Duke Ellington made it a point to master.
  - ♪ He taught Fats Waller and collaborated with him in a stage revue *Keep Shufflin'* (1928).
  - ♪ He accompanied blues singers including Bessie Smith, Ethel Waters, and Ida Cox.
  - ♪ He was a diversified musician who composed a large amount of diverse compositions including classical symphonic works, Broadway musicals, and popular songs.
  - ♪ He was professionally active until 1951 when he suffered a stroke.
- **Willie "the Lion" Smith** (1897–1973) A formidable stride pianist, Smith was much in demand at the rent parties and small clubs of Harlem. He made only a few recordings in the 1920s, and didn't make any recordings under his own name until the 1930s. He played with Mamie Smith's Jazz Hounds, performing with them on one of the first blues recordings made in 1920, "Crazy Blues."
- **Charles "Luckyeth" Roberts** (1887–1968) Arrived in New York City around 1910. He played at the Little Savoy Club, eventually composing and performing in vaudeville shows. He was the owner of the Rendezvous Club from 1940 to 1954.
- **Thomas Wright "Fats" Waller** (1904–1943) Born in New York City, Waller was a stride pianist who was a protegé of James P. Johnson. As a teenager he played at rent parties and recorded piano rolls. Waller could also play organ and celeste. He found work playing these instruments as background music for silent films in some of the most prominent theaters in Harlem. Eventually Fats became famous as a singer, entertainer, and composer of popular songs and Broadway shows. In the 1920s, Waller teamed up with lyricist Andy Razaf to write hit songs such as "Ain't Misbehavin'," "Honeysuckle Rose," and "(What Did I Do To Be So) Black and Blue." He made over 500 recordings, starred in movies, and performed on radio broadcasts. He died suddenly in Kansas City while aboard an express train on its way from Los Angeles to New York City.

- **Jelly Roll Morton** (1890–1941) Born Ferdinand Joseph LaMenthe in New Orleans, Jelly Roll Morton became a stride pianist and one of the first jazz composers and arrangers. He worked in Storyville *district of New Orleans* as a teenager and was also a pimp, pool shark, and gambler. From 1904 to 1917 he was an itinerant musician who traveled the South, going as far east as Atlanta, Georgia. From 1917 to 1922 he performed on the West Coast. In the 1920s Morton made his most significant ensemble recordings on the Victor label with the Red Hot Peppers, a band he formed for the sole purpose of recording. He also made solo piano recordings for the Gennett label from 1923 to 1924. Morton fell out of favor in the 1930s eventually playing in small bars in Washington, D.C. In 1938, he was recorded by Alan Lomax in a series of interviews made for historical documentation at the Library of Congress. Among other subjects in these interviews, Morton speaks from and demonstrates at the piano about the early days of jazz in New Orleans, making him an important jazz historical resource.
- **Earl Hines** (1903–1983) Born and raised in Pittsburgh, Earl Hines found his first professional work in that city in 1921. In 1923, he relocated to Chicago where his style of stride piano playing demonstrated the influences of the trumpet playing of Louis Armstrong. He used creative piano devices to imitate Armstrong's innovations on trumpet such as the following:
    - ♪ Right-hand single-note improvisations that imitated trumpet melodies
    - ♪ Fast right-hand octave tremolos to imitate Armstrong's fast vibrato
    - ♪ Forceful right-hand octave melodies to imitate Armstrong's powerful sound
        - ♩ His Chicago radio broadcasts from 1929 to 1939 helped influenced the style of pianists Art Tatum, Nat "King" Cole, and Teddy Wilson. Hines's style was a precursor to the bop style of Bud Powell in the 1940s.
        - ♩ In the 1930s and 1940s, Hines led an important big band that eventually contained many young bebop musicians who went on to have significant careers, such as Charlie Parker, Dizzy Gillespie, Billy Eckstine, and Sarah Vaughan.
- **Teddy Wilson** (1912–1986) Born in Austin, Texas, Teddy Wilson was raised in Tuskegee, Alabama. He was one of the most influential stride pianists of the 1930s and early 1940s. Influenced by Earl Hines's single-note trumpet style, Wilson perfected the stride style while playing with great jazz musicians including Louis Armstrong, Jimmie Noone, Art Tatum (in piano duets), and Benny Carter. From 1936 to 1939, with the encouragement of John Hammond, Wilson played with Benny Goodman, mostly in trios and quartets, making him part of the first interracial band. Wilson also collaborated on many recordings with Billie Holiday.
- **Art Tatum** (1909–1956) Born in Toledo, Ohio. Tatum was the most extraordinary of all pianists and jazz musicians. Although legally blind, he possessed no musical or technical limitations. He received some formal training in his youth and performed on his own radio show from 1929 through 1930. Although influenced by Fats Waller, Tatum took the stride piano style to a level unattainable by anyone else. His left-hand

control and right-hand double-time lines amazed all who witnessed his playing. He also had the ability to take any popular song and reharmonize it in his own ingenious way. His 1933 virtuosic recordings of popular songs such as "Tiger Rag" served notice to all (including classical pianists) that Art Tatum was simply beyond comparison. He traveled throughout the United States appearing in nightclubs and offering himself to local musicians in friendly cutting sessions where he reigned as superior. In the mid-1940s, Tatum led a trio with guitarist Tiny Grimes and bassist Slam Stewart, performing in New York City nightclubs. He served as an inspiration to the young bebop musicians in New York in the early 1940s. Unfortunately, Tatum's playing was not documented on recordings in any consistent manner until it was almost too late. He was recorded often during the last two years of his life. Earlier recordings, while still definitive, are not always of the best quality.

- Other stride pianists include Eubie Blake, Abba Labba, Mary Lou Williams, and Lillian "Lil" Hardin.

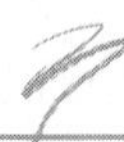

## BOOGIE-WOOGIE PIANO (HONKY-TONK)

- The boogie-woogie piano style has its roots in the blues style and was prevalent with players from the South and Midwest. Many of these players did not have access to formal music training and therefore were self-trained pianists. As a result, they created exciting dance rhythms using repetitive, stationary left-hand patterns instead of the stride style of piano commonly used by players from Chicago and New York.
- Even though there were still four beats per measure, the patterns often used continuous eighth notes (sometimes swing eighth notes) creating a rhythmic feel of eight beats per measure. Typical boogie-woogie piano compositions featured left- hand patterns used to cycle through blues forms an indefinite number of times along with improvised blues riffs with the right hand. For example, listen to "Honky Tonk Train Blues" by Mead Lux Lewis. The repetitive, stationary left-hand pattern is obvious. Lewis initiates a new blues riff at the beginning of each chorus while using the same idea in every B section.
- The boogie-woogie piano style has the following features:
  - ♪ A stationary, repetitive left-hand pattern
  - ♪ Improvised blues riffs in the right hand
  - ♪ Mostly AAB blues forms, which are repeated ad lib
- To discern the difference between the stride style and the boogie-woogie style, listen for the following elements:
  - ♪ A stationary, repetitive left-hand pattern
  - ♪ Improvised blues riffs in the right-hand material
  - ♪ An AAB blues form
- Boogie-woogie pianists played in small bars, saloons, barrelhouses, and honky-tonks throughout the South and Midwest. Many times the pianos

were large uprights that were not in the best condition, giving the overall music a rough edge.

- In 1938, John Hammond organized a legendary Carnegie Hall concert, "From Spirituals to Swing," which featured significant boogie-woogie pianists Meade Lux Lewis, Albert Ammons, and Pete Johnson; the first two were good friends and shared ideas in Chicago during the 1920s. The concert initiated a rebirth of public interest in the boogie-woogie piano style, resulting in many boogie-woogie imitators.

**Meade Lux Lewis** (1905–1964) is the **Father of Boogie-Woogie**. Born in Chicago, Lewis grew up listening to blues pianists including Jimmy Yancey. In 1927 he recorded his famous "Honky Tonk Train Blues," inspired by the trains he heard in his youth pass by his South La Salle Street home. The recording wasn't released until 1929. He was discovered by John Hammond in 1935, and he made recordings in the late 1930s and 1940s. He also appeared in the movie *New Orleans* with Louis Armstrong in 1947.

**Pete Johnson** (1904–1967) was born in Kansas City, Missouri. He grew up playing blues piano styles and accompanying blues singers around Kansas City. In 1936, John Hammond arranged for Johnson and blues singer Joe Turner to play at New York City's club The Famous Door. In 1938, he was featured in a Carnegie Hall concert with Meade Lux Lewis and Albert Ammons. He performed and recorded in the 1940s and 1950s. In 1958 he suffered a stroke that ended his musical career.

**Albert Ammons** (1907–1949) played in Chicago nightclubs during the 1920s and 1930s. He made his first recordings in 1936. He appeared regularly at Café Society in New York in the 1940s and played for President Harry Truman's inauguration in 1949. Ammons was a versatile pianist who was not limited to playing the boogie-woogie style. His son, Gene Ammons, had a prolific career as a jazz tenor saxophonist.

**Jimmy Yancey** (1898–1951) was playing boogie-woogie piano as early as the 1910s and 1920s. He was a self-taught pianist who could also sing and dance. He played at rent parties and entertainment establishments around Chicago. In 1939, he made recordings including "State Street Special" and "Yancey's Stomp." He also had a day job as groundskeeper for the Chicago White Sox for twenty-five years. Jimmy Yancey was inducted into the Rock and Roll Hall of Fame in 1986.

**Clarence "Pine Top" Smith** (1904–1929) was among the first to record a boogie-woogie piano solo when he recorded "Pine Top's Boogie Woogie" in 1928. He toured with minstrel shows and was featured on the TOBA circuit in the 1920s. He also accompanied blues singer Mamie Smith.

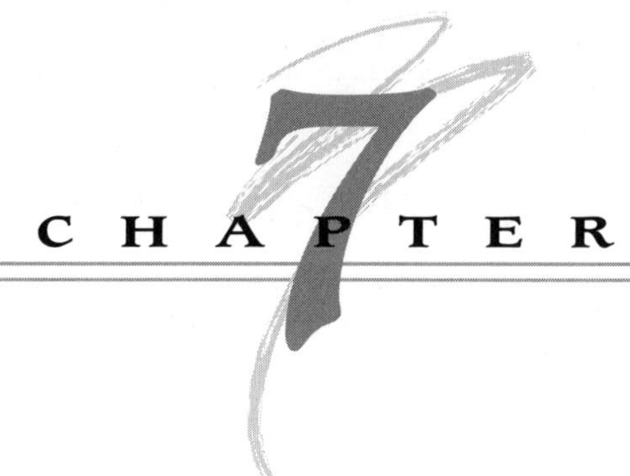

CHAPTER 7

# Two Great Soloists

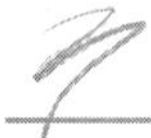

## LOUIS ARMSTRONG

- Louis Armstrong (1901–1971) was born in New Orleans. Even though he maintained throughout his life that he was born on July 4, 1900, it has been determined more recently that he was actually born on August 8, 1901.
- His first exposure to jazz was as a child growing up near the Storyville district of New Orleans, where he pushed around a coal cart to help with the family income. He also performed in spasm bands on street corners. These were small groups made up of kids that sang songs and played homemade instruments for pocket change.
- At age twelve, after being arrested for firing a pistol on New Year's Day, Louis was sent to the Colored Waifs Home, a juvenile reform school, where he was given some structure to his personal life. He also played in the school band under the direction of Peter Davis; there he was first given a bugle, then later a cornet. The Waifs Home would give Louis his first formal musical education.
- Armstrong earned the nickname "Satchel Mouth" (later shortened to "Satchmo") because of his large mouth.
- After leaving the Waifs Home, Joe "King" Oliver, one of the most famous cornet players and bandleaders in New Orleans, became Armstrong's mentor. In exchange for lessons, young Armstrong performed household chores for the Olivers. He eventually began working (substituting) in places for Oliver and other New Orleans trumpet players when they were

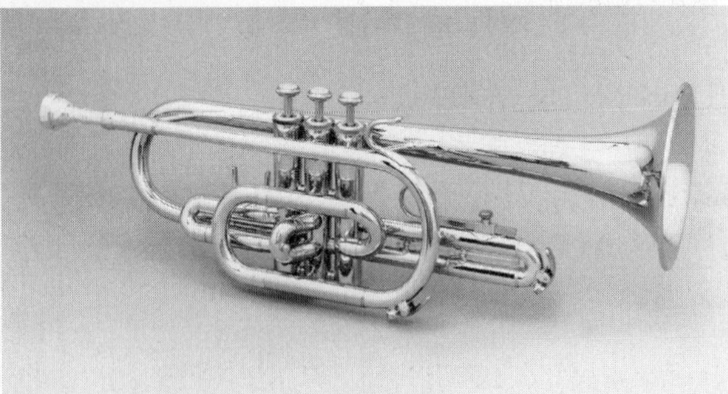

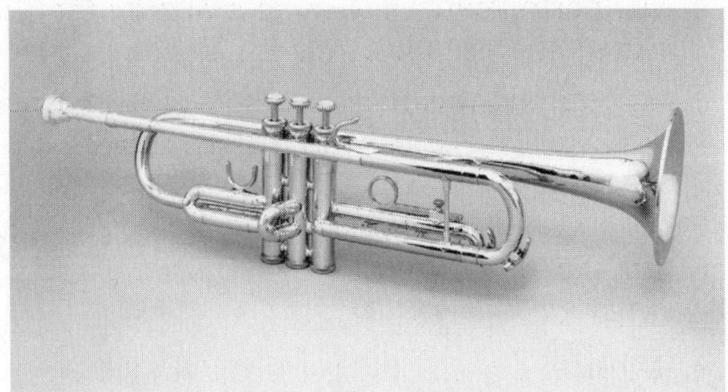

*The cornet (left) and trumpet (right) have the same length of tubing, but the shape of the tubing is different. The cornet has conical tubing (ever expanding) and the trumpet has cylindrical (straight) tubing. The difference in sound is not always apparent, but the cornet typically has a more mellow sound than that of the brighter sounding trumpet. The early high brass players were more inclined to play cornet, but by the early 1920's many had switched to the increasingly popular trumpet which could be heard more easily in the larger bands.*

unable to make an engagement. Manny Perez, Freddie Keppard, and Bunk Johnson were some of the most well-known cornet/trumpet players in New Orleans at the time. Louis developed a reputation as a fine player, which enabled him to find steady employment in New Orleans.

- In 1917 Storyville, the legal red-light district, was closed and with it many of the night spots that provided entertainment. As a result, many New Orleans jazz musicians including King Oliver went to Chicago. These same musicians enjoyed great popularity and success in Chicago's nighttime establishments, partially because of Chicago's corrupt city administration run by mobsters.
- Around 1920, Louis Armstrong was employed by Fate Marable on Mississippi riverboats, where it was mandatory that musicians be able to read music. Louis polished his style and became one of the most sought after musicians in New Orleans.
- In 1922 King Oliver invited Armstrong to relocate to Chicago and join his successful Creole Jazz Band performing at the Lincoln Gardens nightclub. Soon it was apparent that Armstrong would surpass his mentor.
- King Oliver had a female pianist named Lil Hardin in his Creole Jazz Band. She caught Louis's eye and they were soon married.
- Oliver's band made a series of recordings in 1923 with Armstrong playing the second cornet part. Oliver's sound is sweet compared with that of Armstrong. However, Oliver does not have much range or sheer power. (Because of limitations in recording technology at this time, these acoustic recordings do not fully represent the complete tone quality of the instrumentalists.) Oliver was also a master of using mutes to color his sound (tonal manipulation).
- In 1924, at the urging of his wife, pianist Lil Hardin Armstrong, Louis moved to New York City to perform with the famous Fletcher Henderson Orchestra.
- His impact on the New York musicians was strong and influential. These musicians had never heard anyone with Louis's talent and capabilities. His solo improvisations were the most innovative and expressive to date.

His performances were so amazing that he raised the level of expectation of all trumpet players.

- By 1925 he was back in Chicago with great fanfare and was being hailed as the greatest "hot" jazz player alive.
- From 1926 to 1929 Armstrong made a series of recordings in Chicago dubbed "Louis Armstrong and His Hot Five" and "Louis Armstrong and His Hot Seven," featuring many former Creole Jazz Band musicians and other former New Orleans players.
- These are some of the most important recordings in American music, and they changed the course of jazz history. They also helped to establish the primacy of Louis Armstrong as the **first great jazz soloist.** His playing on these recordings influenced all popular and jazz musicians. Whether they were singers or instrumentalists didn't matter.
- The recordings themselves are not always of the highest quality; the arrangements are of minimal quality, and most of the other soloists cannot compare with Armstrong. What is important about these recordings is Armstrong's playing and singing. Armstrong influenced all musicians in the following ways:
  - ♪ **Rhythm**: His sense of swing is exciting and compelling to both players and listeners. He plays groups of eighth notes in a long—short manner and accents or emphasizes the offbeat eighth notes.
    - ♩ To better appreciate swing, try tapping your foot while saying the word "apple" on each tap. Then elongate the first syllable and emphasize the second, and you have swing eighth notes.
  - ♪ The swing eighth note is different from the Western European concept of eighth notes where they are evenly subdivided with the accent on the first eighth note instead of the second. Louis's sense of rhythm seemed more acute than any of his contemporaries. His rhythmic inflection was perhaps the most influential aspect of his playing. Prior to Armstrong, the common rhythms played by jazz instrumentalists more closely resembled the rhythm of ragtime music. Ragtime, while highly syncopated, did not have the long—short lilt or the unusual accents of Armstrong. This new concept in rhythm influenced all subsequent popular instrumentalists and singers.
  - ♪ **Double time** is when twice as many notes are played in the same amount of time. Most improvisers play two notes per beat as they convey the feeling of swing. Sometimes they play three notes per beat. However, once four notes per beat are being played, the swing feel changes and suddenly the beat feels as though it has increased to double the speed. Louis Armstrong used double time in many of his solos, and he could sometimes even create triple time. Double time is standard equipment for today's jazz musicians, but in Armstrong's day, he amazed everyone with his ability to improvise double-time phrases that were both accurate and musically valid.
  - ♪ **Sound**: Louis possessed a large, penetrating, extroverted sound. It was often described as being "hot." His power and projection were far superior to anyone else at the time of the Hot Five and Seven recordings. It is said that even after Armstrong was placed more than twenty feet farther away from the recording apparatus than the other players, his sound was still the most powerful. His

articulation (the way he played his notes) was also clear and precise. Part of his sound may be related to a switch from cornet to trumpet in the mid-1920s.

- **Range**: Armstrong extended the practical, usable range of the trumpet by a fifth. Today, many trumpet players have the ability to achieve Armstrong's range, but at that time it was extremely rare and unprecedented among jazz trumpeters (compare it to the first runner to break the four-minute mile—today all milers are expected to surpass this mark!). Armstrong played with such strength, range, and authority that many trumpet players of his day were in awe of his stamina and abilities.
- **Vibrato**: Louis had a different style of vibrato from that of his contemporaries. He used what is referred to as "terminal" vibrato. Europeans use a constant and consistent vibrato. Early blues singers used a different kind of vibrato, which is often reflected in their guitar playing. Armstrong was one of the first instrumentalists to imitate this kind of vibrato on his trumpet. All subsequent jazz instrumentalists and most popular singers followed suit.
- **Improvisation**: Armstrong was one of the first to move away from paraphrase improvisation and create improvised solos that were completely new and different from the original melody. Paraphrase improvisation is the first step in improvisation where the soloist uses the original melody and more or less paraphrases it. One can readily hear this technique used by many early jazz musicians. When Armstrong improvised, he created new material, sometimes using bits of the original song, but mostly spontaneously creating fresh material not related to the original song. His improvisations were often as memorable and strong as the original song. They were compositions (or recompositions) that stand by themselves. It is both interesting and amazing that Armstrong had few models from which to develop his new approach.
- **Scat singing** is defined as singing using nonsense syllables. Jazz singers who scat sing use and often improvise nonsense syllables such as doo, dah, be, bah, scoo, and so on, in creating instrumental-like melodies. Armstrong is given credit for the first recorded scat solo on his Hot Five "Heebie Jeebies" recording. Legend has it that he accidentally dropped a piece of paper with the words to the song while in the process of recording and rather than waste the recording, he improvised a scat solo. The recording was released with no changes, and more scat solos were included on subsequent recordings. Listen to how Armstrong interacts with the clarinetist on "West End Blues." It is as if he has transformed his voice into an instrument—or perhaps he is imitating his trumpet playing with his voice. Since Armstrong's initiation of scat solos, there have been many singers who have pursued this aspect of vocalization including Cab Calloway, Dizzy Gillespie, Sarah Vaughan, John Hendricks, Al Jarreau, and perhaps the greatest of them all, Ella Fitzgerald.

- Armstrong demonstrated that jazz was a solo improviser's art. The preceding generation of New Orleans musicians utilized collective improvisation. Armstrong established the primacy of the soloist—one who could step forward and move beyond the collective style of the older generation. His playing and singing were unique, expressive, inventive, and easy to identify. Even his ballad playing was lyrical and reflective. His phrases made musical sense and conveyed feeling and emotion.

- These contributions are why Armstrong's 1920s recordings changed the course of jazz history. For someone to have made any one of these contributions would have been sufficient for them to be assessed significant. In Armstrong's case, he is considered either the most significant or at least one of the most significant jazz artists of the twentieth century. Musicians and singers have taken from Armstrong what they thought would fit their own personality. Many have parlayed that into new modes of self-expression through jazz. Most American popular music can be traced back to him.
- In the early 1930s, Louis Armstrong traveled extensively making appearances in Denmark, Sweden, Norway, Holland, England, and all over the United States.
- In 1935, Joe Glaser became Armstrong's manager and remained so until 1969. Glaser managed business affairs while Armstrong concentrated on his music. The Luis Russell Orchestra was hired to back up Armstrong, and the band eventually became known as Louis Armstrong and His Orchestra. Armstrong spent the next ten years fronting the Russell Orchestra and other big bands, achieving a huge amount of popularity. As result, he appeared in several movies as well.
- In 1947, Armstrong performed with a small group called the All Stars, reverting back to playing in his style of the 1920s. The All Stars had some prominent 1920s players such as Earl Hines, Jack Teagarden, Barney Bigard, and Kid Ory.
- In the 1950s and 1960s Armstrong became known as an American ambassador because of his extensive performance tours to Africa, Asia, Europe, and South America.
- In the 1960s Armstrong reached another peak in his career by recording several top hits including "Hello Dolly" in 1963 and "What a Wonderful World" in 1968. By this time, Louis was known more for his singing than his trumpet playing.
- When he died in 1971, most people were unaware that Armstrong had been a leading jazz innovator in the 1920s. However, had he never played another note after 1930, he still would have been considered one of the most significant musicians of the twentieth century.

## BIX BEIDERBECKE

- Bix Beiderbecke (1903–1931) was born and raised in Davenport, Iowa.
- He was showing signs of prodigious musical talent as early as age six. His parents arranged piano lessons; however, Bix's lack of discipline, a recurring theme throughout his adolescence, eventually ended his piano lessons.
- After his older brother brought home recordings of the ODJB, Bix became interested in jazz and, in particular, the cornet. His parents, however, tried to discourage his interest in playing cornet.

- As a result, he was largely self-taught, learning by playing along with recordings. Consequently he learned an unorthodox system of fingerings on the instrument and developed a unique, highly individual sound.
- Bix became infatuated with the sound of the New Orleans bands performing on boats coming up the Mississippi River. He would often skip school to go hear riverboat bands.
- His earliest influences were Nick LaRocca of the ODJB, cornetist Emmet Hardy, and, of course, Louis Armstrong, who he may have heard on the riverboats.
- Bix resisted any kind of formal training during his youth. His frequent absence at school led to poor grades. In 1921, his parents decided to send him to Lake Forest Academy, a private school near Chicago. However, Bix spent many nights in Chicago playing and listening to jazz. Unfortunately, he also developed alcohol-related problems that would plague him for the rest of his life. He was frequently tired and hung over for class the next day. He was soon expelled and sent back home to Davenport. After a short period of working for the family business, Bix moved to Chicago in 1923 and pursued a music career.
- He first spent time in Chicago's South Side listening to black jazz musicians from New Orleans. Then in 1924, he achieved notoriety when he recorded with a band modeled after the New Orleans Rhythm Kings and the ODJB called the **Wolverines.** His solos with the Wolverines were so amazing that he became one of the first white jazz musicians to be widely admired by black jazz musicians.
- From 1925 to 1927, he played with the Detroit-based **Jean Goldkette Orchestra,** teaming up with C-melody saxophonist **Frankie Trumbauer,** who would be an important partner on many recordings.
- In 1927, both Beiderbecke and Trumbauer had relocated to New York City and were hired to perform in **Paul Whiteman's Orchestra.** Both men were important as "hot" jazz soloists within the context of Whiteman's jazz arrangements. The arrival of arranger Bill Challis in 1927 was one reason for Beiderbecke's and Trumbauer's success in the Whiteman band. Challis created arrangements that highlighted Beiderbecke and Trumbauer as preeminent jazz soloists.
- Jazz musicians of the 1920s often were inspired by classical music and sought to incorporate such influences into jazz. Bix and his Whiteman compatriots would often attend New York Philharmonic concerts. Bix was generally unimpressed with classical composers such as Beethoven, Mozart, and Brahms but he was fascinated with modern developments in orchestral music. He was especially attracted to the French impressionistic composers Debussy and Ravel. Their use of whole-tone scales and extended harmonies such as ninth, eleventh, and thirteenth chords were important influences in his improvisations. Bix would often spend time with the conservatory-trained Bill Challis learning about these and other modern composers.
- Bix remained interested in the piano throughout his life. He would often "noodle" at the piano on band breaks, creating impressive improvisations. One such improvisation, later titled "In A Mist," was recorded in 1927. It reveals impressionistic elements such as whole-tone melodies and parallel ninth chords. With Bill Challis's help as transcriber,

several of Bix's "improvisations" were written down and eventually published such as "Candlelight," "Flashes," "In The Dark," and "In A Mist."

- When Bix was not performing or recording with Paul Whiteman's band, he would often be playing with talented jazz musicians from **The Gang.** In the mid-1920s, a loosely knit group of musicians in New York were referred to as The Gang; it comprised the most important white jazz musicians in New York: Bix Beiderbecke, Frankie Trumbauer, Tommy and Jimmy Dorsey, Adrian Rollini, Miff Mole, Red Nichols, Eddie Lang, and others. They would get together to play, exchange ideas, and make their "mark" on jazz.
- Bix was never able to overcome his problems with alcoholism. He had at least one episode of delirium tremens after which Whiteman, although still keeping him on the payroll, sent him home to Davenport to recuperate. However, Bix never returned to Whiteman's band and spent the last two years of his life making recordings under his own name and with songwriter Hoagy Carmichael. He died in his Queens, New York, apartment at the tragically young age of twenty-eight during an alcoholic seizure.
- Beiderbecke has become a cult figure and is often perceived as a tragic-hero figure. His last years, 1929 to 1931, were ones of frustration, because he was unable to perform in appropriate musical contexts. This melancholy attitude is sometimes reflected in his playing.

## Characteristics

- His improvisational style was highly original.
- He was strongly influenced by impressionistic composers Ravel and Debussy.
- He used relatively few blue notes (flat thirds and sevenths).
- His range was limited—he did not possess Armstrong's strong and secure upper register.
- His unorthodox, self-taught system of cornet fingering helped him to achieve a unique, highly personal sound.
- He often worked with inferior musicians or in a context where he had few opportunities to express himself musically.
- Everyone who heard him play commented on his beautiful, round sound.
- He improvised in a more introverted manner compared with the extroverted Louis Armstrong.
- He thought compositionally (sometimes like a pianist) when improvising; he played "alternate melodies."
- He had a very smooth and lyrical approach.
- He played on the beat in contrast to Armstrong's playing, which was more behind the beat.
- He played his eighth notes rather evenly.
- His contribution was the evolution of a complementary white jazz style.
- He was sometimes criticized for not playing hot solos like Armstrong, but he was not trying to imitate Armstrong. Beiderbecke used his own musical sensibilities and experiences to synthesize a highly original and innovative approach that influenced many subsequent jazz musicians.

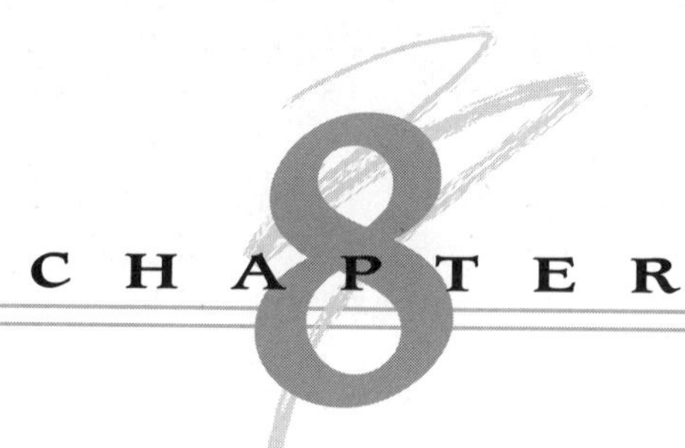

# CHAPTER 8

# Chicago

- Many New Orleans musicians were drawn to Chicago because the city had an abundance of illegal cabarets, dance halls, and speakeasies that provided many playing opportunities.
- Chicago's growth was partially a result of the industrialization of large northern cities after the turn of the century, which was aided by World War I. There was a massive northern migration of blacks from the deep South, many of whom moved to Chicago. This created a large audience for black performers, especially blues artists. Most people who went to Chicago ended up in the South Side, home to a substantial proportion of vice, which gave Chicago its Roaring Twenties reputation. In this area, most of the New Orleans musicians worked in clubs and cabarets. They attracted both white and black audiences. Here is where Chicago musicians first heard authentic New Orleans–style jazz. Both black and white musicians were able to get hands-on exposure at informal jam sessions at a time when black and white musicians were not allowed to perform together in public. After a nightclub closed to the public, white and black musicians would play together in a relaxed and informal setting. Sometimes jam sessions could be very competitive when open to the public, as was the case in Kansas City in the 1930s. In a sense, jam sessions were the first schools of jazz.
- The most important early 1920s band in Chicago was King Oliver's Creole Jazz Band. King Oliver moved to Chicago in 1918, and his group comprised an all-star group of New Orleans musicians. In 1923, the group made a series of recordings with a young Louis Armstrong, which constituted the first important body of jazz recorded by African Americans.

- The heyday of Chicago was short; by 1928 a newly elected city government, promising to clean up the corruption of the previous administration, had swept away all of the illegal cabarets and dance halls. By the following year many musicians left for New York. The New York jazz scene was just coming of age in the late 1920s and would soon become the jazz center of the world.

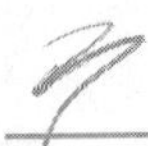

## JAZZ COMBO MUSIC PRIOR TO THE 1930s

- Combo jazz began in New Orleans, but it received national attention when many of the musicians, black and white, moved to Chicago. Many young Chicago musicians of high school age became enamored with the new style of music and began imitating it. The white Chicago jazz musicians were the first group of non–New Orleans–born jazz musicians to make a contribution to this new music. For them it was a new and exciting music. Many of these young Chicagoans were born of immigrant parents of Irish, Polish, Russian, German, and Italian extraction. For many it was also a means of rebellion; parents forbade their children to play jazz. Many musicians from around the country also moved there to be a part of this movement. The music came to be known as **Dixieland** once it moved north of the Mason-Dixon line.
- Early jazz musicians began embellishing the melodies of popular tunes, marches, rags, and so on, to form the basis of jazz. As it evolved, the embellishments became as important as the melodies themselves.
- New Orleans jazz is characterized by collective improvisation, where everyone improvised simultaneously while complementing each other. The delicate balance and interplay found in New Orleans jazz began to disappear in the Chicago style when players became more interested in the **solo improvisation** of one player at a time. Improvising in the newer solo style required a different approach from the older collectively improvised music.
- As a soloist, the improviser must possess good technique, range, sound, understanding of harmony, and the ability to create memorable solos that can stand on their own merit. In collectively improvised music, the musicians were required to blend their improvisations into a single moving texture.
- It was in Chicago that black jazz musicians from New Orleans first recorded in the early 1920s. There are no recordings made by such musicians from New Orleans prior to the early 1920s. This fact has made it difficult to determine exactly what early New Orleans jazz sounded like; all that exists on record is what was played in Chicago by musicians originally from New Orleans. Recordings helped to popularize and disseminate jazz all over the country. Blues singer Bessie Smith became a household name, selling millions of recordings in the early 1920s. The instrumental groups also sold millions of records.

### Differences Between Early New Orleans Style and Chicago Style

- Change in instrumentation:
  - Saxophone gradually becomes part of standard instrumentation.
  - Saxophone and clarinet are interchangeable.

- String bass appears more often and eventually replaces the tuba.
- Trumpet replaces the cornet.
- Banjo gradually disappears from standard instrumentation.
- Piano is standard rhythm section instrumentation with optional guitar.

- Groups begin to rely more on written music and arrangements.
- Paraphrase improvisation transformed into more adventurous improvisation based on harmony.
- Stop-time breaks: The band suddenly stops playing for four beats while one person improvises, providing a change in musical texture.
- Collective improvisation occurs less frequently than solo improvisation.
- Rhythmic feel is often more frantic than the relaxed, blues-oriented New Orleans style, possibly because of the four quick beats underlying what had been a traditional 2/2 march style.
- The drumming style changes from one that is military/rudimental to one that swings and is more cymbal-oriented.
- The modern drum set begins to evolve in the 1920s.

In Chicago, there were three main groups of players:

1. Transplanted black New Orleans musicians (such as King Oliver's Creole Jazz Band)
2. Transplanted white New Orleans musicians (such as the New Orleans Rhythm Kings)
3. White Chicago natives

## THE AUSTIN HIGH GANG

- Inspired by the jazz of the New Orleans Rhythm Kings, Bix Beiderbecke with the Wolverines, King Oliver, and others, there existed a group of young white aspiring jazz players who were, at first, fans and then emulators of the above-mentioned legends. Many of these young jazz musicians attended Austin High School in Chicago. As a result they were given the designation of the "Austin High Gang." Members included cornetist Jimmy McPartland, clarinetist/saxophonist Frankie Teschemacher, saxophonist Bud Freeman, guitarist Eddie Condon, banjo player Dick McPartland, pianist and later bassist Jim Lannigan, drummers Dave Tough and Gene Krupa, and the young clarinetist Benny Goodman. Eventually Austin High Gang members followed one of two possible directions in jazz developments. Some remained loyal to the early New Orleans and Chicago small group styles, one being called the Blue Friars, while others pursued the new big band swing style being pioneered in the 1920s by Duke Ellington, Fletcher Henderson, Ben Pollack, and Bennie Moten. The white Chicago musicians attempted to get as close as possible to the black jazz style in Chicago while at the same time maintaining the white jazz traditions established by the New Orleans Rhythm Kings and the Wolverines.

## Some important musicians in the 1920s

| TRUMPET/CORNET | CLARINET | TROMBONE | SAXOPHONE |
|---|---|---|---|
| Jimmy McPartland | Benny Goodman | Jack Teagarden | Frankie Trumbauer |
| Bix Beiderbecke | Frankie Teschemacher | Tommy Dorsey | Frankie Teschemacher |
| Wingy Manone | Mezz Mezzrow | Glenn Miller | Bud Freeman |
| Red Nichols | Pee Wee Russell | Miff Mole | Jimmy Dorsey |
| Jabbo Smith | | Charlie Green | |
| Muggsy Spanier | | Jimmy Harrison | |
| Henry "Red" Allen | | J. C. Higginbothan | |
| Wild Bill Davidson | | | |

| PIANO | DRUMS | BASS | GUITAR/BANJO |
|---|---|---|---|
| Earl Hines | Dave Tough | Pops Foster | Eddie Lang |
| Lil' Hardin | George Wettling | John Lindsay | Lonnie Johnson |
| Joe Sullivan | Ben Pollack | Steve Brown | Dick McPartland |
| | Ray Bauduc | Bill Johnson | Eddie Condon |
| | Vic Berton | Wellman Braud | |
| | Gene Krupa | Jimmy Lannigan | |

| VIOLIN | BANDLEADERS |
|---|---|
| Joe Venuti | Ben Pollack |
| Stuff Smith | Jean Goldkette |
| | Erskine Tate |
| | Carroll Dickerson |

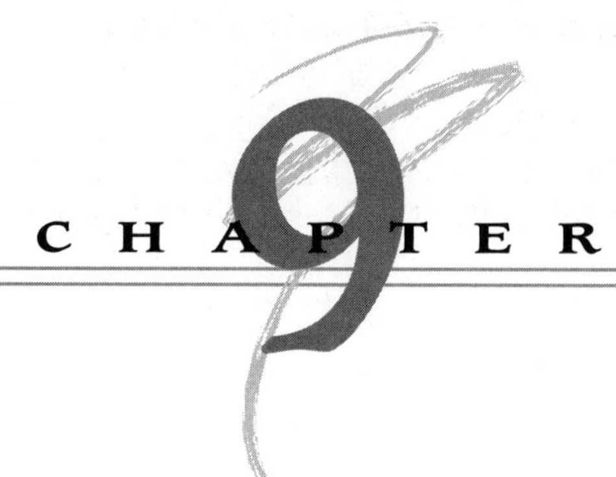

CHAPTER 9

# Early Big Band Swing

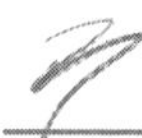

## JAMES REESE EUROPE, WILL MARION COOK

- Before 1920, there were large ensembles that performed arrangements of popular music. Influenced by the brass band tradition, these large ensembles performed what was called "syncopated" music. From a purist's point of view, they were not jazz ensembles, and their output consisted mostly of ragtime and blues arrangements.
- One of the most successful of these large ensembles was led by **James Reese Europe** (1881–1919). Europe was born in Washington, D.C. At age twenty-two he moved to New York City, where he played piano in cabarets and was musical director of several shows. In 1910 he founded the Clef Club, an African-American organization that also had an orchestra. The Clef Club Orchestra made a successful debut at Carnegie Hall on May 2, 1912. As a result, Europe's Clef Club Orchestra performed at elite functions in New York, London, Paris, and other international cities. Eventually, the renowned dance team of Vernon and Irene Castle joined Europe's orchestra. They were joined by composer and arranger Ford Dabney. Europe eventually left the Clef Club Orchestra to pursue other musical ventures. He also led an important band as part of the armed forces during World War I. This band performed in Great Britain, Italy, and France. Tragically, James Reese Europe was knifed to death by one of his dissatisfied percussionists on May 9, 1919.
- Another successful ensemble was Will Marion Cook's Southern Syncopated Orchestra. **Will Marion Cook** (1869–1944) was born in Washington, D.C. He studied violin at the Oberlin Conservatory of Music

and under Professor Joseph Joachim in Germany. He also studied briefly with Antonin Dvorak at the National Conservatory of Music. Cook became successful in New York's musical theater scene in the 1890s. In the early twentieth century, Cook led the Southern Syncopated Orchestra, which included Sidney Bechet when they toured Europe.

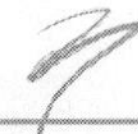

## PAUL WHITEMAN, FERDE GROFÉ

- A major change in dance bands took place around 1914 in a group led by Art Hickman in San Francisco. His pianist was **Ferde Grofé** (1892–1972), a formally trained musician and composer who also played violin. At this time most dance bands, except for New Orleans bands, basically played the melody repeatedly in unison.
- Grofé began to make arrangements for the group, which involved giving separate lines of music to various instruments in a type of contrapuntal fashion. He decided to build this new style around a saxophone choir, motivated by the instrument's novelty. They could also play much softer and had a more mellow (sweeter) tone than brass instruments. Therefore, they could function much like a string section but with significantly fewer people for essentially the same effect. Grofé and Hickman thus created the first seeds of what would eventually become the big band swing style.
- One of the most successful dance bands of the 1920s was formed by **Paul Whiteman** (1890–1967) in 1918 in San Francisco, later moving to Los Angeles and then to New York in 1920. Whiteman was a classically trained viola player whose father was an important music teacher in Denver, Colorado. Paul Whiteman recognized Grofé's talent as an arranger and hired him away from Hickman's band.
- While most bands were playing unimaginative stock arrangements, Grofé took a more creative approach to arranging for Whiteman's band by treating each chorus of an arrangement differently. He might give the melody to one saxophone while harmonizing the same melody using other instruments and perhaps write a countermelody as well. Whiteman allowed Grofé much freedom to create arrangements, borrowing liberally from the symphonic style and fusing it with the more modern jazz sounds that were becoming increasingly popular.
- Whiteman's recordings of the 1920s were a great success and led to his being dubbed the "King of Jazz." He called his music, "symphonic jazz" explaining that it combined elements taken from jazz rhythms and the blues with elements taken from classical harmony and melody.
- Paul Whiteman organized one of the most famous New York concerts of the 1920s. He always had aspirations to elevate the status of jazz and demonstrate that it deserved equal recognition and billing with classical music. It has been written that he tried to "make a lady out of jazz." On February 12, 1924, at one of New York City's premier classical venues, Aeolian Hall, Paul Whiteman's band performed jazz-influenced compositions he commissioned well-known composers to write. The concert was titled "An Experiment in Modern Music." The last piece performed that evening was the premiere of George Gershwin's "Rhapsody in Blue" with the composer at the piano. Many famous and curious musicians were present including the famous Russian composer

and pianist Sergei Rachmaninoff. Favorable critical attention was paid to "symphonic jazz" and to the work of Whiteman, Gershwin, Irving Berlin, and others.

- Another important arranger for the Whiteman band, Bill Challis, was hired in 1927. In his previous job as an arranger for the Jean Goldkette Orchestra, it was obvious he already knew how to highlight talented jazz soloists. Challis used all the instruments in Whiteman's band to create clever arrangements that captured the essence of 1920s jazz in a large ensemble context. In many ways, Challis's significance is equal to Don Redman's contributions as an arranger.
- Whiteman's success was noticed by both black and white bandleaders; his music had more commercial appeal than the authentic sounds of New Orleans jazz.

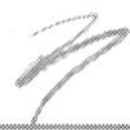

## THE EMERGENCE OF BIG BAND SWING

- By the late 1920s, the swing eighth-note pattern and a looser, less stiff rhythmic feel had become predominant. The seeds of the more organized and less spontaneous big band swing style go back to the 1920s. Some of the finest recordings made in the New Orleans/Chicago collectively improvised style appear in the latter part of the 1920s in the music of Armstrong's Hot Five and Hot Seven groups, Bix Beiderbecke, and Jelly Roll Morton's Red Hot Peppers. However, by 1930 the newer, more highly structured style of big band swing had all but replaced it as the most popular style.
- "The Swing Era was influenced by Louis Armstrong who gave it its language" (*The World of Swing*; Stanley Dance, p. 3). His manner of playing influenced all subsequent instrumentalists, singers, and arrangers. When Armstrong appeared with Fletcher Henderson in 1924 it was to change the way jazz and popular music was performed. His rhythmic inflection, improvisational ability, phrasing, and vibrato would change jazz forever. Henderson's band was transformed from a good commercial dance band to a band that could swing. The soloists in New York took careful note of the way Armstrong played, as did arrangers Fletcher Henderson and Don Redman. The changes in Henderson's band and the new arrangements to accommodate Armstrong's innovative playing did not go unnoticed by other important bandleaders
- The concept of a big band actually began with adding more instruments to the frontline Chicago-style bands. With the increasing commercial success of jazz, it was possible to pay more members in a band. Therefore, bands could increase the numbers of members, following the adage "more is better."
- In the mid-1920s pioneering bands had two trumpets, one trombone, and three saxophones/clarinets. The rhythm section was maintained without any major changes; however, some rhythm sections included guitar, and in the 1930s vibraphone was sometimes present. By the mid-1930s, it was more common to have three trumpets, two or three trombones, and four saxophones. Eventually the standard big band instrumentation grew to four trumpets, four trombones, and five

saxophones plus rhythm section. In addition, there would usually be two tenor saxophones, two alto saxophones, and one baritone saxophone.

- Many jazz musicians got their initial start in professional music as accompanists for blues singers, traveling with minstrel shows or performing in vaudeville or burlesque halls. Armstrong was a major attraction at the Vendome Theatre in Chicago after his return from New York in 1925. The big band was soon to become a major attraction in the theatres and night clubs. The most famous nightclubs, dance halls and theatres in Chicago, New York and other large cities featured lavish floorshows featuring dancers, singers, comedians and the visual aspect of the show became very important. Some bands developed a stage presence that was nothing short of dramatic and the dancers and listening audiences responded in kind. As dance band arrangements became increasingly more sophisticated and complex in New York, bands in the Midwest, primarily Kansas City, stripped away most of the ostentatious trappings. The Kansas City style opted for a more streamlined style that was focused on the ability to swing hard with a smooth underlying structure in the rhythm section. This smooth rhythmic style and uncluttered arrangements were in response to the needs of the dancers and allowed more room for the soloists. (see Chapter 11)
- As the popularity of social dancing was rising in the late 1920s and 1930s so was the musical response of the bands. The music reflected the needs of the dancers and the dancers in turn inspired the musicians.
- All players were expected to be able to read music, but usually there was at least one trumpeter, one trombonist, and two saxophonists who could improvise a "hot" jazz chorus when necessary. These players were characteristically called the "jazz" or "hot" players.
- With the increasing number of players came the necessity for arrangers who would write separate parts for each player, often creating unique arrangements of popular repertoire. It was no longer possible for so many musicians to simply improvise and have the result be anything but chaotic. Arrangers became as important to a big band as the players themselves. Some arrangers were also players in the band, but it was not unusual for arrangers to be employed only for their arranging talents.

## Characteristics of Big Band Swing

- Preferred instrumentation is a larger ensemble (from nine to sixteen players) rather than combo.
- The emphasis is on arrangements (written-out parts for each player) with occasional solo improvisations.
- Saxophones (alto, tenor, baritone) are used.
- The bass replaces tuba (most bassists started their careers on the tuba).
- The banjo is either eliminated or replaced by guitar.
- Drummer's role is expanded with more varied use of cymbals.
- The soloist prevails; little if any collective improvisation takes place.
- There is a smoother, looser rhythmic feel in general.
- The musicians are technically more proficient and must have the ability to read music.

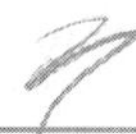

# FLETCHER HENDERSON

- Bandleader/pianist/arranger **Fletcher Henderson** (1897–1952) was born in Cuthbert, Georgia. He grew up learning to play the piano. However, he received a degree in chemistry and mathematics from Atlanta University and moved to New York to pursue a career as a chemist. It soon became apparent he would not be offered a job as a chemist, so he worked as a pianist for the Pace-Handy Music Company. Harry Pace founded the Black Swan record label, and he soon had Henderson organizing and leading recording sessions for bands and blues vocalists. Henderson already had experience playing piano for Mamie Smith's Jazz Hounds and Ethel Waters.
- In 1924, he was leading a dance band at the famous Roseland Ballroom in New York. The ten-piece band featured **Coleman Hawkins** on tenor sax, **Louis Armstrong** on trumpet, and other well-known musicians. (with excellent arrangements by saxophonist **Don Redman**). They started with buying "stock" arrangements of popular songs sold by the big publishing companies. The arrangements, for the most part were not very good, and did not reflect the newly emerging jazz style very well. It was like buying an ill-fitting suit made from a scratchy material. Both Redman and Henderson, who were excellent and well trained musicians, began to "doctor" the arrangements, which made them more suitable and sound better than the published versions. As they both became more adept at this a new sound began to emerge. Redman and Henderson became sought after arrangers.
- Redman's formula of arranging material according to families of instruments became standard arranging procedure and influenced big band arranging throughout the 1930s and 1940s. After Redman left in 1927, Henderson became successful as an arranger following Redman's model. Both Henderson and Redman were successfully building on Jelly Roll Morton's example of combining highly arranged music with improvised jazz solos. It began a trend leading to the big band jazz that would ten years later dominate American popular music.
- Henderson's band was a hit and was the first real jazz-influenced big band in New York. Louis Armstrong's presence in 1924 had a profound impact on every player. After 1924, Coleman Hawkins became a more creative improviser and played hotter than any of Whiteman's musicians. In his solo spots he truly improvised, whereas in most dance bands of that time, soloists played only the written melodies.
- In the early 1930s, the band experienced financial difficulties and strong competition from other orchestras, and eventually Coleman Hawkins left for Europe. As a result, the band broke up in early 1935.
- In 1934, Henderson sold many of his arrangements to Benny Goodman who had started an orchestra. Some of these arrangements, such as "King Porter Stomp," became big hits for Goodman's band. Eventually,

Goodman hired Henderson to arrange for his band, and occasionally Henderson played with Benny Goodman's Sextet.

- Both Paul Whiteman and Fletcher Henderson arrived in New York in 1920 and went on to lead successful bands. However, bandleader and pianist **Sam Wooding** was also making a name for himself in New York in the early 1920s. Although Wooding's greatest successes occurred during his extensive European tours of the mid-1920s, his contributions to the development of big band swing are also important.

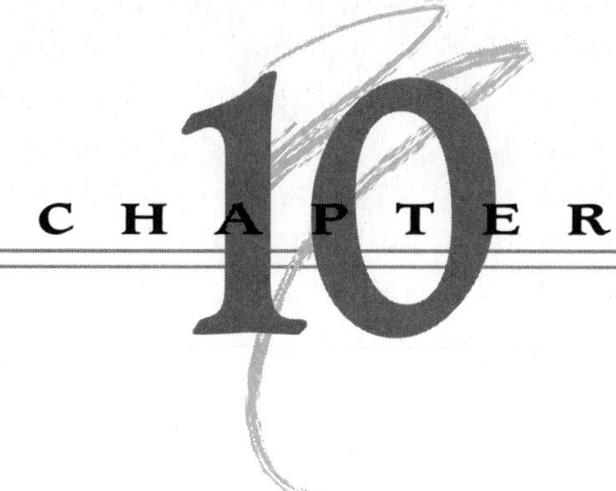


# Duke Ellington

- Edward Kennedy Ellington (1899–1974) was born and raised in Washington, D.C. His family was from the upper middle class. His mother was very protective, and after Ellington had an alarming accident while playing baseball, she decided piano lessons might be a better way for him to spend his time.
- His parents taught him to always present himself with dignity and elegance. As a result, Edward was given the nickname "Duke" for his impeccable manners and good taste. These traits followed Duke for the rest of his life.
- As a teenager he also aspired to be an artist, but he soon turned his attention to becoming an accomplished musician. However, he never lost his appreciation and talent for art. In fact, many of his compositions can be perceived as musical "paintings":
  - ♪ "The Flaming Sword"
  - ♪ "Beautiful Indians"
  - ♪ "Dusk in the Desert"
- He considered each member of his orchestra to be like a color on an artist's palette.
- When composing, he conceived each part mindful of his specific band members and their unique talents and musical personalities. Therefore, Duke created unique and original sounds that could not be duplicated in other bands. In some cases, once a band member departed, his band was no longer capable of producing the same effect because material written for specific band members lost much of its personal identity when played by someone else. This approach to composition and arranging

was in stark contrast to his contemporaries who were simply writing with instrumentation in mind; the players, in essence, could be anyone.

- His arranging technique was also different in that he would often have melodies played by combining instruments from the different sections. This method of arranging is called **voicing across sections**. For example, Duke might have a muted trumpet, trombone, clarinet, and baritone saxophone grouped together to play the same melody. This unusual method of arranging (in contrast to that of Don Redman) created a diverse palette of colors; he even used a singer's voice (such as female vocalist Ivie Anderson) as an instrument by writing wordless vocals for her.
- He might voice the low brass (trombones) above the woodwinds to create new tone colors. The more common method would have been to write for the trumpets and saxes above the trombones.

Much of Ellington's music was first conceived collaboratively, often with band members. For example, Duke might come up with a musical idea or theme; play it first on the piano; then the rhythm section might pick it up; and then a soloist might begin to improvise over it, followed by instrumental backgrounds directed by Duke at the piano accenting harmonies or giving other directions; thus he *created* many compositions. Consequently, much of the music was not written down, posing a problem if a band member were to leave; there was little or no music for the new replacement member.

- Ellington helped his musicians unfold and develop their unique talents and ideas. Then he utilized their highly personal musical styles within the context of his band to help produce the "Ellington" sound.
- Ellington learned how to arrange primarily by trial and error. What seemed to work would be filed away to be expanded on later, and what did not work was discarded; he was constantly experimenting with musical colors and textures. As he broke with traditional methods of composition, he established new practices.
- Ellington was intensely proud of his heritage; many of his large-scale works such as *Black, Brown and Beige* and *Harlem Suite*, took their themes from African-American history.
- His band's first significant job in New York was their stay from 1923 to 1927 at the Kentucky Club, located near Times Square. Duke's band experienced significant transformations during those years. The personnel became reliable and consistent, he became the designated leader, and they began to make recordings.
- Their first notoriety came with an extended stay at the famous Cotton Club in Harlem (1927–1931), where he established much of his style and fame in what is now perceived to be his first great band. The Cotton Club gave nightly floor shows that used exotic African themes as the basis for its material. Duke was expected to compose music to complement these floor shows. Much of the music has an exotic flavor thanks to Duke's creative use of his brass players' talent for using mutes and other devices to change the sound of their horns. This Ellington repertoire has come to be known as **jungle-style** compositions. Much of the success of the Cotton Club band can be

attributed to Ellington's excellent brass and woodwind soloists such as the following:

- Bubber Miley—trumpet (helped establish the **jungle** sound by using a plunger mute and growling into the trumpet, creating an awesome array of colors)
- Cootie Williams—trumpet (another mute specialist who replaced Bubber Miley in 1931)
- "Tricky" Sam Nanton—trombone (helped establish the **jungle** sound by using a plunger mute and growling into the trombone)
- Johnny Hodges—alto sax
- Barney Bigard—clarinet
- Harry Carney—baritone sax

- When Duke was leading his band at the Cotton Club, he was unaware of a fringe benefit that would be included. In the late 1920s, radio became a popular form of entertainment. The first radio stations appeared in 1923. By 1927, there were hundreds of radio stations across the country syndicated by companies based in New York City. At times, the New York stations would broadcast live from major hotels and nightclubs,

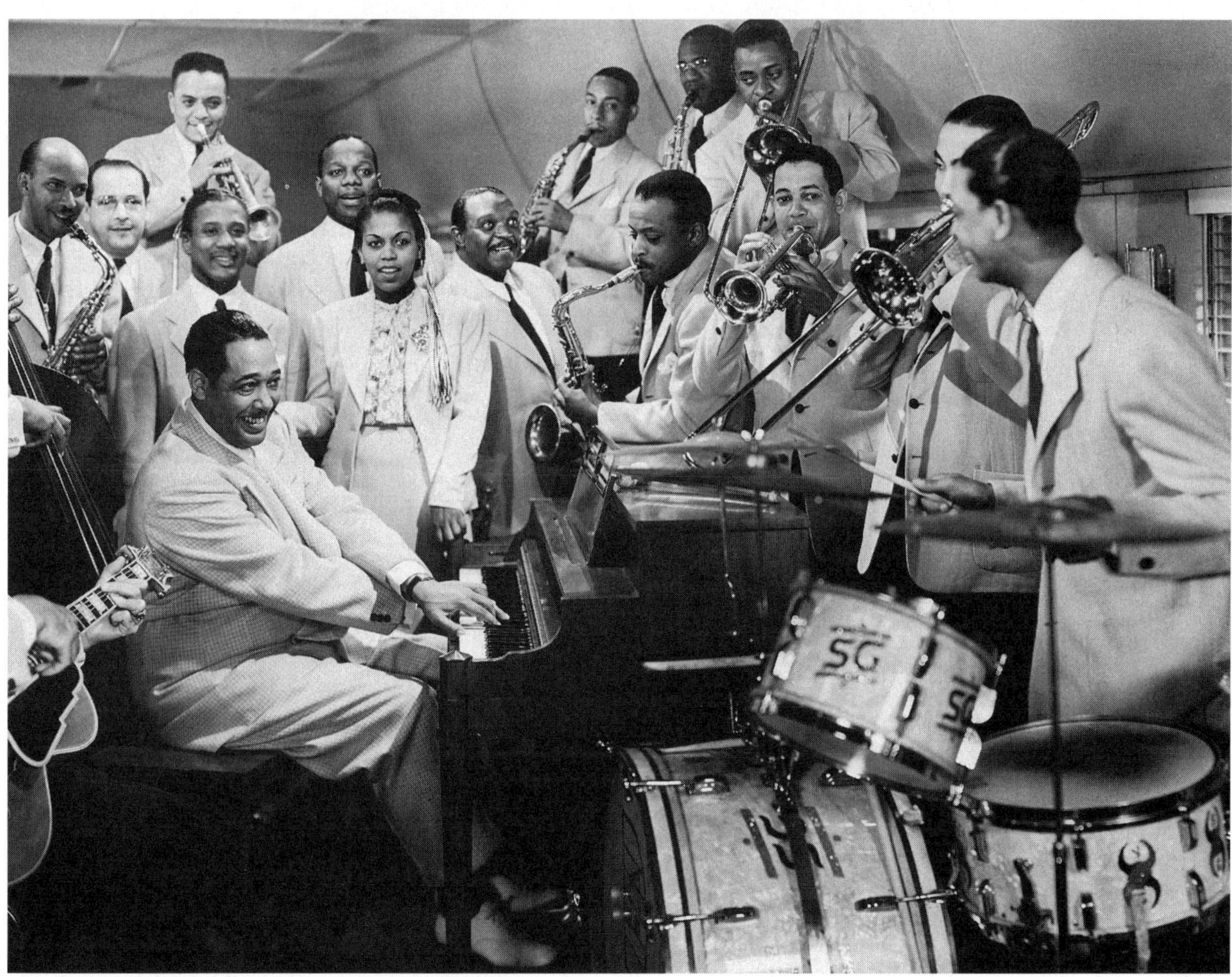


*Duke Ellington Band © Bettmann/CORBIS*

sending the programs to radio stations throughout the country. The Cotton Club was one such venue when Duke took the job in 1927. Without realizing it, he would become nationally famous simply because people all over the country were listening to his Cotton Club band's performances on a regular basis.

- As a result, in the 1930s, when not appearing at the Cotton Club, Ellington's band would embark on commercially successful tours all over America. They were also able to successfully tour Europe several times.

## After the Cotton Club

- A second peak period for Ellington's band was from 1938 to 1941. It is sometimes referred to as the **Blanton/Webster Band** because Ben Webster, a highly regarded tenor saxophonist, and Jimmy Blanton, the most talented and innovative bassist to date, were members of the band.
- **Ben Webster** (1909–1973) was a Coleman Hawkins-influenced player whose improvisations were strong and impressive. He had a rich tone with a wide vibrato and is perhaps best known for his interpretations of ballads. Webster was featured on several Ellington masterpieces including "Cottontail" and "All Too Soon."
- **Jimmy Blanton** (1921–1942) was one of the first bass players not to develop from a two-beat "tuba" approach. Most bass players were originally tuba players. Blanton had been trained in music theory, piano, violin, and alto sax before settling on the bass. As a musician with a strong formal background and a virtuoso of the bass, he was able to play convincing melodies and create a variety of rhythms unprecedented for bass players. Ellington featured Blanton as a soloist in compositions such as "Jack the Bear." He also collaborated with Blanton in bass/piano duets. Blanton, as a major jazz bass innovator, influenced the next several generations of jazz bassists to expand the possibilities of the instrument.
- Another reason why Ellington's band experienced a second peak was the arrival of Billy Strayhorn. Often called "Duke's alter ego," Strayhorn was hired in 1939 to help with composing and arranging, since Ellington had become too busy to handle these duties by himself. Strayhorn's contribution to the Ellington Orchestra is not always easy to determine because his writing and arranging was so close to Duke's. Strayhorn remained with Duke's band until the end of his life in 1967. During that time, he collaborated with Duke on many works including *A Drum Is a Woman, Such Sweet Thunder*, and *Far East Suite*. Strayhorn's composition "Take the 'A'Train" sounded so much like Ellington's writing, it was adopted as the Ellington Band's theme song.
- **Billy Strayhorn** (1915–1967) was born in Dayton, Ohio, but he grew up in Pittsburgh. He became interested in the piano early in his life, and by his teens he was writing songs. "Lush Life," one such song written when he was seventeen, has become a jazz standard and has been recorded countless numbers of times by many significant jazz musicians and singers. Other Strayhorn compositions include "Chelsea Bridge," "Lotus Blossom," "Johnny Come Lately," and "Passion Flower."

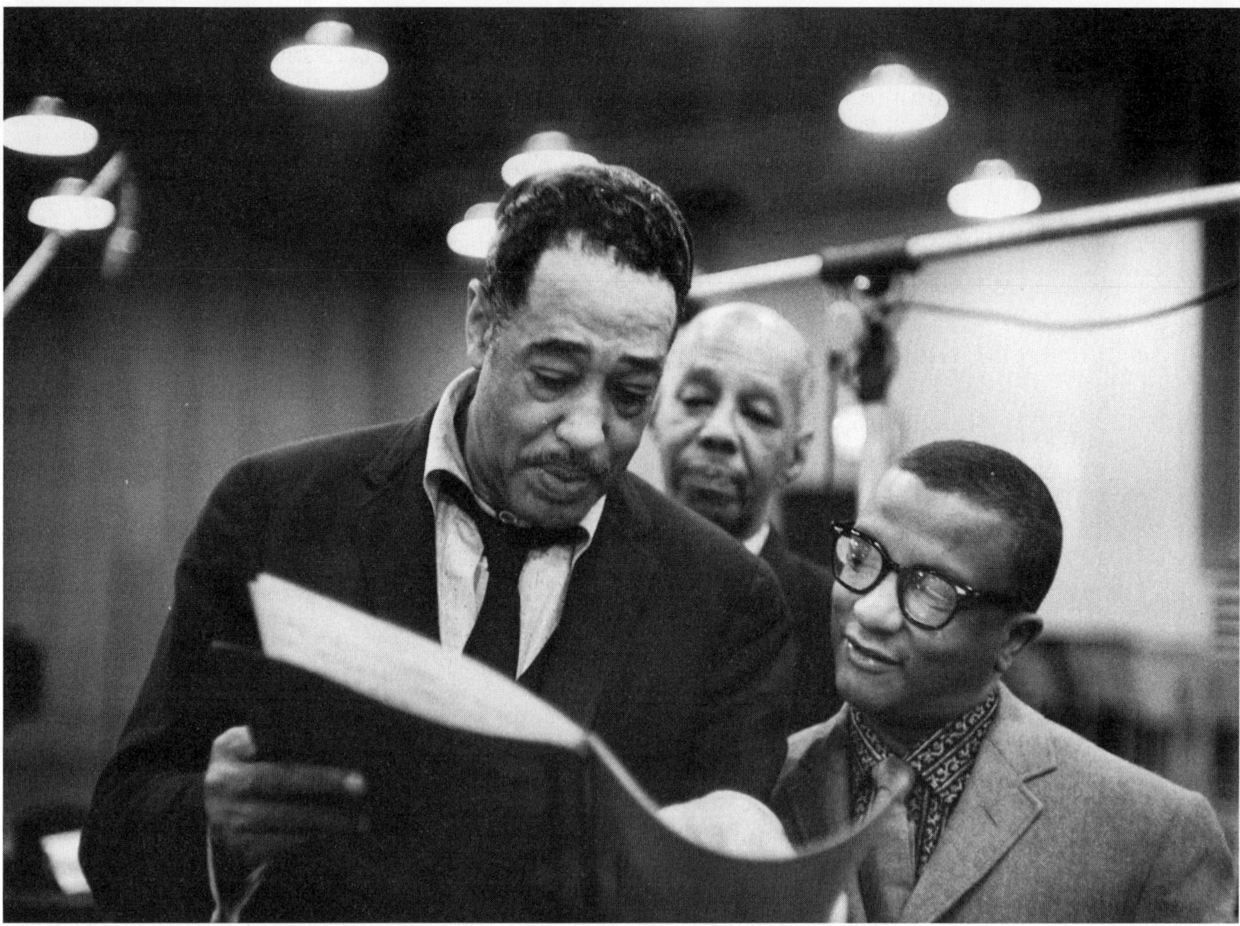

*Duke Ellington and Billy Strayhorn. © Underwood & Underwood/CORBIS*

**Important members of Duke Ellington's Orchestra:**

Harry Carney, baritone sax
Johnny Hodges, alto sax
Cootie Williams, trumpet
Tricky Sam Nanton, trombone
Barney Bigard, clarinet
Billy Strayhorn, arranger/composer
Ben Webster, tenor sax
Bubber Miley, trumpet
Jimmy Hamilton, clarinet
Sonny Greer, drums
Paul Gonsalves, tenor sax
Jimmy Blanton, bass

## After the Blanton/Webster Band

- Ellington was able to keep his band together in the late 1940s while most other bands were either forced to scale down or break up. However, as big bands became less popular and less in demand, Duke turned his attention to more serious compositions focusing more on *extended works* such as suites, sacred concerts, and other classically influenced works. Actually, Ellington wrote extended works throughout his career. He always made attempts to create more orchestral-like large-scale compositions, which were not necessarily bound by the standard three-minute time limit of recordings in the 1920s, 1930s, and 1940s. For example, Ellington wrote *Creole Rhapsody* in 1931, a six-minute work that further helped to establish him as a composer. His first major long work *Black, Brown, and Beige* was premiered in 1942. From the 1950s to the end of his life, Ellington concentrated on multimovement, thematically linked works such as suites and masses.

- Ellington's suites consisted of a collection of related compositions. They were often based on a common idea or theme usually made obvious in their title. For example, Duke's *Far East Suite* was inspired by his trip to that part of the world. In the 1960s and 1970s, Duke sought to create large-scale religious works.
- Ellington's compositions can be broken up into five different categories:
  - **Jungle**—compositions that extensively use muted brass sounds and other devices to capture the exotic flavor of African culture. It was the first and most famous of the Ellington trademark sounds developed around the motif of the famous Cotton Club (1927–1931) and the sound of trumpeter Bubber Miley. Specific characteristics include the following:
    - Relatively slow tempo (almost like a funeral march)
    - Starts in the minor mode and then moves to the major mode
    - Use of plunger mutes and "growling" brass
    - Features plunger muted trumpet solos
    - Composed of many different sections for contrast
    - Three minutes in length (constraints of the ten-inch 78 rpm-record)
  - Examples of Ellington's jungle compositions:
    - "East St. Louis Toodle-oo" (1927)
    - "Jungle Nights in Harlem"
    - "Black and Tan Fantasy" (1927)
    - "The Mooche" (1929)
    - "Echoes of the Jungle"
    - "Koko" (1939–later period)
  - **Mood**—compositions intended to capture or depict a particular mood or setting. Usually the title will be indicative of the composer's intention. Mood compositions include the following features:
    - Pastel-like dissonant harmony
    - Unusual combinations of instruments for color
    - More emphasis on ensemble work
    - De-emphasis of "hot" solos
  - Examples of Ellington's mood compositions:
    - "Mood Indigo" (1931)
    - "Blue Tune"
    - "Blue Mood"
    - "Clouds in My Heart"
    - "Sophisticated Lady" (1933)
    - "Dusk"
    - "Solitude"
    - "Blue Serge"
    - "In a Sentimental Mood" (1935)
    - "Prelude to a Kiss" (1938)

- **Concerto—**compositions intended to feature the talents of a specific band member. Sometimes they were cooperatively written with the featured band member. They often became part of the "standard" jazz band repertoire. Examples of Ellington's concerto compositions:
  - "Concerto for Cootie" (for Cootie Williams) (1939)
  - "Clarinet Lament" (for Barney Bigard) (1936)
  - "Boy Meets Horn" (for Rex Stewart) (1938)
  - "Echoes of Harlem" (Cootie's Concerto) (1936)
  - "Jack the Bear" (prominently featuring bassist Jimmy Blanton)
  - "Jeep's Blues" (for Johnny Hodges)
- **Extended Works—**compositions intended to extend the length and scale of a work. Examples of Ellington's extended works:
  - *Creole Rhapsody* (1931) (first long work; a six minute work—unusual at that time for a jazz composition)
  - *Reminiscing in Tempo* (1935)
  - *Black, Brown and Beige* (1942)
  - *New World a-Comin'*
  - *The Deep South Suite* (1946)
  - *The Tattooed Bride* (1948)
  - *Liberian Suite* (1947)
  - *Harlem Suite* (1950)
  - *Newport Jazz Festival Suite* (1956)
  - *A Drum Is a Woman* (1957)
  - *Shakespearean Suite (Such Sweet Thunder)* (1958)
  - *Suite Thursday* (1960)
  - *Latin American Suite* (1968)
  - *New Orleans Suite* (1970)
  - *The Nutcracker Suite* (1960)
  - *Far East Suite* (1966)
  - *The Queens Suite* (1959)
  - *The Afro-Eurasian Suite* (1971)
  - *Three Sacred Concerts* (1965, 1968, 1973)
- **Dance—**compositions intended for dancing. The majority of most big bands' repertoire consisted of these kinds of compositions. Examples of Ellington's dance compositions:
  - "Black Beauty" (1928)
  - "Creole Love Call" (1928)
  - "Jubilee Stomp" (1928)
  - "Rockin' in Rhythm" (1931)
  - "It Don't Mean a Thing If It Ain't Got That Swing" (1932)
  - "Delta Serenade" (1935)
  - "Reminiscing in Tempo" (1935)
  - "Azure" (1937)

- ♩ "Cottontail" (1940)
- ♩ "Harlem Airshaft"
- ♩ "Mainstem"
- ♩ "Warm Valley" (1941)
- ♩ "Take the 'A' Train" (1941), composed by Billy Strayhorn
- ♩ "I Got It Bad (and That Ain't Good)" (1941)
- ♩ "I Let a Song Go Out of My Heart"
- ♩ "Don't Get Around Much Anymore" (1942)
- ♩ "Crescendo in Blue" (1943), composed by Duke Ellington and Billy Strayhorn
- ♩ "I'm Beginning to See the Light" (1944)
- ♩ "Satin Doll" (1958), composed by Duke Ellington and Billy Strayhorn, lyrics by Johnny Mercer

- Other more unusual compositional categories are as follows:
  - ♪ **Exotic—**brought to mind images of far-away exotic places:
    - ♩ "The Flaming Sword"
    - ♩ "Caravan" composed by Juan Tizol (1937)
    - ♩ "Conga Brava"
    - ♩ "Bakiff" composed by Juan Tizol
  - ♪ **Train—**Ellington loved trains and was able to recreate the sound of them in various compositions:
    - ♩ "Day Break Express" (1934)
    - ♩ "Old Man Blues"
    - ♩ "Happy Go Local Lucky"
  - ♪ **Musical Portraits**
    - ♩ "Bert Williams"
    - ♩ "Mahalia Jackson"
    - ♩ "Wellman Braud"
    - ♩ "Bojangles" (for Bill Robinson)

## THE ELLINGTON LEGACY

- He achieved a balance between written and improvised music.
- His compositions number in the thousands.
- The use of plunger mute/growling brass sound is an Ellington trademark.
- He used a high degree of chromaticism and dissonance for his time.
- He wrote arrangements with specific musicians in mind and sometimes wrote melodies for instruments that would ordinarily not be given the lead melody, for example:
  - ♪ Harry Carney on the baritone sax
  - ♪ Jimmy Blanton playing pizzicato melodies on the string bass
- He established the technique of voicing across sections in jazz arranging.

- He used irregular forms (sometimes making them up as he went along).
- He had an innate ability to hire musicians that could make unique and highly personal contributions to his orchestra.
- He wrote wordless vocals for his singers, utilizing their voices like another instrument.
- He used unusual combinations of instruments for unique timbres.

♪ Ellington was one of the most significant composers of twentieth-century American music. He was not given proper credit for his work during his lifetime. However, since his death, his musical significance has gradually entered the realm of immortal greatness.

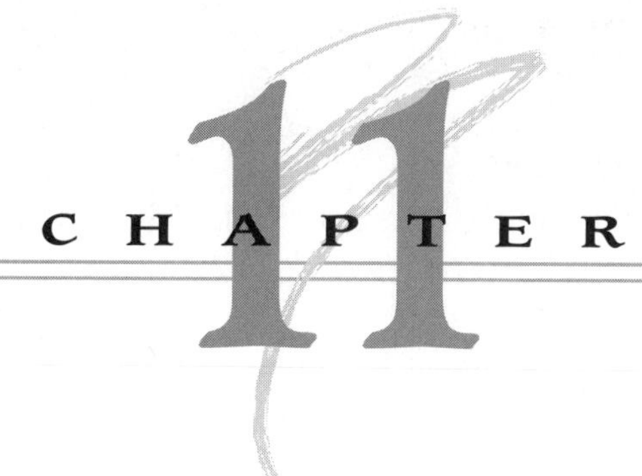

CHAPTER 11

# Kansas City, Bennie Moten, and Count Basie

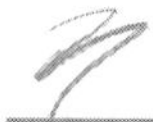

## KANSAS CITY

- In the 1920s and 1930s there was a thriving jazz scene in Kansas City, which was centered in club districts under the control of a corrupt politician known as Tom Pendergast. He allowed speakeasy bars and nightclubs to make prostitution, alcohol, gambling, and other illegal commodities available. His empire was known as the Pendergast Machine, and he controlled Kansas City after the passage of the Volstead Act in 1919. Pendergast maintained control until 1938 when he was indicted for income tax fraud.
- Music was an integral part of Kansas City club districts; therefore musicians found many employment opportunities there. Kansas City was also an important center for traveling carnivals, vaudeville shows, and TOBA theaters. As a result, many musicians who traveled with these shows eventually settled in Kansas City. Bands would also travel to other cities in the Midwest, such as Oklahoma City, Dallas, Omaha, and Denver, for more opportunities to perform. Such bands, not always based in Kansas City, came to be known as **territory bands,** since they were traveling and performing in what had been a territory in the recent past.
- The nineteenth-century brass band tradition and ragtime were important influences of the Kansas City jazz style. However, the most obvious influence comes from the blues tradition, which was strong in the Midwest. Many blues musicians were active in Kansas City, and the

boogie-woogie piano style was also popular and abundant there. As was the case with boogie-woogie piano players, Kansas City bands were expected to provide fast, swinging music that would motivate dancers to move their bodies to the rhythm.

- The blues influence can be discerned by observing how Kansas City bands construct tunes and arrange the material. A large portion of their repertoire consists of blues forms and features blues vocalists; however, there is also a healthy amount of popular song forms such as AABA. Instrumentalists made use of their familiarity with the blues by using **riffs** (short, catchy musical ideas used to create momentum) to create these blues and AABA forms. With riffs being the basis for melodies or accompaniment material, these arrangements were often created spontaneously and developed over a period of several performances, eventually settling into codified entities. Usually not written down on paper, the band members were expected to retain each arrangement in their heads. Thus the term **head arrangement** is sometimes used to refer to this kind of repertoire.
- As dance band arrangements became increasingly more sophisticated and complex in New York, bands in the Midwest, primarily Kansas City, stripped away most of the ostentatious trappings. The Kansas City style opted for a more streamlined style that was focused on the ability to swing hard with a smooth underlying structure in the rhythm section. This smooth rhythmic style with uncluttered arrangements was in response to the needs of the dancers and allowed more room for the soloists.
- Kansas City bands can also be called **riff bands.** With this approach, a strong sense of swinging rhythm with enticing riffs was more important than the more complex melodies and sophisticated arrangements of New York bands.
- Important Kansas City bands include Walter Page and the Blue Devils, Harlan Leonard's Kansas City Rockets, Jesse Stone and the Blues Serenaders, and the Jay McShann Orchestra. There was also Andy Kirk and the Clouds of Joy, who had a black female pianist/arranger from 1929 to 1942 named Mary Lou Williams (1910–1981). She is considered to be one of the most significant female jazz instrumentalists and arrangers of the twentieth century.

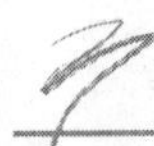

## BENNIE MOTEN

- One of the best-known Kansas City bands was led by pianist **Bennie Moten** (1894–1935). His band's first recordings were made in 1923 and featured a six-piece ensemble. It progressively expanded to ten pieces by 1926. From 1926 until 1935, the Bennie Moten Band was among the most prestigious in Kansas City and dominated the best jobs.
- However, the most exciting band was the **Blue Devils,** led by an Oklahoma City bass player named **Walter Page.** The Blue Devil's success was due in part to its exceptional personnel, which included trumpeter Oran "Hot Lips" Page, saxophonists Ben Webster and Buster Smith, trombonist and arranger Eddie Durham, vocalist Jimmy Rushing, and pianist Bill Basie (later known as Count Basie).

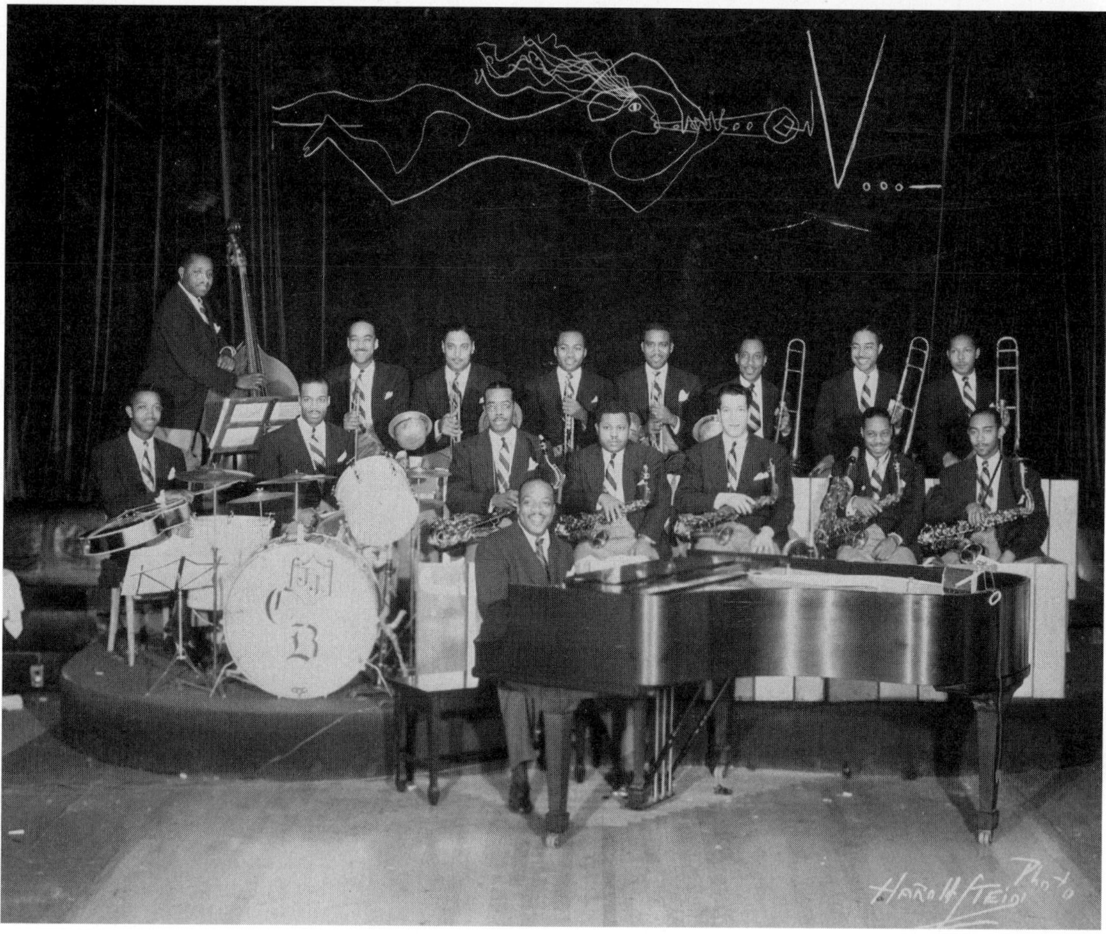

*Count Basie Band. © Bettmann/CORBIS*

- Moten, after losing in 1928 to the Blue Devils in one of the many band contests frequently held at that time, made an unsuccessful attempt to take over the Blue Devils. However, eventually all the previously mentioned players were enticed to join Moten's band after the Blue Devils experienced financial problems. The Bennie Moten band made their last recordings in1932 with most of the former members of the Blue Devils. Their most important recordings include "Toby" and "Moten Swing."
- On April 2, 1935, Bennie Moten suddenly died of complications while having his tonsils removed. If he had lived longer, it is possible his band would have achieved the notoriety Count Basie's band attained, since Basie's band had many of the same players.

## COUNT BASIE

- The most well-known and successful band to come out of Kansas City was led by **Count Basie** (1904–1984). Born in Red Bank, New Jersey, William Basie received his first piano lessons from his mother. After graduating from high school, he found work in New York clubs. At this time he was influenced by Harlem Stride pianists such as James P. Johnson and Willie the Lion Smith. He became friends with Fats Waller and took a few lessons from him.

- From 1923 to 1926 Basie worked with touring vaudeville shows. While on the road with one of these shows, Basie was favorably impressed with the Blue Devils. In 1928 he joined the Blue Devils and in 1929, Bennie Moten's band, settling in Kansas City. He led his own band in 1934, but then rejoined Moten's band. After Bennie Moten's untimely death, his relative Buster Moten unsuccessfully attempted to keep the band together.
- In 1935, Basie formed his own band for a regular engagement at the Reno Club in Kansas City. Many of the band members were Bennie Moten alumni. Drummer Jo Jones and tenor saxophonist Lester Young would join in 1936. Later that same year, record producer John Hammond heard Basie's band on a live radio broadcast from the Reno Club. Hammond immediately traveled to Kansas City to hear the group with the intention of taking them back to New York to sign a record contract with Columbia. After Hammond left Kansas City, a dishonest record company executive tricked Count Basie into signing a contract with Decca. Containing no royalties, the contract was valid until early 1939. Some of the hits Count Basie recorded while with Decca include "One O'Clock Jump" and "Jumpin' at the Woodside."
- Count Basie kept his band together for the rest of his life. However, the personnel changed over the years, including a two-year period from 1950 to 1952 when financial problems caused him to significantly reduce the size of the band. The most crucial years of activity for his band were from 1936 to 1942. Many band members during this time were jazz soloists who went on to have significant careers, such as trumpeters Buck Clayton and Harry "Sweets" Edison, trombonists Dicky Wells and Eddie Durham, tenor saxophonists Herschel Evans and Lester Young, and vocalists Helen Humes and Jimmy Rushing. Eddie Durham and Buck Clayton contributed many arrangements that exemplified the blues/riff style commonly found in Kansas City.
- The preeminent soloist of Count Basie's band was undoubtedly **Lester Young.** Along with Coleman Hawkins, Young is considered to be one of the most significant tenor saxophonists of the 1930s and 1940s. His playing was diametrically opposed to that of Hawkins. Young's sound is more transparent, and his tendency is to play fewer notes than Hawkins in a similar situation. In his youth, Lester listened to Frankie Trumbauer on radio broadcasts who (unknown to Lester at the time) was playing a C-melody saxophone, an instrument different from a tenor or alto saxophone. As Young tried to imitate Trumbauer's sound on the tenor saxophone, he created a unique timbre for which he would be known for the rest of his life. In addition, it is likely Young heard and was influenced by Bix Beiderbecke's smooth approach to jazz improvisation on those same radio broadcasts. As a result, Young offered an alternative to the Coleman Hawkins (strongly influenced by Louis Armstrong) approach to tenor saxophone improvisation. This alternative featured a light tone with little or no vibrato. Lester Young was nicknamed "Prez," short for "President of the Saxophone," by Billie Holiday, with whom he made significant recordings and maintained a close relationship.

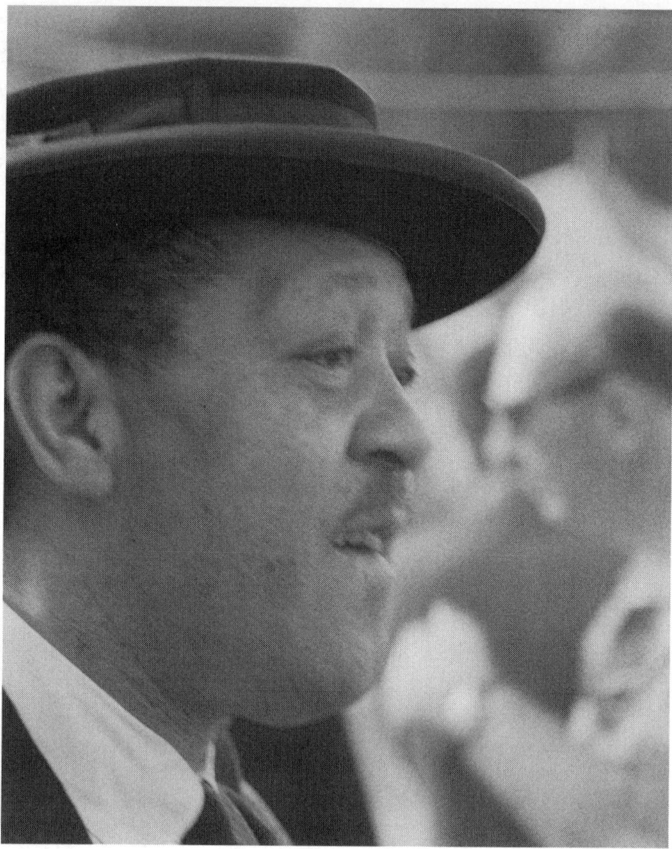

*Lester Young. © Ted Williams/CORBIS*

- While the previously mentioned soloists were important to the success of Count Basie's band, it was the rhythm section that distinguished it from any other ensemble of its kind. By 1938, Count Basie's rhythm section consisted of bassist Walter Page, drummer Jo Jones, guitarist Freddie Green, and Basie on piano. Dubbed "the **All American Rhythm Section,**" it produced some of the most exciting yet refined rhythm section playing of all swing bands.
  - Walter Page established the standard 4/4 walking bass line approach commonly used by swing bass players.
  - Drummer Jo Jones supported Page's bass lines by softly playing the bass drum on each beat. Jones also produced an accurate high-hat *chink* on beats two and four. His hands were then free to create colorful sounds to further enhance the music. Jones helped to establish this standard approach to swing drumming; however, he would sometimes depart from the norm by only using the bass drum for accents and creatively using his cymbals.
  - Freddie Green would forcefully strum chords on his guitar on all four beats of every measure. Since Green's guitar was generally not amplified, he chose to add to the rhythmic texture by supporting the beat with precise chords stroked in a regular fashion.
  - With all of this rhythmic activity, one might think Count Basie would not be needed to play piano or that his playing wouldn't add anything new to the mix. If he had chosen to play in the stride style, it is likely that he wouldn't have been heard very well. Basie had grown up playing

in the stride piano style of mentors such as Fats Waller. However, he developed into a different, thriftier kind of player. His left hand often was used sparingly, and his improvised right-hand melodies used the minimum rather than maximum number of notes. Basie's instincts to take an economical approach to piano playing led him to something entirely different from what any other pianists were doing.

  - ♪ When playing with his band, rather than playing on the same four beats Page, Jones, and Green were articulating, Basie began to jab chords intermittently between beats. In addition, he often used chords in the extreme upper register of the piano to penetrate the texture effectively and therefore be heard.
  - ♪ This method of jabbing chords between beats has come to be known as **comping.** Comping comes from the jazz colloquial term **comp,** which is short for the word *accompany*. Modern jazz pianists have adopted and developed this approach as a way to accompany a jazz soloist or group of soloists.

- All of the previous contributions make Count Basie's rhythm section one of the most significant of all swing bands and is certainly part of the reason why his band is so historically important.
- Count Basie also made recordings with small ensembles under names such as Kansas City Five, Six, or Seven, depending on how many players were involved. Typically the instrumentation featured the Basie rhythm section and Lester Young, Buck Clayton, and/or Dicky Wells. A good example is the classic "Lester Leaps In," recorded in 1939.
- In the 1950s, Basie's band became known for its precision and refinement. It had an amazing dynamic range, and the soft levels were especially impressive. While it was not on the cutting edge of jazz developments, this version of the Basie band enjoyed more popularity and success than the one from the 1930s and 1940s. With excellent soloists and section players such as Frank Foster, Frank Wess, Thad Jones, and Eddie Lockjaw Davis, as well as arrangers such as Neal Hefti, Quincy Jones, Frank Foster, Ernie Wilkins, and Sammy Nestico, selections such as "April in Paris," "Shiny Stockings," and "Corner Pocket" became well-known favorites with audiences.

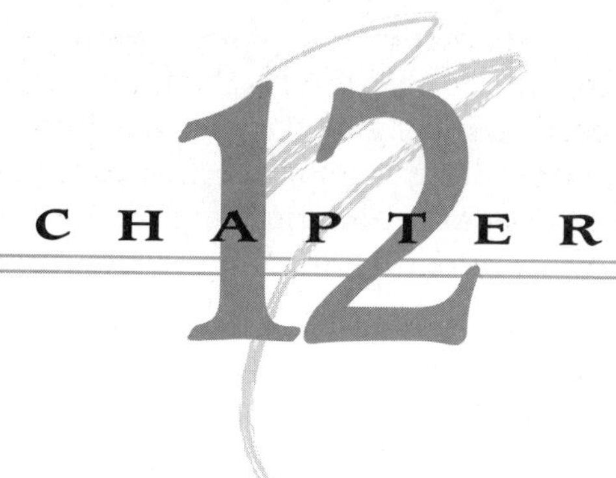

CHAPTER 12

# The Swing Era, 1935 to 1945

- *Swing* was first used by radio broadcasters—instead of referring to it as "hot" music. The term is confusing because it also describes an important rhythmic attribute of jazz performance from that period. Swing was centered on big jazz bands active in cities such as New York and Kansas City. Swing was commercialized, packaged, and sold over the radio airwaves, through records, and through live performance. It became big business.
- By 1935, the Depression had lifted somewhat, and the middle class had money to spend on entertainment. The repeal of Prohibition in 1933 helped to get jazz out of the speakeasies and into public's eye.
- Some reasons for the popularity of swing music:
  - ♪ Swing furnished music for an insatiable desire to dance.
  - ♪ The music helped people forget their problems
  - ♪ Swing catered to a large college market
  - ♪ Swing bands furnished the public with entertainer idols such as Benny Goodman, Cab Calloway, Gene Krupa, Duke Ellington, Artie Shaw, Tommy Dorsey, and Frank Sinatra.
- The big band was soon to become a major attraction in theatres, hotels, dance halls, and night clubs. The most famous such venues in Chicago, New York and other large cities featured lavish floor shows featuring dancers, singers, and comedians. Therefore, the visual aspect of the show also became an integral part of the presentation. Some bands

developed a stage presence that was nothing short of dramatic causing dancers and listening audiences to respond in kind.

- As the popularity of social dancing was rising in the late 1920s and 1930s so was the musical response of the bands. The music reflected the needs of the dancers and the dancers in turn inspired the musicians.

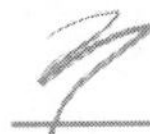

## STYLE

- The use of larger bands with twelve or more musicians:
  - Three to four trumpets
  - Two to three trombones
  - Four to five saxes: two altos, two tenors, one baritone
  - Three to four rhythm: bass, piano, drums, guitar
- The majority of big band swing repertoire consisted of popular songs. As a result these familiar melodies gained more importance. Because it was often necessary to have lyrics, singers became an integral part of the style.
- With a majority of commercial bands improvised solos were less prominent.
- A smooth, sweet sound that became commercially viable.

### Swing Music Features the Following:

- The use of more sophisticated harmonic progressions.
- Arrangers became very important; the influences of Redman and Henderson are apparent:
  - Melodies are supported by block harmonization
  - Harmonized solo lines
  - Call and response between sections
- The music was well-arranged and the bands were carefully rehearsed with an emphasis on precision, teamwork, and blend.
- There is a de-emphasis on improvised solos, although Count Basie, Duke Ellington, and Benny Goodman still placed much emphasis on improvised solos.
- The music requires proficient reading ability.
- The bandleader, or front man, was often a featured player on the piano or another instrument.
- Immediate identification of the band to the listener was of utmost importance.
- Each band had a highly recognizable theme song.
- The bandleaders would strive to establish a unique sound or style.
- Many bands used gimmickry to excess.
- The style of arranging common to the 1930s and 1940s still exists today. Most modern big bands use the same instrumentation and format.
- The great success experienced by bandleaders who wrote their own arrangements and were playing members of their bands is due to their

thorough knowledge of the individual musician's capabilities. This explains the great success of Duke Ellington, Benny Carter, Glenn Miller, Don Redman, and Fletcher Henderson to name a few.

- Other important bandleaders had arrangers who were an integral part of the organization's success: Chick Webb had Edgar Sampson; Jimmie Lunceford had Sy Oliver and Ed Wilcox; Andy Kirk had Mary Lou Williams; Count Basie had Buck Clayton, Eddie Durham, and Dicky Wells. These arrangers were writing for musicians whom they knew. This kind of writing intended to cater to individual players was in contrast with bandleaders who often simply purchased "stock" arrangements written by anonymous arrangers for many of the commercial dance bands; these writers were not writing for individuals, but faceless instrumentalists.

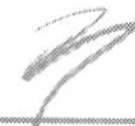

## IMPORTANT BANDS OF THE SWING ERA

### Casa Loma Band

- The Casa Loma Band was formed in Detroit under the leadership of Glen Gray in 1929.
- This band was an important predecessor (late 1920s to early 1930s) to the Benny Goodman and Tommy Dorsey bands. It helped set the stage for the Swing Era.
- It was one of the first white bands to come close to a good swing feel.
- There were no star soloists; the band exhibited good, cleanly executed ensemble playing with good and sometimes flashy arrangements in a variety of styles (also used riffs).
- The band was very popular with the college crowd and remained popular until the end of World War II.

### Benny Goodman Band

- Benny Goodman (1909–1986) was born and raised in Chicago.
- He was an excellent clarinetist and uncompromising bandleader, eventually dubbed the "King of Swing."
- He formed his own band in 1934 and with the help of John Hammond, the Benny Goodman band was hired for a nationally broadcast weekly radio show called *Let's Dance* in 1934.
- In the summer of 1935, after leaving the radio show, the Goodman band embarked on a summer tour. As they made their way west to California, they experienced little success.
- Then, seemingly out of nowhere, they experienced a wildly successful engagement playing mostly Fletcher Henderson arrangements at the Palomar Ballroom in Los Angeles.
- The Palomar Ballroom engagement was favorably reviewed in the press and has since been determined to be the unofficially beginning of the Swing Era.

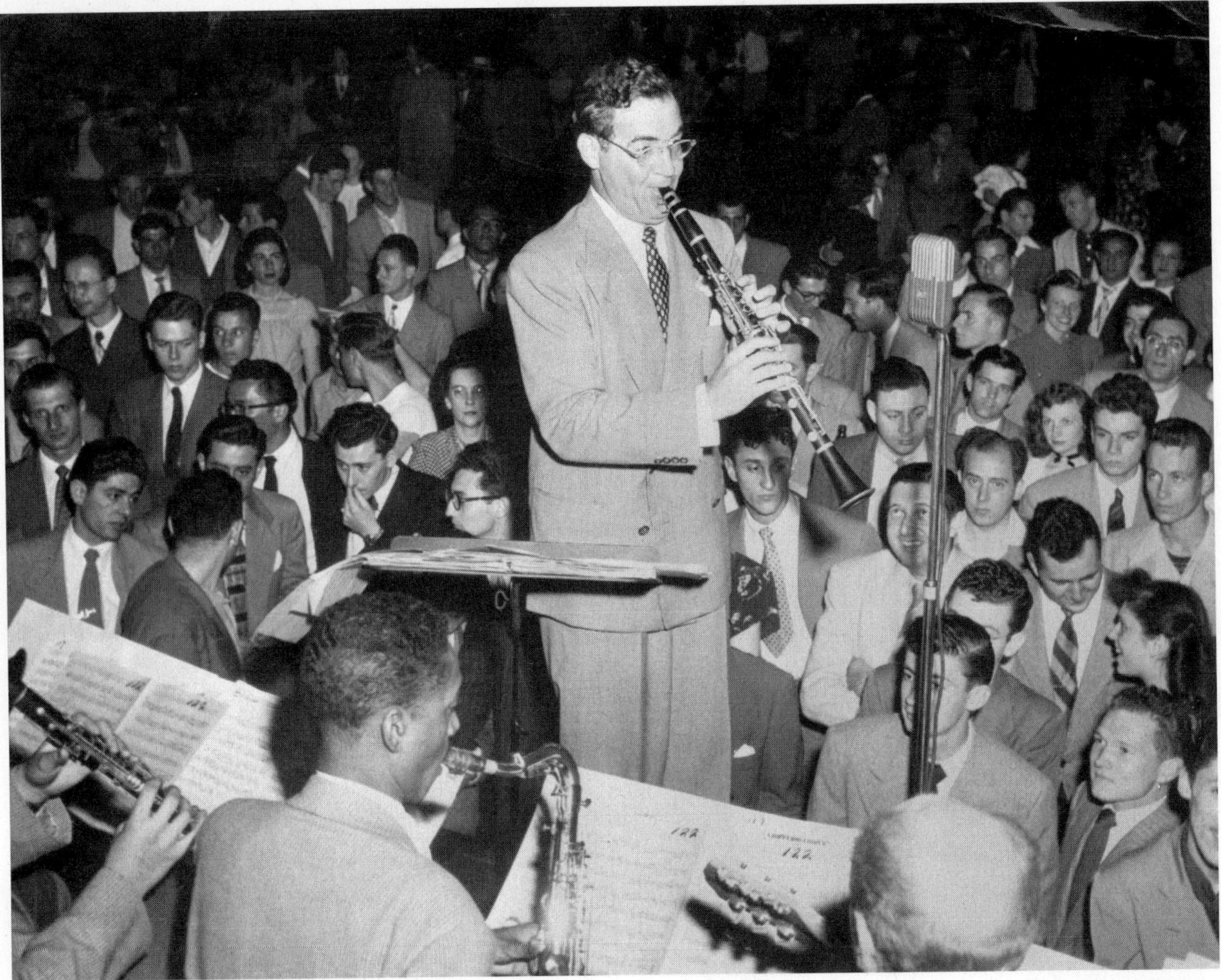

*Benny Goodman.* © *Bettmann/CORBIS*

- The Benny Goodman Band featured the following:
  - Excellent improvising soloists
  - Highly polished arrangements, many written by Fletcher Henderson and Eddie Sauter
  - A strong sense of swing
  - A style that suited the youthful taste of the country
- Beginning in 1936, with the encouragement of John Hammond, Benny Goodman hired African-American jazz musicians for his band, making it the first to be racially integrated. Pianist Teddy Wilson, vibraphonist Lionel Hampton, and later guitarist Charlie Christian performed and recorded with Benny Goodman's small and large ensembles. The small group recordings are among the best of their time and became quite popular.
- Goodman's clarinet work was so well respected that he was able to commission works from twentieth-century classical composers. The following works were written for Benny Goodman:
  - Bela Bartok, *Contrasts*
  - Aaron Copland, *Concerto for Clarinet and String Orchestra*
  - Morton Gould, *Derivations for Clarinet and Band*

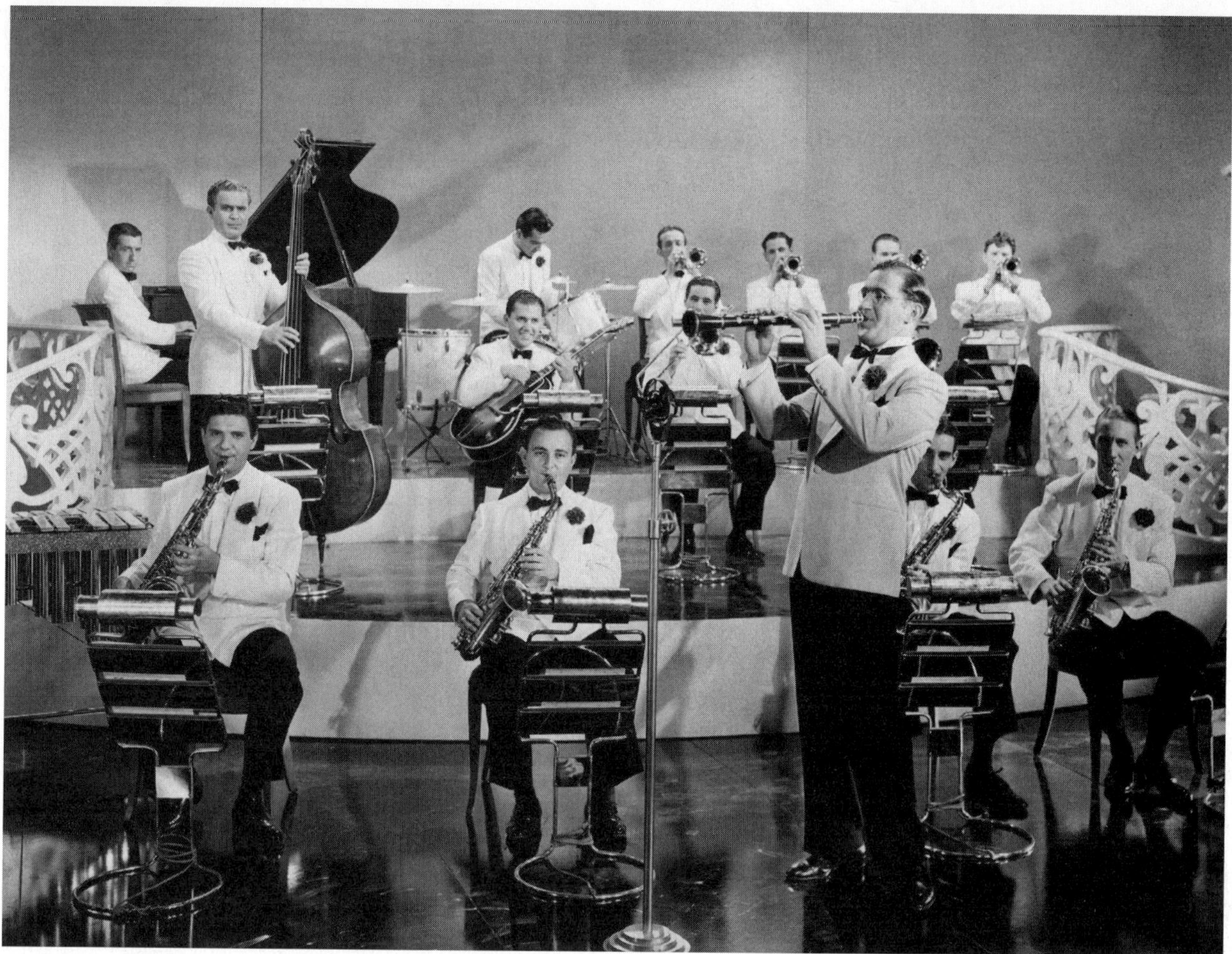

*Benny Goodman Band. © Bettmann/CORBIS*

- Goodman was a demanding bandleader who did not tolerate problems, professional or otherwise, with his band members. Therefore, there were many personnel changes over the years of its existence. The following is a partial list of players who played in the Benny Goodman Band.

### Artie Shaw Band

- Artie Shaw (born 1910) was raised in New Haven, Connecticut. He was first influenced by Louis Armstrong, Frankie Trumbauer, and Bix Beiderbecke.
- In 1930, after a short time in Cleveland and Los Angeles playing with different bands, he moved to New York City. He made his first appearance as a bandleader at a swing concert in 1936 held at the Imperial Theater.
- He led a big band that played refined and subtle jazz in the late 1930s and early 1940s.
- He was an excellent clarinetist, arranger, and improviser, often displaying impressionistic and other classical influences in his playing.
- He was considered a rival to Benny Goodman.
- He hired Billie Holiday to tour with his band in the late 1930s, making his the first white band to perform with a black female vocalist.

- He became a big-name performer with his successful 1938 recording of "Begin the Beguine."
- Some important musicians who were members of his band include the following:
  - Roy Eldridge, trumpet
  - Billie Holiday, vocalist
  - Hot Lips Page, trumpet
  - Johnny Guarneri, piano
  - Max Kaminsky, trumpet
- In 1940, following the lead of bandleaders such as Count Basie and Benny Goodman, Shaw organized a small group named the Gramercy Five. They made many successful and significant recordings.
- In 1954, Artie Shaw, for all practical purposes, retired from the music business and has since then mostly functioned as a jazz spokesman when he feels the urge to make his opinion known.
- As a jazz clarinetist and leader of bands, Artie Shaw was second to none. He is one of the most adventurous and charismatic yet controversial figures of jazz.

### Tommy Dorsey Band

- Tommy Dorsey (1905–1956) was born in Shenandoah, Pennsylvania.
- He was one of the finest trombone players in all of jazz (brother of saxophonist **Jimmy Dorsey**). At first he played with bands led by Jean Goldkette and Paul Whiteman. He also made recordings with Bix Beiderbecke, Red Nichols, Joe Venuti, and Eddie Lang.
- In 1932, he and his brother, Jimmy, formed the Dorsey Brothers Orchestra, which included Glenn Miller and Bob Crosby (Bing Crosby's brother). In 1935, Tommy quit the band and started his own band.
- He was an outstanding interpreter of ballads. "I'm Getting Sentimental Over You" became his band's theme song. His most commercially successful recording was a big band version of "Boogie-Woogie," originally a Pinetop Smith piano composition.
- A hard-swinging band with polished arrangements, the Tommy Dorsey Band was sometimes recognized as one of the greatest all-around dance bands.
- Some important musicians who were members of his band include the following:
  - Buddy Rich, Dave Tough, drums
  - Bunny Berigan, trumpet
  - Frank Sinatra, vocalist
  - Pee Wee Erwin, trumpet
  - Sy Oliver, arranger
- In 1947, both Dorsey brothers were featured in a movie called *The Fabulous Dorseys*. In 1953, the brothers worked out their differences and reformed the Dorsey Brothers Band. They were featured on their own television program in 1955 to 1956.

### Glenn Miller Band

- Glenn Miller (1904–1944) was born in Clarinda, Iowa. He began his professional career as a studio musician and a dance band sideman playing with bands led by Ben Pollack, Red Nichols, the Dorsey Brothers, and English bandleader Ray Noble. He formed his own band in 1937 but did not experience much success until 1939 when the band was broadcast on radio while performing at the Meadowbrook Ballroom in New Jersey and the Glen Island Casino in New York.
- From 1939 to 1944, Miller led one of the most popular and commercially successful bands of the Swing Era.
- The band's emphasis was on arrangements and attractive melodies.
- Improvised solos were not so important, but one exceptionally talented soloist was cornetist Bobby Hackett.
- The popular vocal group the Pied Pipers sang with Miller's band.
- Miller's characteristic arranging technique was doubling the saxophone melody an octave higher on clarinet.
- The Glen Miller Band's best-known recordings are "In the Mood," "Little Brown Jug," and "Moonlight Serenade."

### Jimmy Lunceford Orchestra

- Jimmy Lunceford (1902–1947) was born in Fulton, Missouri, but he grew up in Denver where as a boy, he studied music with Paul Whiteman's father. In the early 1930s he played in Cleveland and Buffalo. The band eventually was hired to play at the Cotton Club in 1934, and by 1935 they were nationally known as the Jimmie Lunceford Orchestra.
- Less known for soloists, Lunceford's band was known for precision, clean execution in its performance of excellent and imaginative arrangements, and showmanship.
- Sy Oliver created the majority of arrangements and is partly responsible for the "Lunceford style." His arrangements of "For Dancers Only" and "Margie" established him as a talented and innovative dance band arranger ahead of his time.
- The band had excellent soloists including the following:
  - ♪ Willie Smith, alto sax
  - ♪ Trummy Young, trombone
  - ♪ Joe Thomas, trumpet

### Chick Webb Orchestra

- Chick Webb (1909–1939) was born in Baltimore, Maryland. As a result of tuberculosis contracted early in life, he had a hunchback and found it difficult to get around. Doctors felt that drumming would be helpful. By the age of seventeen, he was in New York playing with Benny Carter and Duke Ellington. In 1931, he formed the Chick Webb Orchestra.
- He was an outstanding drummer and bandleader made famous through recordings and performances at the Savoy Ballroom in New York City.

- He was one of the most influential drummers of his era, possessing a powerful sense of swing.
- He hired singer Ella Fitzgerald in 1934.
- One of Fitzgerald's first hits was based on a nursery rhyme: "A Tisket a Tasket."
- For two years, Fitzgerald assumed leadership of Webb's band after his untimely death.
- Some important musicians who were members of his band include the following:
  - Bobby Stark, trumpet
  - Taft Jordan, trumpet
  - Louis Jordan, sax and vocals
  - Edgar Sampson, alto sax, arranger

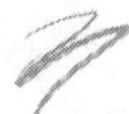

## IMPORTANT SWING ERA TRUMPET PLAYERS

**Roy Eldridge** was born on January 30, 1911 in Pittsburgh, Pennsylvania. Known as "Little Jazz," Roy Eldridge was a fiery, energetic trumpeter who bridged the gap between Louis Armstrong and Dizzy Gillespie. He possessed tremendous range and technique, was an excellent improviser and had a bright brassy tone. He also could "growl" with the best of them. Perhaps because he was originally a drummer, his trumpet playing exhibited great rhythmic drive. He began touring with carnivals when he was 16. His playing was strongly influenced by Armstrong and he was hired by such band leaders as Horace Henderson, Zack Whyte, and Speed Webb. In 1930, he moved to New York and worked with a number of well-known dance bands. In 1934, he left New York to join the Michigan-based McKinney's Cotton Pickers performing with the outstanding tenor saxophonist Chu Berry. He made his first recording in 1935 in New York with the Teddy Hill Orchestra and soon after joined Fletcher Henderson's orchestra where his upper register abilities were featured. Drummer Gene Krupa hired Eldridge in 1941 where he was a featured soloist and singer. He later toured with the Artie Shaw band in 1944 and then later led his own band. Eldridge was a very competitive player who loved playing in jam sessions. His late 1940s work with Norman Granz' "Jazz at the Philharmonic" series was an ideal opportunity to showcase his talents. After the 1940s he freelanced in New York, spent time in Europe, and made many memorable recordings. He died on February 26, 1989.

**Rowland Bernart "Bunny" Berigan** was born November 2, 1908 in Hilbert, Wisconsin. From 1935 to 1939, Berigan, was recognized (along with Eldridge and Armstrong) as one of the top trumpet players in jazz. He had a beautiful tone and a wide range. A great soloist, Berigan brought excitement to every group with which he played. He was an outstanding soloist, full of fire and bravado. Berigan played in many Midwestern territory bands in the mid to late 1920s and in 1930 he was hired to play trumpet in the Hal Kemp Orchestra, but soon left to perform with Paul Whiteman. By the early 1930s, Berigan gained a reputation as a hot jazz soloist appearing on numerous records with the Boswell Sisters and the Dorsey Brothers. In 1935 he performed with Benny Goodman's orchestra, recording classic solos on Goodman's first two hit records "King Porter Stomp" and "Sometimes I'm Happy." As an in-demand studio musician he performed on countless recordings and in 1937 joined Tommy Dorsey, recording more classic solos on "Marie" and "Song of India." After leaving Dorsey, he found enough financial backing to form his own orchestra and record his biggest hit "I Can't Get Started." A great bandleader, but a terrible businessman, he was soon forced to disband and perform for other bandleaders. He died on June 2, 1942 at the much too young age of thirty-three never to achieve his full potential.

**Charlie Shavers** was born August 3, 1917 in New York City. He was one of most well-respected trumpeters to emerge during the Swing Era. He was an excellent trumpet player, possessing great technique, a beautiful "buttery" sound, and an extroverted style along with a great sense of melody. Shavers began as a pianist before switching to trumpet—this may account for his great arranging skills. By the time he was 18 he was performing professionally; first with Tiny Bradshaw's band; later Lucky Millinder's big band. In 1937, he became a key member of John Kirby's Sextet where he became an integral part of the group playing excellent muted solos and arranging many numbers for the band. He also had a major hit with his composition "Undecided." He left Kirby in 1944 and joined Tommy Dorsey's Orchestra from 1945 until Dorsey's death in 1956. He also recorded with the Metronome All-Stars and toured with Jazz at the Philharmonic. A competitive player, his cutting sessions with Roy Eldridge were infamous. Shavers died July 8, 1971 in New York City.

**Harry James** was born March 15, 1916 in Albany, Georgia. He was one of the most outstanding trumpet players of the Swing Era. He possessed excellent technique, tremendous range, big beautiful sound all of which made his trumpet work instantly identifiable. He was also one of the most popular bandleaders of the 1940s, and he continued to lead his band until just before his death. He grew up in Texas around circus performers and his father was a circus bandleader and trumpet player. As a circus musician James developed his prodigious technique and range. He was only 14 when he won a state music contest as a trumpeter and soon after turned professional. In 1935 he became a member of Ben Pollack's band. In 1936, he was a star trumpet player with the Benny Goodman Band. In December 1937, he made recordings under his own name. In early 1939, he left Goodman and formed his own orchestra, soon hiring a young unknown singer named Frank Sinatra. He enjoyed tremendous popularity in the 1940s and 1950s, but was often criticized as being too commercial. His trumpet playing set a very high standard and was universally respected. Harry James died July 5, 1983.

**Charles Melvin "Cootie" Williams** was born on July 11, 1911 in Mobile, Alabama. He was an integral part of Duke Ellington's band and a valued soloist from 1929 to 1940. He replaced trumpeter Bubber Miley whose plunger mute and growl contributed to the Ellington band's distinctive "jungle" sound. Williams was able to expand on that role with his superior technique. His brilliant open horn playing is featured in many of Ellington's recordings, including "Concerto for Cootie," which Ellington wrote specifically for him. Williams frequently recorded on his own with artists such as Teddy Wilson, Billie Holiday, Lionel Hampton, and other fellow Ellingtonians. He played with Benny Goodman in 1941 for a year before leaving in 1942 to form his own band. Williams led his own bands from 1942 until 1959 and employed some of the most outstanding young bebop players of the day such as Bud Powell, Arnett Cobb, "Lockjaw" Davis, and Eddie Vinson. Williams collaborated with Thelonious Monk on the composition "Round Midnight," introducing it in 1944 when it became the band's theme song. In 1948 when times became tough for big bands, Williams reduced the group to a sextet that played the Savoy Ballroom for eleven years. He recorded many albums, two of the best with fellow Ellington cornetist Rex Stewart titled *The Big Challenge* and *Porgy and Bess Revisited*. He rejoined Ellington in 1962 and stayed with the band even after Duke's death in 1974 when his son Mercer Ellington took over. Cootie Williams died September 15, 1985.

**Wilbur Dorsey "Buck" Clayton** was born on November 11, 1911 in Parson, Kansas. He first achieved national notoriety as a trumpet soloist with the Count Basie Orchestra during the 1930s and 1940s. Clayton began his career in California with a band that later ended up traveling to China. In 1936, while visiting Kansas City, he was invited to join the Count Basie orchestra as a replacement for "Hot Lips Page." This band was the same one that John Hammond heard and invited to New York. Clayton was also featured on sessions with tenor saxophonist Lester Young, pianist Teddy Wilson, and the singer Billie Holiday in the late 1930s. He remained in the Basie band until 1943, when he left for army service. After leaving the army, Clayton wrote arrangements for many bands including Basie, Benny Goodman, and Harry James before forming a sextet in the late 1940s. After the 1940s, he was active as a performer, arranger, and teacher. His later career focused on his work as a studio musician, jam session player, writer, and arranger. He had a dry, striking tone and possessed great dexterity. His approach was melodic yet more understated than many of his contemporaries. He died on December 8, 1991.

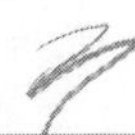

## IMPORTANT SWING ERA TENOR SAXOPHONISTS

### Coleman Hawkins

If historians or scholars ever decide to assign the accolade "Father of the Tenor Saxophone," Coleman Hawkins would undoubtedly be a top contender. Perhaps the reason why he is not already considered such is because of his counterpart, Lester Young, who, in his own way, deserves the same title. Both of these tenor saxophonists, in different ways, made equally important contributions to the instrument around the same time.

Coleman Hawkins (also known as either "Hawk" or "Bean") was born in St. Joseph, Missouri in 1904. His first musical instruments were piano and cello but he eventually settled on saxophone at age 14 While in high school in Topeka, Kansas, he took two years of music theory courses at Washburn College. After spending some time playing in Kansas City theaters, he was hired to play in Mamie Smith's Blues Hounds in 1922. He toured the United States with Mamie Smith and eventually settled in New York City in 1923. Shortly thereafter, he joined the Fletcher Henderson Band and remained with them until 1934. During this ten-year period, Hawkins' developed from a Broadway style slap-tongue player into a swing jazz tenor saxophonist with a robust sound and formidable technique. The beginnings of this transformation can be traced to the year 1924 when Louis Armstrong was a member of the Fletcher Henderson Band. Within two years after 1924, Hawkins had become a leading tenor saxophonist mostly by transferring many of Armstrong's innovations to the tenor saxophone.

From 1934 to 1939, Hawkins was in Europe where he performed with many European and ex-patriot jazz musicians including Jack Hylton and Django Reinhardt. It was during these years that many other tenor saxophonists established themselves in the United States, mostly by emulating Hawkins' accomplishments with the Fletcher Henderson Band. Upon returning to the States, Hawkins found many potential rivals playing his chosen instrument including Ben Webster and Lester Young. In 1939, not to be outdone by these players, he produced perhaps his most significant recording "Body and Soul." It was a perfectly conceived improvisation based on the song's melody and chord progression. It quickly became a sensation with the public and jazz musicians who then and now continue to hold it in high esteem.

In the 1940s Hawkins proved himself to be an important mentor for the younger generation of jazz players as the bebop style was evolving. He was the first musician to use Thelonious Monk on recordings and hire other young players such as Max Roach and Dizzy Gillespie. Although he never developed into a Bebop player himself, he was receptive to the style unlike many of his contemporaries who often gave negative commentary about the Bebop generation. Throughout the 1950s and 1960s, Hawkins continued to perform but his pre-1940s accomplishments have proved to be the most influential on jazz saxophonists. Coleman Hawkins died May 19, 1969.

### Lester Young

Lester Young was born in Woodville, Mississippi, on August 27, 1909. His father, Willis Young, gave him his first music lessons. Willis led a family band that traveled and performed in the Midwest. While a member of his father's band, Lester learned to play the violin, trumpet, and drums before choosing the saxophone as his main instrument. At age 19, he quit the Young family band to play with bands in Phoenix and Minneapolis. After playing with The Thirteen Original Blue Devils in 1932, he moved to Kansas City in 1933 to join the Bennie Moten Band.

Lester Young achieved national recognition after joining Count Basie's band in 1936. For the next eight years, Young toured with the Basie band while making recordings with a variety of small groups. He became a favorite sideman of Billie Holiday on her recordings. She nicknamed him "Prez," short for President of the Saxophone.

In 1944, Young spent a short and unhappy period of time in the U.S. Army. Differing accounts of his experience in the Army indicate he bore emotional scars after his dishonorable discharge later that same year. In the late 1940s, Young led small groups in nightclubs and on recordings. He also performed with Norman Granz' Jazz at the Philharmonic. In the 1950s, he experienced a gradual deterioration in his health resulting in a similar decline in his playing.

Young's style was the antithesis to Coleman Hawkins's Louis Armstrong influenced approach. Influenced by Bix Beiderbecke and Frankie Trumbauer, Young's tone was light and airy; he used an economy of notes while leaving plenty of empty space in his solos. This kind of playing proved to be a starting point for the 1950s cool style jazz musicians. Stan Getz was especially influenced by Young's style. Lester Young died on March 15, 1959 in New York City.

### Ben Webster

Benjamin Francis Webster was born in Kansas City, Missouri, March 27, 1909. He grew up learning several different instruments (violin, piano) before settling on the saxophone. He began his music education on the streets of Kansas City and in jam sessions. He traveled throughout the Midwest playing with many bands including one led by Lester Young's father Willis Young. Webster was able to hear Lester Young at times while being mentored by both Lester and his father who "taught [him] the notes on the horn." In the 1930s Webster played with many well-known big bands including those led by Bennie Moten, Andy Kirk, Fletcher Henderson, Benny Carter, Cab Calloway, and Teddy Wilson.

From 1940 to 1942, Webster was a member of Duke Ellington's band where he established himself as a top soloist on the tenor saxophone. His playing became such an integral part of Ellington's band that it is now referred to as the Blanton/Webster Band. Webster's solos on "Cottontail," "In a Mellow Tone," and "C-Jam Blues" were second to none. After an altercation that resulted in Webster cutting one of Ellington's suits in small pieces, Webster left the Ellington band.

From the mid-1940s to 1964, Webster found work either in New York or Los Angeles. He also was a featured soloist with the Norman Granz' Jazz at the Philharmonic bands. In 1964, Webster moved to Europe where he remained active for the rest of his career.

Even though he encountered Lester Young early in his life, Webster's style was deeply influenced by Coleman Hawkins, especially with regard to his big, rich tone and vibrato. However, there were more subtle differences between the two players due to Webster's tendency to play with less force and use more space. Describing his style as "an alto approach to the tenor," Webster lists Benny Carter and Johnny Hodges, both alto saxophonists, as important influences as well. Webster continues to influence jazz tenor saxophonists of the late 20th and early 21st century. He died in Amsterdam on September 20, 1973.

### Chu Berry

Leon "Chu" Berry was born in Wheeling, West Virginia on September 13, 1908. As the product of a good family, his half sister, a jazz pianist, inspired him to pursue music by learning to play the saxophone. He performed with jazz bands as a teenager in Wheeling and Charleston. By 1929, he was working professionally in New York. Throughout the 1930s he played with many jazz bands including those led by Teddy Hill, Benny Carter, and Fletcher Henderson. In 1937, he began a more long lasting association with Cab Calloway's band. He also appeared on recordings made by well-known artists such as Lionel Hampton, Roy Eldridge, Teddy Wilson, Count Basie, and Bessie Smith. By the late 1930s he was recognized as a leading jazz tenor saxophonist winning an All-Star Band distinction in *Metronome* magazine in 1937 and 1938.

Although Berry was deeply influenced by Coleman Hawkins, he had a unique style that was harmonically advanced and an impressive ability to improvise flawlessly at fast speeds. For this reason, it is assumed Charlie Parker, a Chu Berry disciple, named his son Leon.

Berry's life tragically ended on October 31, 1941 due to an auto accident in Ohio when he was on his way to a Cab Calloway engagement in Canada. His reputation would undoubtedly be far greater had he not died so young. Coleman Hawkins considered him ". . . about the best." Even modern saxophonists such as Branford Marsalis say Berry is a significant influence on jazz tenor saxophonists of today.

## IMPORTANT SWING ERA ALTO SAXOPHONISTS

**John Cornelius "Johnny" Hodges** was born July 25, 1906 in Cambridge, Massachusetts. He is primarily known for his work with the Duke Ellington Orchestra. His alto saxophone sound became an integral part of Ellington's sound when he joined in 1928. He was a masterful improviser, possessed great technique, and had a most distinctive and beautiful tone on the instrument. In fact, his unique tone makes him one of the easiest performers to identify. He began on drums and piano before taking up the saxophone at the age of 14, playing soprano first and later the alto. He took lessons from Sydney Bechet and began his professional career in Boston and New York around 1924. He made hundreds of records with Ellington and recorded with numerous small groups, many of which were comprised of members of Ellington's band. Some titles associated with Hodges include: "Jeep's Blues," "Hodge Podge," and "The Jeep is Jumpin" all cowritten with Duke. Other Ellington recordings that bear Hodges trademark sound include: "Things Ain't What They Used To Be," "Don't Get Around Much Any More'" "Passion Flower," and "Blood Count." His sound was a model for alto sax players of the 1930s and early 1940s and it influenced many younger musicians who would go on to be important in the bebop era and beyond. Johnny Hodges died on May 11, 1970 in New York City.

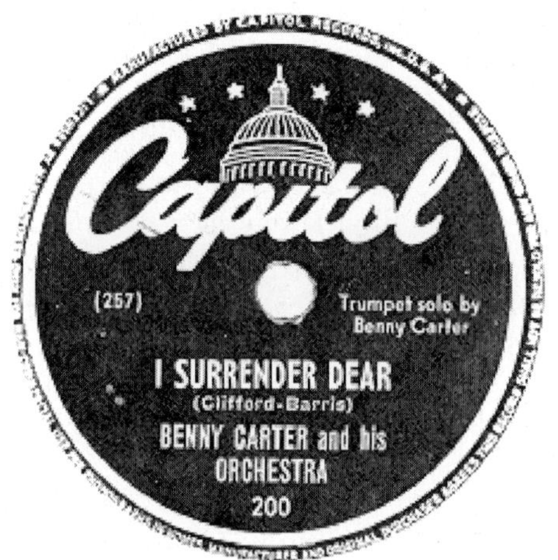


**Bennett Lester "Benny" Carter** was born August 8, 1907. He began as a trumpet player after having heard trumpeters Cuban Bennett and Bubber Miley, but soon switched to the saxophone where he began to emulate C-melody saxophonist Frankie Trumbauer. From 1924 to 1928, Carter worked as a sideman in some of the nation's top bands including Earl Hines and the Charlie Johnson Orchestra. During this period he taught himself the craft of arranging. In 1930, Carter joined Fletcher Henderson's orchestra, assuming the arranging duties previously handled by Don Redman. Carter's innovative scores, particularly his writing for the sax section, helped to revitalize the band. In 1931, Carter became musical director of another important musical organization: the Detroit-based McKinney's Cotton Pickers. In 1932, Carter returned to New York and soon began putting together his own orchestra,

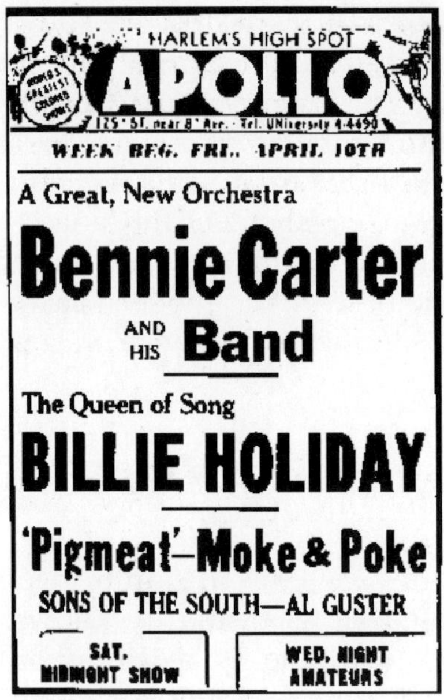


which eventually would include such swing stars as Chu Berry, Teddy Wilson, Sid Catlett, and Dicky Wells. However, this excellent band was not a commercial success. Carter traveled to Europe in 1935 staying until 1938, successfully performing and directing groups in France and England. Upon his return to the States he realized that the country was at the height of the Swing Era and the big band sounds, which he had helped shape, were sweeping the airwaves. He formed another outstanding orchestra, which spent much of 1939 and 1940 at Harlem's famed Savoy Ballroom. As an arranger, his arrangements were in great demand and featured on recordings by Benny Goodman, Count Basie, Duke Ellington, Glenn Miller, Gene Krupa, and Tommy Dorsey. In 1941, Carter cut the group back to a sextet, which included bebop pioneers Dizzy Gillespie and Kenny Clarke. In 1942, he reformed his big band and it included important future bebop stars, such as Miles Davis, J. J. Johnson, Max Roach, and Art Pepper, all having later acknowledged their debt to Carter as a teacher. After settling in California in 1942, Carter found himself writing music for films such as the soundtrack to *Stormy Weather* in 1943. He later arranged music for dozens of feature films and television productions. He has provided arrangements for almost every major popular singer including Billie Holiday, Ella Fitzgerald, Sarah Vaughan, Lou Rawls, Ray Charles, Peggy Lee, Louis Armstrong, Pearl Bailey, Billy Eckstine and Mel Torme.

Benny Carter has made contributions to music in numerous areas. As a soloist, Carter, along with Johnny Hodges, was the model for Swing Era alto saxophonists. He also had the unique ability to double on trumpet, which is very unusual for a saxophonist. As an arranger, he was one of the principal architects of the big band style and helped chart the course of big band jazz during the 1930s. His arrangements for Fletcher Henderson in the early 1930s and McKinney's Cotton Pickers were often emulated by other arrangers. Some of his compositions, such as "When Lights Are Low" and "Blues In My Heart," have become jazz standards. Carter also made major musical contributions to the world of film and television. Benny Carter died July 12, 2003.

**Willie Smith** (1910–1967), originally from Charleston, South Carolina, was considered one of the finest alto saxophonists in jazz together with Johnny Hodges and Benny Carter during the 1930s. He had a distinctive sound, a swinging style, and strong leadership skills, all of which were a major asset to Jimmy Lunceford's orchestra. Smith was also an excellent clarinetist and was considered a very good arranger, having contributed many numbers to the Lunceford band. Willie Smith attended Fisk University in the late 1920s where he met Lunceford. When Lunceford formed his band he asked Smith to join as an alto player in 1929. A superb lead alto saxophonist and the strongest soloist in the Lunceford Orchestra, Smith was one of the stars of the group until 1942. He left Lunceford and over the next few years played with a number of important big bands led by Charlie Spivak, Duke Ellington, and the trumpet player, Harry James. He remained with James in the 1950s and early 1960s, while also occasionally playing with Norman Granz' Jazz at the Philharmonic.

**Henry "Buster" Smith** (1904–1991) was originally from Alsdorf, Texas. He could play the play organ, guitar, alto saxophone, and the clarinet by the time he was 18. He began playing alto saxophone and clarinet professionally in Dallas in the early 1920s. In 1925, he joined the famous Midwestern territory band Page's Blue Devils. He played with some of the best musicians in the Southwest (from Oklahoma City to Kansas City) including Hot Lips Page, Walter Page, Lester Young, Count Basie, and Jimmy Rushing, and by 1931 became the leader of the Blue Devils. In 1933, he joined the Bennie Moten Orchestra. After Moten's sudden death in 1935, Smith remained in the band that eventually became the Count Basie Orchestra. The band's great success in Kansas City led to the group relocating to New York by 1937. Buster Smith is reputed to have used a thicker saxophone reed that produced a louder and "dryer" sound that was different from the sweeter, more refined sound of Johnny Hodges. Smith's sound could carry better in the loud clubs of Kansas City. An excellent blues player he mentored the young Kansas City alto saxophonist Charlie Parker. Smith's tone, attack (the way he played his notes), linear conception, and rhythmic feel strongly influenced Parker who revolutionized jazz in the 1940s.

### Important musicians of the swing era

| TRUMPET | ALTO SAX | TENOR SAX | TROMBONE |
|---|---|---|---|
| Hot Lips Page | Johnny Hodges | Lester Young | Tommy Dorsey |
| Roy Eldridge | Benny Carter | Coleman Hawkins | Glenn Miller |
| Bunny Berigan | Willie Smith | Ben Webster | "Tricky" Sam Nanton |
| Harry James | Buster Smith | Bud Freeman | Lawrence Brown |
| Cootie Williams | Jimmy Dorsey | Vido Musso | J. C. Higginbothan |
| Harry "Sweets" Edison | Russell Procope | Chu Berry | Benny Morton |
| Henry "Red" Allen | | Herschel Evans | Vic Dickenson |
| Buck Clayton | | Don Byas | Dicky Wells |
| Charlie Shavers | | Georgie Auld | Jack Teagarden |
| Ziggy Elman | | | Trummy Young |
| Rex Stewart | | | Jimmy Harrison |
| Jonah Jones | | | Miff Mole |

| BASS | DRUMS | PIANO | ARRANGERS |
|---|---|---|---|
| Walter Page | Sid Catlett | Teddy Wilson | Don Redman |
| Jimmy Blanton | Jo Jones | Duke Ellington | Bill Challis |
| John Kirby | William "Cozy" Cole | Count Basie | Duke Ellington |
| Israel Crosby | Dave Tough | Jess Stacy | Sy Oliver |
| | Chick Webb | Mel Powell | Fletcher Henderson |
| | Gene Krupa | Mary Lou Williams | Mary Lou Williams |
| | Buddy Rich | Nat Cole | Edgar Sampson |
| | Lionel Hampton | Billy Kyle | Billy Strayhorn |
| | | Nat Pierce | Eddie Sauter |
| | | Claude Thornhill | Jerry Gray |
| | | | Glenn Miller |
| | | | Jimmy Mundy |
| | | | Paul Weston |
| | | | Buck Clayton |
| | | | Eddie Durham |
| | | | Spud Murphy |

| CLARINET | VOCALISTS |
|---|---|
| Benny Goodman | Peggy Lee |
| Barney Bigard | Helen Forrest |
| Artie Shaw | Nat Cole |
| Buster Bailey | Frank Sinatra |
| | Mildred Bailey |
| | Jo Stafford |
| | Boswell Sisters |
| | Anita O'Day |

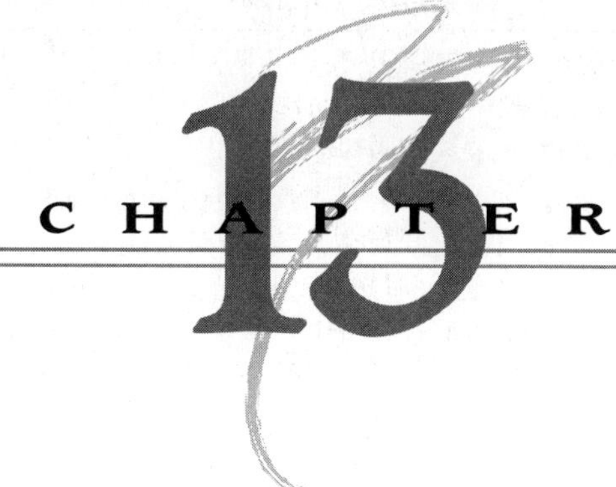

CHAPTER 13

# The Decline of Big Band Swing and Rise of Bebop

- Modern jazz (post-1940s) instrumentation focuses primarily on a combo (small group). The emphasis on small groups emerged for a variety of reasons:
  - **Overcommercialization—**big band swing had become a commercialized business product rather than an artistic genre. The public was saturated with big band swing music after Benny Goodman's 1935 Palomar Ballroom success. It was only a matter of time before a change would be necessary.
  - **Artistic Dissatisfaction—**The improvising jazz soloist was often frustrated by the limitations of big band swing. Emphasis tended to be placed on arrangements and relatively little space was provided for improvising soloists. Coleman Hawkins opened new doors with his 1939 "Body and Soul" recording, whetting the appetite of many young, aspiring jazz improvisers to seek a new mode of self-expression in small-group settings and after-hours jam sessions.
  - **World War II** had an influence and effect on a variety of societal and technological changes:
    - First, the draft left women with few men to dance with. In addition, many band members were drafted.
    - Second, the scarcity of petroleum limited the big band's ability to tour, thus eliminating an important financial source.

- Third, there was a 20 percent amusement tax levied on club owners, who were obviously forced to cut back on the number of musicians hired for engagements.

- **1942–1944 Recording Strike—**In August of 1942, it became necessary for **James Petrillo,** head of the American Federation of Musicians Local 802 New York organization, to call for a strike against the recording industry in order to obtain appropriate payment and royalties for studio musicians. Smaller companies acquiesced in the fall of 1943, while the two big companies, RCA Victor and Columbia, didn't back down until 1944. The two-year strike added to the mounting frustration big bands were experiencing as America entered World War II.
- Changes in jazz are caused by evolution and revolution. During the early 1940s, jazz was in a period of musical maturation and development. Changes dictated by public and musical sentiment made it necessary for big bands to either scale down or disband. In fact, by 1946 many swing bands, who had experienced success in the late 1930s such as those led by Benny Goodman, Harry James, Tommy Dorsey, Benny Carter, and Jack Teagarden, had either significantly reduced the number of members or were no longer together.

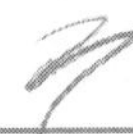

## EVOLUTION OF BEBOP

- There was a concerted effort to raise the status of dance music from functional music to art or chamber music. Many young black musicians wanted to do away with stereotypical images of 1920s and 1930s black entertainers. There was a change in attitude about how these musicians wished to be perceived. They considered themselves **artists** rather than merely **entertainers.** There was an attempt to shed associations with the more commercial aspects of jazz and the aspiration to achieve new musical heights.
- A new style gradually developed that grew out of the playing of a handful of young musicians who were arriving at similar ideas independently of each other at first. The new style did not originate at any one place or time, but many of the "architects" congregated at after-hours jam sessions at Minton's Playhouse and Clark Monroe's Uptown House in the early 1940s.
- This newer, experimental approach to jazz came to be known as bebop. The name is drawn from the fast, angular melodies with unusual accents that were characteristic of the music. It did not develop all of a sudden, but it appeared that way since the first recordings did not occur until 1945 due to the recording ban of 1942–1944. Moreover, developments that brought about bebop took place during World War II when many musicians who had been active during the Swing Era were overseas and not able to witness its evolution. However, some of the old-guard Swing players inspired the young musicians to explore new territory such as the following:
    - Tenor saxophonists Coleman Hawkins, Lester Young, and Don Byas
    - Pianists Art Tatum, Nat Cole, and Earl Hines
    - Trumpeter Roy Eldridge

- ♪ Guitarist Charlie Christian
- ♪ The Count Basie rhythm section
- ♪ Bassist Jimmy Blanton

- Many of the younger musicians were members of the Billy Eckstine or Earl Hines big bands. Unlike many other bandleaders, these men were sympathetic to the plight of the younger jazz musicians and open to experimentation with new sounds and approaches. They expanded on Swing styles and developed a more modern style directly from it. Bebop is a departure from Swing, but not necessarily a reaction against it.
- The unofficial leaders of the bebop movement were Charlie Parker and Dizzy Gillespie. Other young musicians soon joined them, including Thelonious Monk, Charlie Christian, and Kenny Clarke (regulars at Minton's in the early 1940s), in their quest for new avenues of jazz expression.
- Initially bebop was not widely accepted by many older players, critics, and the general public. Because of its harmonic and melodic sophistication, it did not lend itself well to mass public consumption. A New Orleans revivalist movement took place during the 1940s that pitted the younger, more progressive bebop musicians against those who championed the older Chicago and New Orleans styles. In typical fashion, these older players were resistant to change.

## BEBOP

- Bebop is an instrumentally conceived style as opposed to a vocal one. The often fast, angular melodies and improvisations are technically complex and therefore difficult to sing. Much of the repertoire favored by Big Band Swing musicians are songs borrowed from Broadway shows and originally intended to be sung. However, many Swing Era musicians and the general public could not relate to bebop melodies that are often difficult if not impossible to sing. Where earlier musicians such as Louis Armstrong often took the original melody and used it as a basis for a solo, bebop solos often have no connection at all with the original melody. It was often difficult for the uninitiated listener to comprehend the music.
- Ironically, much of the repertoire of bebop musicians was not entirely new. Original melodies of standard popular songs were replaced with angular bebop melodies while the original chord progressions were retained (with perhaps a few small changes and/or substitutions). Therefore, there would be a lingering familiarity. These "new" compositions were known as **contrafactions.** However, the bebop melodies sounded very much like the new style of improvisation. Consequently, it was confusing for the uninitiated listener to get a handle on where the song stopped and the improvisation started.
- In fact, few totally original bebop compositions (original melodies *and* chords) were written during the 1940s. However, two important composers of this era who did write totally original compositions were pianists **Tadd Dameron** and **Thelonious Monk.**

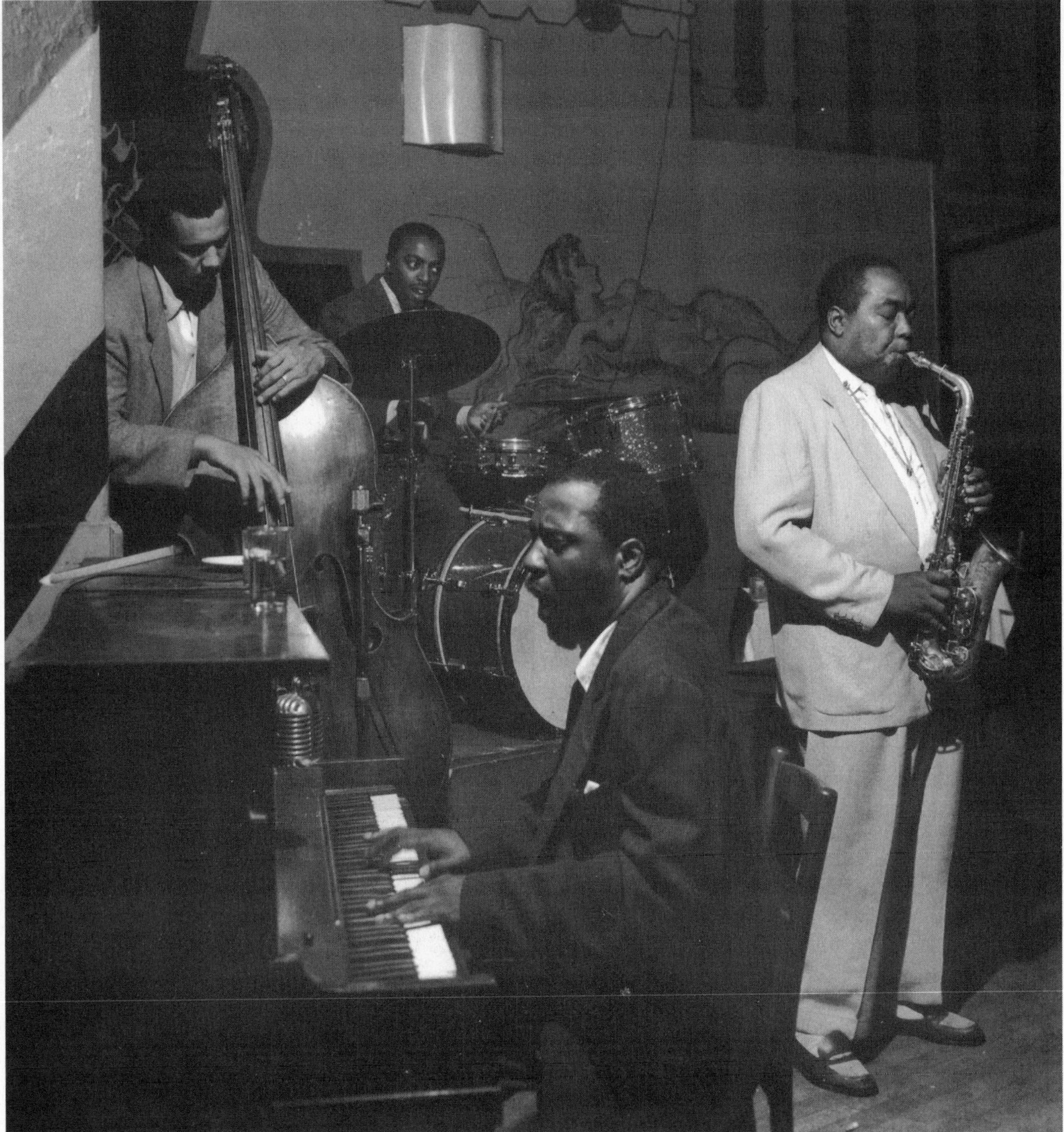

*Charlie Parker Quartet: from left, Charles Mingus (bass), Roy Haynes (drums), Thelonius Monk (piano), Charlie Parker (alto sax). Photograph by Bob Parent. Courtesy of Dale Parent.*

- Reharmonization and substitute chords are common in bebop tunes. Also, harmonies utilize upper extensions and altered tones. For example, flatted fifth and ninth scale degrees are used to add tension, color, and richness.
- Often bebop players would play compositions in unusual keys and at very fast tempos.
- Bebop also had a social aspect about it. A mode of behavior and dress became associated with the leading figures. Players wore pin-striped suits, sunglasses, and berets, and some even sported goatees.

In addition, there was a new code language perpetrated by the players that exhibited an air of exclusion to society in general. For example, such words as hip and cool had special meaning for "initiated" beboppers. Most likely, these individuals sought to separate themselves from their immediate predecessors in more than just musical ways.

## RHYTHM SECTION

- The bebop style of accompanying did not evolve as quickly as solo playing did; many rhythm sections still played in the older Swing style, while the improvisers played in the newer style.
- Bass: Bebop bass players were influenced by Swing Era bassists Jimmy Blanton and Walter Page. In the bebop style, bass players became **the primary timekeeper.** They were expected to maintain very fast tempos while creating smooth, stepwise, melodically interesting lines from one chord change to the next. Unlike Swing bass players who received help from both piano and drums, bebop bass players were expected to occupy the lower end of the harmonic spectrum with little or no support from other rhythm section players. Also, bass players were expected to be competent soloists.
- Drums: Jo Jones and Sid Catlett were precursors to the innovative bebop drumming of Kenny Clarke. Bebop drummers increased the frequency and spontaneity of kicks and "bombs," which helped them deviate from the role of strict timekeepers. "Pops" and "crashes" were called "chatter" to provide an energetic layer of activity. They played the bass drum more lightly with more discretion. Clarke is credited with switching time to the ride cymbal and snapping the high hat cymbals on beats two and four. Bebop drummers were more technically advanced than their predecessors.
- Piano: Initiated by Count Basie's upper register comping style, bebop piano players began to intermittently jab chords in the middle register with their left hands creating mostly syncopated rhythms. As a result, the piano player's left-hand activity was greatly reduced, allowing bass players more freedom and independence. The right hand was left free to either enhance left-hand chord voicings or create melodies. Bud Powell was the most widely imitated bebop pianist. His right hand could improvise convincing bebop melodies while the left hand comped harmony. The result was the first true modern jazz piano style.

### Differences Between Bebop and Big Band Swing

- Bebop used small group format.
- The improvised solo was of great importance.
- Tempos seemed faster.
- The clarinet was used infrequently.
- The average level of proficiency was higher.
- Bebop placed less emphasis on arrangements.
- Melodies and harmonies were more complex.

- Accompaniments were more varied; pianists were comping in the Basie style.
- Generally more interaction took place between the soloist and the rhythm section.
- The drummers kept time on ride cymbal and high hat, leaving the drums for playing accents. The bass drum was used for "dropping bombs" in a more **agitated** style.
- Angular melodies were written based upon existing chord progressions (contrafactions).
- Bebop emphasized surprise and tension in solos.
- Melodic lines were more often jagged with more syncopation.
- Singers were used infrequently; bebop melodies rarely had lyrics.
- Bebop lacked visual appeal.
- The sounds were more "dry" with little vibrato.
- The use of riffs was less than that of swing.

## Charlie Christian—Guitar

- Charlie Christian (1916–1942) was born in Dallas, Texas, but he grew up in Oklahoma City. He came from a musical family and made his first guitar out of cigar boxes. His first professional work came with territory bands in which he sometimes played bass. He began using amplification for his guitar as early as 1937.
- His early style was influenced by the blues; however, he also developed a single-note melody style influenced by Belgian jazz guitarist **Django Reinhardt.** Reinhardt played and recorded with the Quintet of the Hot Club of France, a high-quality ensemble capable of playing authentic jazz even though they were located in Europe. The group often included jazz violinist **Stephane Grappelli.** After losing partial use of his left hand in a fire-related injury, Reinhardt was forced to play single-note melodies using mostly two fingers. Christian took Reinhardt's style and applied it to playing melodies on his amplified guitar.
- In 1939, John Hammond heard Christian performing at the Ritz Café in Oklahoma City. He persuaded Benny Goodman to hear Christian. Goodman was so impressed with Christian's twenty fivc-chorus solo on "Rose Room," a tune Goodman had called to stump Christian, he hired Christian on the spot, mostly to perform in his small groups.
- Christian then moved to New York where he spent many nights at Minton's Playhouse exchanging ideas with the young bebop musicians. His advanced harmonic ideas and asymmetrical or rhythmically displaced phrases were incorporated into the standard bebop vocabulary.
- Unfortunately, Christian developed tuberculosis and was hospitalalized by the end of 1941. He died in March 1942, joining a growing list of jazz geniuses that were never allowed to reach their full potential.

## Charlie Parker—Alto Saxophone

- Charlie Parker (1920–1955) was born and raised by his mother in Kansas City, Missouri. He became especially interested in music at a young age. By the time he was twelve, he was sneaking out (after his mother had gone to a nighttime job) to hear jazz nearby in Kansas City's nightlife district. He especially loved to hide in the balcony of Sol Stibel's Club Reno and listen to his idol Lester Young play with the Count Basie Band.

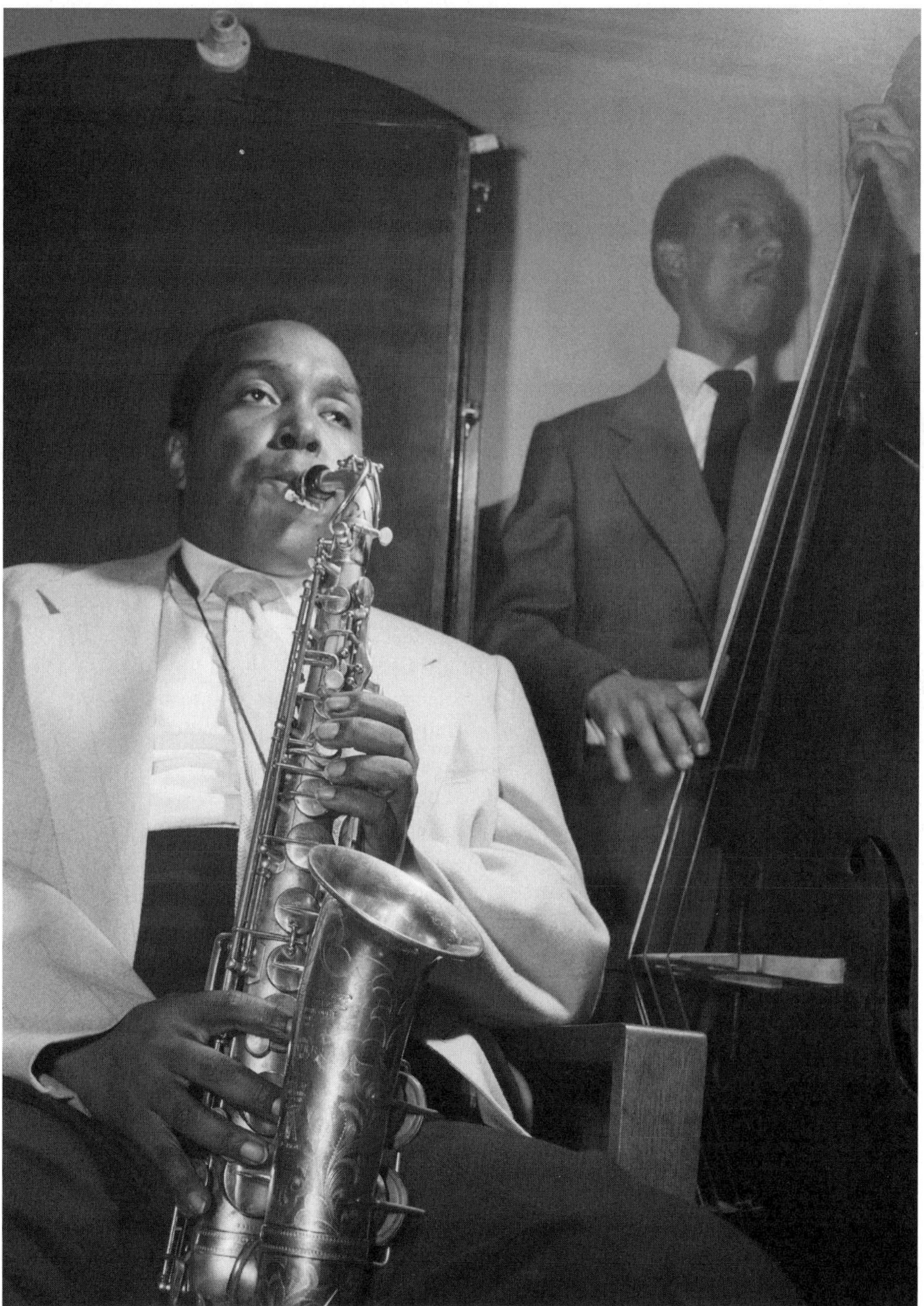

*Charlie Parker. © Bettmann/CORBIS*

- Parker was given some musical training by band teacher Alonzo Lewis while at Lincoln High School. Starting on baritone horn, he quickly became interested in the saxophone. He played in various bands in and around Kansas City from 1935 to 1939. At this time he diligently practiced to become proficient in all twelve keys—something he didn't realize most jazz musicians had not done. He was mentored by several Kansas City musicians including alto saxophonist Buster Smith and bassist Gene Ramey. At some point, Parker was given the nickname **Yardbird,** later shortened to just **Bird,** for his penchant for eating chicken.
- In 1938, Parker joined the Jay McShann Band. He performed in Chicago and New York with McShann's band.
- In 1938–1939, Parker lived in New York and spent time washing dishes at Jimmy's Chicken Shack, where **Art Tatum** gave nightly performances. He studied harmony with guitarist Biddy Fleet. Parker soon returned to Kansas City (for his father's funeral) and rejoined the McShann band. His solo on "Hootie Blues" with McShann's band was the first time he could be heard on a commercial recording. However, it was his improvisation on the popular tune "Cherokee" that displayed a different, more advanced ability and impressive talent.
- McShann's band was periodically in New York in the early 1940s and Parker would always visit Minton's Playhouse and Clark Monroe's Uptown House whenever he was there. In 1943 he was hired by Earl Hines (at the request of Dizzy Gillespie) to play in his band. Then in 1944 he played in the Billy Eckstine Band. In late 1944, Parker and Gillespie co-led a small group at the Three Deuces nightclub. They would perform unison angular bebop melodies at extremely fast tempos, followed by equally impressive solo improvisations using the chord progressions and forms of familiar songs. The "new" songs were given names such as "Groovin' High" (based [a contrafaction] on "Whispering"), "Salt Peanuts" (based on "I Got Rhythm"), and "Ko Ko" (based on "Cherokee"). Many swing musicians were puzzled yet impressed by such an approach to jazz.
- In 1945, Parker participated in recording sessions in February, May, and November. Gillespie was present on most of the recordings as they introduced their new bebop repertoire to the rest of the world. These recordings made a significant impact on jazz musicians not unlike what had occurred twenty years earlier with Louis Armstrong's Hot Five and Hot Seven recordings. In essence, the course of jazz history was forever changed after the Parker/Gillespie 1945 recordings were released.
- In 1946, Parker and Gillespie traveled to Los Angeles to showcase their talents at Billy Berg's nightclub. Parker remained in California for the next year, making recordings for Ross Russell's Dial label. Miles Davis was a sideman on some of these recordings. However, Parker's drug addiction was taking its toll, and he ended up in the Camarillo State Mental Hospital.
- By 1947, Parker had returned to New York. Over the next five years he made numerous recordings with varied personnel including Bud Powell, Miles Davis, Duke Jordan, Tommy Potter, Kenny Dorham, Max Roach, and J. J. Johnson. He also appeared on concerts organized by Norman Granz that featured well-known jazz musicians. These concerts were called "Jazz at the Philharmonic."

- In the late 1940s, Norman Granz organized recording sessions that featured Parker as a soloist in the context of a string orchestra.
- In 1949 and 1950 Parker made two successful European tours. His performances were well received by European critics and audiences. Parker was surprised to find that in Europe, jazz musicians were given the status and respect generally reserved for classical musicians in America.
- During the last three years of his life, drugs and alcohol took their toll and he experienced emotional problems partially due to the death of his daughter Pree. It became more difficult for Parker to find work. His last performance was given on March 5, 1955, at Birdland, a club created in his honor in 1949. He died only a week later while watching the Dorsey Brothers' television show at Baroness Pannonica de Koenigswarter's apartment.
- Even though he died tragically young, Parker, during his short and troubled career, managed to change the direction of modern jazz.

### *Parker characteristics*

- Possessed a linear concept similar to that of Lester Young
- Great technical command and rhythmic dexterity
- Heavily blues influenced; a Kansas City product
- Complex style
- Chose notes based upon upper tetrachords
- Utilized passing and substitute chords
- Utilized flat-5th and flat-9th chord tones implied in his phrases, but not always stated by the rhythm section
- Phrase length was often irregular and phrase contour angular (jagged)
- Subdivision of the beat was very complex (as was Dizzy Gillespie's)
- Placed accents in unusual places, thus giving the impression of greater rhythmic complexity
- Influenced all subsequent modern jazz musicians with his new, creative language

### *Parker's sound*

- Directly contrasted with the warm, dark, wide-vibrato sound of Swing Era alto saxophonists such as Johnny Hodges and Benny Carter
- Often cutting and hard with little vibrato enhancing his unique persona
- He used a slow, wide vibrato in ballads

## Dizzy Gillespie—Trumpet

- John Birks Gillespie (1917–1993) was born in Cheraw, South Carolina. He learned to play trumpet mostly on his own.
- In 1935, he moved to Philadelphia and began to play with local bands where he was dubbed "Dizzy" for his precocious behavior. In 1937, he moved to New York City where he played with several bands including Chick Webb's Orchestra. There he first met Mario Bauza, who would later be an important influence in Dizzy's Afro-Cuban music.

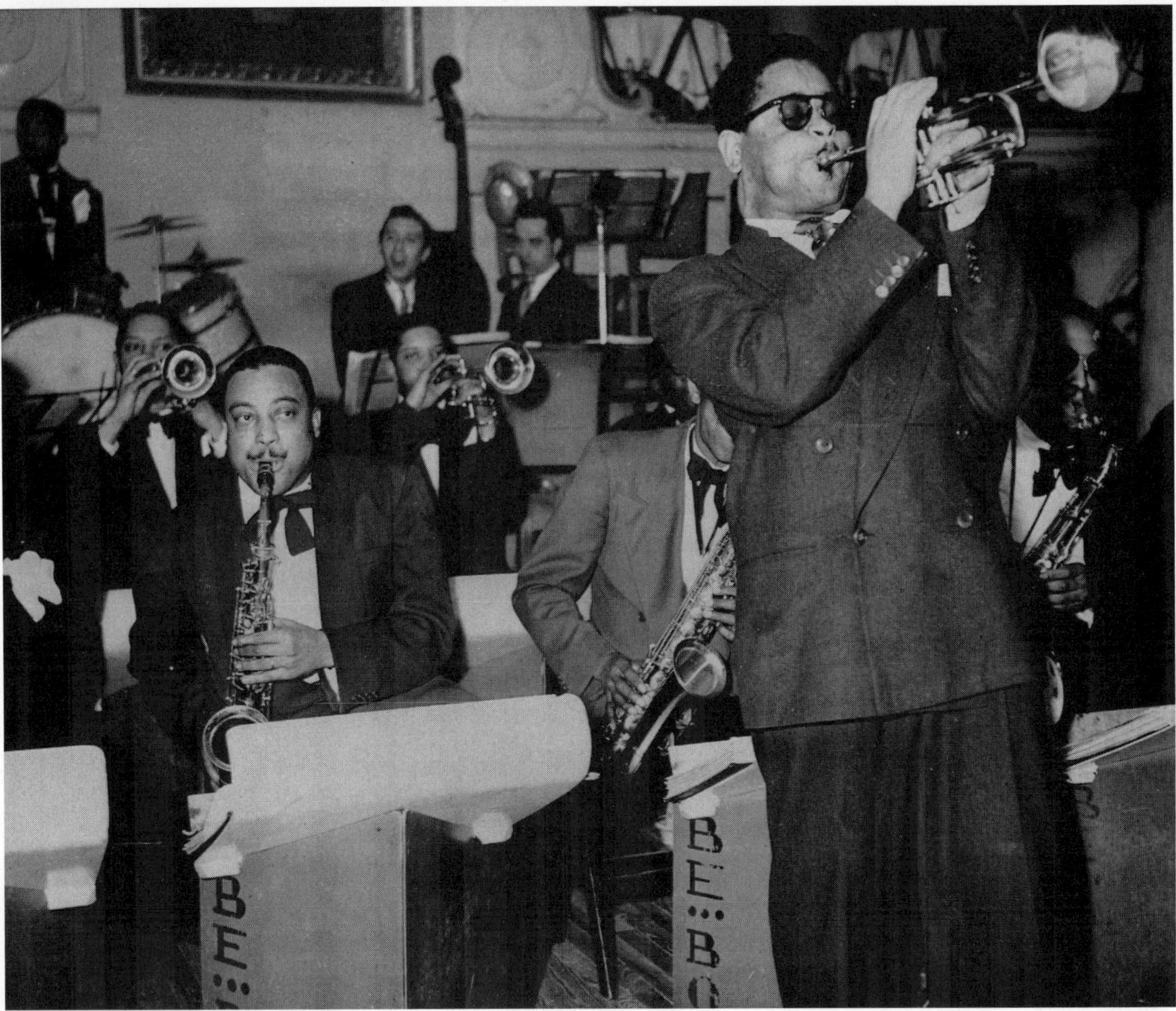

*Dizzy Gillespie. © CORBIS*

- Dizzy's first significant professional job was playing with the Teddy Hill Band in 1937. He replaced one of his idols and significant influences, trumpeter Roy Eldridge. Kenny Clarke, a soon to be important Bebop drummer, was also in the Teddy Hill Band.
- From 1939 to 1941, Gillespie was a member of Cab Calloway's band. Dizzy was able to build a good reputation due to the Calloway band's popularity and commercial success. Eventually a dispute with the leader over Dizzy's behavior led to his dismissal.
- Gillespie was a member of Earl Hines's band from 1941 to 1943. Then he joined an important big band led by Billy Eckstine. Charlie Parker was a member of the Hines and Eckstine bands. Other members of Eckstine's band read like a who's who list of bebop, such as Fats Navarro, Dexter Gordon, Miles Davis, Wardell Gray, and Sonny Stitt. Some musicians referred to Eckstine's band as a "bebop school" since the exchange of ideas between the players helped educate them about the bebop style.
- Gillespie was already familiar with Parker's playing from repeated exposure to him in several contexts. In 1940, he had met Parker in

Kansas City while touring with Cab Calloway. He also was jamming with Parker in informal situations at Minton's Playhouse and Clark Monroe's Uptown House from about 1941 to 1944.

- In 1944, Gillespie and Parker co-led a quintet that performed at the Three Deuces on Fifty-second Street.
- The Three Deuces engagement led to a number of important bebop recordings made with Charlie Parker in February and May of 1945. With the release of these recordings, it became apparent that Gillespie was at ease with the bebop style due to his startling technique and imagination on the trumpet.
- In early 1946, Gillespie and Parker performed in Los Angeles at Billy Berg's nightclub. After the Berg engagement was over, Gillespie returned to New York and formed a bebop big band. However, Parker remained in Los Angeles for the next year.
- From 1946–49, Gillespie led his own bebop big band. In 1947, he hired conga player Chano Pozo in an effort to combine Latin elements with jazz. Unfortunately Pozo was soon killed in a knife fight, but Gillespie continued to hire Latin musicians to play in his big band. He has since been credited with successfully integrating Latin music with jazz. Gillespie wrote several Latin-influenced compositions that have become standards, such, as "Cubano Be," "Cubano Bop," (with George Russell) and "A Night in Tunisia."
- Gillespie also wrote many bebop compositions that have become standards, such as "Woody 'n You" and "Groovin' High."
- In the 1950s Gillespie made many recordings with varied personnel, sometimes in collaboration with Norman Granz's "Jazz at the Philharmonic." It was in 1953 that Gillespie began using a trumpet with the bell pointed upward at a forty five degree angle from the instrument. This kind of trumpet would be his trademark for the rest of his life.
- In the late 1950s, he toured South America, Africa, the Middle East, and Asia as a State Department-sponsored goodwill ambassador.
- For the rest of his career, Gillespie continued to play bebop in many contexts, both small and large. He became a major spokesman for jazz and an important mentor for young, aspiring jazz trumpet players such as Jon Faddis, Wynton Marsalis, and Arturo Sandoval.
- Gillespie contributed to an original jazz vocabulary that influenced most post-1945 trumpet players.

### Bud Powell—Piano, Composer

- Bud Powell (1924–1966) was born and raised in Harlem. He was classically trained to play piano as a child. He began playing professionally around New York City when he was sixteen years old.
- He began participating in jam sessions at Minton's Playhouse in 1941. He was impressed with the advanced harmonic ideas of Thelonious Monk and the asymmetric phrases of Charlie Christian. He quickly became an integral part of the bebop scene.
- Powell was a member of the Cootie Williams Band from 1943 to 1944. At this time, his playing already revealed bebop influences.

- Problems with mental stability plagued Powell throughout his life. They reportedly began with an arrest in Philadelphia (while on tour with the Cootie Williams Band), where he was badly beaten by police officers. Periodically he spent time in mental hospitals, where he sometimes received electroconvulsive therapy (deemed harmful since that time).
- Powell's method of left-hand comping and right-hand bebop melodies influenced all jazz pianists of the 1940s and after. He was the most imitated bebop pianist. His approach set the foundation for modern jazz piano development. When he was at his best, he was able to improvise at remarkably fast speeds while still maintaining amazing technical control.
- Some of his most important recordings as a leader occurred from 1949 to 1951. These Blue Note recordings were either solo piano or with a rhythm section.
- As a composer, Powell contributed creative and unique yet complex bebop compositions such as "Parisian Thoroughfare," "Tempus Fugit," and "Un Poco Loco." Some have become standards, while others, due to their difficulty and eccentricity, have not often been performed or recorded.
- In the 1950s Powell recorded and performed with many leading bebop figures such as Charlie Parker, Charles Mingus, Dizzy Gillespie, and Max Roach. However, he was not always a consistently high-quality performer due to his mental health problems. He also was devastated by the loss of his brother, pianist Richie Powell, in 1956. In the late 1950s he moved to Paris where he experienced more of the same ups and downs, both personally and professionally.

## Kenny Clarke—Drums

- Kenny Clarke (1914–1985) was born and raised in Pittsburgh, Pennsylvania. He played drums in bands around Pittsburgh while still in his teens. He eventually joined the Teddy Hill Band where he collaborated with Dizzy Gillespie, who was sympathetic and receptive to new ideas and approaches.
- Clarke was already approaching jazz drumming in a unique way that apparently led to his eventual dismissal from the Teddy Hill Band. However, a year later, Hill became manager of Minton's Playhouse and hired Clarke for the house band. This time, Clarke was chosen because of his innovative drum techniques.
- Clarke moved the beat from the bass drum to the ride cymbal, achieving a lighter texture. He used the bass drum for intermittent "punches" (called "dropping bombs") that seemed to enhance the angular melodies of his associates at Minton's Playhouse.
- Clarke worked and recorded with Parker, Monk, Powell, Christian, and other bebop musicians in the 1940s. By the late 1940s he was playing with Dizzy Gillespie's bebop big band. His drumming style significantly influenced all bebop drummers.
- In the early 1950s he was a member of the Modern Jazz Quartet, but in 1956 he moved to Paris where he spent most of the rest of his life. He eventually became a drummer who was proficient in many styles, and he frequently performed and recorded in Europe.

### Thelonious Monk—Piano, Composer, Band Leader

- Thelonious Sphere Monk (1917–1982) was born in Rocky Mount, North Carolina, but was raised in New York City in a neighborhood called San Juan Hill. He began playing piano at the age of six and was largely self-taught. His first professional experience was touring with an evangelist when he was in his teens.
- By 1941 Monk was in the house band at Minton's Playhouse along with drummer Kenny Clarke. Many musicians were impressed with Monk's original and advanced musical ideas. However, his unorthodox method of playing the piano was controversial. Many bandleaders and record producers were not confident that his style would be appealing.
- Between 1943 and 1945, Coleman Hawkins was the first to hire Monk for recording sessions.
- In 1947, Monk made his first recordings as a leader for Blue Note Records. These recordings established Monk as both a talented yet unusual pianist and quality composer of bebop compositions that didn't

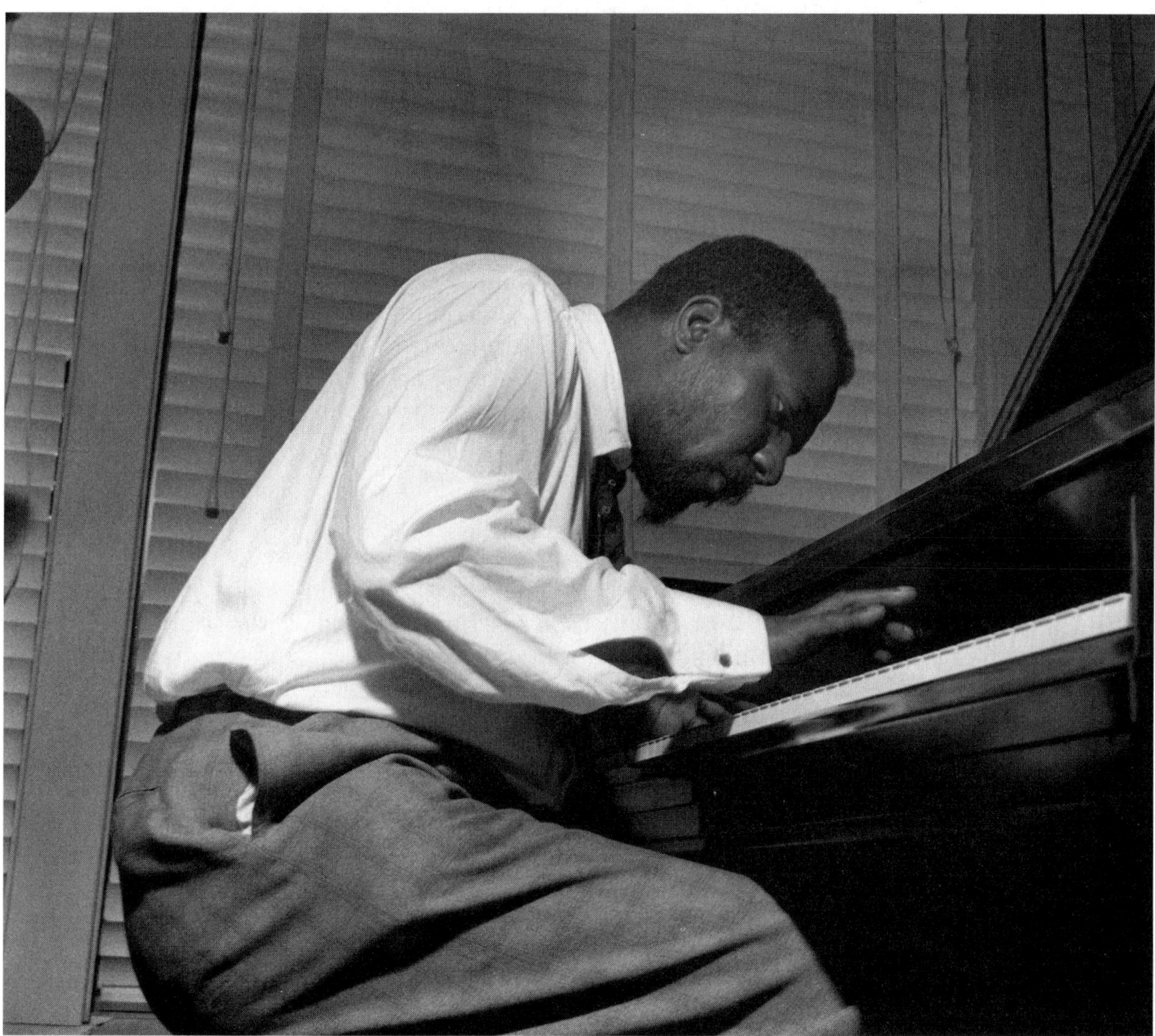

*Thelonious Monk. © Mosaic Images/CORBIS*

always rely on the principle of contrafaction. Worth noting is the playing of vibraphonist Milt Jackson on some of these recordings.

- In 1951, Monk was deprived of a cabaret card (necessary to perform in New York nightclubs) for the next six years because of a drug possession incident. Therefore, he was forced to perform in other cities such as Paris, Philadelphia, and Chicago.
- In 1955, Riverside released recordings of Monk playing Ellington compositions. In 1956, "Brilliant Corners" was released, featuring Monk performing his own original compositions. Many of Monk's compositions have become jazz standards such as "Straight No Chaser," "Round About Midnight," "Well You Needn't," and "Ruby My Dear."
- In 1957, after obtaining a new cabaret card, he appeared at the Five Spot in a band that included tenor saxophonist John Coltrane.
- In the 1960s, Monk performed and recorded regularly with a quartet that featured tenor saxophonist Charlie Rouse, bassist John Ore, and drummer Ben Riley.
- In the 1970s, Monk made appearances at jazz festivals and toured with the Giants of Jazz (1971 to 1972).
- However, illness led to his gradual reclusion from public appearances. He did not perform for the last six years of his life.
- Monk was a unique player who never fit into any definitive stylistic category. His emphasis on dissonance in both his melodic improvisations and his approach to comping separated him from all other jazz musicians of any style. In addition, Monk preferred to use the minimum number of notes necessary to make his point. He was not an excessive player who needed to dazzle an audience with his technical prowess. He tended to organize his material in unusual rhythmic groupings and was frequently unpredictable. In all of these ways, Monk emanated a powerful influence on the bebop musicians around him. However, it is a testimony to his unique and inestimable talent that he has continued to influence jazz musicians beyond the twentieth century.

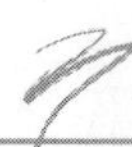

## MORE BEBOP

- The Earl Hines and Billy Eckstine bands served as important training grounds for a new generation of bebop musicians who remained active for at least the next ten years. Such musicians include Fats Navarro, Tadd Dameron, Sonny Stitt, Gene Ammons, Dexter Gordon, Lucky Thompson, Wardell Gray, and Miles Davis.

### Fats Navarro—Trumpet

- Fats Navarro (1923–1950) was born in Key West, Florida. As a self-taught musician, he was already working professionally as a teenager. He represented the first true generation of bebop musicians not originally schooled in Swing.
- In 1945 he replaced Dizzy Gillespie in the Billy Eckstine band. His late 1940s collaborations with pianist/composer Tadd Dameron led to bebop recordings of exceptional quality.

- His sound was rich and his eighth-note lines were smooth. He had good control in the upper register but chose to remain in the midrange most of the time. In general, his playing was melodic, logical, and didn't rely on pyrotechnics so commonly found in Gillespie's style.

### Tadd Dameron—Piano, Composer, Arranger, Bandleader

- Tad Dameron (1917–1965) was born in Cleveland, Ohio. He came from a musical family, receiving his first piano lessons from his mother. He developed into a respected jazz pianist, arranger, composer, and bandleader. He was one of the first jazz musicians to attempt well-crafted arrangements within the context of the bebop style.
- In the early 1940s he wrote and arranged for Harlan Leonard and His Rockets. Later he was hired to arrange for Dizzy Gillespie's bebop big band.
- From the late 1940s to the mid-1950s, Dameron led small groups that featured many of his original compositions including "Good Bait," "Our Delight," "Lady Bird," and "If You Could See Me Now." Some important musicians that played with Dameron's groups include Fats Navarro, Kenny Clarke, Wardell Gray, and Clifford Brown (after Fats Navarro died in 1950).
- Dameron was a proficient jazz pianist who allowed himself minimal solo space. His talents lay more in composing and arranging.

### J. J. Johnson—Trombone

- J. J. Johnson (1924–2001) was born in Indianapolis, Indiana. He played with Dizzy Gillespie, Max Roach, Woody Herman, Illinois Jacquet, Oscar Pettiford, and other important bebop artists in the 1940s and 1950s.
- In the mid-1950s, Johnson and trombonist Kai Winding toured and recorded with a bebop rhythm section.
- Johnson was the first bebop trombonist to move away from the singing, lyrical style of Swing made popular by players such as Tommy Dorsey and Glenn Miller. Johnson also avoided "Tricky" Sam Nanton's plunger style. Rather he was a leader of a modern school of jazz trombone that incorporated the bebop innovations of Parker and Gillespie. It was difficult for most trombone players to execute bebop lines due to the physical limitations of the instrument. Johnson took trombone technique to a new level by playing the instrument with the virtuosity and finesse of bebop saxophonists and trumpeters.

### Sonny Stitt—Alto and Tenor Saxophone

- Sonny Stitt (1924–1982) was born in Boston, Massachusetts but grew up in Saganaw, Michigan. He was a member of Billy Eckstine's band; then he joined Dizzy Gillespie's bebop big band in 1946.
- Stitt established himself first as a bebop alto saxophonist who was so similar to Charlie Parker that he was hailed as the "New Bird." However, Stitt proved himself to be equally proficient on the tenor saxophone.
- He made significant recordings in the late 1940s and throughout the 1950s as both a leader and a sideman.

## Important bebop musicians

| TRUMPET | ALTO SAX | TENOR SAX | TROMBONE |
|---|---|---|---|
| Dizzy Gillespie | Charlie Parker | Dexter Gordon | J. J. Johnson |
| Fats Navarro | Sonny Stitt | Lucky Thompson | Kai Winding |
| Miles Davis | Sonny Criss | Don Byas | Frank Rosolino |
| Red Rodney | | Wardell Gray | |
| Howie McGee | | Allan Eager | |
| Benny Harris | | Stan Getz | |
| Clark Terry | | Sonny Rollins | |
| | | Gene Ammons | |

| PIANO | DRUMS | BASS | GUITAR |
|---|---|---|---|
| Bud Powell | Kenny Clarke | Curly Russell | Charlie Christian |
| Thelonious Monk | Max Roach | Oscar Pettiford | Jimmy Raney |
| Al Haig | Roy Haynes | Charles Mingus | Tal Farlow |
| Tadd Dameron | Denzil Best | Ray Brown | |
| Dodo Marmarosa | Art Blakey | Tommy Potter | |
| John Lewis | | Gene Ramey | |
| Oscar Peterson | | Leonard Gaskin | |
| George Shearing | | Slam Stewart | |
| Billy Taylor | | Milt Hinton | |

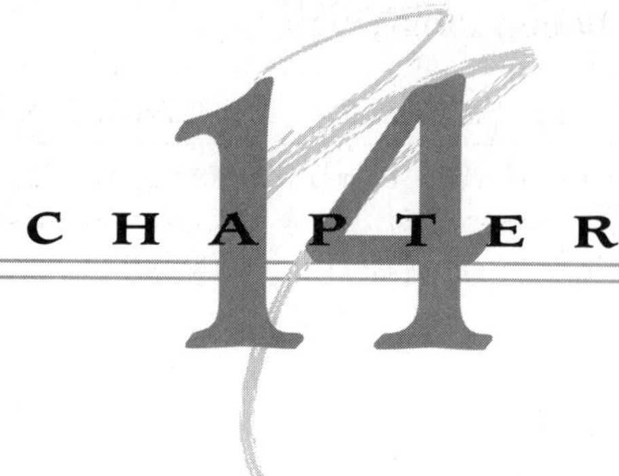

CHAPTER 14

# Cool Style

- Cool jazz is one of the least clearly defined jazz styles to emerge. It encompasses a group of diverse styles rather than just one simple approach. It has been applied to musicians influenced by Bix Beiderbecke, Count Basie, and Lester Young. It is primarily associated with jazz musicians who are perceived to be subdued and/or understated players.
- The bebop style, with its emphasis on improvisation and unpredictability, became trapped within the formulas its practitioners attempted to avoid; many jazz musicians were looking for another component not readily found in bebop.
- In the cool style there is generally more emphasis on the arrangement and counterpoint (multiple melodic lines moving against each other). The term cool can also be used to describe an attitude. *Cool* may have been derived from the lack of high, loud, and aggressive playing.
- The improvisational style comes straight from bebop, but it is more smooth and refined.
- The cool movement began initially in New York, but seemed to find great popularity among many Los Angeles-based jazz musicians; hence *West Coast jazz* is often used as a reference term.
- However, one cannot assume that all jazz played in Los Angeles was cool-style jazz. Many important bebop musicians come from what is known as the Central Avenue scene in Los Angeles, which in the 1940s was the equivalent of Fifty-second Street in New York City.
- The main proponents of this new approach to evolve from bebop were a group of well-known, young New York jazz musicians. Much like the early beboppers at Minton's Playhouse, they began meeting informally at the

apartment of arranger Gil Evans in the late 1940s. They included Miles Davis, John Lewis and Gerry Mulligan—all practitioners of the bebop style and influenced by the sound, lyricism, and rhythmic feel of Lester Young.

- Other important individuals were associated with pianist and teacher Lennie Tristano, including Lee Konitz, Billy Bauer, and Warne Marsh.
- Pianist and composer Dave Brubeck began experimenting with more highly arranged music for his octet in the mid-to late 1940s in northern California. This paralleled the work of Gil Evans, Mulligan, and Davis's Royal Roost Nonet (*Birth of the Cool* band) in New York City.
- There was also a strong division in attitude toward cool and bebop.
- Cool has sometimes been perceived as a white reaction to bebop; however, it also was fostered by African-American musicians (John Lewis and Miles Davis).

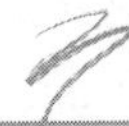

## CHARACTERISTICS OF THE COOL STYLE

- Often little or no vibrato is used
- Sometimes works are criticized for lacking warmth and fire
- Each instrument represents a different tone color
- Use of advanced harmonies
- Works are highly arranged
- The drummer's role is somewhat reduced
- Interest in contrapuntal textures
- Neoclassicism finds its way into music; foreshadows third stream music
- Improvisation, while still important, sometimes plays a lesser role
- Players tend to play in the middle register (avoiding the extreme)
- Jazz form is expanded with an obvious classical influence: rondos, fugues, passacaglias
- Combinations of unusual instruments are used
- Greater use of the flugelhorn and flute in jazz
- Smoother, more melodic improvisations than in bebop
- More laid back, relaxed feeling than in bebop
- Meter is not confined to 4/4 time; 3/4, 5/4, 7/4, and mixed meters are also used
- There were four big bands that provided many of the "seeds" of the cool school. They were led by **Woody Herman, Stan Kenton, Boyd Raeburn,** and, perhaps most important, **Claude Thornhill.** These bands emphasized the following characteristics:
  - Music based on European models; compositional devices taken from European orchestral practice; symphonic in nature
  - Complex, massive arrangements
  - Extended instrumentation: the use of French horn, flute, tuba, clarinet, and oboe
  - Excellent bebop soloists, which helped attract other young, white jazz musicians

## Woody Herman Band

- Woody Herman (1913–1987) was born in Milwaukee, Wisconsin.
- In 1936, he formed his first band, which was influenced by the blues.
- Over the years he had many personnel changes in his bands. Each personnel change resulted in a new band that developed its own identity and unique talents. Each of these bands was referred to as "First Herd," "Second Herd," and so on.
- The First Herd (1945) was possibly the most vital white big band of its time.
- The Second Herd was well known for its four talented saxophonists (listed below). Their successful and popular recording of "Four Brothers" displays the talents of the saxophonists both as individuals and as a cohesive unit.
- At times they were known for their "cool" sound. These saxophonists (especially Stan Getz) went on to become important cool-style players.
- At other times, the Herman band incorporated bebop influences into its arrangements and solos, unlike most other bands of the day.
- His bands became commercially successful from the late 1940s on.
- Herman hired top arrangers, and the band executed the arrangements effortlessly.
- The band always relied heavily on improvised solos and featured some of the best jazz improvisers including the following:
  - ♪ Stan Getz, tenor sax
  - ♪ Al Cohn, tenor sax
  - ♪ Zoot Sims, tenor sax
  - ♪ Serge Chaloff, baritone sax
  - ♪ Sonny Berman, trumpet
- Woody Herman was also an exceptional clarinetist and vocalist. He was often featured as such in his band.
- Influenced most likely by Benny Goodman's similar efforts, Herman commissioned Russian composer Igor Stravinsky to compose the *Ebony Concerto for Clarinet and Orchestra*.

## Stan Kenton Orchestra

- Stan Kenton (1911–1979) was born in Wichita, Kansas, and grew up in Los Angeles, California. After graduating from high school, he played in several small groups in Los Angeles, San Diego, and Las Vegas. He studied piano and composition with Frank Hurst, a theater organist, and with Earl Hines.
- In 1941, Kenton decided to start his own band. He went to the San Jacinto Mountains and wrote arrangements and compositions (including a Maurice Ravel-influenced composition, based on the ballet music from *Daphne and Chloe*, that would become his band's theme song "Artistry in Rhythm") that became the core of the book for his own band.
- Kenton's orchestras produced a string of alumni whose influence on jazz was undeniable: June Christy, Gerry Mulligan, Lee Konitz, Maynard

Ferguson, Kai Winding, Frank Rosolino, Art Pepper, and Laurindo Almeida.

- An excellent jazz pianist, he rarely featured himself. He chose to focus on the great soloists and arrangers in his bands.
- By 1947, his group, now called the **Progressive Jazz Orchestra,** expanded the brass section to five trumpets and five trombones. In the saxophone section he used one alto, two tenors, and two baritones, which was unusual for the time.
- Kenton was also interested in Afro-Cuban music, and in 1947 he hired an extra percussionist—first on bongos, then on congas.
- In 1950, the **Innovations in Modern Music Orchestra** numbered forty musicians, adding French horns and strings. He hired two important composer/arrangers, Bob Graettinger and Shorty Rogers, to contribute new works and feature high-note trumpeter Maynard Ferguson.
- By 1952, he had scaled down to a smaller group of nineteen musicians called the **New Concepts of Artistry in Rhythm Orchestra.** He hired many young arranger/composers to write for the group such as William Russo, Lennie Niehaus, Bill Holman, Gerry Mulligan, Johnny Richards, Gene Roland, Dee Barton, Willie Maiden, Pete Rugolo, Ken Hanna, and Hank Levy.
- In 1965, Kenton decided to showcase his more adventuresome concert music in the **Los Angeles Neophonic Orchestra,** a slightly expanded big band, with French horns and woodwind doubles.
- The band was active through the 1970s, producing many excellent recordings such as *Live at Redlands*. Kenton always embraced the new sounds of contemporary music and was never afraid to fuse new sounds into his groups.
- Kenton was also important in jazz education. He was an important founding member of the National Association of Jazz Educators (now known as the International Association of Jazz Education). As a clinician and performer, he appeared at high schools and colleges all over America.

## Boyd Raeburn Orchestra

- Boyd Raeburn (1913–1966) was born in South Dakota. He became a bandleader in 1933, leading commercial dance bands.
- His group from 1944 to 1948 was, however, different from his previous groups.
- This group featured advanced arrangements, borrowing from bebop and European orchestral music, especially the French impressionists.
- He extended the instrumentation of the group to include French horns.
- He hired many good arrangers and featured major bebop players of the era including: Dizzy Gillespie, Benny Harris, Sonny Berman, and Buddy DeFranco.
- The arrangements were too sophisticated for dancers, consequently the group experienced little success.

### Claude Thornhill Orchestra

- Claude Thornhill (1909–1965) was born in Terre Haute, Indiana. He was a student at the Cincinnati Conservatory and the Curtis Institute of Music. In the 1930s, he worked in both New York and Los Angeles with well-known jazz musicians such as Benny Goodman, Paul Whiteman, and Glenn Miller.
- In 1940, Thornhill formed his own band. It eventually contained an unusual instrumentation including seven clarinets, two French horns, and a tuba. Gil Evans joined the group and wrote arrangements that were considered progressive.
- World War II and the draft caused the band to break up for a few years. Thornhill enlisted in the navy as a musician.
- In 1946, the original Thornhill band was reorganized. However, it was too difficult for a big band to survive at the time and they disbanded in 1948.
- The innovative arrangements and unusual instrumentation of the Claude Thornhill Band was the inspiration for the Miles Davis Nonet *Birth of the Cool* recordings.

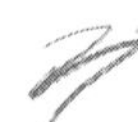

## BIRTH OF THE COOL

- After leaving Charlie Parker in 1949, Miles Davis rarely appeared as a sideman. From 1948 to 1950, he made a series of historic recordings with a nine-piece band (Nonet) for Capitol Records, which was to have a profound effect on jazz in the 1950s. The group initially met informally at the apartment of Gil Evans to discuss music and exchange ideas. They eventually formed a band based on the Claude Thornhill Orchestra model. In essence, arrangers Gerry Mulligan and Gil Evans created a scaled-down big band.
- The influences stemmed from the arranging style of Gerry Mulligan and Gil Evans, both Thornhill alumni. Also important were the light, airy tone of alto saxophonist Lee Konitz, the nonaggressive sound of trumpeter Miles Davis, and Gerry Mulligan's smooth baritone sax sound. A very unusual instrumentation was used, including tuba, French horn, and trombone, but absent were the tenor sax and guitar. Composer and pianist John Lewis, who would later co-lead the Modern Jazz Quartet, was also an important member of the group, contributing cool-style, understated piano solos to the repertoire.
- Miles Davis consolidated the influences of Claude Thornhill, Gil Evans, and Lennie Tristano in these sessions. The subdued feeling, limited range, moderate tempos, medium dynamic range they brought to their solos, and the textures achieved by the instrumentation created a delicate, cool sound.
- The music, at times, resembled classical chamber music. The tunes played were influenced by the bebop idiom, but the emphasis on arrangements set them apart from other late-1940 band arrangements. Short solos were interwoven between the written ensemble lines, much as Duke Ellington had done. Orchestral textures can be found throughout each selection. It was serious music for dedicated listeners

and was not necessarily intended for dancing. These individuals continued the practice of borrowing from various sources, this time more European in context.

## Lennie Tristano and Lee Konitz

- Lennie Tristano and Lee Konitz were important pioneers of the cool style, although their playing was not detached or subdued; it was intense. The impact of the cool style was initially felt on Miles's recording *Birth of the Cool*. After *Birth of the Cool*, a category called West Coast cool began to evolve in the early 1950s. The term *West Coast cool* is a bit misleading because many cool-style players were initially from New York. Cool style was also played in New York and bebop in Los Angeles, but many prominent West Coast players were involved with the cool style. This style dominated much West Coast jazz of the 1950s.
- Lennie Tristano grew up in Chicago before relocating in New York. He was a pianist, composer, leader, and teacher who created an alternative style to bebop during the late 1940s. He was influenced by Art Tatum and Lester Young; his lines were less jumpy and jagged than those of Charlie Parker and Dizzy Gillespie. His improvisations were smoother with more straight-line contours. His music was harmonically complex, using many chord changes per measure. His most talented students were alto saxophonist Lee Konitz, tenor saxophonist Warne Marsh, and guitarist Billy Bauer. He was a demanding teacher well versed in both classical and jazz styles. He was primarily interested in the creation of pure melodic line. He had his students play smooth lines, with little or no accents and steady tempo. This sometimes gave a "nonsuggestion" of bar lines.
- Bass and drums played a very conservative role in Tristano's music, as with most cool-style recordings.
- Lee Konitz was one of the few alto saxophonists not to be influenced by Charlie Parker; his sound was more reminiscent of Lester Young. He was a product of Tristano's piano style—played on top of the beat, with less syncopation. Konitz influenced many West Coast alto saxophonists including Bud Shank, Art Pepper, Lennie Niehaus, and Paul Desmond.
- The Tristano group was among the first to attempt improvisation with no preset chord progressions. Sounding similar to the *Free Jazz* recordings of ten years later, this work culminated in the 1949 recording of "Intuition."
- Lennie Tristano influenced the work of pianist Bill Evans.

## Modern Jazz Quartet

- The Modern Jazz Quartet began as the rhythm section of the late-1940s Dizzy Gillespie Big Band. The rhythm section (piano, bass, drums, and vibraphone) played intermissions to let the horn players rest. They played so well together that they eventually formed a working quartet in the early 1950s.
- The leader of the group eventually became pianist and composer John Lewis. He was a college-educated pianist thoroughly schooled in European music, especially Renaissance and Baroque music. Other members of the original group included drummer Kenny Clarke, bassist Ray Brown, and vibraphonist Milt Jackson.

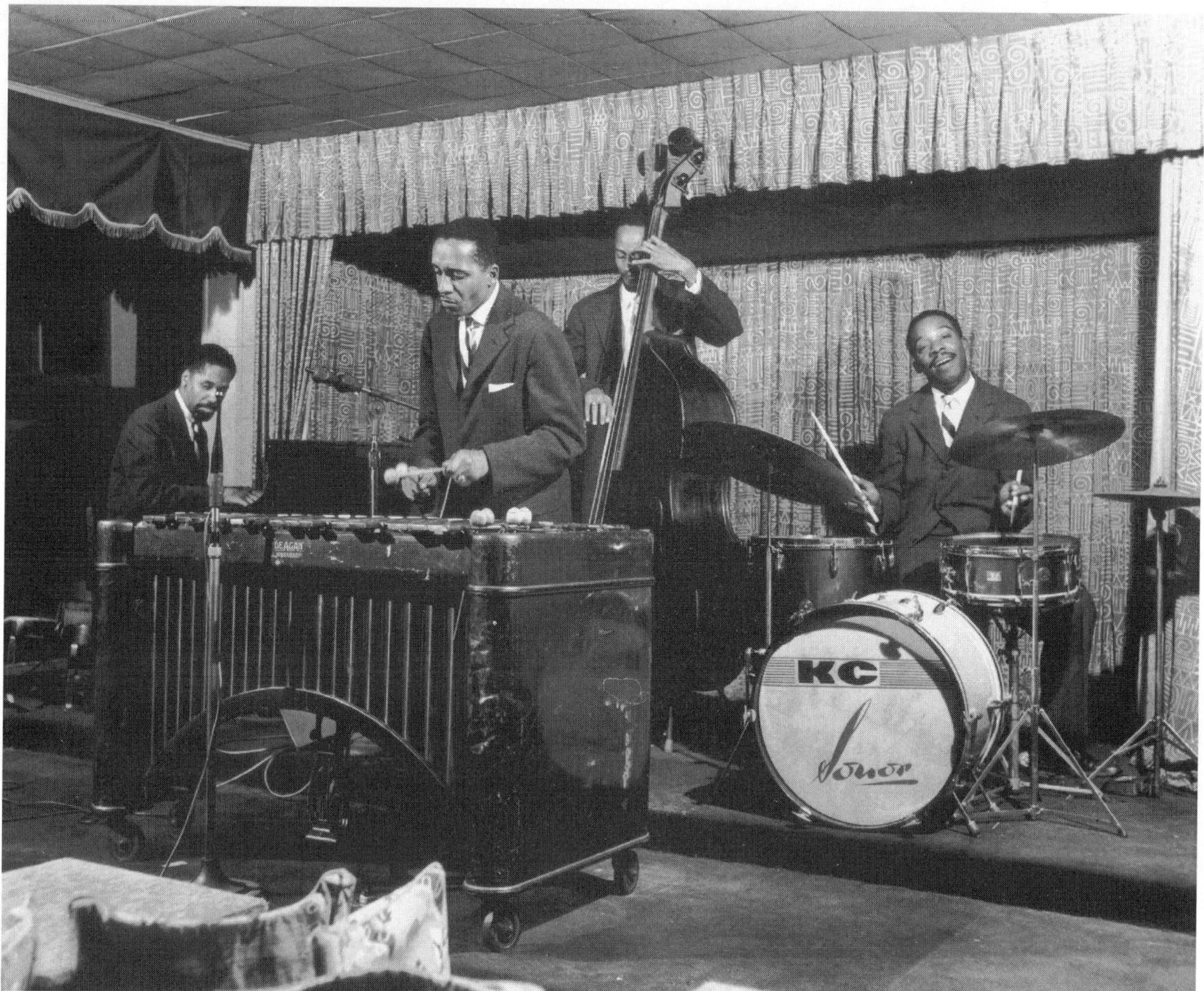


*Modern Jazz Quartet. Photograph by Bob Parent. Courtesy of Dale Parent.*

- Soon after Ray Brown was replaced by bassist Percy Heath. Then after Kenny Clarke moved to Europe, the band discovered drummer Connie Kay while playing a two-week engagement in California. They had originally planned to hold formal auditions for the drum chair, but after spending two weeks with Kay, it was obvious they didn't need to look any further. Connie Kay remained with the Modern Jazz Quartet until his death in the early 1990s.
- Lewis attempted to feature the improvisations of the group in more interesting settings using tempo, mood, and formal structure changes based upon symphonic and chamber forms. He was making explorations that were long overdue because jazz had not really explored form or structure as deeply as European music.
- The dichotomy of the group was the result of Jackson's strong bebop roots and Lewis' more European-influenced formal approach to jazz: in other words, intellect versus emotion. Lewis's models were the classical music scenes in eighteenth-century Paris and seventeenth- century Venice, while Jackson's were from Minton's Playhouse and New York City's Fifty-second Street bebop jazz scene.

- Jackson was always a bit frustrated by Lewis's writing and arranging. Jackson found classical music to be confining and not conducive to improvised jazz soloing. Therefore, Jackson would not permit Lewis to go too far, thus keeping him from allowing European formalism to rule their music. The Modern Jazz Quartet has been criticized because at times they were overly concerned with structure at the expense of jazz feeling.
- They used titles such as "Vendome," "Versaille," "La Ronde," and "Fontessa." Possibly their best work was the composition "Django."
- The group played more softly than most other bands from the same time period. Milt Jackson's vibraphone and his strong bebop roots helped to define the sound of the band. Lewis's improvisation is in stark contrast to Jackson's. Lewis does not play many notes and leaves much space between ideas.
- The Modern Jazz Quartet remained together until 1974 when Milt Jackson quit. They reformed in the late 1980s and performed together until the deaths of Jackson, Lewis, and Kay.

## Dave Brubeck Quartet

- Dave Brubeck (born 1920) was born near San Francisco, California. He grew up on a farm and first learned piano from his mother, who was a piano teacher. He first attended the College of the Pacific where his father intended for him to become a veterinarian so he could help out with the

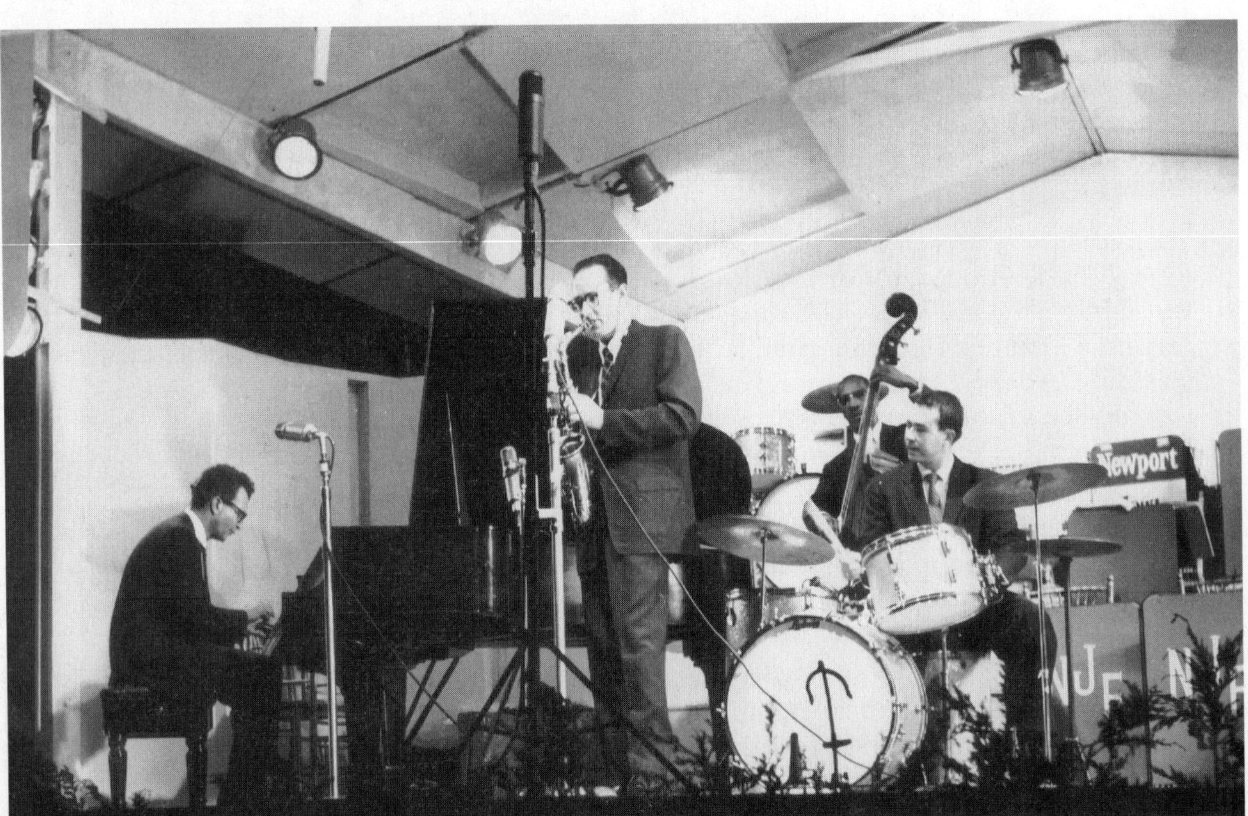


*Dave Brubeck Quartet. Photograph by Bob Parent. Courtesy of Dale Parent.*

farm. However, Brubeck quickly decided to major in music instead. His college education, however, was interrupted by World War II.

- After World War II, he attended Mills College where he studied composition with French composer Darius Milhaud. (In 1923, Darius Milhaud was one of the first European composers to write a jazz-influenced classical composition. It is called *La Creation du Monde*.) In 1946, Brubeck formed his Octet, creating arrangements of jazz standards and many of his own original works. The group performed in the San Francisco Bay area through 1948. Many of these original works can be considered third stream music (classical elements and jazz elements combined to create a new style), and they were very avant-garde for their time. The repertoire is similar in scope and style to the Miles Davis Nonet *Birth of the Cool* recordings.
- In 1949, Brubeck formed a trio, and in 1951, he added alto saxophonist Paul Desmond, forming the commercially successful and eventually world-renowned Dave Brubeck Quartet.
- Paul Desmond was a significant cool-style alto saxophonist. His mellow tone and frequent understated improvisations were the epitome of the cool style.
- With the help of Darius Milhaud, Dave Brubeck's groups performed college concerts on the West Coast of California. They were the first jazz group to perform formal jazz concerts for college audiences. The Quartet recorded a series of albums entitled *Jazz Goes to College* in the 1950s.
- The album *Time Out* (1958) was one of their most successful recordings. It showcases jazz compositions in meters other than the usual 4/4 time signature. For example, "Take Five," written by Paul Desmond, is in a 5/4 time signature. Partly because of its huge commercial success, it has been said that "Take Five" taught America how to swing (or dance) in five. "Three to Get Ready" alternates a 3/4 time signature with a 4/4 time signature. "Blue Rondo a la Turk" uses a 9/8 time signature but arranges the eighth notes into three measures of 2 + 2 + 2 + 3 subgroups followed by one measure of 3 + 3 + 3.
- The Dave Brubeck Quartet compositions are carefully arranged. His piano playing does not show the influence of Bud Powell, but rather he is more reliant on block chord voicings. It sometimes has a dense quality and can be heavy-handed.
- Dave Brubeck's significance is mostly as a composer and bandleader. Many of his jazz compositions have become part of the standard jazz repertoire. He has also written works for orchestra, ballet, and various chamber ensembles.

## Chet Baker/Gerry Mulligan Quartet

- The quintessential West Coast cool jazz quartet featured baritone saxophonist/composer/arranger Gerry Mulligan and trumpeter/singer Chet Baker. Mulligan, originally from New York City, had worked with the Claude Thornhill Orchestra where he met arranger Gil Evans. Later in the 1940s, he worked with the Miles Davis Nonet on the *Birth of the Cool* sessions. In 1952, he was in Los Angeles leading a band at a club

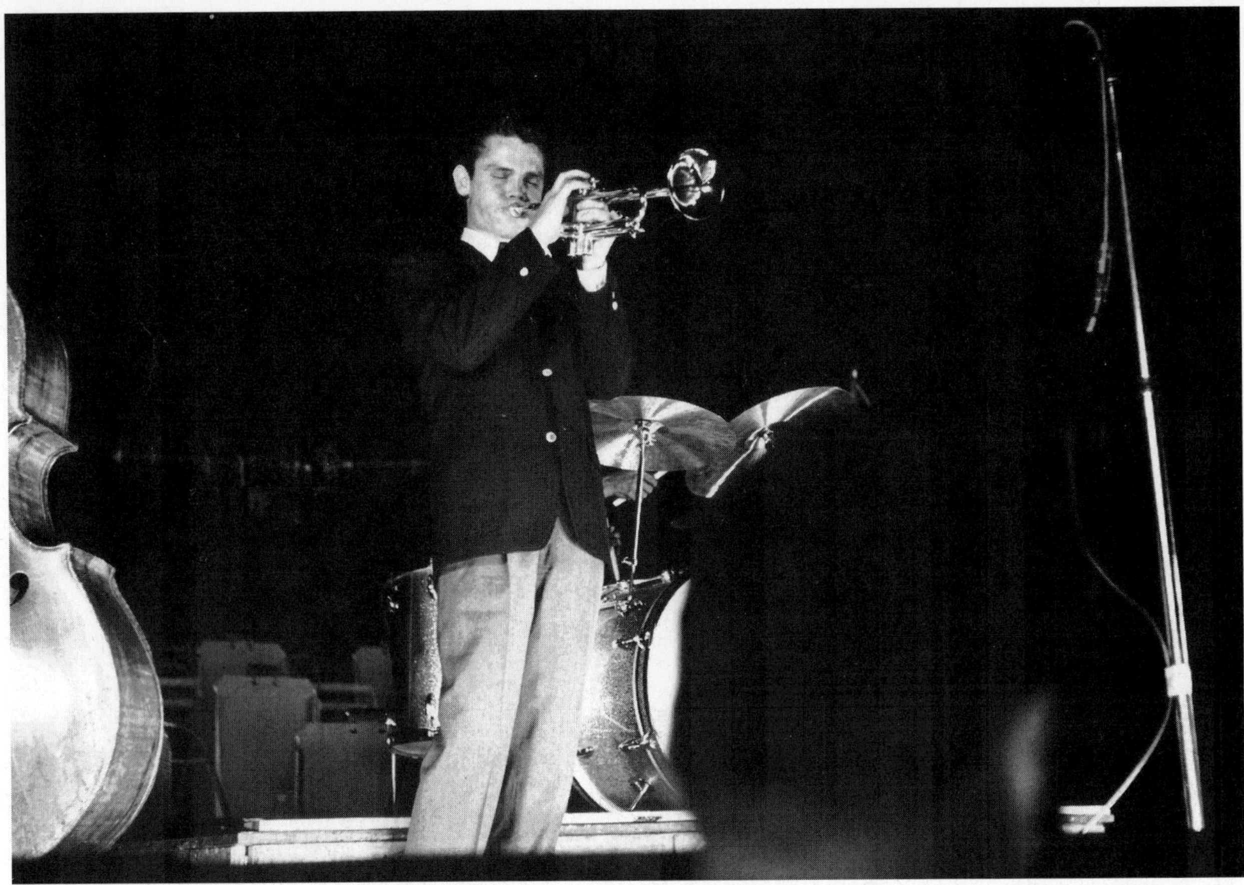

*Chet Baker. Photograph by Bob Parent. Courtesy of Dale Parent.*

called The Haig. Chet Baker, originally from Oklahoma, had secured his reputation in the early 1950s playing with Charlie Parker in California.

- Mulligan and Baker formed a quartet that featured trumpet, baritone sax, drums, and bass—an unusual instrumentation for the time, since piano was absent from the rhythm section. It has become known as the "pianoless quartet." Without the piano, Mulligan and Baker were able to weave contrapuntal lines to create a clear texture without obscuring each other. They were able to create new combinations of instrumental colors. Mulligan's arrangements proved to be just as important as the improvised solos. Mulligan had already established himself as composer and arranger with the Miles Davis Nonet; now he had only three voices and drums with which to work.
- Baker's soft tone, sense of lyricism, and logically improvised solos provided an excellent foil to Mulligan's baritone saxophone sound. The band found immense popularity with this chamber-like approach to jazz. As jazz transformed from functional dance music to serious chamber-like music in the 1940s, the Mulligan/Baker Quartet was an excellent example of how jazz could function as a marketable product. Though the group was together for less than two years, it helped to codify the sound known as West Coast jazz. Baker and Mulligan went their separate ways, but both enjoyed much success throughout their careers.

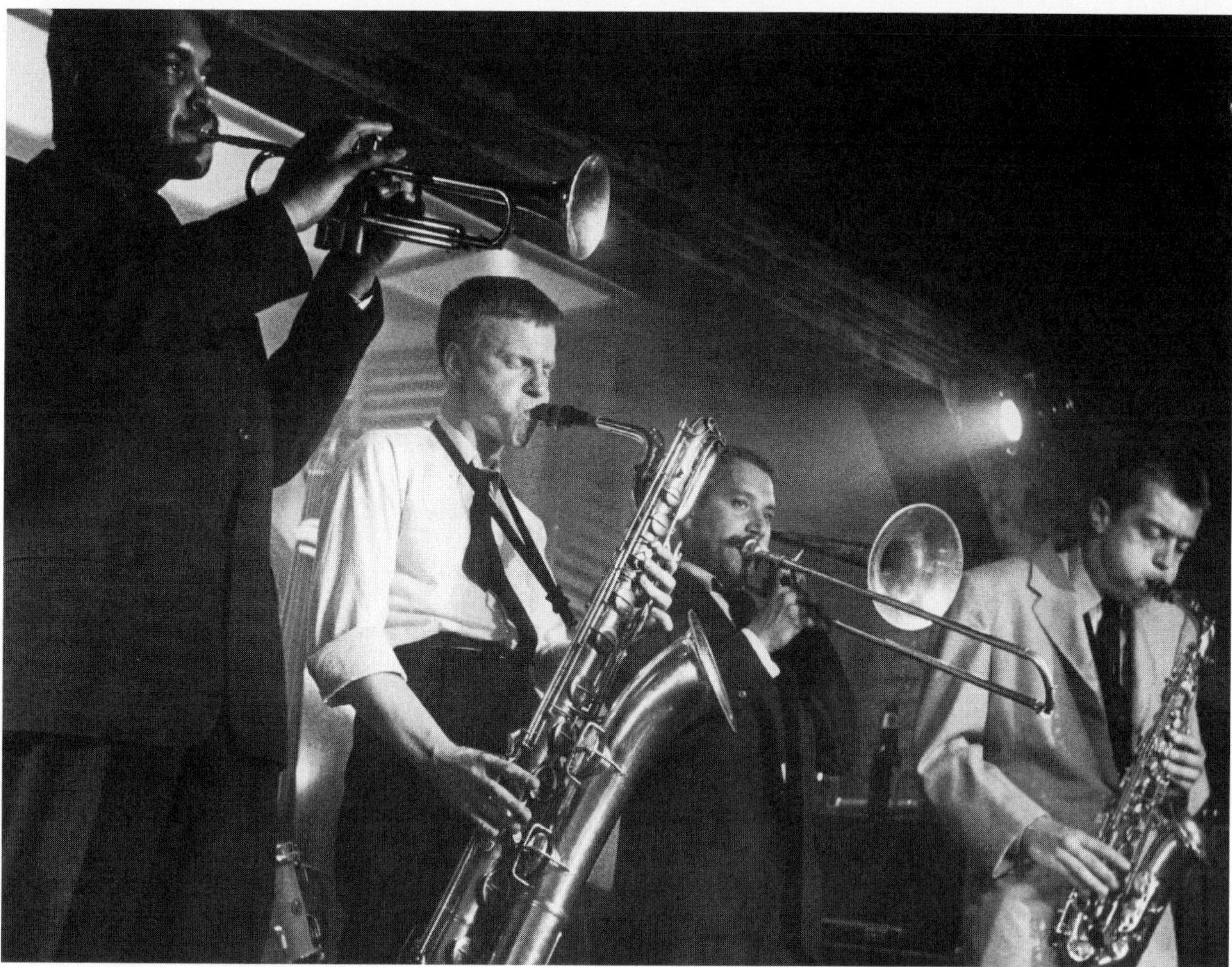

*Gerry Mulligan, Art Farmer, Bud Shank. © Bettmann/CORBIS.*

## Lighthouse All Stars

- The Lighthouse All Stars was a group of talented West Coast jazz players that performed in a seaside club on Hermosa Beach called the Lighthouse during the 1950s. Bassist Howard Rumsey was the musical director for the Lighthouse. He collaborated with a long list of varied personnel from week to week and month to month as he put together small jazz groups to perform there throughout the 1950s.
- At any given time, his rhythm section might contain drummer Shelly Manne; pianists Hampton Hawes, Sonny Clark, or Stan Levey; and guitarist Barney Kessel. Horn players might include Chet Baker, Conte Condoli, Jimmy Giuffre, Bud Shank, Pepper Adams, Frank Rosolino, or Shorty Rogers.
- Jazz musicians first became interested in instruments such as the flute and oboe when Bud Shank, Buddy Collette, and Bob Cooper began to use them. Many of these players had grown up in California and settled there playing studio sessions by day and improvising jazz, often at the Lighthouse, by night. Many of these "All Stars" went on to have significant careers as either leaders or sidemen in many other jazz contexts.

**Important west coast cool jazz musicians**

| TRUMPET | TENOR SAX | ALTO SAX | TROMBONE |
|---|---|---|---|
| Miles Davis | Stan Getz | Lee Konitz | Frank Rosolino |
| Chet Baker | Jimmy Giuffre | Paul Desmond | Bob Brookmeyer |
| Jack Sheldon | Warne Marsh | Art Pepper | Bob Envoldsen |
| Shorty Rogers | Zoot Sims | Bud Shank | Carl Fontana |
| Conte Condoli | Bill Perkins | Lennie Niehaus | |
| | Bill Holman | Buddy Collette | |
| | Joe Maini | Herb Geller | |

| PIANO | DRUMS | BASS | GUITAR |
|---|---|---|---|
| Lennie Tristano | Shelly Manne | Howard Rumsey | Billy Bauer |
| Dave Brubeck | Chico Hamilton | Red Mitchell | Barney Kessel |
| John Lewis | Larry Bunker | Carson Smith | Jim Hall |
| Hampton Hawes | | Joe Mondragon | Johnny Smith |
| Russ Freeman | | | |
| Vince Guaraldi | | | |
| George Shearing | | | |
| Lou Levy | | | |
| Clare Fischer | | | |
| Pete Jolly | | | |

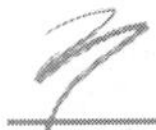

## LATIN JAZZ

- Much of today's Latin jazz is referred to as salsa (which literally means "hot sauce") and is a hybrid of much Cuban/Puerto Rican/African music and jazz. Salsa is not one specific style, but encompasses a wide variety of approaches and styles of Afro-Latin music. The Afro-Latin qualities manifest themselves in characteristic rhythms (such as the clave), while the jazz qualities reside more in the area of harmony and melody.
- The powerful and rhythmic influence of Afro-Cuban music in jazz reached a peak in 1947 when bandleader Dizzy Gillespie hired the famous Cuban drummer Chano Pozo to perform with his big band for a Town Hall concert in New York City. Pozo was famous in Cuba as a dancer, drummer, and composer. As a boy, Chano was fascinated by West African music that survived practically intact in the slums of Havana; these were the rhythms that Pozo brought to the Gillespie band.
- Pioneering jazz drummers such as Art Blakey and Max Roach were so taken with Chano's playing that they went to Africa and Haiti to study African rhythm. Pozo was another example of the influence of African music on American jazz by way of South America, the West Indies, Puerto Rico, and particularly Cuba.
- From the earliest days of jazz, many Creole (Spanish and French) songs in New Orleans used a rhumba beat or tango rhythm. The influence of Latin music was not limited to New Orleans. It was felt in New York and other large metropolitan cities. The same music in a diluted form had reached Tin Pan Alley by 1915. W. C. Handy's "St. Louis Blues" contains a tango rhythm. In the 1930s, the rhumba and conga became popular in

the United States, the samba during the 1940s, and the cha-cha and mambo in the 1950s.

- Bandleaders like Xavier Cougat (the Paul Whiteman of Latin music) helped to popularize Latin music by making it simpler and easier to dance to, thus creating a new blend. Cougat always recruited top-quality Cuban musicians to play in his band.
- The real Latin music, however, was found in the Spanish sections of New York, Miami, and Los Angeles where large Latin populations lived.
- Some American bandleaders experimented with Latin music in the 1930s. Cab Calloway and Duke Ellington, under the influence of Mario Bauza and Juan Tizol, who were top arrangers for these bands respectively, incorporated Latin-style selections into their bands' repertoire.
- The Afro-Cuban bands that played for these dances used rhythms based on the traditional off-center accents of the claves (wooden sticks that make a penetrating sound when struck together). There are specific rhythms played by these sticks and these rhythms are simply called clave rhythms. The clave rhythm (which can actually be played on a variety of percussion instruments) is the soul of Cuban music and occurs in bolero, guaracho, mambo, charanga, cha-cha, and other dance-related styles. On top of the clave rhythm, other rhythms played on the bongos, congas, cowbell, timbales, bass, maracas, and piano are superimposed.
- These rhythms are not random, but are carefully conceived and executed. Each instrument has an assigned role and function. Rarely do any of them overlap. Individually each rhythm is simple, but all together the rhythms swing. At times, there are *montuno* or solo sections where players are given the opportunity to improvise using one or two chords. The rhythm in these montuno sections can be complex, but the harmonies are relatively simple.
- The bass line can be confusing because it is rarely played on any beat. The notes fall somewhere in between beats three and four in 4/4 time. Salsa is the basis for much of today's Latin jazz and has helped to expose jazz musicians to the beautiful intensity of this style.
- Jazz players initially may have problems learning to play with a Latin rhythm section; the beats are confusing, and staying on one or two chords seems unnecessarily limiting. In turn, Latin players may find jazz harmonies too complicated. The practical result is a situation where soloists are jazz musicians and rhythm section players are Latin musicians, as was the case in the 1940s with Dizzy Gillespie and Stan Kenton. These bandleaders hired Latin percussionists. On the other hand, Latin bandleaders such as Machito, Tito Puente, and Eddie Palmieri hired jazz players to do the solo work. This is no longer the case.
- One of the best bands to blend both jazz and authentic Latin styles was led by Machito (Frank Grillo). He had one of the best bands in New York City, and much of the credit can be given to arranger/trumpeter Mario Bauza. Originally from Cuba, Bauza played with Chick Webb's and Cab Calloway's bands where he became good friends with Dizzy Gillespie. When Bauza left Calloway's band to organize Machito's band, he was well versed in both Cuban and jazz styles of music. Machito's band played progressive Latin music and built a large following. Charlie Parker, Flip Philips, Brew Moore and Howie McGee recorded with him.

- Afro-Cuban music has brought a large and enthusiastic audience along with the blending of jazz with the styles of other South American countries and islands in the West Indies. The music is gaining popularity with non-Latins due to the wonderful fusion of the two styles and its dance appeal.
- Each of the Caribbean Islands as well as Central and South American countries have a style of indigenous music derived from West African music brought over to the New World by slaves.
- During the early 1960s, guitarist **Charlie Byrd** and saxophonist **Stan Getz** discovered Brazilian **bossa nova.** This subtle combination of Brazilian rhythm (samba) with cool jazz was attractive to American jazz artists. The performances of Brazilian guitarists Laurindo Almeida, Joao Gilberto, and singer Astrud Gilberto, combined with the compositions of **Antonio Carlos Jobim,** proved to be very popular in the United States. Many of Jobim's compositions have become standards in the jazz repertoire.
- Latin music has directly influenced jazz-rock fusion and was the basis (even eighth notes on the high-hat) for the disco craze of the 1970s. Many American jazz fusion bands of the 1970s and 1980s such as Weather Report, the Yellowjackets, the Pat Metheny Group, and the Word of Mouth Orchestra borrow from this style.

## Important Latin jazz musicians

| BAND LEADER | COMPOSER | PERCUSSION | PIANO |
|---|---|---|---|
| Tito Puente | Tito Puente | Tito Puente | Eddie Palmieri |
| Eddie Palmieri | Antonio Carlos Jobim | Ray Barretto | Antonio Carlos Jobim |
| Machito | Hermeto Pascal | Mongo Santamaria | Charlie Palmieri |
| Xavier Cugat | Mario Bauza | Jery Gonzales | Michel Camilo |
| Sergio Mendes | | Pancho Sanchez | Hilton Ruiz |
| Jerry Gonzales | | | Gonzalo Rubalcaba |
| Pancho Sanchez | | | Chucho Valdez |

| GUITAR | VOCALIST | TRUMPET | SAXOPHONE |
|---|---|---|---|
| Laurindo Almeida | Celia Cruz | Jerry Gonzales | Paquito D'Rivera |
| | | Arturo Sandoval | David Sanchez |

# Hard Bop

- Cool-style jazz quickly gained momentum after the *Birth of the Cool* recordings and experienced its most success and popularity during the first half of the 1950s. While many jazz musicians were drawn to the cool style of playing, there was a separate group of mostly young black jazz musicians who instead continued to develop along the lines of bebop. However, many of these young players had their first experiences with music in the sanctified church where gospel music was the norm. They sought to simplify what was perceived as a growing complexity in jazz since its beginnings. They achieved a more expressive, less intellectual style labeled hard bop. It incorporates influences from gospel music and the blues.
- The late 1940s and the early 1950s saw an emergence of rhythm and blues (R&B) jump bands (e.g., Earl Bostic and Louis Jordan). Many musicians who later became significant hard bop players spent time working in rhythm and blues bands in large urban centers such as Detroit, Philadelphia, and New York City. In fact, one could perceive these rhythm and blues bands to be a kind of dividing partition between bebop and hard bop.
- These players had obviously not been satisfied with certain aspects of bebop. Rhythm and blues was perhaps, at first, perceived to offer new possibilities. However, in the end, the style lacked the challenge necessary to stimulate sophisticated jazz musicians. Therefore, a new style developed based on bebop but with obvious rhythm and blues influences.
- Hard bop bands placed more emphasis on small-group arranging and lengthy solos than bebop bands. Thanks to technological advancements in recording format, musicians were no longer limited to three minutes

for each recording. It was now possible for jazz soloists and arrangers to create longer recordings. As a result, many hard bop recordings had longer, more structured improvised solos. A typical hard bop improvisation might begin with little or no intensity, then take as long as three minutes or more to build up to a high level of intensity before allowing the next player to improvise. Soloists depended on sensitive support and reaction from the rhythm section in creating different levels of intensity. The interplay between the rhythm section and the soloist is an important aspect of hard bop.

- Before long a derivative style known as *funk* evolved, which featured earthy blues-oriented piano riffs accompanied by aggressive rhythmic playing. This style has almost completely shed itself of bebop devices and depends heavily on blues and gospel music for its material.

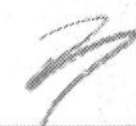

## HARD BOP CHARACTERISTICS

- Standard group instrumentation: tenor sax, trumpet, bass, drums, piano
- Elements of gospel music
- Elements of blues
- Early 1950s R&B influence
- Hard-driving rhythmic feel
- Simpler melodies
- Small-group arranging important for melody presentation
- Original compositions using challenging chord progressions and forms
- More frequently occurring songs in minor keys
- Philadelphia, Detroit, and New York are important centers of activity
- Generally slower tempos than bebop
- Dominated by black musicians
- Danceable and popular sounding
- Latin influence sometimes present

The hard bop groups discussed next are all important contributors to the development of jazz during the 1950s leading into the 1960s.

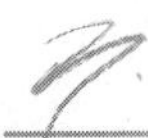

## ART BLAKEY AND THE JAZZ MESSENGERS

- Art Blakey (1919–1990) was born and raised in Pittsburgh, Pennsylvania. He first learned to play the piano but then became more interested in the drums. In the early 1940s he played in swing bands. In 1944, he was in the Billy Eckstine Band that contained Charlie Parker and Dizzy Gillespie. He subsequently played in bands led by Thelonious Monk, Charlie Parker, and Fats Navarro.
- In the late 1940s Blakey traveled to Africa to learn about Islamic culture and African music. Blakey incorporated African drumming concepts in his approach to playing jazz. He used African devices such as rapping on

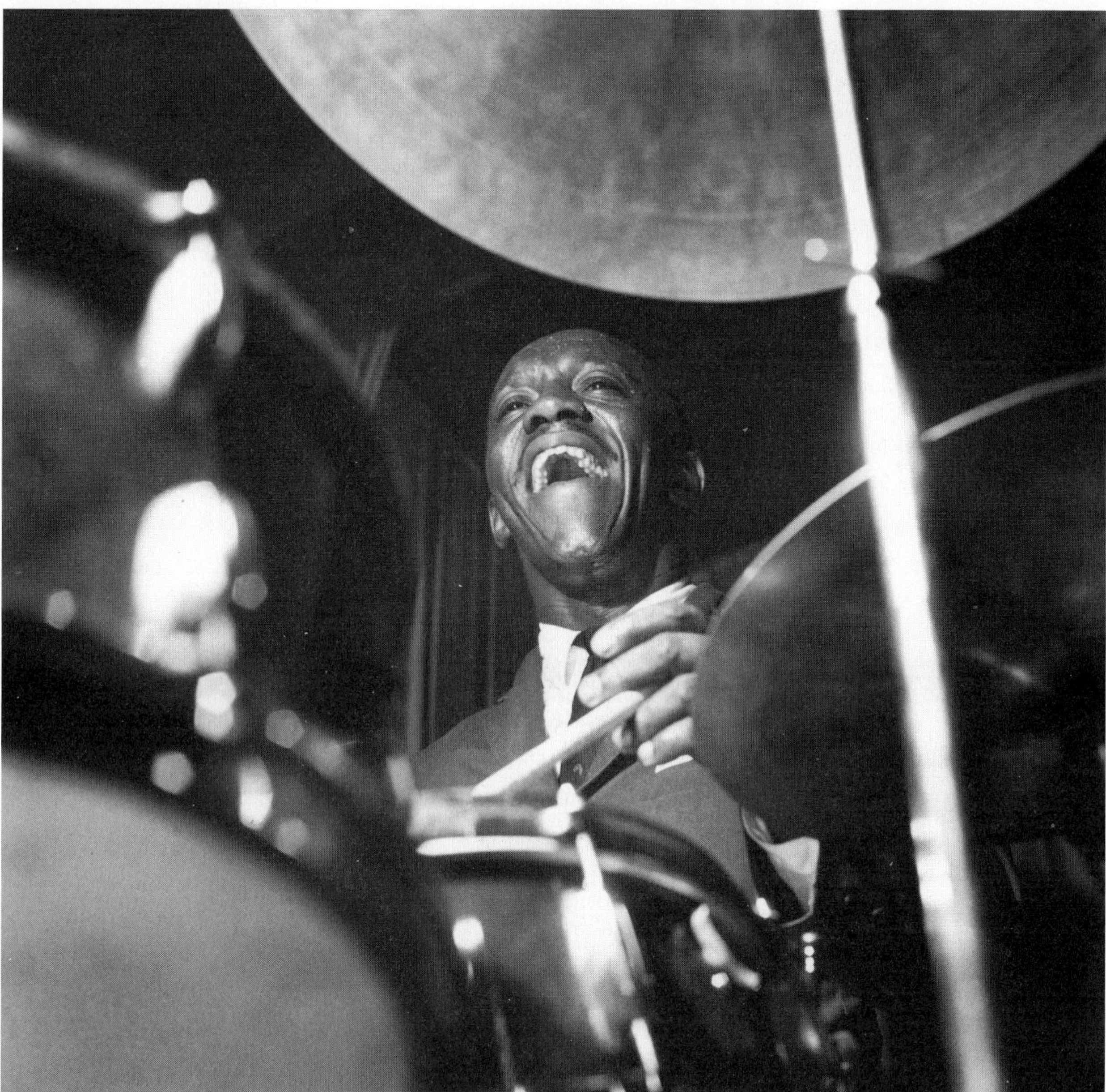

*Art Blakey. © Mosaic Images/CORBIS.*

the side of the drum, using his elbow on a tom-tom to alter the pitch, and perhaps even his forceful closing of the high-hat on beats two and four. In essence, his style became more aggressive and heavy. He eventually was nicknamed "Thunder."

- In 1955, Blakey and pianist Horace Silver formed the Jazz Messengers. Tenor saxophonist Hank Mobley and trumpeter Kenny Dorham were also members. They played an aggressive style of jazz influenced by the blues and gospel church traditions.
- In 1956, Horace Silver left the Messengers to lead his own band, and Art Blakey became the leader for the rest of his life. Because Blakey's Jazz Messengers had a large number of personnel changes over the years, he developed into someone with a keen eye for talent and the ability to shape it to his liking. He would encourage his players to be daring in

their approach to improvisation. He, in turn, was responsive and in this way, he was often able to mold players from his drum set, often pushing them toward their highest levels of intensity. As a result, many of his band members became great jazz musicians and went on to their own significant careers after leaving Blakey's band.

- The Jazz Messengers alumni reads like a who's who list of jazz post-1955. Only Miles Davis could be compared with Art Blakey as an important jazz mentor in this way.
- The following are some Jazz Messengers alumni:

| TRUMPET | ALTO SAX | TENOR SAX | PIANO |
|---|---|---|---|
| Kenny Dorham | Jackie McLean | Hank Mobley | Horace Silver |
| Lee Morgan | Lou Donaldson | Benny Golson | Bobby Timmons |
| Clifford Brown | | Wayne Shorter | Cedar Walton |
| Freddie Hubbard | | Johnny Griffin | Keith Jarrett |
| Donald Byrd | | Branford Marsalis | James Williams |
| Woody Shaw | | | Bennie Green |
| Wynton Marsalis | | | JoAnne Brackeen |

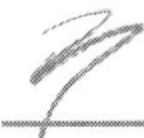

## HORACE SILVER QUINTET

- Horace Silver (born 1928) was born in Norwalk, Connecticut. He grew up influenced by his father's folk music of Cape Verde, but he was also exposed to jazz, blues, and gospel music. He was especially interested in Thelonious Monk and Bud Powell. He played with Stan Getz in 1950.
- In 1951, Silver was a freelance musician in New York where he played and recorded with Coleman Hawkins, Lester Young, and Oscar Pettiford.
- In 1952, he joined Lou Donaldson to make recordings for Blue Note. Subsequently Silver would release his own Blue Note recordings over the next twenty-eight years.
- From 1953 to 1955, Silver co-led the Jazz Messengers with Art Blakey.
- In 1956, Silver formed the Horace Silver Quintet and, as much as Art Blakey's Jazz Messengers, it afforded excellent training for young, talented jazz musicians such as Art Farmer, Blue Mitchell, Woody Shaw, Junior Cook, and Joe Henderson. Accompanied by trumpeter Blue Mitchell and tenor saxophonist Junior Cook, the Horace Silver Quintet enjoyed great success in the 1950s.
- As a funk-style pianist, Silver's playing is rhythmic and bluesy sounding. He plays short, catchy, melodic phrases, many of which are influenced by boogie-woogie pianists' right-hand blues riffs.
- Silver established himself as a major jazz composer by featuring many of his compositions in his quintet. He is one of the most prolific jazz composers to come out of the 1950s. His compositions are categorized as follows:
  - ♪ Blues/gospel-sounding works:

    "The Preacher"

    "Sister Sadie"

    "Filthy McNasty"

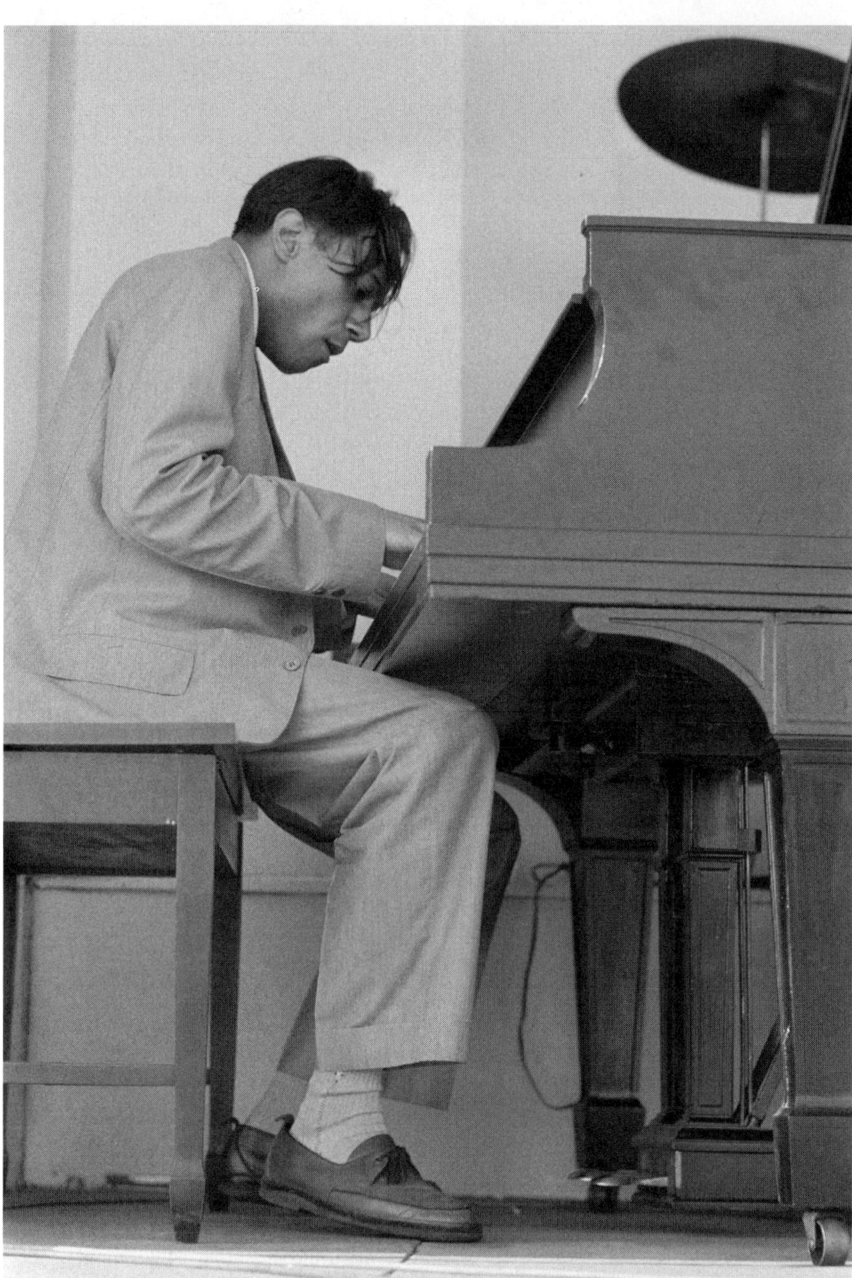

*Horace Silver. © Ted Williams/ CORBIS.*

- Latin-influenced compositions:
  "Song For My Father"
  "The Gringo"
  "Nica's Dream"
- Lyric ballads:
  "Peace"
  "Melancholy Mood"
  "Lonely Woman"
- Harmonically challenging up-tempo pieces:
  "Room 608"
  "Ecaroh"

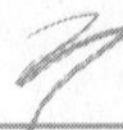

## CLIFFORD BROWN/MAX ROACH QUINTET

- Clifford Brown (1930–1956) was born in Wilmington, Delaware. He began playing trumpet when he was fifteen years old. Only three years later he was playing gigs in Philadelphia while majoring in math at Delaware State College. In Philadelphia, Brown played with accomplished jazz musicians including Kenny Dorham, Max Roach, J. J. Johnson, and Fats Navarro. A year later Brown transferred to Maryland State College, playing in the college sixteen-piece band and taking music courses. Unfortunately, his education was cut short by an auto accident in June 1950. He spent the next year recovering.

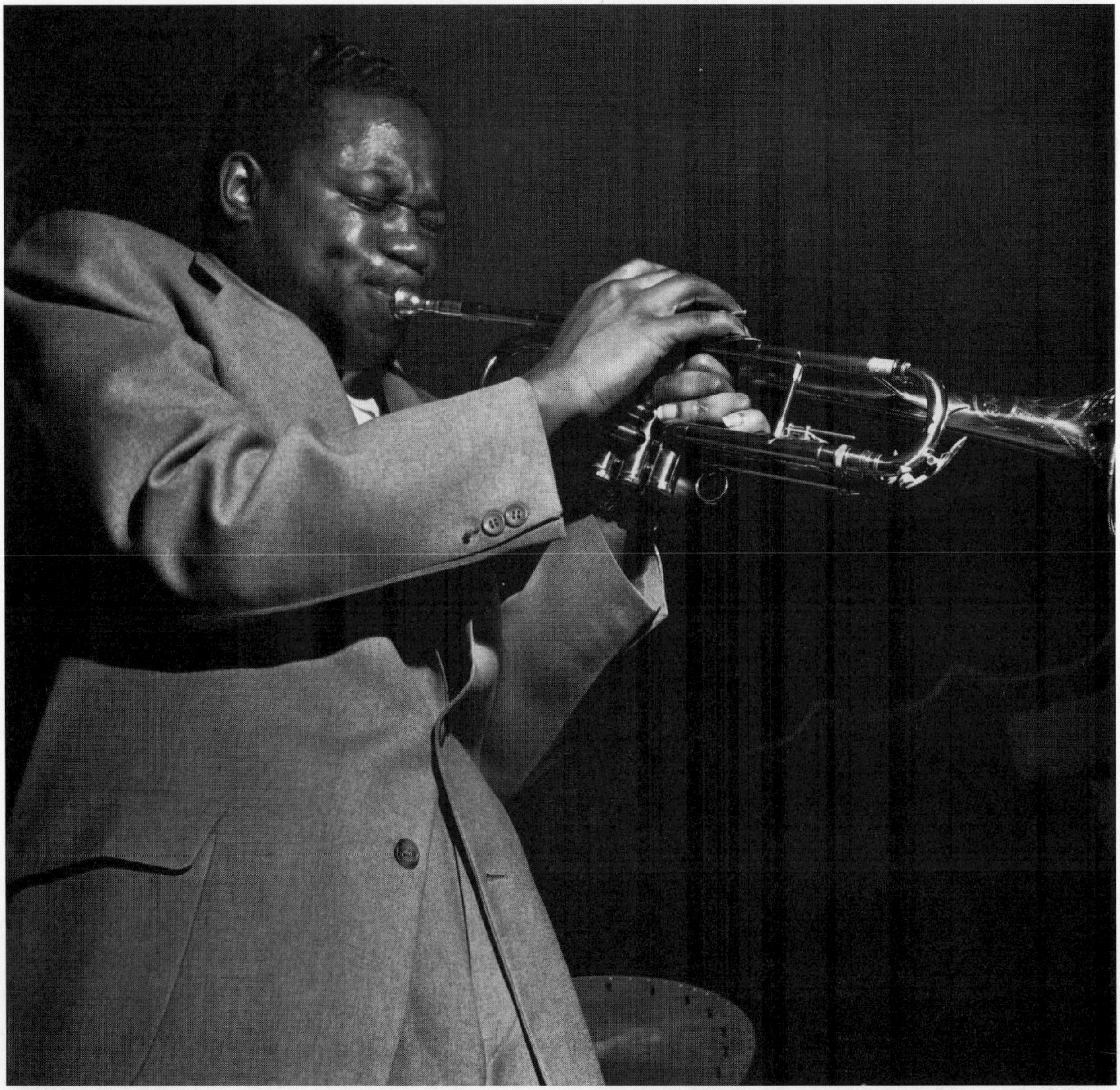

*Clifford Brown. © Mosaic Images/CORBIS.*

- In the early 1950s, Brown played with Chris Powell's Blue Flames, Tadd Dameron in Atlantic City, and Lionel Hampton's band while touring Europe in the fall of 1953. Brown also made small group-recordings with French rhythm section players while in Europe. These recordings show him to already be a unique artist with great technical mastery of his instrument. As a result, in 1954 he won a *Down Beat* Magazine Critics Poll.
- In 1954, after playing with Art Blakey, Brown formed a band with drummer Max Roach called the Clifford Brown/Max Roach Quintet. The Quintet also had Richie Powell (younger brother of Bud Powell), bassist George Morrow, and originally tenor saxophonist Harold Land when the group was based in California, but he was replaced by Sonny Rollins in 1955 when they went to New York. The group utilized interesting arrangements with clever introductions and endings. They made a number of important recordings between 1954 and 1956 that helped define the parameters of hard bop.
- Brown proved to be the epitome of a hard bop trumpet player. His facile technique, imaginatively improvised lines, fat sound, and joyful demeanor made him the archetype trumpeter of the 1950s. Strongly influenced by trumpeter Fats Navarro, Brownie (as he was known) established a highly personal approach to the trumpet that influenced the next generation of trumpet players to come out of the second half of the 1950s. He was also a fine composer and wrote a number of compositions that have become jazz standards.
- In June of 1956, Brown, Powell, and Powell's wife, Nancy, were driving from Philadelphia to Chicago when they had a tragic accident in which all three people were killed. Jazz lost a player with incredible potential who was only beginning his career. In addition, Brown's clean and responsible lifestyle made him an excellent role model for future generations. Sonny Rollins commented, "Clifford was a profound influence on my personal life. He showed me that it was possible to live a good, clean life and still be a good jazz musician."

## SONNY ROLLINS–TENOR SAXOPHONE

- Sonny Rollins (born 1930) grew up in the Sugar Hill section of Harlem. He began his piano studies at age eight and then took up the saxophone at age eleven. He had a band in high school that included Jackie McLean, Art Taylor, and Kenny Drew. He was influenced by Charlie Parker, Dizzy Gillespie, and Bud Powell. In the late 1940s and the early 1950s, he recorded with such significant jazz musicians as Charlie Parker, Bud Powell, Thelonious Monk, Fats Navarro, Tommy Potter, Roy Haynes, and Miles Davis. In 1955, he replaced Harold Land in the Clifford Brown/Max Roach Quintet.
- In the late 1950s, Rollins made a series of Blue Note recordings with varied personnel that established him as a top-quality hard bop tenor saxophonist. Sometimes he worked within the context of a pianoless trio giving him more leeway to develop his improvisations. One of his most important albums was *Saxophone Colossus*. It contained "Blue

Seven," a work about which music historian Gunther Schuller wrote favorably. Schuller commented on Rollins's approach to improvisation, recognizing his ability to take themes and develop them spontaneously. In 1957, he won a *Down Beat* Magazine Critics Poll as new star of the tenor saxophone.

- From 1959 to 1961, Rollins did not perform in public attempting to refine his craft in private. He spent many evenings practicing on the Williamsburg Bridge in Manhattan.
- In 1962, Rollins returned to recording and performing sometimes allowing himself to collaborate with musicians associated with the then new Free Jazz movement.
- In 1966, Rollins took a second sabbatical that lasted until 1972. Since then he has released numerous recordings on the Milestone label and performs regularly in concert halls, night clubs, and jazz festivals. Some of Rollins' jazz compositions have become jazz standards such as "Oleo," "Doxy," and "St. Thomas."

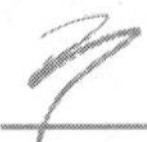

## CANNONBALL ADDERLEY QUINTET

- Julian "Cannonball" Adderley (1928–1975) was born in Tampa, Florida. He was a high school band director in Florida for several years before moving to New York in 1955. He was influenced by Benny Carter and Charlie Parker.
- Cannonball played with Miles Davis from 1957 to 1959 and was the featured alto saxophonist on Miles Davis's legendary *Kind of Blue* album.
- In 1959, Cannonball formed his own group with his brother, cornetist Nat Adderley. They became an immediate success after a live performance from San Francisco's Jazz Workshop was released. Pianist Bobby Timmons, a former Jazz Messenger member, contributed a funk piano style equal to that of Horace Silver. The Cannonball Adderley Quintet proved itself to be popular and another prototypical hard bop group in the soul or funky jazz vein. Bobby Timmons and later Joe Zawinul wrote many compositions and helped to create an identifiable sound for the group. Some compositions associated with the Adderley Quintet include the following:
    - ♪ "This Here"
    - ♪ "Hi Fly"
    - ♪ "Jive Samba"
    - ♪ "Mercy, Mercy, Mercy"
    - ♪ "Work Song"
- Cannonball's saxophone playing was an extension of Charlie Parker combined with perhaps a dose of rhythm and blues plus gospel music. As an important spokesperson for jazz, Cannonball often gave intelligent, well-organized explanations to the audience before playing a composition, helping him to become a popular, well-respected jazz musician. He also made numerous television appearances and spent time giving clinics at universities.

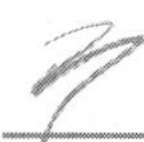

## JIMMY SMITH ORGAN TRIO

- Jimmy Smith (1928–2005) was born in Norristown (just outside Philadelphia), Pennsylvania. His father taught him to play stride piano, and they performed together for a dance team when he was 14 years old. Smith went into the navy at fifteen years of age and remained with the service until 1947 when he studied piano at the Ornstein School of Music on a GI bill, string bass at the Hamilton School of Music, and music theory at the Halsey Music School.
- In 1951, Smith played with the R&B band Don Gardner's Sonotones. He spent time listening to organ players Wild Bill Davis and Bill Doggett, who served as important early influences. In 1955, Smith bought his first organ, placing it in a warehouse where he practiced for three months.
- Some jazz and R&B performers were attracted to the sound of the Hammond B-3 organ. It produced a unique sound that could be altered and played at loud volumes, and the foot pedals provided a viable alternative to the upright bass. Played through a Leslie Tone Cabinet, the novel sound appealed to audiences. Smith was inspired by horn players Coleman Hawkins and Don Byas to play horn lines with his right hand using the first three drawbars and the percussion feature of the Hammond B-3.
- In 1955, Jimmy Smith formed a trio of guitar, drums, and organ. In 1956, he signed a contract with Blue Note Records playing blues to bebop styles. At times he added important hard bop tenor and trumpet players to round out his groups, including Lou Donaldson, Stanley Turrentine, Lee Morgan, George Coleman, Curtis Fuller, Jackie McLean, and Blue Mitchell.
- In 1962, he released recordings of Oliver Nelson arrangements with guitarist Wes Montgomery on the Verve label.
- The majority of his repertoire consisted of down home blues compositions. The sound of the organ trio was popular through the early 1970s and had all but disappeared until the recent work of Joey DeFrancesco, Larry Goldings, and Hank Marr brought it back into the public spotlight.

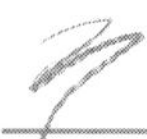

## WES MONTGOMERY—GUITAR

- Wes Montgomery (1923–1968) was born in Indianapolis, Indiana. His family did not have enough money for music training, so he was self-taught. His mother bought a tenor guitar (four-string guitar) for him in 1935. In 1943, he bought an electric guitar and amplifier after hearing a recording of Charlie Christian's "Solo Flight." He spent the next year learning Christian's solos and was then hired by the 440 Club in Indianapolis.
- In 1948, he played with Lionel Hampton's band. He occasionally recorded with his brother's West Coast group (bassist Monk Montgomery and vibraphonist Buddy Montgomery) called the Mastersounds.

- In 1959, Cannonball Adderley heard Montgomery and was so impressed, he recommended him to Riverside Records. Montgomery subsequently released *A Dynamic New Sound; The Wes Montgomery Trio* and *The Incredible Jazz Guitar of Wes Montgomery*, earning him instant fame and success. On these albums, Montgomery included original tunes such as "West Coast Blues," which established him as a legitimate jazz composer.
- In 1961, Montgomery joined John Coltrane's quartet for a performance at the Monterey Jazz Festival. Coltrane offered Montgomery a place in his band, but he declined as he did not feel he could consistently reach Coltrane's high levels of intensity. In 1962, Montgomery recorded *Full House*, an album featuring pianist Wynton Kelly, bassist Paul Chambers, drummer Jimmy Cobb, and tenor saxophonist Johnny Griffin. In 1960, '61, '62, and '63, Montgomery won the *Down Beat* Critics Poll Award for best jazz guitarist.
- Montgomery later released *Fusion*, an album featuring him in the context of string orchestra arrangements. Beginning in 1965, Verve Records released recordings that emphasized Montgomery in "easy listening" arrangements of popular songs. Although he experienced tremendous commercial success with these kinds of recordings, they precipitated negative commentary among the jazz community. However, he received a Grammy in 1966 for the best instrumental jazz performance on "Going Out of My Head." He also won the *Down Beat* Critics and Readers Poll in 1966 and 1967.
- Montgomery is particularly known for a style that featured the following:
  - ♪ A rich tone due to his use of the thumb rather than a pick to initiate the guitar string's sound
  - ♪ Melody lines voiced in octaves
  - ♪ Melody lines voiced in block chords
- Wes Montgomery died suddenly of a heart attack on June 15, 1968.

### Important hard bop musicians

| TRUMPET | ALTO SAX | TENOR SAX | TROMBONE |
|---|---|---|---|
| Miles Davis | Cannonball Adderley | Benny Golson | Curtis Fuller |
| Clifford Brown | Charles McPherson | Frank Foster | Frank Rehak |
| Lee Morgan | Gigi Gryce | Harold Land | Frank Rosolino |
| Art Farmer | Jackie McLean | Jimmy Forest | J. J. Johnson |
| Booker Little | Lou Donaldson | Hank Mobley | Slide Hampton |
| Donald Byrd | Phil Woods | James Moody | Jimmy Knepper |
| Freddie Hubbard | Sonny Stitt | Jimmy Heath | |
| Thad Jones | Eric Dolphy (flute, bass clarinet) | John Coltrane | |
| Kenny Dorham | | Junior Cook | |
| Blue Mitchell | | Sonny Rollins | |
| | | Booker Ervin | |
| | | George Coleman | |
| | | Joe Henderson | |
| | | Johnny Griffin | |
| | | Oliver Nelson | |
| | | Sonny Stitt | |

| PIANO | DRUMS | ORGAN | GUITAR |
|---|---|---|---|
| Barry Harris | Art Blakey | Jack McDuff | Wes Montgomery |
| Bobby Timmons | Max Roach | Jimmy Smith | Kenny Burrell |
| Horace Silver | Elvin Jones | John Patton | Grant Green |
| Kenny Drew | Jimmy Cobb | Larry Young | Joe Pass |
| Roland Hanna | Louis Hayes | Richard "Groove" Holmes | Herb Ellis |
| Tadd Dameron | Philly Joe Jones | Shirley Scott | |
| Tommy Flanagan | Roy Haynes | Charles Earland | |
| Red Garland | Art Taylor | | |
| Wynton Kelly | Mickey Roker | | |
| Les McCann | | | |
| Ramsey Lewis | | | |
| Andrew Hill | | | |

| BASS | R&B TENOR SAXOPHONE | BARITONE SAX |
|---|---|---|
| Charles Mingus | Eddie "Lockjaw" Davis | Pepper Adam |
| Paul Chambers | Gene Ammons | Nick Brignola |
| George Morrow | Arnett Cobb | Ron Cuber |
| Jimmy Garrison | Red Holloway | |
| Reggie Workman | Ike Quebec | |
| Doug Watkins | Jimmy "Night Train" Forrest | |
| Jymie Merritt | Stanley Turrentine | |
| Sam Jones | Houston Person | |
| Art Davis | | |

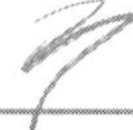

## CHARLES MINGUS—BASS, COMPOSER, BANDLEADER

- Charles Mingus (1922–1979) was a bassist who has come to be known primarily as a bandleader and composer. In many respects, his music stands apart from the mainstream jazz of the 1950s. It represents a variety of original sounds performed by many creative musicians. It features a blend of pre-swing, bebop, free jazz, third stream, programmatic music, twentieth-century classical music, and Duke Ellington concepts. He was also strongly influenced by gospel church music giving much of his music an exciting and spontaneous quality. In retrospect, Charles Mingus is difficult to categorize in terms of jazz styles because his work reflects the influences of so many different genres.
- Mingus was raised in Watts, a ghetto section of Los Angeles, California. He first learned to play the trombone and cello, eventually becoming a member of the Los Angeles Junior Orchestra. He took a lot of verbal and sometimes even physical abuse from neighborhood gangs as he carried his cello back and forth from rehearsals. Eventually, he decided to switch to acoustic bass when he learned it would be difficult for African-American cellists to find work.
- He studied with bassist Red Callendar and quickly became proficient enough to find work in dance bands in the Central Avenue scene in Los Angeles. In the 1940s, he played with Louis Armstrong, Kid Ory, Barney

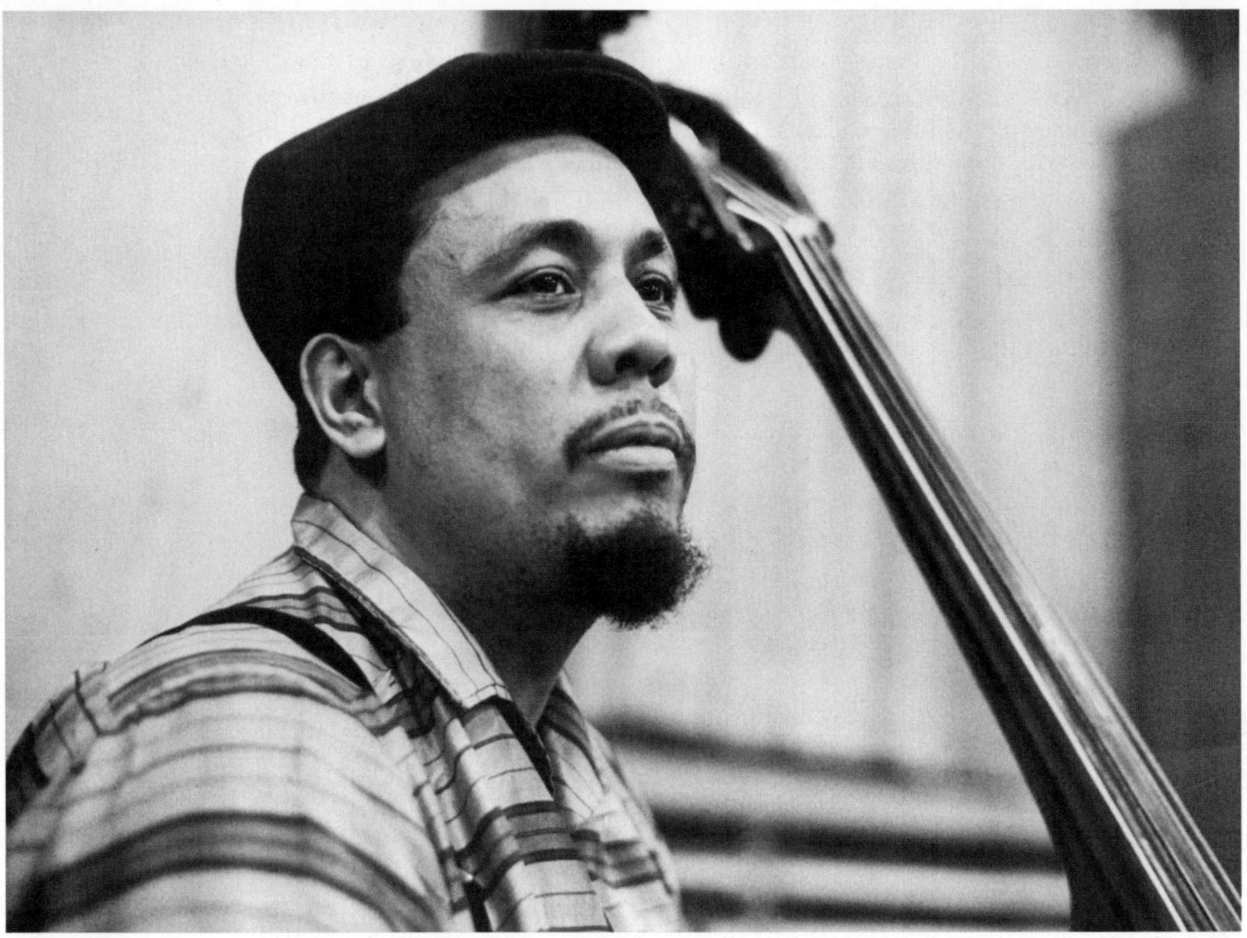

*Charles Mingus. © Bettmann/CORBIS.*

Bigard, Lionel Hampton, and Duke Ellington. In 1947, while with Lionel Hampton, Mingus composed "Mingus Fingers," his first composition and arrangement for Hampton's band.

- Eventually Mingus moved to New York City where he performed with Charlie Parker, Dizzy Gillespie, Stan Getz, Bud Powell, and the Red Norvo Trio. Mingus quit the Norvo Trio after a frustrating experience with racial discrimination while performing for a television show.
- Mingus experienced an inner mental turmoil for most of his life. His early childhood frustrations were only the beginning of what would be many more confrontational episodes during his life. Racial tension was frequently a source of conflict. As a result, many of his compositions contain some kind of emotional message or content. For example, "Fables of Faubus" is Mingus's commentary on former Arkansas governor Faubus's handling of the 1957 Little Rock school integration

crisis; "Pithecanthropus Erectus" reflects Charles Darwin's theories of evolution in that Mingus depicts man's transformation from a primate dependent on all four limbs for travel to a creature standing erect on two legs; "Goodbye Porkpie Hat" is Mingus's tribute to the recently deceased Lester Young; and "Self-Portrait in Three Colors," Mingus's musical depiction of himself.

- Eventually in 1969, Mingus published an autobiography titled *Beneath the Underdog* in which he tells the story of his life from his psychologist's chair.
- Charles Mingus is one of the most interesting and enigmatic figures of jazz history. The unique aspects of his life and personality are evident in his music.
- For a time Mingus studied bass with great dedication and purpose, resulting in a prodigious technique that set him apart from most other bass players. However, even with all his talent and ability as a bass player, what interested him most was composition.
- In the mid-1950s, Mingus founded his Jazz Workshop, due in part to this developing interest in composition. Somewhat related to the "head charts" of earlier Kansas City swing bands, his unusual method of composing included dictating melodies to the individuals in his ensemble. The Jazz Workshop was drawn from a pool of musicians ranging from four to more than fifteen. In addition, the instrumentation featured diverse combinations.
- Duke Ellington's influence is present in much of Mingus's music in the following ways:
  - ♪ He hired alto saxophonists who were capable of emulating the **sound** of Johnny Hodges.
  - ♪ His brass players used plunger mutes, creating "jungle" timbres.
  - ♪ He recorded many Ellington compositions.
  - ♪ He composed works either as a tribute or dedication to Ellington.
  - ♪ He achieved a balance between composed and improvised music.
  - ♪ He hired musicians for their unique capabilities within the context of his band.
- Mingus was able to break away from standard hard bop accompaniments by using preset musical figures to break the flow of the music. By writing specific figures or short chunks of music to be played when he dictated, the soloists were forced to play around these background figures. In some ways it was like an obstacle course for the improviser, but it produced solos that were more fresh and original. He was able to manipulate the way his soloists played by writing these figures; they could not rely on typical 1950s hard bop approaches. With this technique he could change the style of a composition in mid-performance. Sometimes he would move from 6/8 to 4/4 time or have the band drop out and accompany the soloists with hand clapping. He utilized many unusual methods to keep the music fresh and spontaneous. Thus, Mingus was able to get the most out of his musicians by utilizing unorthodox methods.

## Personnel of Mingus's bands

| TRUMPET | TENOR SAX | ALTO SAX | TROMBONE |
|---|---|---|---|
| Ted Curson | Booker Ervin | Eric Dolphy | Jimmy Knepper |
| Richard Williams | Roland Kirk | Charles Mariano | Britt Woodman |
| Thad Jones | Yusef Lateef | John Handy | |
| Jack Walrath | George "Pepper" Adams | Jackie McLean | |
| | J. R. Monterose | Charles McPherson | |

| PIANO | DRUMS |
|---|---|
| Jaki Byard | Dannie Richmond |
| Roland Hanna | Willie Jones |
| Don Pullen | |
| Mal Waldron | |

## Important Mingus compositions include

| COMPOSITIONS | ALBUM | YEAR | PERSONNEL |
|---|---|---|---|
| "Fables of Faubus" | *Mingus Ah Um* | 1959 | |
| "Hora Decubitus" | | | |
| "Jelly Roll" | *Mingus Ah Um* | 1959 | |
| "Peggy's Blue Skylight" | | | |
| "Moanin'" | | | |
| "Revelations" | | | |
| "An Open Letter to Duke" | *Mingus Ah Um* | 1959 | |
| "Reincarnation of a Lovebird" | | | |
| "Better Get It in Yo' Soul" | *Mingus Ah Um* | 1959 | |
| "Epitaph" | | | |
| "Haitian Fight Song" | *Clown* | 1957 | |
| "Goodbye Porkpie Hat" | *Mingus Ah Um* | 1959 | |
| "Pithecanthropus Erectus (The Story of Man)" | *Pithecanthropus Erectus* | 1956 | Charles Mingus, bass; Jackie McLean, alto sax; J. R. Monterose, tenor sax; Mal Waldron, piano; Willie Jones, drums |
| "Nostalgia in Times Square" | | | |
| "Conversation" | *East Coasting* | 1957 | Charles Mingus, bass; Jackie McLean, alto sax; J. R. Monterose, tenor sax; Mal Waldron, piano; Willie Jones, drums |

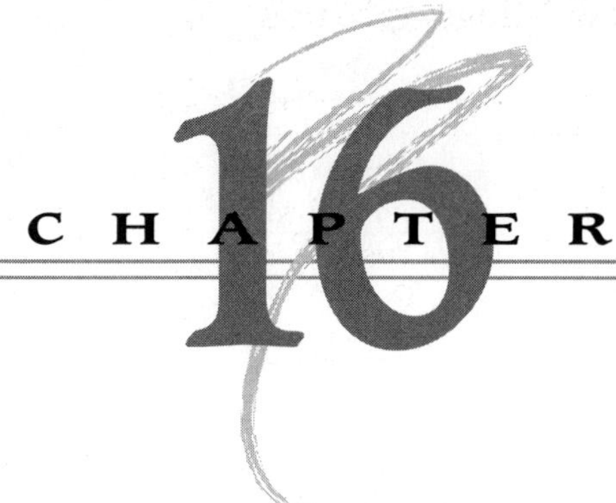

# Jazz Singers

What is a jazz singer?

- A jazz singer has assimilated the (instrumental) jazz phrasing of Louis Armstrong.
- Jazz singers can approximate the rhythmic feel of jazz instrumentalists.
- Their interpretation and execution of lyrics reflect individuality.
- They reinterpret melodies of songs into highly personal *recompositions*.
- A jazz singer is not required to scat sing (vocal improvisation).
- Jazz singers usually have a standard jazz rhythm section accompanying them, but they might be accompanied by a pianist or a bassist only.
- Jazz singers do not have to possess a *great* voice, but they must be *familiar* with the inflections and nuances of other established jazz instrumentalists and singers.

♪ There is a fine line between a jazz singer and a pop singer. They both may, for instance, sing the same song. Sometimes a pop singer may attempt a more jazz-like rendition of a song—is he or she then a jazz singer? Certain singers have been accepted into the jazz category while others remain on the periphery—what is the difference?

♪ Louis Armstrong was perhaps the first authentic jazz vocalist. Through his playing and singing he influenced all subsequent jazz singers and instrumentalists. It was his phrasing, approach to rhythm, and the liberties he took reinterpreting the melody of songs that made such a great impact on jazz.

# THREE PROFILES

## Billie Holiday "Lady Day"

- Billie Holiday (1915–1959) was born Eleanor Fagan in Baltimore, Maryland.
- Her voice had a limited range and it was not very strong. She did not scat sing, but her innovative behind-the-beat phrasing made her one of the most famous and influential jazz singers.
- The emotional intensity that she achieved in her songs (particularly in later years) was very memorable; she often really did live the words she sang.
- Holiday was discovered by producer John Hammond when she was singing in Harlem clubs. He arranged for her to record a couple of titles

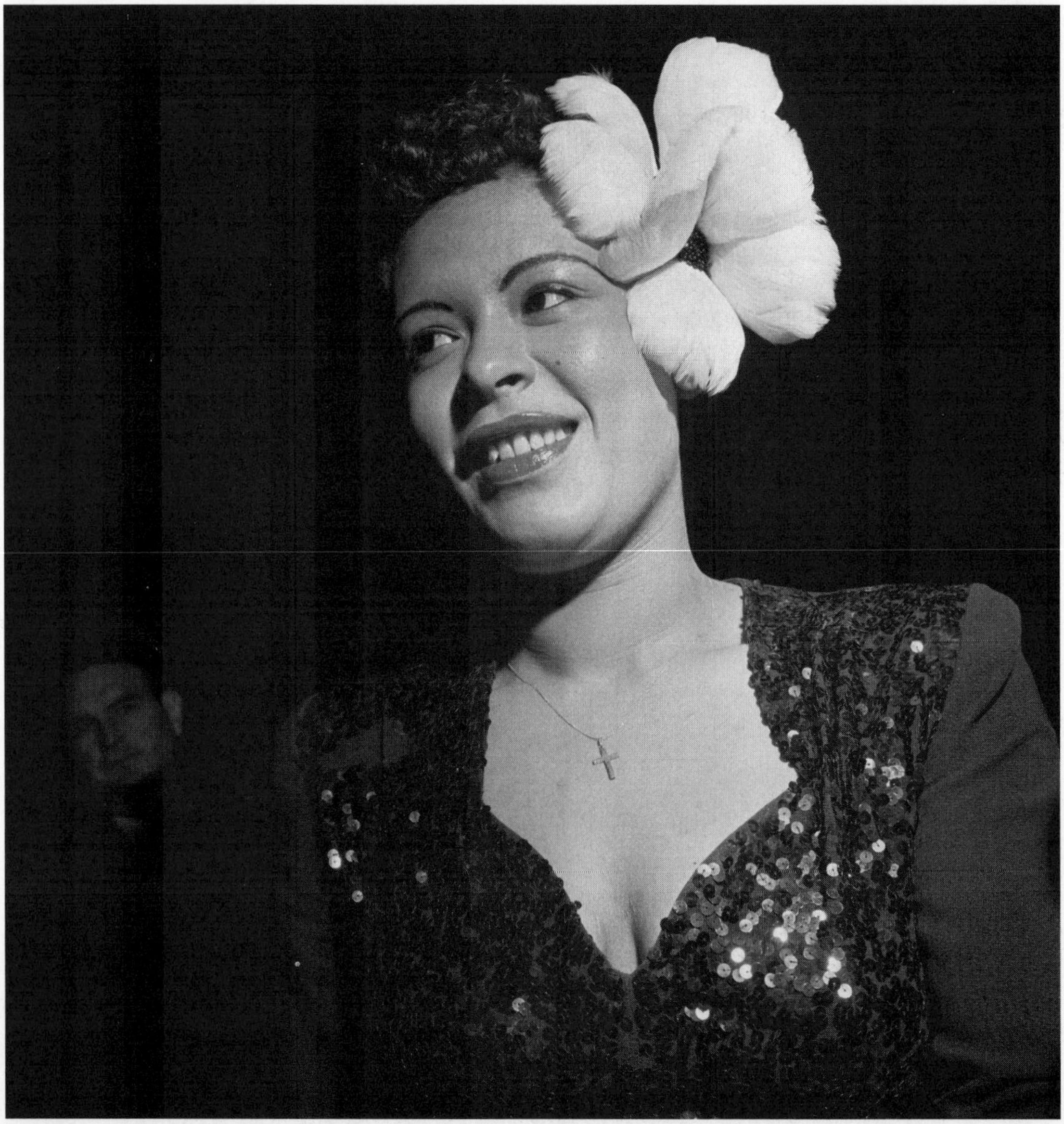

*Billie Holiday. © Bradley Smith/CORBIS*

with Benny Goodman in 1933, and although the recordings had limited success, they helped to establish her career.

- Two years later she joined a pickup band led by Teddy Wilson and the combination clicked. From 1935 to 1942, she would make some of the finest recordings of her career with some of the top Swing Era players.
- Holiday sought to combine Louis Armstrong's swing and Bessie Smith's sound; the result was her own fresh approach.
- In 1937, Lester Young and Buck Clayton began recording with Holiday.
- She performed with Count Basie's Orchestra during much of 1937, but all that exists of the collaboration are three songs from a radio broadcast.
- She worked with Artie Shaw's Orchestra in 1938, but only one song was recorded.
- She became the star attraction at New York's Cafe Society in 1939. Holiday's performance of the graphic "Strange Fruit," a strong antiracism statement, became a permanent part of her repertoire and one of her trademark songs.
- Some of her most memorable recordings were made with Decca Records (1944–1949). She had already introduced "Fine and Mellow" (1939) and "God Bless the Child' (1941), but it was with Decca that she first recorded "Lover Man," "Don't Explain," "Good Morning Heartache," "Ain't Nobody's Business If I Do," "Them There Eyes," and "Crazy He Calls Me."
- Some time in the early 1940s, she became a heroin addict, and she spent much of 1947 in jail. The negative publicity made her a notorious celebrity, and her audience greatly increased.
- Billie Holiday's health and performing ability gradually declined after 1950. In late 1957, she sang "Fine and Mellow" on *The Sound of Jazz* telecast with Lester Young, Ben Webster, and Coleman Hawkins. Holiday's 1958 album *Lady in Satin* found her voice sounding weak, and the following year she died.

## Ella Fitzgerald

- Ella Fitzgerald (1918–1996) was born in Newport News, Virginia, and she grew up in Yonkers, New York.
- Dubbed "the First Lady of Song" she had a long and productive career.
- She is known for her superb musicianship, tonal clarity, wide range, and inventive rhythmic drive.
- She often used her voice as a musical instrument; thus, she became known for her wordless scat vocals. Her ability to improvise with her voice as other jazz musicians did on their instruments has yet to be surpassed by anyone else.
- While still in her teens, she sang at the Apollo Theater's amateur competition and was heard by Benny Carter and Bardu Ali, the conductor of the Chick Webb Orchestra. They recommended her to Webb, with whom she earned great popularity at the Savoy Ballroom and other venues. She made her recording debut with Webb's band on "Love and Kisses" for Decca in June 1935 and had her first major success in 1938 with "A-Tisket, A Tasket," a swinging adaptation of the nursery rhyme.

- After Webb's untimely death in 1939, Ella became nominal leader of the band for two years. Then she pursued a solo career in clubs and theaters. From 1946 to 1957, she worked often with Norman Granz, touring in the United States, Europe, and Japan as a member of his "Jazz at the Philharmonic" cast. From 1948 to 1952, she was married to bassist Ray Brown, the leader of her accompanying trio.
- In the 1950s, she recorded songs by well-known composers Harold Arlen, Irving Berlin, Duke Ellington, George Gershwin, Jerome Kern, Cole Porter, and Richard Rodgers. These have become known as her "Songbooks."
- 1n 1955, she began recording for the Verve label in a variety of concert and studio situations, which established her with a much wider audience. In the 1970s, she appeared with more than forty symphony orchestras in the United States, including the Boston Pops in 1972.
- Health problems, beginning with her eyes in the 1970s and continuing with her heart in the 1980s, slowed but did not strongly curtail her career until the end of the latter decade. By the mid-1990s she had ceased performing but the popularity of her invaluable body of recordings did not diminish.

## Sarah Vaughan

- Sarah Vaughan (1924–1990) was born in Newark, New Jersey. She grew up learning about music through her experiences in the Mt. Zion Baptist Church.
- She possessed a great sense of rhythm and harmony, and an innate ability to reinterpret lyrics in a highly personal manner that seemed to make them come alive.
- She combined exquisite elegance, an impressive range, and an effortless delivery. Also a fine jazz pianist, Vaughan used her voice with great musical creativity, as if it were an instrument.
- In 1942, she won a talent competition at the Apollo Theater Amateur Night, which led to a number of professional performance opportunities. Billy Eckstine, a vocalist with the Earl Hines Orchestra, heard her performance and was so impressed that he recommended her for the position of second pianist in Hines's band.
- When Billy Eckstine left the Earl Hines Orchestra to form his own big bebop band, he took Sarah Vaughan with him, along with trumpeters Dizzy Gillespie and Fats Navarro, saxophonists Dexter Gordon and Sonny Stitt, bassist Oscar Pettiford, and drummer Art Blakey. These band members were many of the pioneers of the bebop style. Vaughan developed an ear for the intricate harmonies and melodies of bebop.
- In 1945, she recorded what are now considered classic tunes, such as "Lover Man" and "East of the Sun and West of the Moon." By the time she was twenty she was well known by her fellow musicians, the new wave of bebop musicians.
- She was given a place as a serious musician in the male-dominated world of jazz rather than being considered *only* a vocalist by her fellow musicians. Her 1945 recording of the song "Lover," performed with Gillespie and saxophonist Charlie Parker, established her reputation as a leading jazz singer.

- She has earned two nicknames both appropriate to her uniqueness as a performer: "Sassy" and "The Divine One."
- Sarah Vaughan was signed to Mercury Records in 1954 and embarked on the most prolific years of her life. It was with Mercury that she made her classic recordings of "Misty," and "Tenderly."
- In the late 1950s, Vaughan was signed by Roulette Records where she recorded with the Count Basie Orchestra. They recorded several jazz standards: "Lover Man," "I Cried for You," and the classic "Perdido."
- She continued to perform and record through the 1970s and 1980s and received numerous accolades.

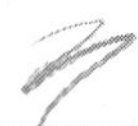

## IMPORTANT SINGERS

### Pre-jazz Blues

Ma Rainy
Mamie Smith
Bessie Smith
Trixie Smith
Alberta Hunter

### Tin Pan Alley/Broadway

Ethel Waters
Eva Taylor
Florence Mills

### Louis Armstrong Influenced

Louis Prima
Roy Eldridge
Jack Teagarden
Bing Crosby (considered to be more *pop* oriented in his later years)

### Swing Era (mid-1930s–present)

Many of these singers began their careers singing with big bands. With the end of the Big Band Swing Era in the late 1940s, many were performing as leaders of their own bands. Some of these singers enjoyed success well into the 1980s.

Mildred Bailey
Helen Forrest
Ella Fitzgerald
Peggy Lee
Cab Calloway
Frank Sinatra
Lee Wiley
Billie Holiday
Jo Stafford
Lena Horne
Billy Eckstine
Nat "King" Cole
Louis Jordan (early predecessor to R&B singers)

### Blues Shouters (Primarily Kansas City/Count Basie-style)

Jimmy Rushing
Big Joe Turner
Joe Williams

### Bebop/Cool Male singers (post–1945)

This group takes bebop instrumental conception and applies it to the voice. Few, if any, of these singers are considered to possess a fine voice, but their jazz rhythmic conception and ability to scat sing put them in this category. A number of them were outstanding instrumentalists.

King Pleasure
Babs Gonzales
Jon Hendricks
Mark Murphy
James Moody (saxophone)
Clark Terry (trumpet)
Chet Baker (trumpet)
Dizzy Gillespie (trumpet)
Frank Rosolino (trombone)
Eddie Jefferson
Joe Carroll
Oscar Brown, Jr.
Bob Dorough

### Male Singers (1950–present)

These are singers with good voices that use jazz phrasing and repertoire.

Mel Torme
Tony Bennett

### Female Bop-oriented (Late 1940s–present)

This group of female singers uses modern jazz phrasing, although some of them began singing at the end of the Swing Era. Some of the songs these artists have recorded may fall outside the standard jazz repertoire. Many of them continued performing through the 1990s. A number are also fine jazz pianists.

Sarah Vaughan
Nina Simone
Chris Connor
Abbie Lincoln
Rosemary Clooney
Betty Carter
Sheila Jordan
Anita O'Day
June Christy
Dinah Washington
Blossom Dearie
Shirley Horn
Carmen McRae

### Vocal Jazz Groups

These are vocal duos, trios, and quartets that sing jazz repertoire, using jazz harmonies and phrasing. Some also employ vocal (scat) singing.

Slim and Slam (Slim Galliard and Slam Stewart)
Lambert, Hendricks, and Ross
The Hi-Los

Swingle Singers
Singers Unlimited
The Four Freshmen
Manhattan Transfer
New York Voices
Take Six

## Modern

These are contemporary artists that draw from many different sources. Not all of them utilize standard jazz-swing rhythm, but their work does fall into the jazz category because of the wide scope of their work.

Ursula Dudziak
Tania Marie
Diane Reeves
Vanessa Rubin
Diane Krall
Flora Purim
Diane Schuur
Cassandra Wilson
Harry Connick, Jr.
Bobby McFerrin

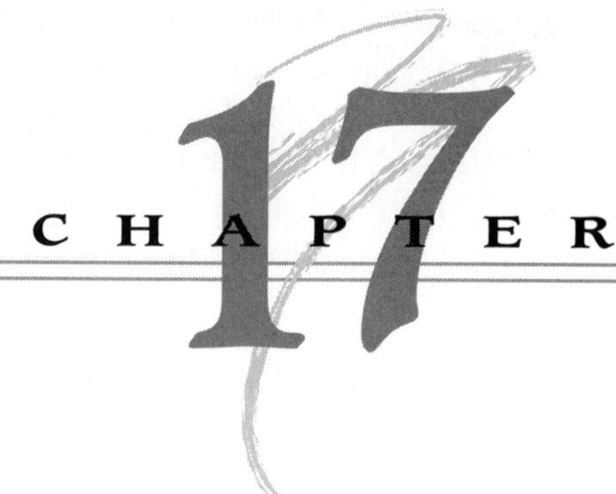

CHAPTER 17

# Miles Davis

- Miles Davis (1926–1991) was born in Alton, Illinois, and grew up in East St. Louis. He began playing trumpet at age thirteen and two years later he was working in Eddie Randall Blue Devils, a local band.
- In 1944, he moved to New York and enrolled at the Julliard School of Music. However, he spent most of his time on Fifty-second Street, where he met Charlie Parker and other great bebop jazz musicians. Soon Davis was enmeshed in the New York jazz scene. He played with big bands led by Benny Carter and Billy Eckstine. He was a sideman in many Parker-led recording sessions from 1945 to 1948.
- From 1948 to 1950, he was involved in the *Birth of the Cool* sessions that influenced the cool/West Coast style with its emphasis on composition and its understated sound featuring solos woven into the texture of the arrangements (see Chapter 14).
- From 1950 to 1955, Davis performed and recorded with many significant jazz musicians including Sonny Rollins, Art Blakey, J. J. Johnson, and Horace Silver. However, his playing suffered due to a heroin addiction problem he finally kicked, in 1953.
- Davis was one of the most significant and innovative bandleaders and composers of the 1950s, 1960s, and 1970s. A large portion of modern jazz history is recorded on Davis-led sessions during this time. The sound of his bands constantly changed, and these continual innovations influenced the direction of post-1950 jazz.
- The first Miles Davis **classic quintet,** with Philly Joe Jones on drums, Paul Chambers on bass, Red Garland on piano, and John Coltrane on tenor sax, epitomized the mid-1950s hard bop-derived sound.

- *Kind of Blue*, recorded in 1959, was important in the development of modal improvisation and represented a move away from the sound of hard bop. The Davis group had expanded to a sextet with the addition of Cannonball Adderley and replaced Red Garland with pianist Bill Evans and later Wynton Kelly. Drummer Jimmy Cobb also appeared on a few of the selections. Their sound influenced the next generation of jazz musicians.
- The second Miles Davis classic quintet, with Herbie Hancock on piano, Ron Carter on bass, Wayne Shorter on tenor and soprano saxophone, and Tony Williams on drums, redefined rhythm section concepts and led the way for the development of the post-bebop acoustic sound and later the electric sound of the 1970s. This band was considered modern in the 1960s and they continue to sound modern today.
- *In a Silent Way* and *Bitches Brew* were albums that broke new ground as Miles looked to the sounds of popular dance music for inspiration in forming one of the early jazz-rock fusion bands. Many members of his fusion groups later led some of the most influential fusion bands of the 1970s and 1980s such as Weather Report, Return to Forever, Tony Williams Lifetime, Mahavishnu Orchestra, and Herbie Hancock's Headhunters.
- Although Davis was not personally responsible for all the ideas and innovations produced at these sessions, he was the overseer, and therefore has been credited with many significant developments in modern jazz.
- Miles Davis, like Duke Ellington, had an innate ability to recognize talent and hire some of the most important and influential musicians in jazz to play in his groups. He always had an ear for musicianship and at crucial times chose musicians who were, or would later become, leading innovators in jazz. Some of these Miles Davis sidemen include John Coltrane, Cannonball Adderley, Bill Evans, Wayne Shorter, Herbie Hancock, Tony Williams, Chick Corea, and Keith Jarrett.
- As a trumpet player, Davis's early playing shows the influences of Dizzy Gillespie, Charlie Parker, Clark Terry, and Freddy Webster. It must have been quite intimidating for the young nineteen- year-old to be playing with Charlie Parker, filling in for Dizzy Gillespie in 1946.
- One should not be obsessed with the limitations of his playing; he used them to his advantage. The fact that he missed or cracked notes did not detract from the beauty of his playing. His lines were more varied and original than those of most trumpet players.
- Miles was always a melodic soloist whose work was characterized by skillful timing and dramatic construction of line. As a master of self-restraint, he never wasted a note or relied on special effect. His trumpet playing was unique, personal, and easily identified by the following:
    - His use of silence (or space) in his solos allowed them to *breathe*
    - The Harmon mute, which gives an esoteric, far-off sound one immediately recognizes
    - His flugelhorn playing; he was one of the first jazz musicians to popularize this instrument
    - The use of little or no vibrato, a characteristic of the cool style
    - His playing is generally confined to the middle register of the trumpet

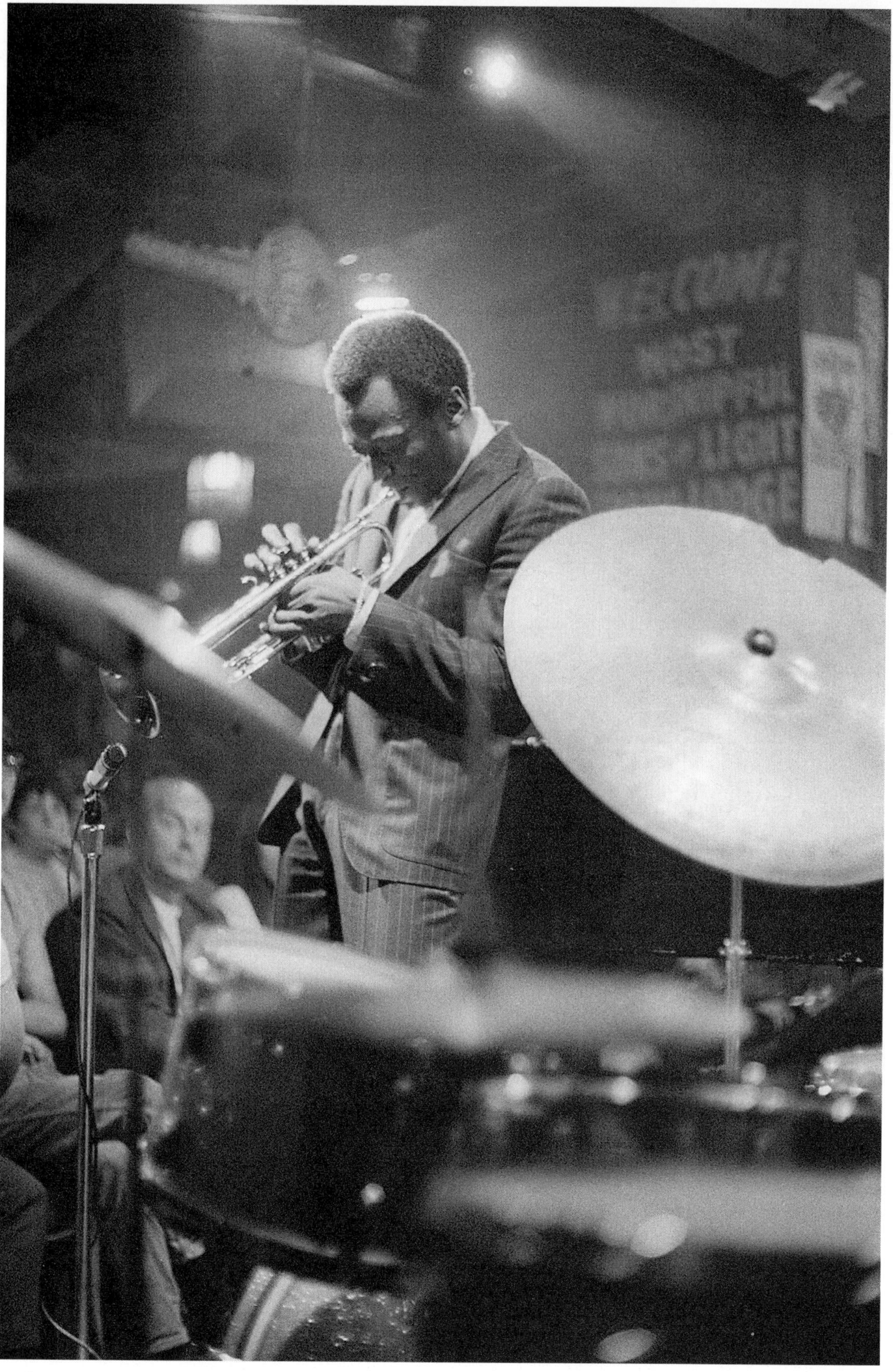

*Miles Davis. © Bettmann/CORBIS*

- ♪ His ability to phrase well-known compositions/melodies in such a distinctive and original manner that he could often make them sound like new compositions
- ♪ His redefinition of the tempo of a jazz composition in the mid-1950s; he generally avoided very fast tempos and adhered to medium tempos
- ♪ His avoidance of musical cliché.
- ♪ His alteration of pitch and tone color, and the bending of pitches
- ♪ His ability to play notes at unexpected places

- All of the above characterize much of what we associate with Miles's playing, especially in the 1950s. As his playing changed in the mid-1960s, he began playing with a brighter, more sharp-edged tone and began to utilize the high register more often. As he struggled with the trumpet on his late 1940s recordings; he realized his limitations and used them to establish his own unique voice and way of playing. His approach was somewhat of a novelty when compared with the cascades of notes coming from Clifford Brown, Dizzy Gillespie, and Fats Navarro.
- The **first classic quintet** consisted of Red Garland on piano, Philly Joe Jones on drums, and Paul Chambers on bass. Initially Miles Davis wanted to hire tenor saxophonist Sonny Rollins, but due to previous commitments, he was not available. Davis instead hired John Coltrane. Five albums were released on Prestige between 1954 and 1956 containing some of the most exciting combo work of the 1950s. Especially important was the appearance of the Miles Davis Quintet at the 1955 Newport Jazz Festival. It was one of the most important events in reestablishing Miles's dominance on the jazz scene. When Miles left Prestige, he was signed by Columbia, and he added alto saxophonist Cannonball Adderley to the group. He chose his sidemen to contrast with his spare style of playing.

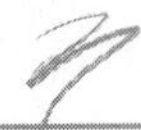

## BEBOP/COOL—1945–1954

### Major Influences

- Freddy Webster
- Clark Terry
- Dizzy Gillespie
- Charlie Parker

### Important Recordings

| ALBUM | YEAR | PERSONNEL |
|---|---|---|
| *Birth of the Cool* | 1948–1950 | Gil Evans, Gerry Mulligan, arrangers; Miles Davis, trumpet; J. J. Johnson, Kai Winding, trombone; Sandy Siegelstein, French horn; Bill Barber, tuba; Lee Konitz, alto sax; Gerry Mulligan, baritone sax; John Lewis, piano; Nelson Boyd, Al McKibbon, bass; Kenny Clarke, Max Roach, drums |
| *Dig* | 1951 | Sonny Rollins, Jackie Mclean, Walter Bishop Jr., Tommy Potter, Art Blakey |
| *Miles Davis and the Modern Jazz Giants* | 1954 | Milt Jackson, Thelonious Monk, Kenny Clarke, Percy Heath |

## 1956–1963

### Major Influences

- Gil Evans (collaborator)
- Ahmad Jamal
- John Coltrane
- Bill Evans

### Important Recordings

| ALBUM | YEAR | PERSONNEL |
|---|---|---|
| *Steamin'* | 1956 | Chambers, Jones, Garland, Coltrane |
| *Workin'* | 1956 | Chambers, Jones, Garland, Coltrane |
| *Cookin'* | 1956 | Chambers, Jones, Garland, Coltrane |
| *Round Midnight* | 1956 | Chambers, Jones, Garland, Coltrane |
| *Milestones* | 1958 | Chambers, Jones, Garland, Coltrane, Adderley |
| *Kind of Blue* | 1959 | Chambers, Jones/Cobb, Evans/Kelly, Coltrane, Adderley |
| *Miles Ahead* | 1957 | Gil Evans (arranger and conductor) |
| *Porgy and Bess* | 1958 | Gil Evans (arranger and conductor) |
| *Sketches of Spain* | 1959–1960 | Gil Evans (arranger and conductor) |
| *Someday My Prince Will Come* | 1961 | Chambers; Cobb; Kelly; Hank Mobley/Jimmy Heath, tenor sax |
| *Seven Steps to Heaven* | 1963 | Ron Carter, bass; Tony Williams, Frank Butler, drums; Victor Feldman, Herbie Hancock, piano; George Coleman-tenor sax |

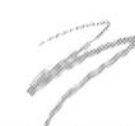

## GIL EVANS

- In 1957, Davis renewed his association with Gil Evans. They produced four albums of music arranged by Evans for an expanded jazz orchestra. Evans used the orchestra to feature Miles as a trumpet soloist much in the same way classical concertos feature soloists. The instrumentation included extensive use of woodwinds, French horns, and other brass instruments.
- Compared with other big band writing of the 1950s and 1960s, Gil Evans's arrangements were more reflective and almost third stream (classical and jazz) in nature. Evans mastered the effective use of shading, color, and programmatic technique. He wove open solo sections for Davis into the texture of his startling arrangements. Evans freed himself from formula writing and voiced freely across sections, weaving improvisation into the framework of each arrangement.
- On *Miles Ahead*, Davis plays flugelhorn throughout. On *Porgy and Bess* Evans arranges songs taken from the popular George Gershwin folk opera. On *Sketches of Spain* Evans uses Spanish composer Joaquin Rodrigo's *Concerto for Orchestra and Guitar* as the basis for many of the arrangements. Another similar Davis/Evans collaboration was *Quiet Nights*.

## KIND OF BLUE

- Most pre-1959 recordings were either popular tunes, bebop, or hard bop tunes. Each player on *Kind of Blue* had already contributed or would soon contribute to a new approach that would significantly influence jazz for many years afterward. The construction of some tunes was remarkably different because the improvisations were based on modes. (Sometimes referred to as "church modes," this concept goes back as far as ancient musicians from Greece.) The influence of pianist Bill Evans is apparent because of his interest in modes at that time and the fact that he wrote or cowrote some of the compositions on the album. For example, all one has to do is listen to Bill Evans's recording of "Peace Piece" on his album *Everybody Digs Bill Evans* to hear the similarity to "Flamenco Sketches" on *Kind of Blue*.
- Before the late 1950s, jazz used chord progressions as the basis for harmony and improvisation in any given tune. A typical jazz composition would use a series of different chords, each one lasting a specific number of beats. "So What" was constructed as the antithesis of this approach. It used only one harmony (D-minor seventh) for the A section of an AABA form tune. The B section used a slightly different chord (E-flat-minor seventh). Therefore, there are only two chords used for the entire selection.
- In addition, two modes (one for D-minor seventh, the other for E-flat-minor seventh) were used as the basis for all the improvisation in "So What." This approach was unprecedented and, in the past perhaps, not considered sophisticated enough to warrant validity. However, "So What" provided over eight minutes of exciting yet accessible jazz. Practically anyone, musician or not, can hear and understand what is happening at any given point in the tune; yet musicians as advanced as John Coltrane, Cannonball Adderley, and Miles Davis were conveying improvisation in deep and convincing ways.
- Another modal selection on *Kind of Blue*, "Flamenco Sketches," was constructed with five preset modes as the basis for improvisation. The soloist would progress from one mode to the next only when ready to go on. For Miles Davis, who already had made a point of simplicity, modal compositions were a perfect vehicle.
- With "So What," "Flamenco Sketches," and other modal selections, a door was suddenly opened for all jazz musicians to take a new approach to jazz improvisation and composition. Much post-1959 improvisational music employed some of these alternatives first used by Davis, where frequent chord changes were rejected in favor of performances based on only one or two chords. Of all the musicians who performed on *Kind of Blue*, John Coltrane was the most comfortable with this new approach, and modal improvisation would manifest itself in many of his recordings released with his own quartet in the 1960s.

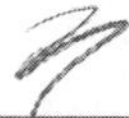

## MILES DAVIS QUINTET—1964–1968

### Major Influences

- Bill Evans (1959–1961 Trio)
- Herbie Hancock
- Wayne Shorter
- Ornette Coleman

### Stylistic Characteristics

- Advanced and modern harmonic knowledge/complexity
- Advanced and creative concepts of rhythm and melody
- More freedom in playing
- Songs with few chords—modal tunes or complex structures
- Little use of mutes
- Performance of mostly original material
- Music is still swing oriented, but sometimes the even eighth-note rhythmic feel is used
- Miles's trumpet playing becomes more aggressive than his 1950s recordings

### Important Recordings

| ALBUM | YEAR | PERSONNEL |
|---|---|---|
| *Four and More* | 1964 | Ron Carter, Tony Williams, Herbie Hancock, Wayne Shorter |
| *My Funny Valentine* | 1964 | Ron Carter, Tony Williams, Herbie Hancock, Wayne Shorter |
| *E.S.P.* | 1965 | Ron Carter, Tony Williams, Herbie Hancock, Wayne Shorter |
| *Miles Smiles* | 1966 | Ron Carter, Tony Williams, Herbie Hancock, Wayne Shorter |
| *Nefertiti* | 1967 | Ron Carter, Tony Williams, Herbie Hancock, Wayne Shorter |
| *The Sorcerer* | 1967 | Ron Carter, Tony Williams, Herbie Hancock, Wayne Shorter |
| *Filles de Kilimanjaro* | 1968 | Ron Carter, Tony Williams, Herbie Hancock, Wayne Shorter |

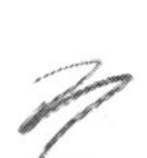

## WAYNE SHORTER/TONY WILLIAMS/ RON CARTER/HERBIE HANCOCK

- In 1963 Miles had two rhythm sections: his Los Angeles based group and his New York group. The album *Seven Steps to Heaven* was interesting in that he used both rhythm sections on different selections.
- In 1964, Miles hired the New York group as his permanent rhythm section; this young group featured drummer Tony Williams (only seventeen years old at the time), bassist Ron Carter, pianist Herbie Hancock, and saxophonist Wayne Shorter. Shorter was probably the most experienced, having already spent some years with Art Blakey and the Jazz Messengers. The interaction of this rhythm section was comparable with that found in the Bill Evans Trio. Both the Davis and

Coltrane rhythm sections consolidated the innovations of modern jazz up to that point. Then the Davis rhythm section moved to the next level.

- Davis's trumpet sound changed from the well-known dark, introspective sound to a more bright and edgy sound. He began to play more in the upper register of the trumpet and moved away from boplike swinging rhythms.
- This group could play at very fast tempos and in the context of slow tunes avoid stating the tempo in an obvious manner, which gave the renditions a floating, dreamlike effect. Their rapport allowed them to change rhythms, textures, and moods spontaneously; their versatility and quick responsiveness were extraordinary. The freedom and flexibility they displayed influenced jazz for the next two decades.
- Most of the compositions Davis played in the 1950s fit conventional song forms except for the groundbreaking work with pianist Bill Evans on *Kind of Blue.* After the departure of Evans and prior to Wayne

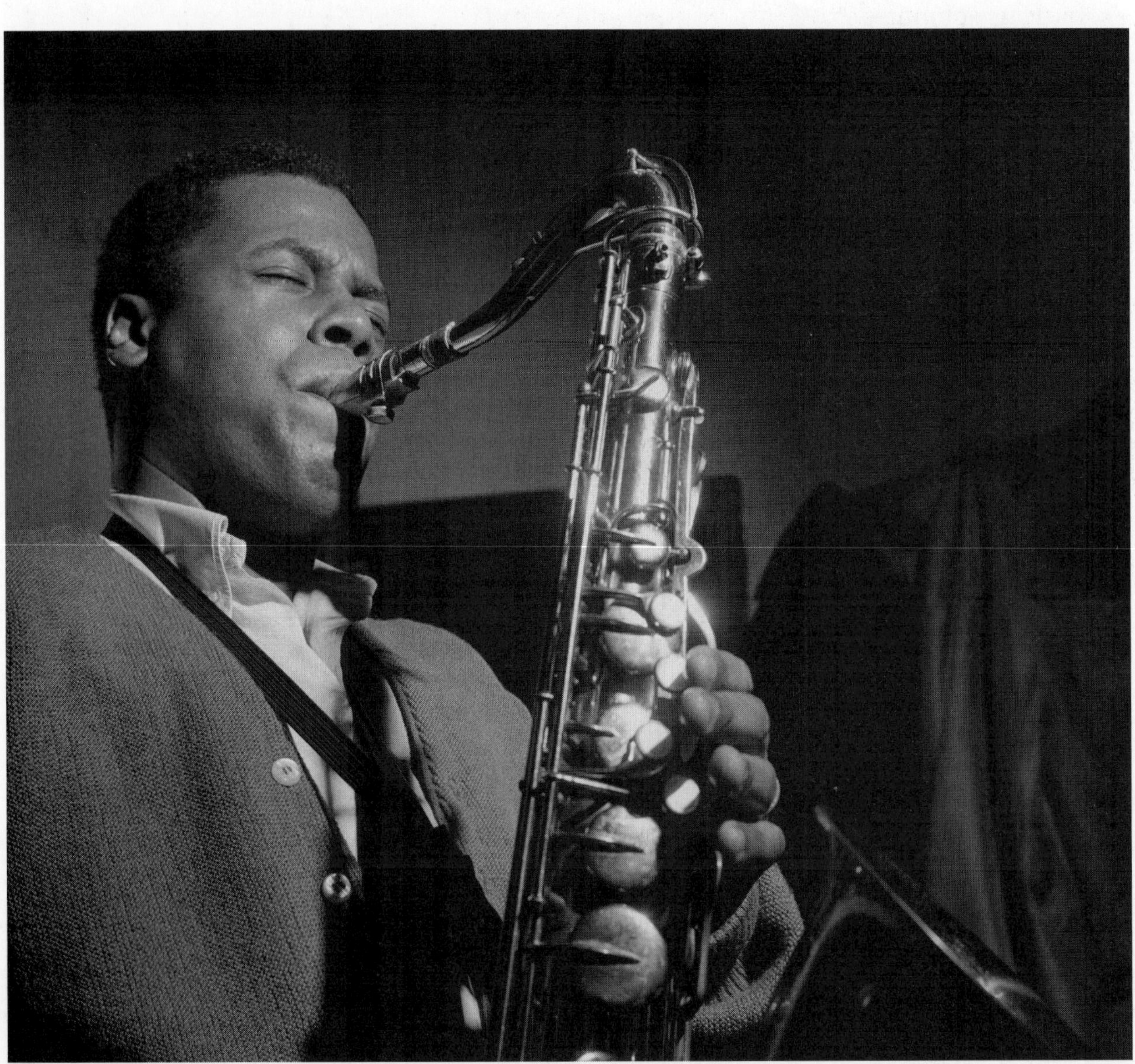

*Wayne Shorter. © Mosaic Images/CORBIS*

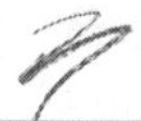

# JAZZ-ROCK—NEW DIRECTIONS (POST-1969)

Shorter joining the band, Davis did not explore much new territory in the area of song forms. With the addition of saxophonist and composer Wayne Shorter, however, Miles stopped recording standard jazz repertoire from the 1950s. Instead, he recorded new material composed primarily by band members Shorter and Hancock. Much of the new material did not fit into the category of conventionally constructed music. Some compositions were more modal in nature, while others had no preset harmonic sequence. Some of the compositions exhibited a transparent texture. Hancock's piano comping style changed to reflect this new style by playing sounds on the piano for mood, color, and dramatic effect.

- Wayne Shorter's saxophone style was initially influenced by John Coltrane. However, by the early 1960s he had developed a unique sound and approach that was all his own. Shorter's contribution as a composer had a dramatic effect on the overall sound of the group. His compositions such as "Nefertiti," sometimes featured complex chord structures. Other Shorter compositions had few chords.
- Tony Williams was one of the most influential drummers to come out of the 1960s. He made extensive use of his cymbals, using the ride cymbal to create a distinctive texture of high-intensity sound. He would sometimes close his high-hat on all four beats, a technique adopted later by jazz fusion drummers. Williams had a daring approach to playing the drums. He liberated the time-keeping role of the drummer in much the same way as Elvin Jones.
- Ron Carter was the foundation of the Miles Davis 1960s quintet. Influenced by Scott LaFaro, his style of bass playing could be either traditional or interactive. As a bassist with few technical limitations, he has been in demand for recordings and performances in New York since the 1960s.
- After 1968, Miles began to draw his sidemen from a pool of very talented young musicians. The music from this period reflects his interest in keeping his music sounding current. Miles Davis has always been aware of changes in popular music and has never been content to play in the same style for a long period of time.

## Major Influences

- Joe Zawinul
- Wayne Shorter
- John McLaughlin
- Motown funk rhythm sound

## Style

- More freedom of melody, harmony and rhythm
- Rock/funk time feel
- Few chord changes or song section demarcations
- Thickly textured music
- Music focused on moods; programmatic music to create illusions

- Use of electronic instruments (e.g., electric guitar, electric bass, electric keyboards)
- Reflects changes in popular music
- Long, extended performances

### 1969 Rhythm Section

Chick Corea, piano/keyboard
Joe Zawinul, keyboards
Keith Jarrett, piano/keyboard
Dave Holland, bass
Jack DeJohnette, drums
John McLaughlin, guitar

### Recordings

*Bitches Brew* (1969)
*Silent Way* (1969)
*Big Fun* (1972)
*Live Evil* (1970)
*Jack Johnson* (1970)
*Pangea* (1975)

- From 1975 to 1980, Miles Davis dropped out of public sight. During that time there were many rumors about the reasons for his sabbatical from performing. However, Miles had some physical problems that were forcing him to retire. He would undergo several hip operations before his return in the 1980s.
- He made a slow return to recording in 1980. Then he began touring in the summer of 1981. He suffered a stroke in 1982, but continued with his performing and recording career later that same year. He received an honorary doctorate of music from the New England Conservatory in 1986.

### 1982–1991 Recordings

*Man with the Horn* (1982)
*Decoy* (1983)
*Tutu* (1986)
*Amandla* (1989)
*Aura* (1989)

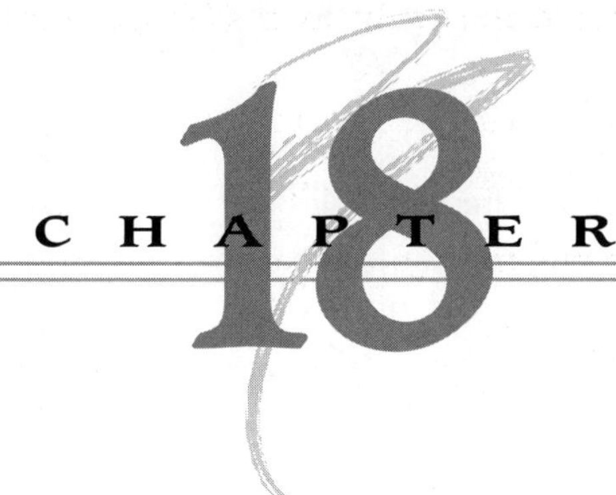

CHAPTER 18

# Free Jazz

- In the late nineteenth and early twentieth centuries, European orchestral composers began to stretch the limits of traditional harmony. Jazz musicians waited until the late 1950s to do the same.
- Pianist Lennie Tristano experimented with his group in a musical format that did not adhere to the rules of improvisation and traditional harmony in the manner of his contemporaries in the late 1940s. He decided that the musicians would be free to direct the music as they were playing it. The results were interesting, but few in the jazz community took serious note.
- In the late 1950s, another group of musicians became interested in playing in a manner that had few or no strict rules about improvisation or harmony.
- This new approach has been dubbed **free jazz** or **avant-garde jazz** and it is usually associated with approaches taken by saxophonist Ornette Coleman and pianist Cecil Taylor.
- The term *free jazz* is taken from the 1960 album recorded by Ornette Coleman's double quartet by the same name.
- Musicians who perform in this genre espoused greater freedom than their predecessors, generally playing music that contains no chord progressions, but they did follow some rules regarding performance practice.
- Free jazz is not totally free of all organization; if it was, the result would be *musical chaos*.

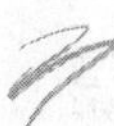

## CHARACTERISTICS OF FREE JAZZ

- Steady tempo—usually consistent meter, but sometimes free or dirgelike
- Written melodies are used for instruments and backgrounds.
- Chording instruments are often omitted because they can suggest tonal centers or chord progressions by their very nature.
- Improvisations are based upon the melody of the composition or a single note or tonal center
- Utilization of unusual or nontraditional instrumental techniques for sound production
- Greater use of tonal manipulation than in previous genres
- Utilization of collective improvisation
- Improvisation of texture and mood play important role
- A high level of energy and activity is often present in the performance
- A move away from the traditional swing feel and little use of bebop-derived musical language
- There is greater interest in music of non-European cultures: Africa, China, India, Middle East, Caribbean, South America
- Often there are nonmusical aspects of performance such as theatrical components

### Ornette Coleman—Alto Sax/Trumpet/Violin/Composer

- Ornette Coleman is one of the most important jazz musicians to emerge from the late 1950s and a central figure in the free jazz movement.
- He is a prolific composer and generally stays away from using preset chord changes for improvisation and omits chording instruments. Most of his compositions serve as the basis for the ensuing improvisations.
- His groundbreaking albums from 1958 through 1960 helped bring about a new approach to jazz improvisation.
- He writes strong melodies, but without an accompanying chord progression or specific length of form, the musicians cannot rely on harmony to create interest in their solos. They rely on the interplay or musical dialogue between the musicians to create interest and give the music direction.
- With Coleman, melody is more important than harmony—he plays his melodies freely, taking cues from the other musicians, especially bass players.
- His quartet recordings from the late 1950s use alto sax, trumpet, bass, and drums. Later he also recorded with his trio: alto, drums, and bass.
- The musicians he chose to work with had to understand his concepts and play accordingly. They include the following:

  Ed Blackwell, drums
  Charlie Haden, bass
  Scott LaFaro, bass
  Eric Dolphy, bass clarinet
  Billy Higgins, drums
  David Izenson, bass
  Don Cherry, trumpet
  Freddie Hubbard, trumpet

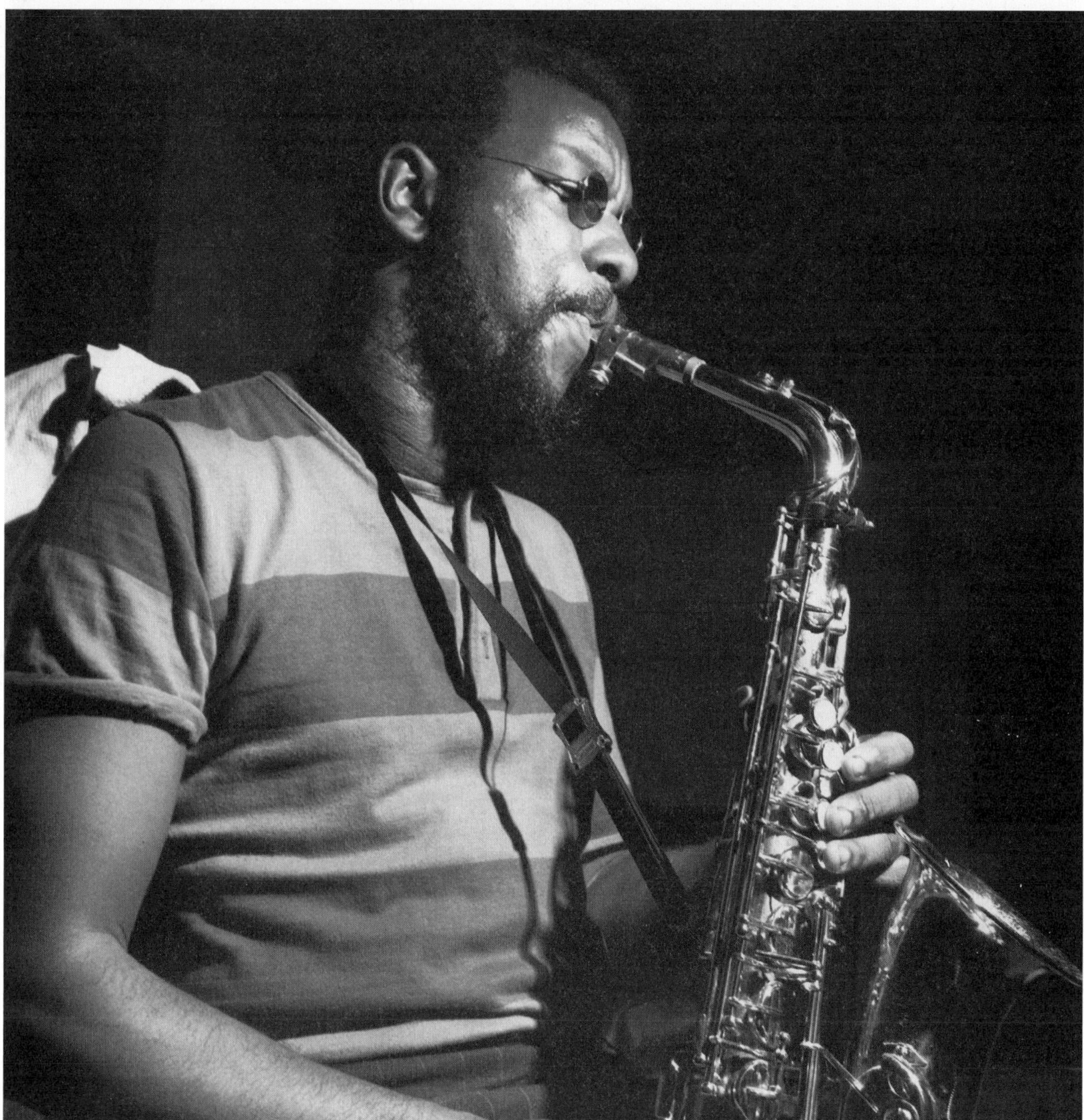

*Ornette Coleman. © Mosaic Image/CORBIS*

- His approach to improvisation greatly impacted jazz post-1960. This approach influenced John Coltrane, Miles Davis, and many other well-established musicians.
- His decision to discard progressions and the style he developed without them have influenced many improvisers since the early 1960s.
- Coleman's legacy: Many musicians post-1960 realized they did not have to adhere to the conventions of traditional harmony and form; this allowed improvisers the opportunity to let melody evolve on its own without the confinement of set harmonies. It also brought about changes in the way rhythm sections functioned.

### Important Recordings

*Something Else* (1958)
*Tomorrow is the Question* (1959)
*Change of the Century* (1959)
*The Shape of Jazz to Come* (1959)
*Free Jazz* (1960)
*Ornette on Tenor* (1961)
*Dancing in Your Head* (with Prime Time) (1975)
*Of Human Feelings* (with Prime Timc) (1979)

### Cecil Taylor—Piano/Composer

- Cecil Taylor is a pianist, composer, and bandleader who developed an alternative piano style during the second half of the 1950s.
- He emphasizes musical textures rather than playing bebop-derived melodic lines. His music can be percussive and sometimes creates a violent effect.
- He does not follow preset chord progressions.
- He made numerous quartet and trio recordings in the 1960s, calling his group the Cecil Taylor Unit.
- Sometimes he uses unusual instrumentation, as in the abstract recording *Unit Structures.*
- Best known for his solo improvisations, they do not have the characteristic swing feel, nor do they follow preset chord progressions. His music sounds atonal (lacking tonal center) and at times has more in common with twentieth-century composers Charles Ives and Karlheinz Stockhausen than with Taylor's jazz predecessors.

### Eric Dolphy (1928–1964)—Alto Saxophone, Bass Clarinet, Flute

- Between 1960 and 1964, Eric Dolphy recorded frequently with Charles Mingus. Dolphy was an accomplished alto saxophonist, flutist, and bass clarinetist; he had mastered each instrument and utilized every sound they could produce. Dolphy is one of the first jazz bass clarinetists.
- His full sound and vibrato on alto saxophone were reminiscent of Johnny Hodges, but Dolphy's improvisational style was different. Dolphy's playing was originally rooted in bebop, but by the late 1950s his work was characterized by an approach bearing neither bebop phrasing nor swing feel.
- As a composer, Dolphy's melodies use unusual intervals and are highly syncopated. This unpredictable approach can be rather disconcerting to listeners. His improvisational style, while sometimes sounding free, is more or less rooted in traditional harmony.
- His work with trumpet player Booker Little, John Coltrane, Oliver Nelson, and Charles Mingus reflects some of his best performances.

### Albert Ayler (1936–1970)—Tenor Sax

- Albert Ayler was a very passionate and original stylist who emerged from the 1950s. His playing evolved from the important saxophonists of the

1940s and 1950s, but had little in common with them. He acknowledged bebop, but did not play in the bebop style.

- His melodic and rhythmic approach had more in common with classical and folk music than jazz. He did not swing in the conventional manner.
- His playing exhibits a continuously high level of tension with little relief.
- One of the most unique aspects of his playing was his sound and use of vibrato. It was very wide, at times uncontrolled, and had little in common with the typical sound of the tenor sax of the 1950s.
- He played the entire range of the tenor sax from the lowest notes to the extreme high range and often would screech and squeal in utter abandonment.
- Most of his music was free of preset harmonies, but contained written melodies with specific sections to be played.
- The music of his groups, at times, is rhythmically free and seems to lack meter
- He often used violinists to augment his group.

### Don Cherry (1936–1996)—Trumpet/Pocket Trumpet

- Don Cherry was one of the most important and sought after free jazz trumpet players.
- He worked with Ornette Coleman in the late 1950s through the 1960s playing on numerous recordings.
- He has strong bebop and hard bop roots, but he also mastered playing without preset chord progressions.
- He possesses an original approach to improvisation; he was one of the first to make the transition from hard bop to free jazz.
- He was strongly influenced by Indian and Third World music.
- Many of his performances in the "world music" genre fall outside the realm of jazz

### Sun Ra (Herman Blount) (1914–1993)—Bandleader, Composer, Pianist

- Active as a pianist since the 1930s, he became a bandleader in the 1950s. The members of the band were drawn from a large pool of musicians who had rehearsed with him over the years.
- His group, known as the Arkestra, could vary in size from a trio to twenty or more musicians.
- He incorporated the use of singing, dancing, lighting, and costumes in his performances and often addressed nonmusical themes such as space travel, astronomy, and astrology.
- Sun Ra's music was extremely varied and drew from many sources such as the following:
    - Free jazz
    - Third World music
    - Electronic music and electronic instruments
    - Traditional big-band music

- Multimedia
- Modal music

- Sun Ra successfully employed collective improvisation within the big band setting.
- His music exhibits a wide range of color and texture due to the use of many different instruments.
- Two of the most important musicians to work with him were tenor saxophonist John Gilmore and alto saxophonist Marshall Allen.

### Association for the Advancement of Creative Musicians (AACM)

- Based in Chicago, the AACM was founded by Muhal Richard Abrams and Fred Anderson. The members of this collective draw their inspiration from the avant-garde movement in jazz. The organization helps arrange the performance, training, and promotion of its members.

### Art Ensemble of Chicago

- This group's music is not always within the standard jazz tradition's boundaries.
- Its members include the following:

  Lester Bowie, trumpet
  Joseph Jarman, saxophone
  Roscoe Mitchell, saxophone
  Malachi Favors, bass
  Don Moye, drums/percussion

- The group performs a wide variety of styles, many of which are not within the accepted jazz tradition.
  - Utilized music from around the world
  - Improvised in the free style
  - Performed dramatic sketches and recited poetry
  - Used staging and makeup
  - Played nonwestern musical instruments
  - Used standard instrumentation to make unusual sounds

### Anthony Braxton—Composer/Woodwind Player

- Anthony Braxton plays all of the woodwind instruments. His playing does not fall into the standard jazz mainstream and is not bebop derived.
- A creative improviser, he leans heavily toward atonality and does not swing in the traditional sense.
- Much of his work is outside the jazz idiom.
- He has written orchestral works that are reminiscent of twentieth-century classical composers and nonwestern sources.

### World Saxophone Quartet (WSQ)

- Saxophonists Julius Hemphill, Oliver Lake, Hamiet Bluiett were original members of the St. Louis-based Black Artists Group (BAG), formed in 1968.
- BAG also included dancers, poets, singers, and actors.
- This group's musical philosophy was similar to that of the AACM.

- The World Saxophone Quartet (WSQ) was formed in the mid 1970s when the three were joined by saxophonist David Murray.
- The four saxophonists blended freely improvised music with written music and performed without a rhythm section.

**Musicians often associated with free jazz**

| TRUMPET | SAXOPHONE | TROMBONE | PIANO |
|---|---|---|---|
| Leo Smith | Jimmy Lyons | Julian Priester | Paul Bley |
| Ted Curson | Steve Lacy | Albert Manglesdorf | Don Pullen |
| Bobby Bradford | Archie Shepp | Ray Anderson | Carla Bley |
| Olu Dara | Eric Dolphy | Roswell Rudd | Muhal Richard Abrams |
| Don Ellis | Sam Rivers | Robin Eubanks | Keith Jarrett |
| Lester Bowie | David Murray | George Lewis | Jaki Byard |
| Don Cherry | Marion Brown | | |
| Bill Dixon | Anthony Braxton | | |
| Bakaida Carroll | Hamiet Bluiett | | |
| | John Tchicai | | |
| | Dewey Redman | | |
| | George Adams | | |
| | Pharoah Sanders | | |
| | Oliver Lake | | |
| | Henry Threadgill | | |
| | Roscoe Mitchell | | |
| | Von Freeman | | |

## Drummers

- Free Jazz drummers often do not state the beat or imply tempo. They utilize the entire drum set and play in an unpredictable style that displays great varieties of color, texture, and energy.
- Drummers in this style do not rely on the traditional manner of playing time on the high hat or ride cymbal, instead they play in an interactive and unpredictable manner.

| DRUMS | BASS |
|---|---|
| Andrew Cyrille | Charlie Haden |
| Milford Graves | Malachi Favors |
| Ed Blackwell | Dave Holland |
| Ronald Shannon Jackson | David Izenson |
| Steve McCall | Henry Grimes |
| Rashied Ali | Fred Hopkins |
| Sunny Murray | Jimmy Garrison |
| Billy Higgins | Scott LaFaro |
| Paul Motian | Buell Neidlinger |
| Barry Altschul | Gary Peacock |
| | Richard Davis |
| | Charles Mingus |

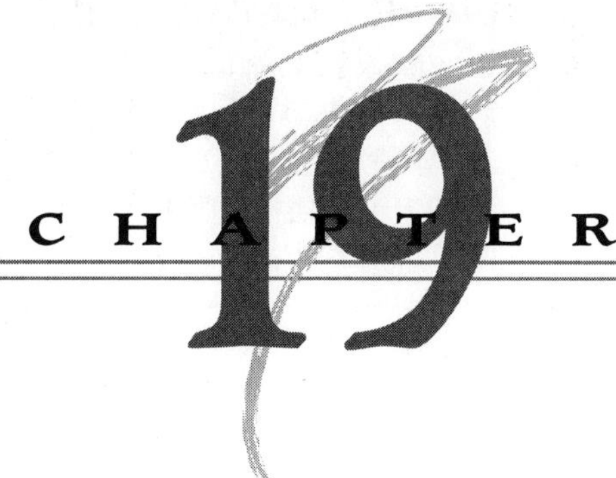


# Bill Evans

- Bill Evans (1926–1980) was born in Plainfield, New Jersey. He began piano lessons when he was six years old, but he was also interested in flute and violin. From 1946 to 1950, he majored in music at Southeastern Louisiana University where he studied mostly classical piano literature. He also worked with local bands in and around the New Orleans area. He spent 1951 in the military during the Korean War. Then he moved to New York, attending the Mannes College of Music, and working with local bands including one with guitarist Mundell Lowe.
- In 1956, Mundell Lowe recommended Evans to Orrin Keepnews at Riverside Records. As a result, Evans's first album, *New Jazz Conceptions,* was released later that same year on the Riverside label. This album contained "Waltz for Debbie," an original composition written for his niece by that name. "Waltz for Debbie" is but one of many Evans compositions that demonstrate his talent and originality as a jazz composer.
- Two years later Evans released his second album, *Everybody Digs Bill Evans*. It contained more impressive original compositions and demonstrated a unique, inventive approach to the performance of jazz standards within the context of the jazz piano trio.
- In 1958, Evans performed with Miles Davis's Quintet. In 1959, Evans recorded several modal selections on *Kind of Blue*. Even though Evans was only with the Davis band for eight months, his sensitive playing and influence on the band members, especially with regard to using modes as a melodic and harmonic source for composition and improvisation, was potent and deep.

- From 1959 to 1961, Evans led one of the most significant jazz piano trios of the twentieth century. The legendary trio had bassist **Scott LaFaro** and drummer **Paul Motian.** Their innovative and interactive approach to improvisation influenced all post-1960 jazz musicians. At times, each member was given an equal amount of importance within the overall context, and they frequently engaged in a "jazz conversation" responding to each other's "input." The end result was a new kind of freedom that still adhered to the boundaries of melody, harmony, time, and form but allowed each member's personality to assert itself at any given moment.
- **Scott LaFaro** (1936–1961) was one of the most important bass players to emerge in the late 1950s. He had the strings of his bass altered (they were brought closer to the fret board) to make it easier to play in the upper register where melodies are more pleasing and clear. As a result,

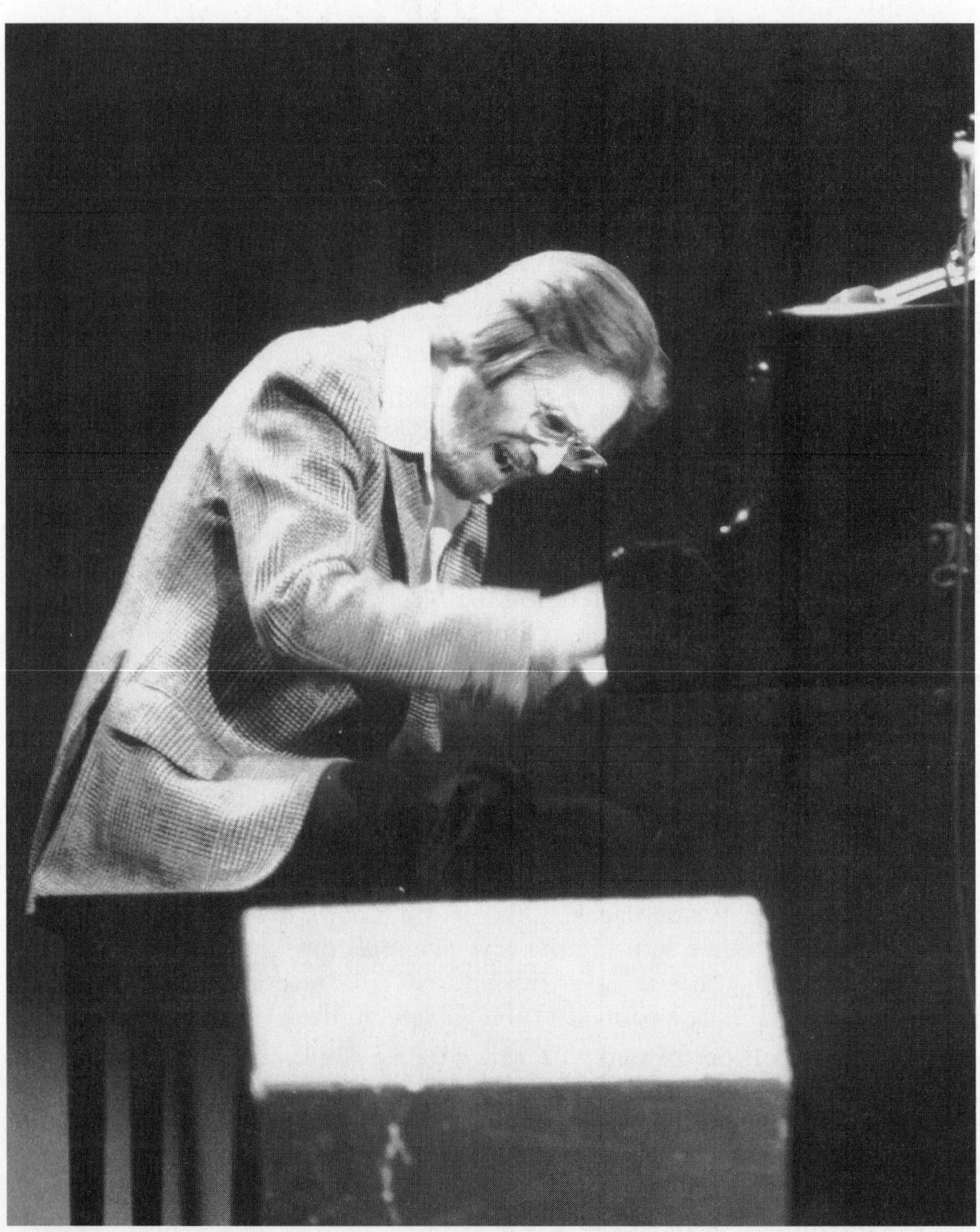

*Bill Evans. © Michael Ullman*

his prodigious bass solos demonstrated no technical limitations and were of an exceptional quality. In addition, rather than simply walking a bass line or playing a funk bass pattern, LaFaro would often depart from his traditional role as time keeper and engage in a melodic exchange with Evans contributing small melodic phrases to the overall texture.

- Paul Motian took the same approach in his drumming. He presented ideas using all the drums and cymbals at his disposal, implying melodies rather than just rhythms. He would, in essence, interject his "two cents" in the trio's "jazz conversation."
- The 1959 to 1961 Bill Evans Trio established a new approach to small-group jazz performance. Its influence on subsequent small groups would have far-reaching implications. *Portrait of Jazz* and *Explorations,* released in 1960 and 1961 by Riverside Records, are albums that featured both Evans compositions and jazz standards. The trio also recorded a live performance in June of 1961 at the Village Vanguard. Their momentum had quickly built to an exciting pace, and Bill Evans was especially optimistic about future developments. However, only two weeks after the Village Vanguard engagement, Scott LaFaro was tragically killed in a car accident.
- Evans dropped out of public sight for a year before returning to his trio format with Chuck Israels on bass. Evans continued to lead and develop his trio over the rest of his career. However, the magic chemistry of the LaFaro/Motian trio was never again duplicated.
- Evans developed an excellent rapport with bassist Eddie Gomez, who played with the Evans trio from 1966 to 1977. Other drummers that played with Evans include Philly Joe Jones, Jack DeJohnette, and Marty Morrell. His last trio, formed in 1978 with bassist Marc Johnson and drummer Joe LaBarbara, perhaps more accurately captured the essence of the 1960 trio than any other.
- Taking advantage of technological innovations in studio recording, Evans created recordings of multiple pianos that were all actually done by one person: himself. Using a process of overdubbing, he was able to play one part; then play the next part while listening to the first part; and so forth. He released these efforts using the word *conversations* in the titles:
  - *Conversations with Myself* (1963)
  - *Further Conversations* (1967)
  - *New Conversations* (1978)
- Evans also collaborated with Claus Ogerman in string orchestra arrangements that featured his trio. The album was titled *Bill Evans Trio with String Orchestra* and was released in 1965.
- Bill Evans was the most influential jazz pianist of the second half of the twentieth century. Bud Powell, Nat Cole, and Lennie Tristano were important influences in his development. However, he spent significant amounts of time studying the compositions of Maurice Ravel, Claude Debussy, Alexander Scriabin, Frederic Chopin, and other classical composers. These influences are apparent in both his compositions and his playing.
- Using a highly developed sense of touch, his style of playing was deeply personal and colorful. He tended to sustain his harmonies while creating

secondary melodies inside his left-hand chord voicings. His right-hand improvisations often rhythmically displaced phrases, creating the effect of complexity and sophistication. He also made extensive use of voicing melodies using the block chord method associated with Milt Buckner, George Shearing, and Errol Garner.

- Evans struggled with a heroin addiction throughout most of his career. He was able to kick the habit in the 1970s, but other drug and alcohol problems undoubtedly led to his untimely death in 1980.

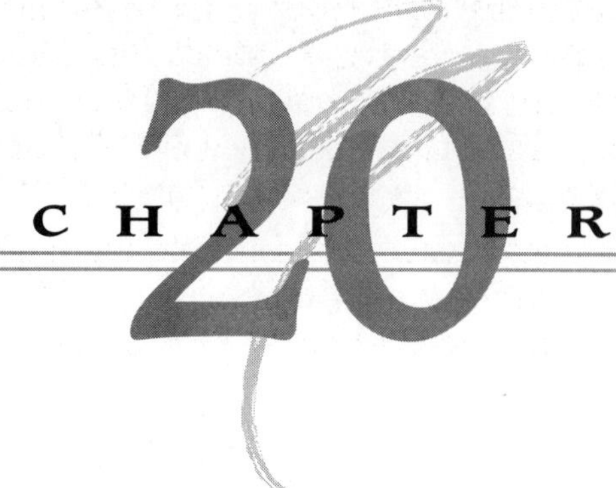

# CHAPTER 20

# John Coltrane

- John Coltrane was one of the most important musicians to come out of the 1950s. His full impact was felt in the 1960s and his playing directly influenced subsequent generations of improvisers.
- A creative artist second to none, he helped move jazz improvisation to a new level. He had great endurance, tremendous technique, and the ability to use the entire range of the saxophone. He played with great passion and power. His concepts of improvisation have been absorbed by saxophonists, pianists, trumpet players, and guitarists. He also helped extend the length of solos on recordings. Because of the length of many of his live recordings, we can hear how he was able to develop his ideas during his solos.
- He did not begin to receive much critical recognition until the late 1950s, although he began playing professionally after World War II, playing alto sax around Philadelphia. He performed with Dizzy Gillespie, Johnny Hodges, and numerous rhythm and blues bands in the early 1950s.
- Miles Davis added him to his quintet in 1955, and for the next five years he would record and perform mostly with the Davis quintet. Several important recordings were made with Miles, including *Kind of Blue*.
- Coltrane also spent several months in the fall of 1957 performing at the Five Spot with Thelonious Monk. Monk encouraged him to play long solos that allowed great latitude for musical exploration. Coltrane once commented about his association with Monk, "Working with Monk brought me close to a musical architect of the highest order. I would talk to Monk about musical problems and he would show me the answers by playing them on the piano. He gave me complete freedom in my playing, and no one ever did that before." It cannot be a coincidence that

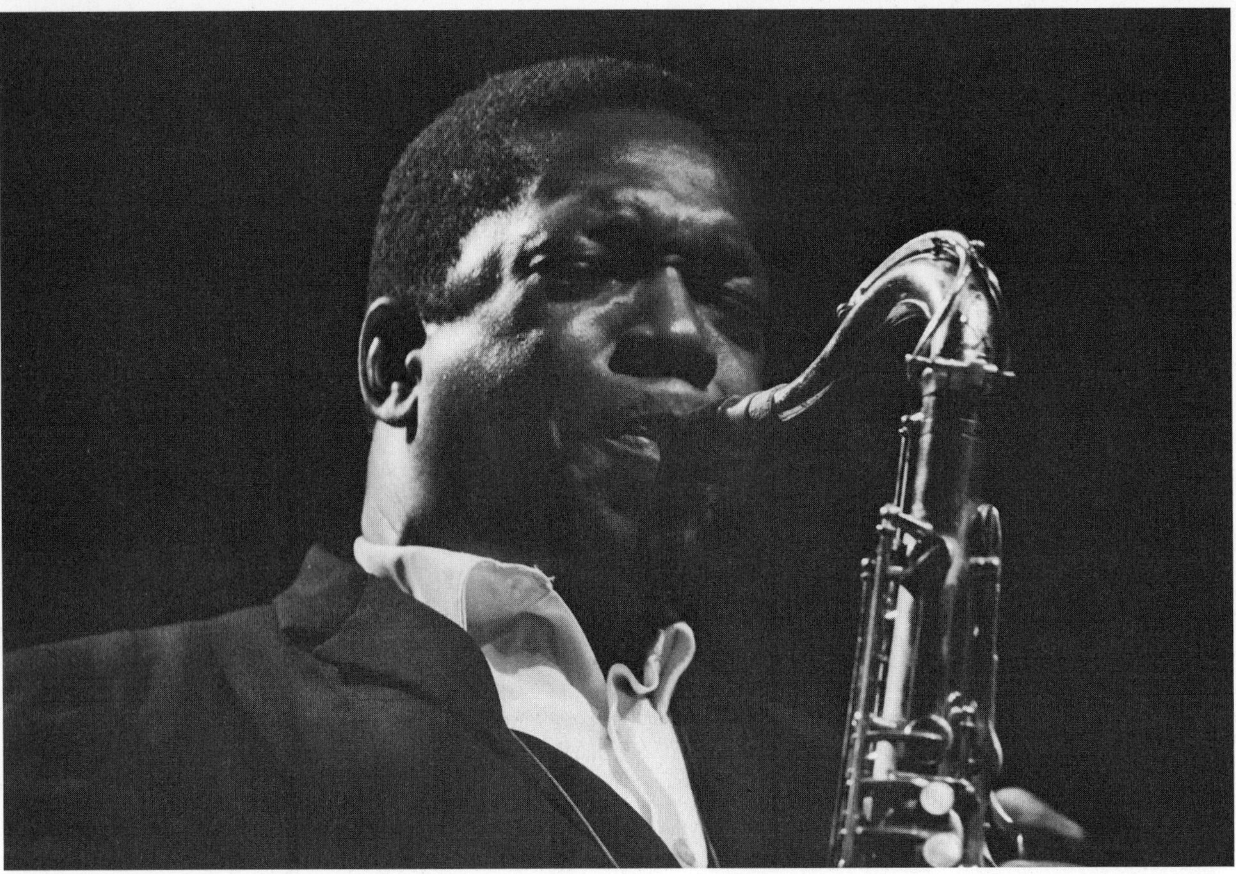

*John Coltrane. © Ted Williams/CORBI*

Coltrane began to assert himself as a formidable jazz virtuoso not long after spending time as a Monk sideman.

- During his time with Miles Davis, Coltrane also made important recordings under his own name, including *Blue Train, Lush Life, Coltrane Jazz,* and *Giant Steps*.
- Coltrane's first influences include Charlie Parker, Coleman Hawkins, Lester Young, Dexter Gordon, and Johnny Hodges. Coltrane's sound came from Hawkins, Hodges, and Gordon, while his bebop influence came from Parker and Sonny Stitt. His preference for intricate chord progressions was reminiscent of Coleman Hawkins.
- Coltrane's saxophone solos were so packed with ideas that they seemed to cascade out of his horn. He tended to fill every bar with as many notes as one could possibly play. This kind of playing has been described by jazz critics as "sheets of sound."
- Many of his pre-1960 compositions demonstrate an infatuation with complex chord changes and harmonic complexity. A famous chord progression he used on the composition "Giant Steps" is based on a major third relationship. This seemingly mathematical approach proved to be very challenging for his contemporaries. His ability to play with great ease over these difficult progressions at fast tempos set new standards for hard bop improvisers in the 1960s and is a significant part of the Coltrane legacy.
- In addition to his ability to play these complex compositions, he was one of the most sensitive interpreters of ballads and a master of playing the

blues. His composition "Naima" from *Giant Steps* is a wonderful example of his sensitive ballad playing, and its use of pedal points (drone effect) in the harmonic progression foreshadowed developments of 1960s Coltrane compositions.

- His post-1960 music changed dramatically. His compositions from this period do not reflect his interest in complicated chord progressions. He abandoned the complex harmonies of "Giant Steps" in favor of more loosely constructed pieces.
- His playing after 1960 shows the influence of avant-garde musicians such as Ornette Coleman, John Gilmore, and Albert Ayler.
- Coltrane began to utilize the high (altissimo) range of the tenor sax indicating a preference for this range. An important related development, he chose to play the soprano saxophone on two selections of his album *My Favorite Things* in 1960. The soprano saxophone has since become a standard instrument in jazz.
- In the late 1950s, Coltrane underwent a spiritual transformation that was strongly reflected in his music. He was also interested in the exploration of Indian and African music. By the early 1960s, there appeared a change in the character of much of his music; there was a meditative, prayerlike quality to many of his compositions and playing. He had abandoned the hard bop style of the 1950s in favor of this new approach.
- Many of his recordings (*Favorite Things, Meditations, Expressions, Love Supreme*) are characterized by the swaying, hypnotic feeling of Elvin Jones's drumming style coupled with simple harmonic structures.
- Much of his music after 1960 is based on modal (one or two tonal centers) or free jazz (no or loosely preset harmonies). His solos remain extremely complex, and at times he seems to spontaneously create chord progressions. Fewer numbers of chord changes gave him the freedom to generate his melodies with less restriction.
- By 1965, his music was becoming more abstract while moving further away from traditional chord-based improvisation. The experimental nature of the group brought textural density, dissonance, and high levels of intensity to the forefront of modern jazz.
- Many of his compositions use pedal point, or drone effects. A pedal point effect is created when the bassist repeats one note for an indefinite period of time, as opposed to playing in a "walking" style. The drone effect helps build tension. Sometimes bassist Jimmy Garrison would strum a number of strings on the bass to create the drone.

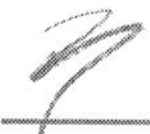

## JOHN COLTRANE QUARTET (1960–1965)

- John Coltrane formed his groundbreaking quartet with outstanding young musicians. He felt that they could provide him with the energy, drive, and appropriate musical background that he required. The group consisted of a number of bassists until he settled on Jimmy Garrison, McCoy Tyner on piano, and Elvin Jones on drums. He would occasionally augment the group with bass clarinetist/alto saxophonist Eric Dolphy.

- Tyner, Garrison, and Jones broke new ground in the way they played together. They provided extreme levels of energy and intensity necessary to match Coltrane's intense playing.
- Pianist McCoy Tyner developed an innovative way to voice chords based on the interval of a fourth, sometimes referred to as quartal voicings. By combining the quartal voicings in the middle register of the piano with the interval of a fifth in the low register used as a drone, this open, hollow sound gave Coltrane great latitude for his improvisations. Tyner would often let notes on the piano ring by holding the keys down or using the sustain pedal. This new approach to chord voicings has had a major impact on jazz pianists since the 1960s.
- Elvin Jones's drumming style was based on the triplet figure. Instead of consistently playing swing ride rhythms, he would usually play some variation of moving triplets on different parts of the drum set. Often triplet figures would occupy several measures. He rarely played anything on the beat. This created the swaying and hypnotic feel that characterizes much of Coltrane's music. At other times, Jones played so forcefully that he seemed to overwhelm the other musicians.
- In 1965, Coltrane began using musicians more associated with free jazz such as drummer Rashied Ali and saxophonists Pharaoh Sanders and Archie Shepp. Eventually Elvin Jones and McCoy Tyner became dissatisfied and quit Coltrane's group.
- Coltrane was searching for new modes of expression that took him far beyond what most 1950s jazz musicians could comprehend. The search took him through many phases of development, ultimately to his most abstract recordings such as *Ascension, Expression,* and *Interstellar Space*. Some of this music was well received, but often it was met with resistance from jazz critics.
- Although Coltrane died in 1967, many saxophonists continue to be influenced by him in terms of sound and improvisational style. The following is a partial list of Coltrane-influenced tenor saxophonists:

  Albert Ayler
  Pharaoh Sanders
  Jerry Bergonzi
  Michael Brecker
  Steve Grossman
  Charles Lloyd
  Branford Marsalis
  Joshua Redman
  Archie Shepp
  Bob Berg
  Joe Lovano
  Joe Farrell
  Dave Liebman
  Wayne Shorter
  Booker Ervin
  Joe Henderson

## SUMMARY OF JOHN COLTRANE'S IMPORTANCE

- Repertoire of improvisational patterns that have become basic to modern jazz
- Extended the techniques of saxophone playing
- Use of soprano sax

- Modal improvisation
- New rhythm section concepts
- Emphasis on technique and intensity
- Body of original compositions
- Model for tone color and rhythmic conception on sax
- System for juxtaposing/superimposing distantly related chords
- Extremely complex subdivisions of rhythm: groupings of seven, nine, or eleven notes per beat, resulting in "sheets of sound"

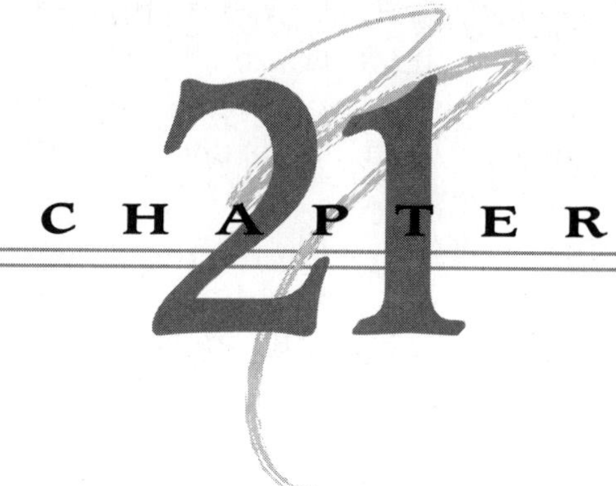

# CHAPTER 21

# (Jazz-Rock) Fusion

- Fusion covers a wide variety of approaches to post-1960s jazz. It combines jazz with the sounds of rock and funk music (nonjazz) from the 1960s and other sources. This may include the Motown sound, James Brown rhythm section style, the Beatles, psychedelic rock to folk rock, and the Afro-Cuban Latin style.
- The mid-1960s brought about a revolution in popular music with the British invasion of 1964. The invasion was the Beatles and a number of other British pop-rock bands that gained widespread popularity the following year.
- This was important to the jazz scene because record companies saw the potential for quick money in rock music versus jazz. The public's taste in music had been moving away from the sound of jazz for at least a decade. This left many jazz musicians and their record companies in a quandary.
- Free jazz, although exciting, groundbreaking, and abstract, did not approach near the popularity of cool or hard bop. In fact, it alienated many audiences. Even the biggest names in jazz were having difficulty filling venues, while rock acts were filling baseball stadiums.
- Nightclubs that formerly featured jazz were closing or were featuring rock or Motown-style acts. Many jazz musicians found employment working for these artists.
- Acoustic jazz and its accoutrements seemed old and dated to teenagers in the 1960s. The strongly visual aspect of rock music is important to the audience, and most jazz musicians were unable or unwilling to move in that direction.

- Many jazz musicians were not willing to address pop music, and they ran the risk of being forgotten. That is not to say that well-established jazz groups/artists did not release outstanding recordings during this period. Other jazz musicians chose to move to Europe to find employment there.
- Several British bands from the mid-1960s began fusing elements of modal jazz, rock, and blues. Some of them achieved a huge success, such as the Cream, the Graham Bond Organization, John Mayall's Blues Breakers, Soft Machine, Jethro Tull, King Crimson, and Emerson Lake, and Palmer. Two important British musicians from this period who would make a lasting impression were guitarist John McLaughlin and bassist Dave Holland.
- Some jazz musicians continued to play as if it were still the 1950s, but others were receptive to the new sounds on the radio. Motown, the Beatles, Sly Stone, Jimi Hendrix, and the psychedelic sound of the late 1960s had an effect on jazz musicians.
- Black R&B music of the 1950s, the basis of rock and roll, took a different turn in the 1960s. R&B often contained more complicated rhythms than rock. Out of this genre came the intricate bass and drum patterns that were the trademark of artists like James Brown and other famous Motown groups. The Motown sound of the 1960s draws heavily from this approach; most of the session musicians on these recordings were jazz musicians. Very few of the big-name Motown artists played instruments.
- Much of the early jazz-rock sound centered on slow moving or modal harmony. This shows the jazz influence of:
    - Miles Davis's *Kind of Blue* (modal improvisation)
    - John Coltrane's modal-based improvisations
    - Indian music
    - Ornette Coleman's free jazz approach
- The emergence of a new style of rhythm section playing that moved away from swing eighth notes and ride rhythms to the feel of rock (even eighth notes) or R&B rhythms altered the style of improvisation. Some of it was still chord based, but the bop cliches of the 1950s were no longer appropriate. With some improvisers, technique became as important as substance.
- Keyboard players' comping styles changed. They began to use the new electronic instruments such as electric pianos or synthesizers to create new sounds, colors, and textures. Bassists used more repetitive staccato figures. Drummers utilized more Latin flavors, played more actively, moved away from traditional swing rhythms, and used fewer cymbals and more drums.
- John Coltrane, Freddie Hubbard, Chick Corea, McCoy Tyner, and Herbie Hancock continued to be role models for the new generation of improvisers. Coltrane, in particular, was the inspiration for many rock guitarists of the 1960s and early 1970s.
- A few jazz musicians utilized the new rock-influenced sounds: Miles Davis, Gary Burton, Larry Coryell, Herbie Mann, Herbie Hancock, Tony Williams, and Joe Zawinul were among the best-known jazz

musicians to fuse elements of the popular sound with their own in a highly original way.

The following are some popular artists/groups that influenced jazz musicians:

- ♪ Sly and the Family Stone
- ♪ James Brown (rhythm section)
- ♪ Jimi Hendrix
- ♪ Ravi Shankar (Indian sitarist)

- Guitar players began to move away from the sound of Wes Montgomery to a rock sound, complete with sound-altering devices such as a wa-wa pedal, echoplex, and fuzz tone. The technique was still jazz oriented, but the sound was completely different. The acoustic bass was often eliminated in favor of the electric bass.
- In the mid-1960s, a group of young jazz musicians with similar interests living in New York formed a loose alliance that began mixing elements of rock/funk with jazz. The group included the following:

| | |
|---|---|
| Larry Coryell, guitar | Bob Moses, drums |
| Joe Beck, guitar | Randy Brecker, trumpet |
| Mike Mainieri, vibes | Warren Bernhardt, piano |
| Gary Burton, vibes | Michael Brecker, tenor saxophone |

- Important bands of the 1960s and early 1970s that fused elements of rock and jazz from this period include the following:

| | |
|---|---|
| Larry Coryell's Free Spirits | Gary Burton Quartet |
| Steve Marcus' Count's Rock Band | Fourth Way |
| Jeremy Steig and the Satyrs | Mike Manieri's White Elephant |
| Blood Sweat and Tears | Dreams |
| Al Kooper/Mike Bloomfield | Electric Flag |
| Chicago (early period) | The Flock |
| Chase | Charles Lloyd Quartet |
| Tony Williams Lifetime | |

## Soul Jazz

| | |
|---|---|
| Cannonball Adderley Quintet | Lee Morgan's "The Sidewinder" |
| Ramsey Lewis Trio | Herbie Mann Quartet |

- The following are groups from the 1970s who integrated the latest technological innovations into their overall concept:

| | |
|---|---|
| The Brecker Brothers | Return to Forever |
| Mahavishnu Orchestra | Weather Report |
| Prime Time (Ornette Coleman) | Headhunters (Herbie Hancock) |
| The L.A. Express (Tom Scott) | |

### Jazz-Flavored Artists/Bands

The Crusaders
Jeff Lorber Fusion
Grover Washington
George Benson
Kenny G
Hubert Laws
Spyrogyra
Steely Dan
Tower of Power
Chuck Mangione
Tom Browne
Herbie Mann

### Post-1980s

The YellowJackets
Steps Ahead
Pat Metheny Group
Chick Corea Elektric Band
Dave Grusin
Bela Fleck and the Flecktones

### Important figures in jazz-rock fusion

| TRUMPET | ALTO SAX | TENOR SAX | VIOLIN |
|---|---|---|---|
| Miles Davis | Dave Sanborn | Michael Brecker | Jon Luc Ponty |
| Randy Brecker | Hank Crawford | Grover Washington | Jerry Goodman |
| | Paul McCandless | Wayne Shorter | Michael Urbaniak |
| | | Tom Scott | |
| | | John Klemmer | |
| | | Dave Liebman | |
| | | Branford Marsalis | |
| | | Joe Farrell | |

| KEYBOARD | BASS | DRUMS | GUITAR |
|---|---|---|---|
| Herbie Hancock | Jaco Pastorius | Billy Cobham | John McLaughlin |
| Chick Corea | Stanley Clarke | Lenny White | John Scofield |
| Joe Zawinul | Michael Henderson | Jack DeJohnette | Pat Metheny |
| Don Grolnick | John Patitucci | Tony Williams | Al DiMeola |
| Bob James | Marcus Miller | Steve Gadd | Larry Coryell |
| George Duke | Jimmy Haslip | Peter Erskine | Bill Frisell |
| Mike Nock | Abe Laboriel | Alphonse Mouzon | Scott Henderson |
| Jan Hammer | Miroslav Vitous | Dave Weckl | Ralph Towner |
| Dave Grusin | Jeff Berlin | | George Benson |
| | Eddie Gomez | | |
| | Marc Johnson | | |

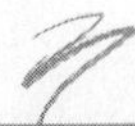

## MILES DAVIS FUSION BANDS

- Miles Davis was one of the first well-established jazz musicians to experiment with mixing musical devices of rock and funk with jazz. In hindsight it should not come as a surprise to anyone who has followed Davis's career. Miles was always looking for new means to express his music and saw a way to reach the audience by coming up with yet another way to express his music.

- In 1968, Miles changed the way he organized his group by inviting guests to sit in on his recording sessions, creating a jam session-like atmosphere. The year 1968 was the end of his well-established bands in terms of personnel. He frequently drew from a pool of like-minded musicians. He combined members of his mid-1960s-era group with younger musicians who were comfortable in the new jazz-rock idiom.
- His recordings of "Eighty-One" from the album *E.S.P* or "Freedom Jazz Dance" from the album *Miles Smiles* feature straight eighth notes played by drummer Tony Williams on cymbals and simple repetitive Motown-like bass figures played by Ron Carter that bear a striking resemblance to popular dance music.
- Miles insisted that electric piano be used in place of the acoustic piano beginning with the 1968 recording *Miles in the Sky.* His next album, *Filles de Kilimanjaro,* marks a move further away from the sound of his mid-1960s quintet.
- The albums *In a Silent Way* and *Bitches Brew,* released in 1969, helped change the direction of much jazz in the 1970s. Miles sometimes utilized as many as three keyboard players simultaneously and several percussionists on each recording. The melodies were more in the realm of rock, and the overall texture suggests a dark, floating, motionless feel.
- Miles met keyboardist Joe Zawinul in the late 1960s, and they began a series of collaborative efforts that were reminiscent of Davis's relationship with Gil Evans in the late 1940s and 1950s. Zawinul was the keyboard player with Cannonball Adderley's quintet and is the composer of the well-known composition "Mercy, Mercy, Mercy." Zawinul cowrote or wrote a number of pieces recorded by Davis in the late 1960s.
- Miles Davis's post-1968 recordings differ greatly from the previous period in the following ways:
- The electric piano, synthesizers, and organ replaced acoustic piano.
- Electric bass replaced acoustic bass.
- Studio overdubs and spliced recordings were used.
- Started using guitar players whose sound was influenced by Jimi Hendrix.
- Sax players spent more time on soprano saxophone in order to be heard.
- Often employed two to three drummers/percussionists.
- Improvisation was more concerned with color, texture, spontaneity, and mood.
- Did not utilize conventionally constructed compositions, nor did the musicians improvise on traditional harmony in the postbop style.
- Miles utilized the high register more often and used sound-altering devices such as a wa-wa pedal or an echoplex.
- Miles's playing was sometimes free of a steady pulse.
- Most of the complexity centered on the way the rhythm section functions.

Many of the musicians who worked with Davis from the mid-1960s went on to become bandleaders and formed their own fusion bands.

Wayne Shorter, tenor and soprano sax
Tony Williams, drums
Herbie Hancock, keyboard
Chick Corea, keyboard
Jack DeJohnette, drums
Bill Evans, tenor saxophone
Bob Berg, tenor and soprano saxophone
Joe Zawinul, keyboard
John Scofield, guitar
John McLaughlin, guitar
Dave Liebman, tenor saxophone
Mike Stern, guitar
Bennie Maupin, bass clarinet
Don Alias, congas
Dave Holland, bass

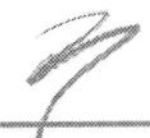

## JOHN McLAUGHLIN

- Important British guitarist whose career started in the early 1960s.
- Played with drummer Tony Williams Lifetime (1969)—one of the first "power" trios emulating Jimi Hendrix mixed with a dose of free jazz.
- Recorded with Miles Davis where his playing was an integral part of *In a Silent Way, Jack Johnson*, and *Bitches Brew*.
- Possesses tremendous technique.
- Influenced many subsequent guitarists because of his cutting sound, unlike the typical warm jazz sound.
- Shows the influence of John Coltrane.
- Does not play swing eighth notes, but instead plays rather evenly.
- Interested in Indian music, employing many Indian instruments and musicians.
- His work with the Mahavishnu Orchestra reflects his interest in Indian music with its busy themes, changing meters, high volume, and *sheets of sound* approach to improvisation.

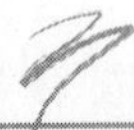

## WEATHER REPORT

- Keyboardist Joe Zawinul, together with Wayne Shorter and bassist Miroslav Vitous, joined together to form a new group called Weather Report. The group had two drummers, one playing traditional drum set and the other playing exotic percussion instruments from around the world. Together they formed this band to explore new ideas in improvised music.

- All three were well-established jazz musicians who could play in the postbop idiom. Shorter and Zawinul were two of the most important jazz composers of the 1960s and 1970s. They intended to focus on improvised music, but not in a traditional postbop style. Each member of the group was an exceptional improviser and could spontaneously create highly original music.
- Weather Report was one of the most original fusion bands because they looked not only to rock and funk but also to the entire musical world for inspiration. Each successive album was different from the previous, as were the selections within each album.
- Their music is difficult to categorize because it represents a combination of many different approaches, which even include nonjazz styles:
  - ♪ Twentieth-century orchestral music
  - ♪ Funk music
  - ♪ Collective improvisation
  - ♪ Improvisation of texture and timbre
  - ♪ Music of other cultures and countries
  - ♪ More emphasis on improvisation than typical fusion bands
  - ♪ Extensive use of synthesizers
  - ♪ Use of exotic percussion instruments
  - ♪ Overdubbing in recording studios
  - ♪ Free-form music
- Weather Report abandoned the concept of individuals taking solos while the rhythm section accompanied. Wayne Shorter's saxophone playing became rather sparse, and solo interjections could come from any member of the band in order to complete an idea or create a mood or texture.
- In 1976, the brilliant electric fretless bassist and composer Jaco Pastorius joined the band. He brought another new dimension to the band by way of his compositions and innovative bass playing.
- By 1980, Pastorius had revolutionized the way the bass was played and set a new standard for bass players, continuing an evolution of innovative bass playing that began with Walter Page and Jimmy Blanton in the 1930s through Scott LaFaro in the early 1960s. After one exposure to Weather Report when Jaco was playing bass, the listener came away in awe of his prowess. He was capable of producing the same effect that Louis Armstrong created with his amazing trumpet solos many years earlier.

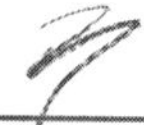

## HERBIE HANCOCK—KEYBOARD, COMPOSER

- Herbie Hancock (born 1940) was born in Chicago, Illinois. He began piano lessons at age seven and quickly demonstrated prodigious talent by giving his first performance two years later. He performed with the Chicago Symphony Orchestra at eleven years of age. He is well versed in classical music, but he has emphasized mostly jazz throughout his

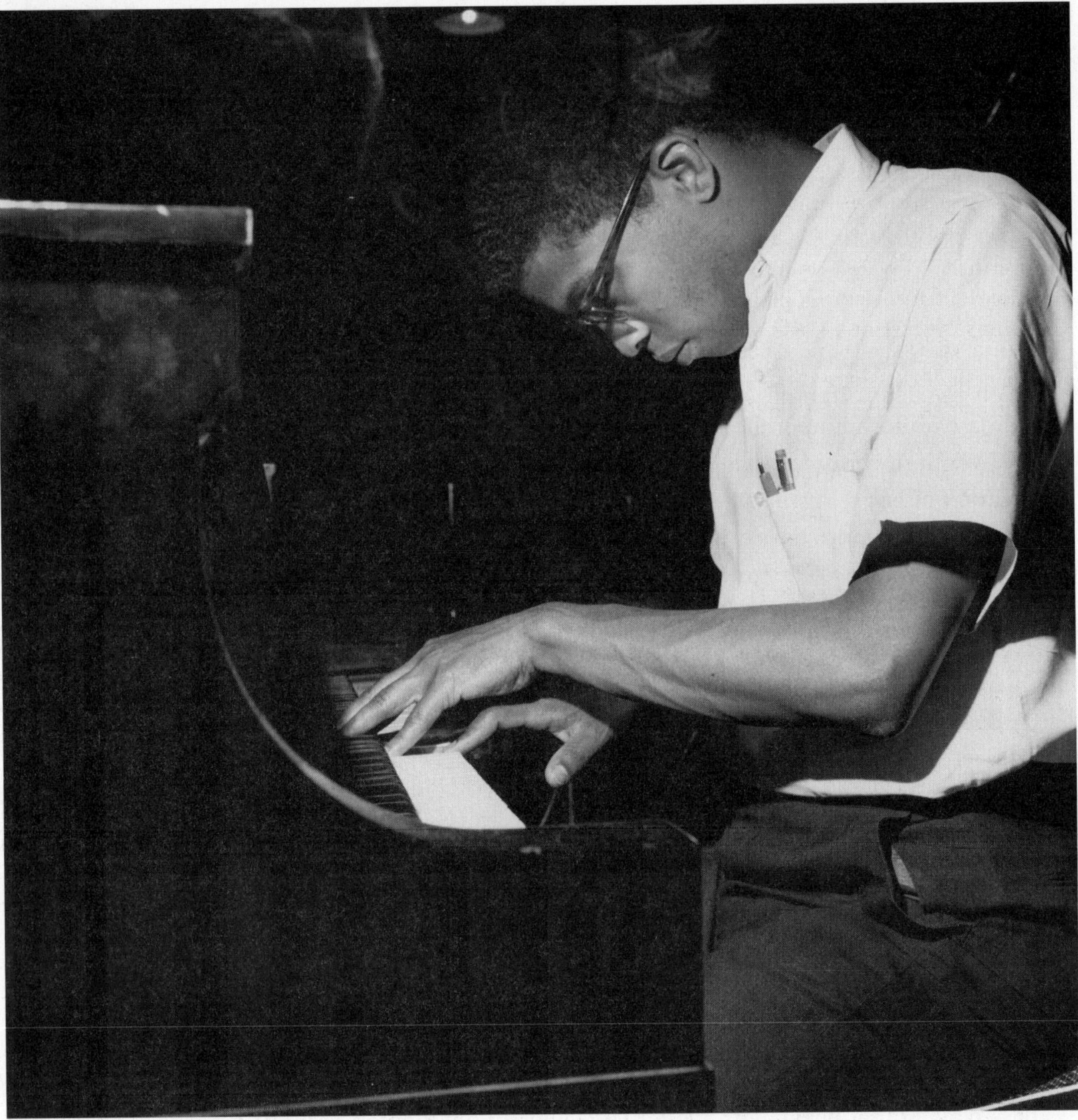

*Herbie Hancock.* © *Mosaic/CORBIS*

career. While in high school and college (Grinnell College), he played with local jazz groups and occasionally accompanied well-known jazz musicians. He graduated from Grinnell College with a degree in music composition in 1960.

- In 1960, Hancock moved to New York where he played and recorded with a band led by Donald Byrd.
- In 1963, Blue Note Records released Hancock's first solo album, *Taking Off* with trumpeter Freddie Hubbard and tenor saxophonist Dexter Gordon. Hancock's compositional skills became apparent when "Watermelon Man," a funk-influenced selection on the album, was recorded by Mongo Santamaría and became a Top 10 hit.

- From 1963 to 1968, Hancock was a member of the now-legendary Miles Davis Quintet.
- In 1965, Hancock released *Maiden Voyage*, an album of Hancock compositions featuring drummer Tony Williams, bassist Ron Carter, tenor saxophonist George Coleman, and trumpeter Freddie Hubbard. "Maiden Voyage," the title selection, uses four different modes in creating an oceanlike texture in order to depict one's first voyage out to sea. "Eye of the Hurricane" uses hard bop effects as it gets across the experience of being in a hurricane. "Dolphin Dance" is a lovely ballad that creates the carefree nature of dolphins at sea. Hancock's ability to combine influences from different jazz styles on *Maiden Voyage* established him as one of the most prominent jazz pianists and composers among the current generation of jazz musicians. Miles Davis described Hancock as the heir to the Bud Powell and Thelonious Monk legacy.
- In 1969, Hancock used electric piano on Miles Davis's double album *Bitches Brew*. In the 1970s, he performed and recorded jazz that combined electric instruments with the rhythms of rock music.
- In 1973, his album *Headhunters* was an instant success, and its hit single, "Chameleon," became popular with both jazz and rock audiences. As a talented musician at home with electric instruments and the latest technological innovations for keyboards, Hancock used a keyboard synthesizer, an ARP String Ensemble, a Fender Rhodes electric piano, and a Hohner clavinet on the album.
- In the late 1970s, Hancock returned to a more traditional acoustic instrumentation as he recorded and performed with the V.S.O.P. Quintet (the Miles Davis 1960s Quintet with Freddie Hubbard on trumpet rather than Miles), the Herbie Hancock Quartet, and a series of duo piano concerts with Chick Corea.
- In the 1980s, Hancock released several albums that again demonstrated he could incorporate current developments in popular music into his music. *Future Shock* was one such album and included a "record scratcher" as part of the band. "Rockit," a highlight of the album, won a Grammy Award for best R&B instrumental.
- Herbie Hancock, as one of the preeminent jazz musicians of the second half of the twentieth century, has demonstrated he is a creative and convincing musician regardless of the style or context of his music.
- Hancock has also written music for movies (Antonioni's *Blow Up*, Bertrand Tavernier's *Round Midnight, A Soldier's Story, Jo Jo Dancer, Action Jackson, Harlem Nights, Colors*) and television (Bill Cosby's *Hey, Hey, It's Fat Albert*).

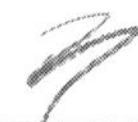

## KEITH JARRETT—PIANO

- Keith Jarrett (born 1945) was born in Allentown, Pennsylvania. He began playing piano at the age of three. He studied classical music in his youth and was an acknowledged child prodigy by the time he was twelve. He briefly attended the Berklee School of Music in Boston when he was fifteen years old. When he was in his late teens, he moved to New York.

- For a brief period in the mid-1960s, he played with Art Blakey's Jazz Messengers. Then in 1966 he joined the Charles Lloyd Quartet. From 1970 to 1971, he played electric piano and organ with the fusion band led by Miles Davis.
- Jarrett released significant recordings in the 1970s of his solo improvisations on acoustic piano. He vehemently disliked using electronic instruments and established himself as an exclusively acoustic artist. He toured all over the world presenting himself as a solo jazz pianist who could improvise an entire concert. In addition, Jarrett often did not use the standard jazz repertoire (or any other repertoire) as vehicles for improvisation, but instead he improvised entirely new compositions in each performance. Such performances were recorded live and have been released as *Solo Concerts, The Köln Concert, Sun Bear Concerts, Paris Concert, Dark Intervals,* and *Vienna Concert.*
- In 1983, Jarrett formed a Bill Evans-influenced trio with bassist Gary Peacock and drummer Jack DeJohnette. They use the standard jazz repertoire as a point of departure for their trio improvisations.
- Jarrett has made numerous recordings of the compositions of such classical composers as J. S. Bach, Dmitri Shostakovich, Béla Bartòk, Paul Hindemith, and Igor Stravinsky. He has also performed with world-renowned orchestras including the San Francisco Symphony, Philadelphia Orchestra, Brooklyn Philharmonic, and the Beethovenhalle Orchestra Bonn.

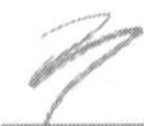

## CHICK COREA—KEYBOARD, COMPOSER, BANDLEADER

- Anthony Armando (Chick) Corea (born 1941) was born in Chelsea, Massachusetts. Inspired by his father, who was a bandleader in the 1930s and 1940s, he began playing piano at four years of age. Corea's early influences include Bud Powell, Horace Silver, Lester Young, and Charlie Parker. He also listened to classical music.
- Corea first played with bands led by Willie Bobo, Cal Tjader, Herbie Mann, and Mongo Santamaria. Corea's experience with Santamaria's band produced a love for Latin music that would influence much of his playing and composing in the 1970s and 1980s.
- Latin pianists play the piano in a percussive manner. In fact, the piano is perceived to be an equal member of the percussion section in Latin bands. Salsa rhythms are commonly used as a means of comping for Latin pianists. Corea incorporated these and other Latin techniques into his jazz playing.
- In the late 1960s, Corea recorded *Now He Sings, Now He Sobs* with bassist Miroslav Vitous and drummer Roy Haynes. Influenced by Bill Evans trios, this album established Corea as an important bandleader and composer.
- In 1968, Corea joined Miles Davis's fusion band participating in the highly successful *Bitches Brew* sessions.
- From 1969 to 1971, Corea led an avant-garde group called Circle with bassist Dave Holland, drummer Barry Altschul, and saxophonist

Anthony Braxton. Circle was influenced by Ornette Coleman but also incorporated ideas taken from the music of John Cage and Karl Stockhausen.

- In 1972, Corea used the Fender Rhodes electric piano in his group Return to Forever, a jazz fusion band. With band members Stanley Clarke on bass, Airto Moreira on drums, Joe Farrell on flute and tenor saxophone, and Flora Purim on vocals, Return to Forever recorded mostly Corea compositions. Corea's electric piano sound often combined with Farrell's flute to create a unique timbre. The electric piano often used salsa rhythms to accompany Flora Purim's airy vocals. The light, Latin-influenced sound they created was most effective on "Spain" from *Light as a Feather* (1973) and "La Fiesta" on *Return to Forever* (1972).
- From 1974 to 1976, Corea changed personnel and instrumentation in his second version of the Return to Forever band. Al DiMeola played acoustic and electric guitar, Stanley Clarke played bass, and Lenny White played drums. Corea used an assortment of keyboard instruments including the Micromoog synthesizer, Hohner clavinet, Fender Rhodes electric piano, and acoustic piano. Albums such as *No Mystery* (1975) and *Romantic Warrior* (1976) had a modern-sounding instrumentation with sophisticated Corea compositions and arrangements that demonstrated both classical and jazz influences.
- In 1985, Corea formed the Elektric Band with bassist John Patitucci and drummer Dave Weckl. The Elektric Band has made use of the latest technological innovations on all instruments. Corea made extensive use of the latest digital technology available to keyboard players. Patitucci used a six-string electric bass, making it more possible for him to build on the accomplishments of Jaco Pastorius. Dave Weckl incorporated electronic drums into his acoustic drum setup. Albums such as *The Chick Corea Elektric Band* (1986), *Light Years* (1987), *Eye of the Beholder* (1988), *Inside Out* (1990), *Beneath the Mask* (1991), and *Paint the World* (1993) have established Chick Corea as a top fusion bandleader, keyboard player, and composer of the 1980s and 1990s.
- In 1989, Corea, Patitucci, and Weckl released *The Akoustic Band*, an album of jazz standards performed in the traditional jazz piano trio setting. These musicians demonstrated they were just as comfortable playing acoustic instruments, implying perhaps that it's the music that matters most, not necessarily the instrumentation.

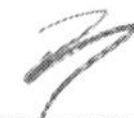

## PAT METHENY—GUITAR, BAND LEADER, COMPOSER

- Pat Metheny (born 1954) was born and raised near Kansas City. He began playing trumpet at age eight and became interested in guitar at age thirteen. When he was fifteen he was already working with professional jazz musicians in the Kansas City area.
- In 1972, he attended the University of Miami where he came into contact with many top- quality jazz musicians including Jaco Pastorius, with whom he would later collaborate. From 1974 to 1977, he performed with vibraphonist Gary Burton. He also founded a trio with bassist Jaco

Pastorius and drummer Bob Moses, which performed together from 1975 to the end of 1976.

- Metheny's first album, *Bright Size Life*, recorded with his trio, was released in 1975. It established him as a new, up-and-coming jazz guitarist with a unique, original sound. His conception was modern yet derivative of traditional styles such as bebop, hard bop, blues, and rock.
- In 1977, Metheny formed the Pat Metheny Group with pianist Lyle Mays, bassist Mark Egan, and drummer Danny Gottlieb. They released their first album entitled *The Pat Metheny Group* in 1978.
- With the release of *American Garage* in 1980, the Pat Metheny Group was voted "Top Group" and Pat Metheny "Best Jazz Guitarist of the Year" by the New York Jazz Awards and Cashbox. Since that time, Pat Metheny and his group have traveled all over the world giving concerts and receiving awards and recognition for their high quality of music.
- Metheny has also been active as a jazz educator. He has taught at the University of Miami and Berkelee College of Music (in Boston), two of the top jazz educational institutions in the world. As a musician on the cutting edge of technology, Metheny has endorsed synthesizers and MIDI instruments as a viable means of musical expression. He has been a consistent winner of polls for "Best Jazz Guitarist," and he received an honorary doctorate in 1996.

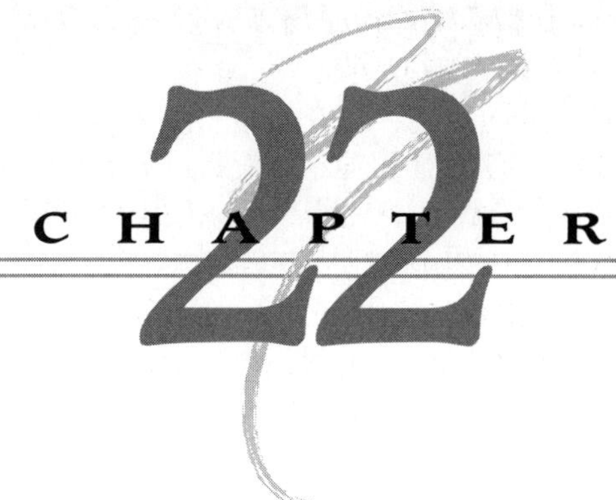


# The Future of Jazz

- Jazz is a universal language that does not obey geographic boundaries. It may not remain "America's only art form" forever. Jazz is changing and being changed by the music from around the world.
- For most creative musicians, it is no longer sufficient to be familiar with conventional jazz formats: play the melody, take solos, trade fours, and take the song out. In order for jazz to grow, it must change and continue to evolve.
- The alliance of jazz and the ethnic music of different cultures is taking place. Many musicians do not consider themselves strictly jazz musicians. Some of the most creative combine improvisation with classical, folk (ethnic), funk, bebop, and odd meters to come up with an original fusion.
- There are highly original fusions of jazz with klezmer music of Eastern Europe as well as music from Turkey and India.
- Jazz musicians are no longer strictly American born. The Middle East, Europe, Africa, and Asia have produced musicians capable of highly original approaches. At the same time, virtuoso musicians from far-off cultures/countries are collaborating with American jazz musicians with interesting and original results.
- One can now go to just about any city in the modern world and hear excellent jazz musicians performing.
- The combination of jazz with essentially nonjazz elements gives music new life and direction. New boundaries are being crossed and others erased.

## IMPORTANT AND INNOVATIVE JAZZ ARTISTS/GROUPS PERFORMING TODAY

- Cassandra Wilson—vocalist blending blues, folk music, and jazz.
- Medeski, Martin, and Wood—eclectic trio blending many sources into an original fusion.
- Steve Coleman and Five Elements—mixing elements of hip hop, funk, complex rhythms, and meters with traditional jazz to form M-Base. The group includes:
  - ♪ Graham Haynes, trumpet
  - ♪ Greg Osby, alto sax
  - ♪ Robin Eubanks, trombone
  - ♪ Marvin "Smitty Smith," drums
  - ♪ Cassandra Wilson, vocals
- Dave Douglas—trumpet/composer/bandleader. He leads a number of groups including Tiny Bell Trio. He often uses unusual instrumentation including string instruments and accordion.
- Trilok Gurtu—percussionist. He has mixed Indian music with elements of jazz.
- John Zorn—alto sax. This eclectic musician borrows freely from many styles including: klezmer music, hard bop, classical composition, free form improvisation, rock, and more. Some of his music can be dissonant, but he often intends for his music to shock the listener. Zorn is associated with two avant-garde groups:
  - ♪ Masada
  - ♪ Naked City
- Special Edition led by drummer Jack DeJohnette—funk rock/world music.
- Prime Time led by Ornette Coleman—electric free/rock fusion.
- Last Exit—free avant-garde music. Members include:
  - ♪ Peter Brotzmann, alto saxophone
  - ♪ Bill Laswell, bass
  - ♪ Ronald Shannon Jackson, drums
- There is an active jazz scene in Europe. Much original and creative music is coming from Italy, France, Germany, and northern Europe.
- The neo-hardbop movement started in the early 1980s through the work of Wynton Marsalis. This movement has given rise to a school of young musicians steeped in the sensibilities of late 1950s and 1960s acoustic jazz.
- There are big bands that recreate the classic work of important composers/arrangers such as Duke Ellington, Fletcher and Horace Henderson, Sy Oliver, and other 1920s and 1930s artists.
- Knitting Factory—A club in New York established in the 1980s to feature experimental jazz groups. This venue has given a forum to the new jazz conceptualists and a haven for the avant-garde.

- Acid Jazz—A phrase used to describe a very wide genre of jazz flavors mixed with contemporary dance rhythms and minimal improvisation

The effect of technology on jazz:

- Sampling of sounds from previously recorded albums
- The looping of rhythms on tape to create a new set of rhythms
- Overdubbing tracks to create new textures and music
- Drum and bass-computer/synthesizer music generated by programmers

The following are some important musicians whose approach may offer new directions in jazz in the twenty-first century:

| TRUMPET | ALTO SAX | TENOR SAX | TROMBONE |
|---|---|---|---|
| Dave Douglas | Kenny Garrett | Joe Lovano | Conrad Herwig |
| Tom Harrell | Vincent Herring | Michael Brecker | Bill Watrous |
| Arturo Sandoval | Greg Osby | James Carter | Steve Turre |
| Kenny Wheeler | Steve Coleman | Jerry Bergonzi | Andy Martin |
| Tim Hagans | John Zorn | Don Byron (clarinet) | Ray Anderson |
| Ryan Kisor | Dave DiPietro | Eddie Daniels (clarinet) | Hal Crook |
| Randy Brecker | Wes Anderson | Chris Potter | Wycliffe Gordon |
| Russell Gunn | Jon Gordon | David Sanchez | Ed Neumeister |
| Terence Blanchard | Donald Harrison | Tony Malaby | Robin Eubanks |
| Nicholas Payton | Steve Slagle | George Garzone | John Allred |
| Claudio Roditi | | Joshua Redman | David Gibson |
| Wynton Marsalis | | Bob Mintzer | |
| Roy Hargrove | | Ralph Moore | |
| Joe Magnarelli | | Branford Marsalis | |
| Bill Mobley | | Dick Oatts | |
| | | Chris Speed | |
| | | Bob Sheppard | |
| | | Ravi Coltrane | |

| GUITAR | BASS | DRUMS | VIOLIN |
|---|---|---|---|
| John Scofield | Christian McBride | Jeff "Tain" Watts | Regina Carter |
| Bruce Forman | Dave Holland | Joey Baron | Billy Bang |
| Russell Malone | James Genus | Terri Lynn Carrington | Mark Feldman |
| Bill Frizell | Stanley Clarke | Adam Nussbaum | Matt Glaser |
| John Abercrombie | George Mraz | Billy Hart | Darol Anger |
| Ralph Towner | John Patitucci | Marvin Smith | Randy Sabien |
| Mike Stern | Marc Johnson | Dennis Chambers | David Balakrishnan |
| Pat Martino | Harvie Swartz | Brian Blade | Didier Lockwood |
| Pat Metheny | Reginald Veal | Jack DeJohnette | |
| Kurt Rosenwinkel | Taurus Mauteen | Lewis Nash | |
| John Hart | | Winard Harper | |
| | | Peter Erskine | |
| | | Bill Stewart | |
| | | Carl Allen | |
| | | Billy Cobham | |

| PIANO | ORGAN |
|---|---|
| Brad Mehldau | Joey De Francesco |
| Cyrus Chestnut | Larry Goldings |
| Danilo Perez | Dan Wall |
| Renee Rosnes | |
| Jim McNeeley | |
| Kenny Werner | |
| Joey Calderazzo | |
| Marc Copland | |
| Elaine Elias | |
| Mulgrew Miller | |
| Marcus Roberts | |
| Uri Caine | |
| Richie Beirach | |
| James Williams | |
| Sascha Perry | |
| Geoff Keezer | |
| Michel Camilo | |
| Geri Allen | |
| Andy LaVerne | |

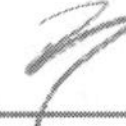

## JAZZ FLAVORED MUSIC

Jazz flavored music is nothing new. The term *smooth jazz* has seen widespread usage since the late 1980s, but the concept of music with certain jazz elements has been around since the Original Dixieland Jazz Band made their first recordings. Paul Whiteman had a jazz "flavored" orchestra (symphonic jazz). Numerous bands in the 1930s and 1940s during the height of the Swing Era were jazz flavored ensembles. These groups utilized some elements of jazz: short improvised solos in otherwise bland arrangements, the presence of swing eighth notes in a specific section of the arrangement, a blues flavored written ensemble section, or the use of plunger muted brass. These are elements found historically in jazz, but don't always help to identify the performance as "real jazz," or jazz flavored music. It is a rather complex issue further complicated by an individual's definition of jazz.

Today's smooth jazz retains some elements of improvisation, but it is more clearly identified by the funk dance rhythms that predominate. The solos are more melodic than adventuresome and the overall sound is pleasant and accessible to the noninitiated jazz listener. Even the great hard bop guitarist Wes Montgomery made numerous jazz flavored recordings in the late 1960s shortly before he passed away. The basic rhythm of smooth jazz does not reflect traditional swing rhythms. Some of the best known artists associated with smooth jazz include Kenny G, Bob James, Dave Koz, Najee, David Sanborn, and George Benson. Some of the older musicians who play in this genre have also recorded in the traditional 1950s hard bop style.

### Acid Jazz

Acid jazz refers to a conglomeration of danceable groove-soul oriented musical styles that share the influences of soul jazz, jazz funk, and Latin jazz. In contrast to the majority of 1990s dance music, acid jazz most often takes the form of a live band commonly featuring a rhythm section, horns, keyboard, and vocals. The music started in the 1980s, but its roots can be traced further back to the jazz fusion albums of Miles Davis and Herbie Hancock. In the 1980s, British club culture became fascinated with American soul jazz of the 1960s and jazz funk of the 1970s all of which was referred to as "rare groove." These sounds inspired a group of young musicians and producers who began to create music in a similar vein. In 1991, the group Brand New Heavies with their combination of jazz, funk, and hip hop achieved widespread success and other groups followed including US3 and the catchy pop-jazz-funk sound of the artist Jamiroquai.

Americans soon discovered this sound and many groups emerged influenced by this style. Today acid jazz encompasses a very wide range of styles from:

- Experimental electronic music
- Minimalism
- Drum and bass (much of it computer generated)
- Back beat funk
- Sounds of 1960s soul jazz
- Highly improvisational music
- Third world music (Latin)
- Sampling (recording portions or phrases of previously recorded old albums and mixing them back as sections of the new music)
- Looping (recording sections of old albums and them continuously repeating, or *looping* them to create rhythms or dancelike grooves)

Some acid jazz contains few or no recognizable elements of jazz. The most important element of the music is the rhythm or the way it "feels." The harmonies are most often very simple and complex improvisation is avoided. The New York and West Coast acid jazz scene produced such groups as Groove Collective, Slide Five, The James Taylor Quartet, The Greyboy Allstars as well as groups Medeski, Martin, and Wood, and Charlie Hunter whose strong jazz background cannot be denied.

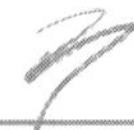

## JAZZ AND EDUCATION

- There are jazz programs at most American universities and some outstanding ones in Europe. In some ways these jazz programs have replaced the jazz scene on New York's 52nd Street.
- The all-important jam sessions of the past are still found in large metropolitan centers, but young jazz musicians are learning much of their craft in schools. The tendency might be for jazz to allow itself to become homogenized.
- More and more non-Americans are studying jazz. A large percentage of students at the Berklee College of Music in Boston, for instance, are foreign born.
- Countries far removed from the American experience have a much greater understanding of jazz than ever before. There are now many more good musicians playing jazz all over the world.
- There may be no more Louis Armstrongs, John Coltranes, or Charlie Parkers on the horizon, and jazz is not as popular as it was fifty years

ago, but that does not diminish the quality or character of the music that is being produced today. There are many substyles under the jazz "umbrella," and many more will undoubtedly emerge.

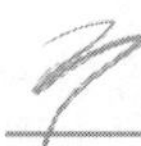

## IS IT JAZZ?

The one constant factor in jazz over the last 100 years has been *change*. The initial changes that took place in jazz occurred over long periods of time, but since the 1950s, changes in jazz have been numerous and have occurred at an accelerated rate. One style of jazz sounds very different from another—often musicians and critics from one era of jazz will repudiate jazz from another era. The emergence of bebop in the 1940s was seen as "blasphemous" by many musicians of the Swing Era; they referred to it as antimusic. This has occurred many times throughout history. What ties all of this music together and makes it jazz? What constitutes the jazz tradition?

- The presence of improvisation?
- The swing feeling?
- Blue notes?

There is a rich history of jazz that all *jazz* musicians acknowledge. The names of the musicians in the hierarchy include Louis Armstrong, Duke Ellington, Charlie Parker, Miles Davis, John Coltrane, Ornette Coleman, and many others. Each innovator acknowledged what had occurred in the past while looking to the future. Changes in jazz are often the result of two factors: evolution and revolution. Artists find new modes of expression by building upon what is already established and then moving forward into "uncharted waters." A new style evolves when all of the musical possibilities within an established genre are exhausted. Change is painful, frightening, and takes courage; each one of the aforementioned musicians faced these issues, persevered, and helped to change the direction of jazz. Having said all of the above, it appears the jazz tradition is simply something that is constantly moving forward while at the same time acknowledging the past.

### What Is Jazz?

An obstacle in defining jazz is that people have different criteria for identifying it. Never have there been so many subcategories in the jazz family. What sounds "jazzy" to some may be perceived differently by others (with a deep understanding of the jazz tradition). Given this dilemma, it is no wonder that some new age music, acid jazz, and smooth jazz end up in the jazz sections of the local CD store. Most people feel very strongly about the music they like and are easily offended when such music is criticized or deemed not worthy of being considered "true" jazz. Jazz combines easily with other types of music and this also facilitates change. This moves us into a very gray subjective area, but there are some helpful guidelines.

### Jazz

- Acknowledges the jazz performance tradition
- Musicians understand the history and are familiar with the important innovators

- *Sometimes* falls into easily identified genres such as big band, hard bop
- Is not resistant to change
- Sometimes sounds experimental
- Often combines music of diverse origins
- Musicians don't always play music that swings in the traditional sense, but it should have a strong sense of forward momentum

What is jazz? In the end, there are as many definitions of jazz as there are people listening to it. As you become familiar with the jazz tradition with its music, musicians, and other parameters, you will develop your own unique concept based on your own experience. The jazz tradition is also inclusive of its listeners and their input taken and given from their point of view. Therefore, your own definition will be important to that tradition. Enjoy your adventure as you become an experienced and knowledgeable jazz enthusiast.

. . . Music reflects the cultural health of a society and jazz has done this with aplomb.

# BIBLIOGRAPHY


Berendt, Joachim. *The Jazz Book*. 6th ed. Lawrence Hill Books, 1992.

Blesh, Rudi and Harriet Janis. *They All Played Ragtime*. New York: Oak Publications, 1971.

Blesh, Rudi, *Shining Trumpets*. New York: Da Capo, 1958.

Bushell, Garvin. *Jazz: From the Beginning*. University of Michigan Press, 1990.

Charters, Samuel, and Leonard Kunstadt. *Jazz: A History of the New York Scene*. New York: Da Capo, 1981.

Chambers, Jack. *Milestones: The Music and Times of Miles Davis*. New York: William Morrow, 1985.

Clark, Andrew, ed. *Riffs and Choruses: a New Jazz Anthology*. London: Continuum Books, 2001.

Collier, James Lincoln. *The Making of Jazz*. Dell Publishing, 1979.

Collier, James Lincoln. *Duke Ellington*. New York: Oxford University Press, 1987.

Collier, James Lincoln. *Louis Armstrong: An American Genius*. New York: Oxford University Press, 1987.

Defaa, Chip. *Voices of the Jazz Age*. Urbana, IL: University of Illinois Press, 1990.

Deveaux, Scott. *The Birth of Bebop*. University of California Press, 1997.

Feather, Leonard. *Encyclopedia of Jazz*. New York: Bonanza Books, 1955.

Feather, Leonard. *Inside Jazz*. New York: Da Capo, 1977

Friedwald, Will. *Jazz Singing*. New York: Charles Scribner's Sons, 1990.

Gerard, Charley. *Jazz in Black and White*. Praeger, 1998.

Gioia, Ted. *West Coast Jazz*. New York: Oxford University Press, 1992.

Goldberg, Joe. *Jazz Masters of the Fifties*. New York: Da Capo, 1965.

Gottlieb, Robert, ed. *Reading Jazz*. New York: Pantheon Books, 1996.

Gitler, Ira. *Jazz Masters of the Forties*. New York: Da Capo, 1966.

Gitler, Ira. *Swing to Bop*. New York: Oxford University Press, 1985.

Gourse, Leslie. *Louis' Children: American Jazz Singers*. New York: Quill, 1984.

Gridley, Mark. *Jazz Styles*. 7th ed., Englewood Cliffs: Prentice-Hall, 2000.

Hadlock, Richard. *Jazz Masters of the Twenties*. New York: Da Capo, 1988.

Hasse, John Edward. *Beyond Category: The Life and Genius of Duke Ellington*. New York: Simon and Schuster, 1993.

Jones, Leroi. *Black Music*. William Morrow, 1967.

Jones, Leroi. *Blues People*. William Morrow, 1963.

Kernfeld, Barry, ed. *The New Grove Dictionary of Jazz*. New York: St. Martin's Press, 1986.

Kirchner, Bill, ed. *A Miles Davis Reader*. Smithsonian Institution Press, 1997.

Koch, Lawrence. *Yardbird Suite: A Compendium of the Music and Life of Charlie Parker*. Bowling Green State University Press, 1988.

Kofsky, Frank. *Black Nationalism and the Revolution on Music*. Pathfinder Books, 1979.

Keil, Charles. *Urban Blues*. University of Chicago Press, 1966.

Lee, Gene. *Singers and the Song*. New York: Oxford University Press, 1987.

Leonard, Neil. *Jazz and the White Americans*. University of Chicago Press, 1962.

Litweiler, John. *The Freedom Principle*. New York: Da Capo, 1984.

Lomax, Alan. *Mister Jelly Roll*. University of California Press, 1973.

Marquis, Donald. *In Search of Buddy Bolden*. New York: Da Capo, 1978.

Nicholson, Stuart. *Jazz Rock: A History*. Schirmer, 1998.

Ostransky, Leroy. *Jazz City*. Englewood Cliffs: Prentice-Hall, 1978.

Pearson, Nathan. *Goin' to Kansas City*. University of Illinois Press, 1987.

Peretti, Burton. *The Creation of Jazz*. University of Illinois Press, 1994.

Porter, Lewis. *John Coltrane*. University of Michigan Press, 1999.

Porter, Lewis. *Jazz—A Century of Change*. New York: Schirmer, 1997.

Priestly, Brian. *Mingus: A Critical Biography*. New York: DaCapo, 1982.

Rattenbury, Ken. *Duke Ellington, Jazz Composer*. Yale University Press, 1990.

Rosenthal, David. *Hard Bop*. New York: Oxford University Press, 1992.

Schuller, Gunther. *Early Jazz*. New York: Oxford University Press, 1968.

Schuller, Gunther. *The Swing Era*. New York: Oxford University Press, 1989.

Shapiro, Nat, and Nat Hentoff. *Hear Me Talkin' to Ya*. New York: Dover, 1966.

Shaw, Arnold. *The Jazz Age*. New York: Oxford University Press, 1987.

Simon, George. *The Big Bands*. MacMillan, 1968.

Southern, Ann. *The Music of Black Americans*. Norton, 1971.

Stearn, Marshall. *The Story of Jazz*. New York: Oxford University Press, 1956.

Stewart, Rex. *Jazz Masters of the Thirties*. MacMillan, 1972.

Stowe, David. *Swing Changes*. Harvard University Press, 1994.

Sudhalter, Richard. *Lost Chords*. New York: Oxford University Press, 1999.

Sudhalter, Richard, and Philip Evans. *Bix: Man and Legend*. Arlington House Publishers, 1974.

Tirro, Frank. *Jazz: A History*. Norton, 1977.

Tucker, Mark, ed. *The Duke Ellington Reader*. New York: Oxford University Press, 1993.

Walser, Robert, ed. *Keeping Time—Readings in Jazz History*. New York: Oxford University Press, 1999.

Williams, Martin. *Jazz Masters in Transition*. New York: Da Capo, 1970.

Woideck, Carl. *Charlie Parker: His Music and Life*. University of Michigan Press, 1999.

# JAZZ CONCERT/ PERFORMANCE REVIEW

A two-page, typewritten review must be completed and handed in by the specified dates. A ticket stub or program must be stapled to the review. Use the third person when writing the review. Take into consideration the organization of the performance, quality of the solos, ensemble playing, and overall sound.

In addition to whatever you feel is significant about the performance, you must also list the following:

Date:

Location:

Instrumentation:

Performers' names:

Titles of some of the pieces performed:

The structural form of at least one piece you heard (pick one selection and try to analyze it to the best of your ability). Discuss one or more solo improvisations pointing out strengths and/or weaknesses. Determine influences of major jazz musicians based on what or how you hear a soloist play.

At the end, include a brief overall account of your personal impressions of the music (what you liked or disliked and why, what style(s) you heard, how the musicians communicated and interacted with each other, stage presence, etc.).

# INDEX

## A


Abercrombie, John, 193
Abrams, Muhal Richard, 166, 167
A cappella, blues, 23
Acid Jazz, 193, 194–95
Acoustic bass, 181
Acoustic guitar, 189
Acoustic jazz, 179
Acoustic piano, 188, 189
Adams, George "Pepper", 125, 139, 142, 167
Adderley, Julian "Cannonball", 136, 138, 152, 154, 155, 156, 181, 183
Adderley, Nat, 136
Aesthetic experience, 3
Aesthetic systems, 1
African aesthetic, 1
African-American music
 the blues, 23–26
 field holler, 27
 folk, 17
 minstrel show, 21–22
 ragtime, 27–29
 spirituals, 27
 work songs, 22
African influences, in early New Orleans jazz, 34
African music
 American experience, 18–19
 Blakey and, 130–31
 characteristics of, 17
 elements borrowed by modern jazz, 17
 influence of, 126
 Latin jazz, 128
 pitch inflection, 16–17
 roots, 15–16
 slave experience, 17–18
Afro-Cuban Latin style, 179
Afro-Cuban music, 118
*The Afro-Eurasian Suite* (Ellington), 73
Afro-Latin music, 126
Agitated style, 104
"Ain't Misbehavin'" (Waller/Razaf), 44
"Ain't Nobody's Business If I Do" (Holiday), 145
*The Akoustic Band* (Corea), 189
Ali, Bardu, 145
Ali, Rashied, 167, 176
Alias, Don, 184
All American Rhythm Section, 81
Allen, Carl, 193
Allen, Geri, 194
Allen, Henry "Red", 60, 97
Allen, Marshall, 166
Allred, John, 193
All-Star Band, 94
All Stars, 53
"All Too Soon" (Ellington), 70
Almeida, Laurindo, 118, 128
Alternate melodies, by Beiderbecke, 55
Alto saxophone, 9, 10, 64, 69, 89, 90, 105–07, 113, 118, 119, 120, 123, 141, 154, 162–64, 166, 175, 192
Alto saxophonists
 bebop, 114
 cool style, 126
 fusion, 182
 future, 193
 hard bop, 138
 Jazz Messengers, 132
 Mingus's bands, 142
 swing era, 95–97
Altschul, Barry, 167, 188
*Amandla* (Davis), 160
American experience, 18–19
American Federation of Musicians Local 802 New York, 100
*American Group* (Corea), 190
American idiom, jazz as, 3
American jazz, influence of African music on, 126
Ammons, Albert, 47
Ammons, Gene, 47, 112, 114, 139
Analysis, of jazz, 3
Anderson, Fred, 166
Anderson, Ivie, 68
Anderson, Ray, 167, 193
Anderson, Wes, 193
Andy Kirk and the Clouds of Joy, 78
Anger, Darol, 193
Animal tusks, 15
Animation, in swing, 5
"An Open Letter to Duke" (Mingus), 142
"April in Paris" (Basie), 82
Arada tribe, 18
Arkestra, 165
Arlen, Harold, 146
Armstrong, Louis, 4, 25, 35, 36, 37, 38, 45, 47, 49–53, 54, 57, 63, 64, 65, 80, 87, 90, 96, 101, 106, 139, 143, 145, 147, 196
ARP String Ensemble, 187
Arrangements
 cool style, 116
 in early New Orleans jazz, 34–35
 hard bop, 130
Arrangers
 big band style, 64, 65
 Ellington as, 67–68
 hard bop, 129–30
 swing era, 84, 85, 97
Art Ensemble of Chicago, 166
Articulation, Armstrong and, 52
Artie Shaw Band, 87–88, 90
Artie Shaw's Orchestra, 145
Artistic dissatisfaction, of big band swing, 99
"Artistry in Rhythm" (Kenton), 117

*Ascension* (Coltrane), 176
Association for the Advancement of Creative Musicians (AACM), 166
"A-Tisket, A Tasket" (Fitzgerald), 145
Atonal music, 164
Attitudes, American, change in, 40–41
Audience, participation of, 4, 16
Auld, Georgie, 97
*Aura* (Davis), 160
Austin High Gang, 59–60
Avant-garde jazz, 161
Ayler, Albert, 164–65, 175, 176
"Azure" (Ellington), 73

## B

Bach, J. S., 188
"Back Water Blues" (Smith), 25
Bailey, Buster, 25, 37, 98
Bailey, Mildred, 98, 147
Bailey, Pearl, 96
Baker, Chet, 2, 123–24, 125, 126, 148
"Bakiff" (Ellington), 74
Balakrishnan, David, 193
Ballads, 88
Bandleader, 111–12, 128, 189–90
Bandleaders, 60, 84–85, 123, 127, 139–42, 165–66, 188–89, 192
Bands, New Orleans funeral, 19
Bang, Billy, 193
Banjo, 33, 34, 59, 64
Banjo players, 38, 60
Bar, defined, 8
Barbarian, Paul, 37
Barber, Bill, 154
Baritone saxophone, 9, 10, 64, 68, 69, 74, 118, 119, 123, 124
Baritone saxophonists, 139
Baron, Joey, 193
Baroque music, 120
Barretto, Ray, 128
Bartòk, Béla, 86, 188
Barton, Dee, 118
Basie, Count (William), 78, 79–82, 84, 85, 88, 94, 96, 97, 103, 115
Bass, 11, 64, 70, 84, 103, 120, 121, 124, 125, 127, 130, 134–35, 137–42, 146, 151, 152, 154, 170, 171, 175, 180, 184, 188, 189, 190
Bass clarinet, 10, 164
Bass drum, 11, 34, 81, 104, 110
Bassists
  bebop, 101, 114
  Chicago style, 60
  cool style, 126
  fusion, 182
  future, 193
  hard bop, 139
  swing era, 97
Bass line, Latin jazz, 127
Bass notes, 34
Bassoon, 9
Bauduc, Ray, 60
Bauer, Billy, 116, 120, 126
Bauza, Mario, 107, 127, 128
Beat
  defined, 8
  early New Orleans jazz, 33
  Latin jazz, 127
  subdivision of, 107
  swing, 5
Beatles, 179, 180
"Beautiful Indians" (Ellington), 67
Bebop, 93, 129–30, 139, 146
  cool style and, 115–16
  vs. big band style, 103–04
  evolution of, 100–101
  history, 99–100
  musicians, 112–14
  rhythm section, 103–12
  singers, 148
  style, 101–03
Bechet, Sidney, 36–37, 62, 95
Beck, Joe, 181
Beethovenhalle Orchestra Bonn, 188
"Begin the Beguine" (Shaw), 88
Beiderbecke, Bix, 53–55, 59, 60, 63, 80, 87, 88, 94, 115
Beirach, Richie, 194
Bela Fleck and the Flecktones, 182
Bells, 15
*Beneath the Mask* (Corea), 189
*Beneath the Underdog* (Mingus), 141
Bennett, Cuban, 95
Bennett, Tony, 148
Bennie Moten Band, 78, 79, 80, 93
Bennie Moten Orchestra, 97
Benny Goodman Band, 85–87, 91
Benny Goodman Orchestra, 91
Benny Goodman Sextet, 66
Benson, George, 182, 194
Berg, Billy, 106, 109
Berg, Bob, 176, 184
Bergonzi, Jerry, 176, 193
Berigan, Bunny (Rowland Bernart), 88, 90–91, 97
Berkelee College of Music, 190
Berklee School of Music, 187
Berlin, Irving, 146
Berlin, Jeff, 182
Berman, Sonny, 117, 118
Bernhardt, Warren, 181
Berry, Chu (Leon), 90, 94–95, 96, 97
Berton, Vic, 60
"Bert Williams" (Ellington), 74
Best, Denzil, 114
"Better Get It in Yo' Soul" (Mingus), 142
Bigard, Barney, 37, 53, 69, 71, 98, 139–40
Big band style, vs. bebop, 103–04
Big-band swing style, 3, 4, 61–66, 83–84
*The Big Challenge*, 92
*Big Fun* (Davis), 160
Bill Evans Trio, 157, 171
*Bill Evans Trio with String Orchestra* (Evans), 171
Billy Eckstine Band, 106, 130
Bird. *See* Parker, Charlie "Bird"
*Birth of the Cool*, 119, 120, 123, 151, 154
Bishop, Walter Jr., 154
*Bitches Brew* (Davis), 152, 160, 183, 184, 187, 188
"Black and Tan Fantasy" (Ellington), 72
Black Artists Group (BAG), 166
"Black Beauty" (Ellington), 73
*Black, Brown and Beige* (Ellington), 68, 71, 73
Blackwell, Ed, 162, 167
Blade, Brian, 193
Blake, Eubie, 46
Blakey, Art, 114, 126, 130–32, 135, 139, 146, 151, 154, 157, 188
Blanchard, Terence, 193
Bland, James, 22
Blanton, Jimmy, 70, 71, 73, 74, 97, 101, 103, 185
Blanton/Webster Band, 70, 94
Bley, Carla, 167
Bley, Paul, 167
Block chord voicings, 123
Block harmonization, 84
"Blood Count" (Ellington), 95
Blood, Sweat, and Tears, 181
Bloomfield, Mike, 181
Blount, Herman, 165–66
Blue Devils, 78, 79, 80, 97
Blue Flames, 135
Blue Friars, 59
"Blue Mood" (Ellington), 72
Blue Note recordings, 110, 111, 132, 135
Blue notes, 2, 16–17, 22, 33, 55
"Blue Rondo a la Turk", 123
Blues, 17, 23–26, 33, 61, 77, 129, 130, 147
Blues Breakers, 180
"Blue Serge" (Ellington), 72
"Blue Seven" (Rollins), 135–36
Blues Hounds, 93
"Blues In My Heart" (Hodges), 96
Blues shouters, 148
*Blue Train* (Coltrane), 174
"Blue Tune" (Ellington), 72

Bluiett, Hamiet, 166, 167
Bobo, Willie, 188
"Body and Soul" (Hawkins), 93
"Bojangels" (Ellington), 74
Bolden, Buddy, 35
Bolero, 127
Bongos, 10, 118, 127
"Boogie-Woogie" (Dorsey), 88
Boogie-woogie piano, 46–47, 78
Boogie-woogie style, vs. stride style, 46
Bossa nova, 128
Bostic, Earl, 129
Boston Pops, 146
Boswell Sisters, 91, 98
Bowie, Lester, 166, 167
Boyd, Nelson, 154
Boyd Raeburn Orchestra, 118
"Boy Meets Horn" (Ellington), 73
Bracken, JoAnne, 132
Bradford, Bobby, 167
Bradshaw, Tiny, 91
Brand New Heavies, 195
Brass band march form, 28
Brass bands, 38, 43
Brass band tradition, 33, 77
Brass instruments, 9, 141, 155
Braud, Wellman, 60
Braxton, Anthony, 166, 167, 188–89
Brazil, 18
Brazilian rhythm, 128
Brecker, Michael, 176, 181, 182, 193
Brecker, Randy, 181, 182, 193
The Brecker Brothers, 181
*Bright Size Life* (Corea), 190
Brignola, Nick, 139
"Brilliant Corners" (Monk), 112
Broadway singers, 147
Brooklyn Philharmonic, 188
Brookmeyer, Bob, 126
Broonzy, Big Bill, 24
Brotzmann, Peter, 192
Brown, Clifford, 113, 132, 134–35, 138, 154
Brown, James, 179, 180, 181
Brown, Lawrence, 97
Brown, Marion, 167
Brown, Oscar Jr., 148
Brown, Ray, 114, 120, 121, 146
Brown, Steve, 60
Browne, Tom, 182
Brubeck, Dave, 116, 122–23, 126
Brunies, George, 37
Buckner, Milt, 172
Bunker, Larry, 126
Burlesque halls, 64
Burrell, Kenny, 139
Burton, Gary, 180, 181, 189
Butler, Frank, 155
Byard, Jaki, 142, 167
Byas, Don, 97, 100, 114, 137
Byrd, Charlie, 128
Byrd, Donald, 132, 138, 186
Byron, Don, 193

## C

Cabarets, 31, 41, 57
Cage, John, 189
Caine, Uri, 194
Calderazzo, Joey, 194
Call and response
  African music, 17
  early New Orleans jazz, 34
  spirituals, 27
  swing era, 84
  work songs, 22
Callendar, Red, 139
Calloway, Cab, 52, 83, 94, 108, 127, 147
Calypso, 18
Camilo, Michel, 128, 194
"Camptown Races" (Foster), 22
"Candlelight" (Beiderbecke), 55
Cannonball Adderley Quintet, 136, 181
"Caravan" (Tizol), 74
"Careless Love Blues" (Smith), 25
Caribbean, 18
Carmichael, Hoagy, 55
Carney, Harry, 69, 71, 74
Carnivals, 77
"Carolina Shout" (Johnson), 44
Carrington, Terri Lynn, 193
Carroll, Bakaida, 167
Carroll, Joe, 148
"Carry Me Back to Old Virginny" (Bland), 22
Carter, Benny (Bennett Lester), 45, 85, 89, 94, 95–96, 97, 100, 107, 136, 145, 151
Carter, Betty, 148
Carter, James, 193
Carter, Regina, 193
Carter, Ron, 152, 155, 157–58, 183, 187
Casa Loma Band, 85
Cashbox, 190
Castle, Irene, 61
Castle, Vernon, 61
Catlett, Sid, 96, 97, 103
Cecil Taylor Unit, 164
Cello, 10, 139
Cha-cha, 127
Challis, Bill, 54, 63, 97
Chaloff, Serge, 117
Chamber-like approach, 124
Chamber music, 119
Chambers, Dennis, 193
Chambers, Paul, 138, 139, 151, 154, 155
"Chamelion" (Hancock), 187
Chandler, D.D., 35
Change, 1, 2, 3, 40–41, 197
*Change of the Century* (Coleman), 164
Charanga, 127
Charles, Ray, 96
Charles Lloyd Quartet, 181, 188
"The Charleston" (Johnson), 44
Charlie Johnson Orchestra, 95
Charlie Parker Quartet, 102
Chase, 181
Chatter, 103
"Chelsea Bridge" (Strayhorn), 70
"Cherokee", 106
Cherry, Don, 162, 165, 167
Chestnut, Cyrus, 194
Chicago, 57–60
Chicago-style jazz, 2, 58–59
Chicago Symphony Orchestra, 185
Chick Corea Elektric Band, 182
*The Chick Corea Elektric Band* (Corea), 189
Chick Webb Orchestra, 89–90, 107, 145
Chopin, Frederic, 171
Chord roots, 34
Chords
  bebop, 102, 104
  defined, 7
  free jazz, 162
  hard bop, 130
  jabbing, 82
  Miles Davis Quintet, 157
Chorus, 12, 23, 62
Christian, Charlie, 86, 101, 104, 109, 110, 114, 137
Christy, June, 117, 148
Christy Minstrels, 22
Chromaticism, 74
Church modes, 156
Church songs, 27
Cincinnati Conservatory, 119
Circle, 188–89
Circus, 22
"C-Jam Blues" (Webster), 94
Clarinet, 9, 33, 34, 58, 63, 68, 69, 86, 103–04, 116, 119, 175
Clarinetists
  Chicago style, 60
  cool style, 117
  early New Orleans jazz, 36–37
  swing era, 98
"Clarinet Lament" (Ellington), 73
Clark, Sonny, 125
Clarke, Kenny, 96, 101, 103, 108, 110, 111, 113, 114, 120, 121, 154
Clarke, Stanley, 182, 189, 193
Classical composition, 192
Classic quintet, 151
Claude Thornhill Orchestra, 119, 123

Clave rhythms, 127
Claves, 126, 127
Clayton, Buck (Wilbur Dorsey), 80, 82, 85, 92, 97, 145
Clef Club Orchestra, 61
Clifford Brown/Max Roach Quintet, 134–35
Clooney, Rosemary, 148
"Clouds in My Heart" (Ellington), 72
C-melody saxophone, 80
Cobb, Arnett, 92, 139
Cobb, Jimmy, 138, 139, 152, 155
Cobham, Billy, 182, 193
Cohesive group sound, 5
Cohn, Al, 117
Cole, Nat "King", 45, 97, 98, 100, 147, 171
Cole, William "Cozy", 97
Coleman, George, 137, 138, 155, 187
Coleman, Ornette, 157, 161, 162–64, 165, 175, 180, 181, 189, 192, 196
Coleman, Steve, 192, 193
Collective improvisation
- Armstrong and, 52–53
- big band style, 64
- early New Orleans jazz, 33, 34, 35
- free jazz, 162
- by Oliver, 36
- Weather Report, 185

Collective participation, 17
Collette, Buddy, 125, 126
Coltrane, John, 37, 112, 138, 151, 152, 154, 155, 156, 159, 163, 164, 173–77, 180, 184, 196
Coltrane, Ravi, 193
*Coltrane Jazz* (Coltrane), 174
Combo jazz, 58–59
Common time (C), 8
Communal participation, 17
Comping, 82, 103, 104, 180
Composer, 109–12, 128, 139–42, 162–66, 185–90, 192
Composers' art, European music as, 4
Compositions, Dave Brubeck Quartet, 123
Concerto compositions, 73
*Concerto for Clarinet and String Orchestra* (Copland), 86
"Concerto for Cootie" (Ellington), 73, 92
*Concerto for Orchestra and Guitar*, 155
Condoli, Conte, 125, 126
Condon, Eddie, 59, 60
"Conga Brava" (Ellington), 74
Congas, 10, 118, 126–27, 127
Congos, 18
Congo Square, 18–19
Connick, Harry Jr., 149
Connor, Chris, 148
*Constrasts* (Bartok), 86
Contrafactions, 101, 104, 112
Contrapuntal fashion, 62
Contrapuntal lines, 124
Contrapuntal textures, 116
Conventional chords, 7–8
"Conversation" (Mingus), 142
*Conversations with Myself* (Evans), 171
Cook, Junior, 132, 138
Cook, Will Marion, 38, 61–62
*Cookin'*, 155
Cool style
- birth of, 119–25
- characteristics of, 116–19
- history, 115–16
- important musicians, 126
- singers, 148

Cooper, Bob, 125
Cootie Williams Band, 109
Copland, Aaron, 86
Copland, Marc, 194
Corea, Chick (Anthony Armando), 152, 160, 180, 182, 184, 187, 188–89
"Corner Pocket" (Basie), 82
Cornet, 9, 33, 34, 59
Cornetists, 35–36, 136
Cornish, Willie, 35
Coryell, Larry, 180, 181, 182
Cotton Club, 68–69, 72, 89
"Cottontail" (Ellington), 70, 74, 94
Count Basie band, 93
Count Basie Band, 105
Count Basie Orchestra, 92, 97, 101, 145, 147
Count Basie-style singers, 148
Countermelody, 62
Counterpoint, 34, 115
Country blues, 24
Count's Rock Band, 181
Cowbell, 127
Cox, Ida, 26, 44
Crawford, Hank, 182
"Crazy Blues", 44
"Crazy He Calls Me" (Holiday), 145
Cream, 180
Creole Jazz Band, 35, 36, 37, 40, 50, 57, 59
"Creole Love Call" (Ellington), 73
*Creole Rhapsody* (Ellington), 71, 73
Creoles, 32
Crescendo, 8
"Crescendo in Blue" (Ellington/Strayhorn), 74
Criss, Sonny, 114
Critical writings, 3
Crook, Hal, 193
Crosby, Bing, 147
Crosby, Bob, 88
Crosby, Israel, 97
Cross-rhythm, 16, 17, 34
The Crusaders, 182
Cruz, Celia, 128
"Cubano Be" (Gillespie), 109
"Cubano Bop" (Gillespie), 109
Cuber, Ron, 139
Cugat, Xavier, 127, 128
Cultural formulas, for sounds, 1
Curson, Ted, 142, 167
Curtis Institute of Music, 119
Cycle, through piece of music, 12
Cymbals, 10, 11, 33, 34, 64, 81, 103, 104, 159, 171, 183
Cyrille, Andrew, 167


## D


Dabney, Ford, 61
Dahomey, 17, 18
Dahomian tribe, 17
"Dallas Blues" (Handy), 24
Dameron, Tadd, 101, 112, 113, 114, 135, 139
Dance bands, 62, 64, 88
Dance compositions, 73–74
Dance halls, 31, 41, 57, 64
Dance music, 100
*Dancing in Your Head* (Coleman), 164
Daniels, Eddie, 193
*Daphne and Chloe* (Kenton), 117
Dara, Olu, 167
*Dark Intervals* (Jarrett), 188
Darwin, Charles, 141
Dave Brubeck Quartet, 122–23
Davidson, Wild Bill, 60
Davis, Art, 139
Davis, Eddie "Lockjaw", 82, 92, 139
Davis, Miles, 96, 106, 108, 112, 114, 116, 119, 120, 126, 132, 135, 136, 138, 151–60, 163, 173, 174, 180, 182–84, 188, 195, 196
Davis, Peter, 49
Davis, Richard, 167
Davis, Wild Bill, 137
"Day Break Express" (Ellington), 74
Dearie, Blossom, 148
Debussy, Claude, 54, 55, 171
*Decoy* (Davis), 160
Decrescendo, 8
*The Deep South Suite* (Ellington), 73
DeFrancesco, Joey, 137, 194
DeFranco, Buddy, 118
DeJohnette, Jack, 160, 171, 182, 184, 188, 192, 193
de Koenigswarter, Pannonica, 107
"Delta Serenade" (Ellington), 73
*Derivations for Clarinet and Band* (Gould), 86

Desmond, Paul, 120, 123, 126
Dickenson, Vic, 97
Dickerson, Carroll, 60
*Dig*, 154
DiMeola, Al, 189
DiMeola, Pat, 182
DiPietro, Dave, 193
Dirge, 16, 19
Disco, 128
Dissatisfaction, artistic, of big band swing, 99
Dissonance, 74
"The Divine One" (Vaughan), 147
Dixieland, 32, 58
Dixon, Bill, 167
Dizzy Gillespie Big Band, 120
"Django" (Modern Jazz Quartet), 121
Doc Cook's Dreamland Orchestra, 36
Dodds, Baby, 37
Dodds, Johnny, 25, 36, 37
Doggett, Bill, 137
"Dolphin Dance" (Hancock), 187
Dolphy, Eric, 138, 142, 162, 164, 167, 175
Donaldson, Lou, 132, 137, 138
Don Gardner's Sonotones, 137
"Don't Explain" (Holiday), 145
"Don't Get Around Much Anymore" (Ellington), 74, 95
Dorham, Kenny, 106, 131, 132, 134, 138
Dorough, Bob, 148
Dorsey, Jimmy, 55, 60, 88, 89, 91, 97
Dorsey, Tommy, 55, 60, 83, 85, 88, 89, 91, 96, 97, 100, 113
Dorsey Brothers Band, 88
Dorsey Brothers Orchestra, 88
Double bass, 10
Double entendre, 22
Double time, 51
Douglas, Dave, 192, 193
*Down Beat* magazine, 135, 136, 138
"Down Hearted Blues" (Smith), 25
"Doxy" (Rollins), 136
Dreams, 181
Drew, Kenny, 135, 139
D'Rivera, Paquito, 128
Drone effects, 175
Dropping bombs, 104, 110
*A Drum Is a Woman* (Ellington/Strayhorn), 70, 73
Drummers
  bebop, 103, 114
  Chicago style, 60
  cool style, 126
  early New Orleans jazz, 37
  free jazz, 167
  fusion, 182
  future, 193
  hard bop, 139
  Mingus's bands, 142
  swing era, 97
Drums, 10, 11, 15, 33, 34, 64, 84, 88, 110, 116, 120, 124, 125, 126, 130, 137, 138, 146, 151, 152, 154, 171, 175, 176, 180, 183, 184, 187, 188, 189, 190, 192
Drum set, 11, 59
Dudziak, Ursula, 149
Duke, George, 182
Duke Ellington's Orchestra, 38, 70, 71, 91, 94, 95
Durham, Eddie, 78, 80, 85, 97
"Dusk" (Ellington), 72
"Dusk in the Desert" (Ellington), 67
Dutrey, Honore, 37
Dvorak, Antonin, 62
*A Dynamic New Sound* (Montgomery), 138
Dynamics, defined, 8


## E


Eager, Allan, 114
Earland, Charles, 139
Earl Hines Orchestra, 146
"East of the Sun and West of the Moon" (Vaughan), 146
"East St. Louis Toodle-oo" (Ellington), 72
Easy listening arrangements, 138
*Ebony Concerto for Clarinet and Orchestra* (Stravinsky), 117
"Ecaroh" (Silver), 133
"Echoes of Harlem" (Ellington), 73
"Echoes of the Jungle" (Ellington), 72
Echoplex, 181, 183
Eckstine, Billy, 45, 96, 101, 108, 112, 146, 147, 151
Eddie Randall Blue Devils, 151
Edison, Harry "Sweets", 80, 97
Egan, Mark, 190
"Eighty-One" (Miles), 183
Eldridge, Roy, 88, 90, 91, 94, 97, 100, 108, 147
Electric bass, 181, 183
Electric Flag, 181
Electric fretless bass, 185
Electric guitar, 189
Electric microphone, 2
Electric pianos, 180, 183, 187
Elektric Band, 189
Elgar's Creole Orchestra, 36
Elias, Elaine, 194
Ellington, Duke (Edward Kennedy), 38, 39, 44, 59, 67–75, 83, 84, 85, 89, 91–92, 96, 97, 119, 127, 139, 140, 141, 146, 192, 196
Ellis, Don, 167
Ellis, Herb, 139
Elman, Ziggy, 97
Embellished filigree, 34
Embellishments, 33, 58
Emerson Lake, and Palmer, 180
Emotion, 3, 121
Empress of the Blues (Smith), 25
Emulation, 12
Energy, in swing, 5
Ensemble
  big band style, 64
  instruments in, 11
  mood compositions, 72
Ensemble chorus, early New Orleans jazz, 34
Ensemble melody, early New Orleans jazz, 35
Envoldsen, Bob, 126
"Epitaph" (Mingus), 142
Erskine, Peter, 182, 193
Erskine Tate's Orchestra, 36
Ervin, Booker, 138, 142, 176
Erwin, Pee Wee, 88
*E.S.P.* (Davis), 157, 183
Eubanks, Robin, 167, 192, 193
Europe, James Reese, 61
European aesthetic, 1
European influences, early New Orleans jazz, 34
European music, vs. jazz, 4
Evaluation, of jazz, 3
Evans, Bill, 120, 152, 155, 156, 157, 158, 169–72, 184
Evans, Gil, 116, 119, 123, 154, 155, 183
Evans, Herschel, 80, 97
*Everybody Digs Bill Evans* (Evans), 156, 169
Excelsior Brass Band, 38
Exotic compositions, 74
Experience, of swing, 4
"An Experiment in Modern Music", 62
Explorations, 171
Expression, of feelings, 2
Expressions (Coltrane), 175, 176
Extended works, 73
*Eye of the Beholder* (Corea), 189
"Eye of the Hurricane" (Hancock), 187


## F


"Fables of Faubus" (Mingus), 140–41, 142
*The Fabulous Dorseys*, 88
Fagan, Eleanor. *See* Holiday, Billie
*Far East Suite* (Ellington/Strayhorn), 70, 72, 73

Farlow, Tal, 114
Farmer, Art, 125, 132, 138
Farrell, Joe, 176, 182, 189
Father of Boogie-Woogie (Lewis), 47
Father of the Blues (Handy), 24
Favors, Malachi, 166, 167
Feelings, expression of, 2
Feldman, Mark, 193
Feldman, Victor, 155
Female singers, 148
Fender Rhodes electric
 piano, 187, 189
Ferguson, Maynard, 117–18
*ff* symbols, 8
Field holler, 17, 27
*Filles de Kilimanjaro*
 (Davis), 157, 183
"Filthy McNasty" (Silver), 132
"Fine and Mellow" (Holiday), 145
First classic quintet, 154
First Herd, 117
First Lady of Song (Fitzgerald), 145
Fischer, Clare, 126
Fitzgerald, Ella, 52, 90, 96,
 145–46, 147
Fitzgerald, F. Scott, 41
Five Spot, 173
"Flamenco Sketches" (Davis), 156
"The Flaming Sword" (Ellington), 67
Flanagan, Tommy, 139
"Flashes" (Beiderbecke), 55
Fleck, Bela, 182
Fleet, Biddy, 106
Fletcher Henderson Band, 93
Fletcher Henderson Orchestra, 50
The Flock, 181
Flugelhorn, 116, 152, 155
Flutes, 9, 15, 116, 125, 164, 189
Fontana, Carl, 126
"Fontessa" (Modern Jazz
 Quartet), 121
"For Dancers Only" (Oliver), 89
Forest, Jimmy, 138
Form
 blues, 23
 defined, 11–12
 jazz, 12
 Kansas City style, 78
 marches, 28
 ragtime, 28
Forman, Bruce, 193
Formulas, for music, 1
Forrest, Helen, 98, 147
Forrest, Jimmy "Night Train", 139
Foster, Frank, 82, 138
Foster, Pops, 60
Foster, Stephen, 22
*Four and More*, 157
The Four Freshman, 149
Fourth Way, 181
Freedom, jazz as symbol of, 3
"Freedom Jazz Dance" (Davis), 183
Free form improvisation, 192
Free-form music, 185
Free improvisation, vs. melodic
 variation, 4
Free Jazz, 136, 139, 161–67
*Free Jazz* (Coleman), 164
Freeman, Bud, 59, 60, 97
Freeman, Russ, 126
Freeman, Von, 167
Free Spirits, 181
French horn, 9, 116, 118, 119, 155
Frisell, Bill, 182, 193
"From Spirituals to Swing", 47
Front line, 33
*f* symbols, 8
Fugues, 116
Fuller, Curtis, 137, 138
*Full House* (Montgomery), 138
Functional music, 15, 21, 22
Funeral dirges, 19
Funk music, 130, 185
*Further Conversations*
 (Evans), 171
Fusion bands, 152, 182–84
*Fusion* (Montgomery), 138
Fusion music, 2, 179–90
Future of jazz, 191–97
*Future Shock* (Hancock), 187
Fuzz tone, 181

## G

Gadd, Steve, 182
Galliard, Slim, 148
Gardner, Don, 137
Garland, Red, 139, 151, 152,
 154, 155
Garner, Errol, 172
Garrett, Kenny, 193
Garrett, Lloyd, 24
Garrison, Jimmy, 139, 167, 175, 176
Gary Burton Quartet, 181
Garzone, George, 193
Gaskin, Leonard, 114
Geller, Herb, 126
Genus, James, 193
Georgia Minstrels, 22
Gershwin, George, 12, 62, 63,
 146, 155
Gelly Mulligan/Chet Baker Quartet,
 123–124
Getz, Stan, 94, 114, 117, 126, 128,
 132, 140
Ghana, 17
Giants of Jazz, 112
*Giant Steps* (Coltrane), 174, 175
"Giant Steps" (Coltrane), 174, 175
Gibson, David, 193
Gilberto, Astrud, 128
Gilberto, Joao, 128
Gillespie, Dizzy, 45, 52, 90, 93, 96,
 101, 106, 107–09, 110, 113,
 114, 118, 120, 126, 127,
 130, 135, 140, 146, 148,
 152, 154, 173
Gilmore, John, 166, 175
Gimmickry, 84
Giuffre, Jimmy, 125, 126
Glaser, Joe, 53
Glaser, Matt, 193
Glenn Miller Band, 89
"God Bless the Child" (Holiday), 145
"Going Out of My Head"
 (Montgomery), 138
Goldings, Larry, 137, 194
Goldkettle, Jean, 54, 60, 88
Golson, Benny, 132, 138
Gomez, Eddie, 171, 182
Gonsalves, Paul, 71
Gonzales, Babs, 148
Gonzales, Jerry, 128
"Good Bait" (Dameron), 113
"Goodbye Porkpie Hat" (Mingus),
 141, 142
Goodman, Benny, 25, 45, 59, 60,
 65–66, 83, 84, 85–87, 88, 92, 96,
 98, 99, 100, 104, 119, 145
Goodman, Jerry, 182
"Good Morning Heartache"
 (Holiday), 145
"Good Night" (Foster), 22
Gordon, Dexter, 108, 112, 114, 146,
 174, 186
Gordon, Jon, 193
Gordon, Wycliffe, 193
Gospel music, 129, 130
Gottlieb, Danny, 190
Gould, Morton, 86
Graettinger, Bob, 118
Graham Bond Organization, 180
Gramercy Five, 88
Granz, Norman, 90, 94, 96, 106, 107,
 109, 146
Grappelli, Stephane, 104
Graves, Milford, 167
Gray, Glen, 85
Gray, Jerry, 97
Gray, Wardell, 108, 112, 113, 114
Green, Bennie, 132
Green, Charlie, 60
Green, Freddie, 81
Green, Grant, 139
Greer, Sonny, 71
The Greyboy Allstars, 195
Griffin, Johnny, 132, 138
Grillo, Frank, 127
Grimes, Henry, 167
Grimes, Tiny, 46
"The Gringo" (Silver), 133
Grofé, Ferde, 62
Grolnick, Don, 182

Groove Collective, 195
"Groovin' High" (Gillespie), 106, 109
Grossman, Steve, 176
Group participation, in African music, 16
Groups, vocal jazz, 148–49
Growling, 69
Growls
 early New Orleans jazz, 33
 Eldridge and, 90
 as Ellington trademark, 74
 jungle style, 72
Grusin, Dave, 182
Gryce, Gigi, 138
Guaracho, 127
Guaraldi, Vince, 126
Guarneri, Johnny, 88
*A Guest of Honor* (Joplin), 29
Guitar, 11, 33, 34, 59, 63, 64, 81, 84, 104, 120, 125, 128, 137–38, 169, 181, 184, 189–90, 194
Guitarists
 bebop, 101, 114
 Chicago style, 60
 cool style, 126
 early New Orleans jazz, 38
 fusion, 182
 future, 193
 hard bop, 139
 Latin jazz, 128
"Gulf Coast Blues" (Smith), 25
Gunn, Russell, 193
Gurtu, Trilok, 192

## H

Hackett, Bobby, 89
Haden, Charlie, 162, 167
Hagans, Tim, 193
Haig, Al, 114
"Haitian Fight Song" (Mingus), 142
Half steps, in the scale, 16
Hal Kemp Orchestra, 90
Hall, Jim, 126
Halsey Music School, 137
Hamilton, Chico, 126
Hamilton, Jimmy, 71
Hamilton School of Music, 137
Hammer, Jan, 182
Hammond, John, 45, 47, 80, 85, 86, 92, 104, 144–45
Hammond B-3 organ, 137
Hampton, Lionel, 86, 92, 94, 97, 135, 137, 140
Hampton, Slide, 138
Hancock, Herbie, 152, 155, 157–58, 180, 181, 182, 184, 185–87, 195
Handy, John, 142
Handy, W.C., 22, 24–25, 126
Hanna, Ken, 118
Hanna, Roland, 139, 142
"Happy Go Local Lucky" (Ellington), 74
Hard bop, 129–39, 192
Hardin, Lillian "Lil", 46, 50, 60
Hardy, Emmet, 54
Hargrove, Roy, 193
Harlan Leonard and His Rockets, 113
"Harlem Airshaft" (Ellington), 74
"Harlem Rag" (Turpin), 28
Harlem stride piano, 43–47
*Harlem Suite* (Ellington), 68, 73
Harmon Mute, 152
Harmonies
 bebop, 102
 cool style, 116
 Davis and, 159
 defined, 4, 7–8
 early New Orleans jazz, 34
 free jazz, 161
 Miles Davis Quintet, 157
 mood compositions, 72
 swing era, 84
Harmony-based improvisation, 59
Harper, Winard, 193
Harrell, Tom, 193
Harris, Barry, 139
Harris, Benny, 114, 118
Harrison, Donald, 193
Harrison, Jimmy, 60, 97
Hart, Billy, 193
Hart, John, 193
Haslip, Jimmy, 182
Hawes, Hampton, 125, 126
Hawkins, Coleman, 25, 65, 70, 80, 92–93, 94, 95, 97, 99, 100, 111, 132, 137, 145, 174
Hayden, Scott, 29
Hayes, Louis, 139
Haynes, Graham, 192
Haynes, Roy, 102, 114, 135, 139, 188
Head arrangement, 78
Headhunters, 152, 181
*Headhunters* (Hancock), 187
Heath, Jimmy, 138, 155
Heath, Percy, 121, 154
"Heebie Jeebies" (Armstrong), 52
Hefti, Neal, 82
"Helly Dolly" (Armstrong), 53
Hemphill, Julius, 166
Henderson, Fletcher, 25, 50, 59, 63, 65–66, 84, 85, 86, 94, 95, 96, 97, 192
Henderson, Horace, 90, 192
Henderson, Joe, 132, 138
Henderson, Michael, 182
Henderson, Scott, 182
Hendricks, John, 52
Hendricks, Jon, 148
Hendrix, Jimi, 180, 181, 183, 184
Herbie Hancock Quartet, 187
Herbie Mann Quartet, 181
Herman, Woody, 113, 116, 117
Herring, Vincent, 193
Herwig, Conrad, 193
Hickman, Art, 62
"Hi Fly" (Adderley), 136
Higginbothan, J. C., 60, 97
Higgins, Billy, 162, 167
High hat cymbals, 11, 37, 81, 103, 104, 159
Hill, Andrew, 139
Hill, Teddy, 94
Hi-Los, 148
Hindemith, Paul, 188
Hines, Earl, 45, 53, 60, 95, 100, 101, 106, 108, 112, 117
Hinton, Milt, 114
"Hodge Podge" (Ellington/Hodges), 95
Hodges, Johnny, 37, 69, 71, 73, 94, 96, 97, 107, 141, 164, 173, 174
Hodges, Johnny (John Cornelius), 95
Hohner clavinet, 187, 189
Holiday, Billie, 45, 80, 87, 88, 92, 93, 96, 144–45, 147
Holland, Dave, 160, 167, 180, 184, 188, 193
Hollers, 32
Holloway, Red, 139
Holman, Bill, 118, 126
Holmes, Richard "Groove", 139
"Honeysuckle Rose" (Waller/Razaf), 44
Honky-tonk, 31, 46–47
"Honky Tonk Train Blues" (Lewis), 46, 47
"Hootie Blues", 106
Hopkins, Fred, 167
Horace Silver Quintet, 132–33
"Hora Decubitus" (Mingus), 142
Horn, Shirley, 148
Horne, Lena, 147
Hot bands, 33
Hot Five, 37, 38, 51, 63, 106
"Hot" jazz chorus, 64
Hot Seven, 37, 38, 51, 63, 106
House, Son, 24
Hubbard, Freddie, 132, 138, 162, 180, 186, 187
Humes, Helen, 80
Hunter, Alberta, 147
Hunter, Charlie, 195
Hurst, Frank, 117
"Hustlin' Blues" (Rainey), 25
Hylton, Jack, 93

## I


Ibos, 18
"I Can't Get Started", 91
"I Cried for You" (Vaughan), 147
Idiosyncracies, musical, 12
"If You Could See Me Now" (Dameron), 113
"I Got It Bad (and That Ain't Good)" (Ellington), 74
"I Got Rhythm" (Gershwin), 12
"I Let a Song Go Out of My Heart" (Ellington), 74
"I'm Beginning to See the Light" (Ellington), 74
"I'm Getting Sentimental Over You" (Dorsey), 88
Imitation, 12
Imperial Orchestra, 36
Improvisation
  Armstrong and, 52
  bebop, 101
  big band style, 64
  Coleman, 163
  Coltrane and, 176
  combo jazz, 58, 59
  cool style, 115, 116
  early New Orleans jazz, 33
  free jazz, 161, 162
  fusion, 180
  hard bop, 130
  Jarrett and, 188
  in jazz, 4, 12–13
  Miles Davis fusion bands, 183
  ragtime and, 27
  swing era, 84
  Weather Report, 185
"In a Mellow Tone" (Webster), 94
"In A Mist" (Beiderbecke), 54, 55
"In a Sentimental Mood" (Ellington), 72
*In a Silent Way* (Davis), 152, 183, 184
*The Incredible Jazz Guitar of Wes Montgomery*, 138
Indian music, 180, 184
Innovation, 12
Innovations in Modern Music Orchestra, 118
*Inside Out* (Corea), 189
Instrumental music, African, 15
Instrumentation, 9, 33, 116
Intellect, vs. emotion, 121
Intensity, hard bop, 130
International Association of Jazz Education, 118
*Interstellar Space* (Coltrane), 176
"In The Dark" (Beiderbecke), 55
"In the Evening by the Moonlight" (Bland), 22
"In the Mood" (Miller), 89
"Intuition", 120
Israels, Chuck, 171
"It Don't Mean a Thing If It Ain't Got That Swing" (Ellington), 73
Ives, Charles, 164
Izenson, David, 162, 167


## J


*Jack Johnson* (Davis), 160, 184
Jackson, Milt, 112, 120–22, 154
Jackson, Ronald Shannon, 167, 192
"Jack the Bear" (Ellington), 70, 73
Jamal, Ahmad, 155
James, Bob, 182, 194
James, Harry, 91, 92, 96, 97, 100
The James Taylor Quartet, 195
Jamiroquai, 195
Jam sessions, 57, 90, 100, 183
Jarman, Joseph, 166
Jarreau, Al, 52
Jarrett, Keith, 132, 152, 160, 167, 187–88
Jay McShann Band, 106
Jay McShann Orchestra, 78
Jazquet, Illinois, 113
Jazz
  chamber-like approach to, 124
  education and, 195–96
  vs. European music, 4
  future of, 191–97
  meanings of, 3
  modern, elements borrowed from African music, 17
  vs. ragtime, 34
Jazz Age, 1920s as, 3, 41
Jazz at the Philharmonic, 90, 91, 94, 96, 106, 109, 146
Jazz conversation, 170
Jazz-flavored artists/bands, 182
Jazz funk, 194
*Jazz Goes to College*, 123
Jazz Hounds, 44, 65
Jazz Messengers, 130–32, 157, 188
Jazz piano trios, 170
Jazz rhythm section, 11–12
Jazz rock, 160
Jazz singers, 143–49. *See also* vocalists
Jazz Workshop, 141
Jean Goldkettle Orchestra, 54, 63
"Jeanie with the Light Brown Hair" (Foster), 22
"Jeep's Blues" (Ellington/Hodges), 73, 95
Jefferson, Blind Lemon, 24
Jefferson, Eddie, 148
Jeff Lorber Fusion, 182
"Jelly Bean Blues" (Rainey), 25
"Jelly Roll" (Mingus), 142
Jeremy Steig and the Satyrs, 181
Jess Stone and the Blues Serenaders, 78
Jethro Tull, 180
Jew's harp, 19
Jim Crow laws, 32
Jimmy Lunceford Orchestra, 89
Jimmy Smith Organ Trio, 137
"Jive Samba" (Adderley), 136
Joachim, Joseph, 62
Jobim, Antonio Carlos, 128
John Coltrane Quartet, 175–76
John Kirby's Sextet, 91
John Mayall's Blues Breakers, 180
"Johnny Come Lately" (Strayhorn), 70
Johnson, Bill, 41, 60
Johnson, Bunk, 36, 50
Johnson, James P., 44, 80
Johnson, J. J., 96, 106, 113, 114, 134, 138, 151, 154
Johnson, Lonnie, 38, 60
Johnson, Marc, 171, 182, 193
Johnson, Pete, 47
Johnson, Robert, 24
Jolly, Pete, 126
Jones, Elvin, 139, 159, 175, 176
Jones, Jo, 80, 81, 97, 103
Jones, Jonah, 97
Jones, Philly Joe, 139, 151, 154, 171
Jones, Quincy, 82
Jones, Sam, 139
Jones, Thad, 82, 138, 142
Jones, Willie, 142
Joplin, Scott, 28–29, 43
Jordan, Duke, 106
Jordan, Louis, 90, 129, 147
Jordan, Sheila, 148
Jordan, Taft, 90
"Jubilee Stomp" (Ellington), 73
Julliard School of Music, 151
Jump bands, 129
"Jumpin' at the Woodside" (Basie), 80
"Jungle Nights in Harlem" (Ellington), 72
Jungle sound, 92, 141
Jungle-style compositions, 68, 69, 70, 72


## K


Kaminsky, Max, 88
Kansas City Five/Six/Seven, 82
Kansas City Rockets, 78
Kansas City style, 64, 77–78, 148
Kay, Connie, 121
Kazoo, 19
Keepnews, Orrin, 169
*Keep Shufflin'*, 44
Keezer, Geoff, 194

Kelly, Wynton, 138, 139, 152, 155
Kenny G, 182, 194
Kenton, Stan, 116, 117–18, 127
Keppard, Freddie, 36, 37, 50
Kern, Jerome, 146
Kessel, Barney, 125, 126
Keyboardists, 182, 184, 185–87, 188–89
*Kind of Blue* (Davis), 136, 152, 155, 156, 158, 169, 173, 180
King Crimson, 180
King of Jazz (Whiteman), 62
King of Swing (Goodman), 85
"King Porter Stomp" (Henderson), 65–66, 91
Kirby, John, 97
Kirk, Andy, 85, 94
Kirk, Roland, 142
Kisor, Ryan, 193
Klemmer, John, 182
Klezmer music, 191, 192
Knepper, Jimmy, 138, 142
Knitting Factory, 192
"Ko Ko", 106
"Koko" (Ellington), 72
Konitz, Lee, 116, 117, 119, 120, 126, 154
Kooper, Al, 181
Koz, Dave, 194
Krall, Diane, 149
Krupa, Gene, 59, 60, 83, 90, 96, 97
Kyle, Billy, 97

## L

LaBarbara, Joe, 171
Labba, Abba, 46
Laboriel, Abe, 182
*La Creation du Monde* (Milhaud), 123
Lacy, Steve, 167
"Lady Bird" (Dameron), 113
*Lady in Satin* (Holiday), 145
The L.A. Express, 181
LaFaro, Scott, 159, 162, 167, 170–71, 185
"La Fiesta" (Corea), 189
Laine, Papa Jack, 37
Lake, Oliver, 166, 167
Lamb, Joseph, 29
LaMenthe, Ferdinand Joseph, 45
Land, Harold, 134–35, 138
Lang, Eddie, 38, 55, 60, 88
Lannigan, Jim, 59, 60
LaRocca, Nick, 36, 40, 54
"La Ronde" (Modern Jazz Quartet), 121
Larry Coryell's Free Spirits, 181
Last Exit, 192
Laswell, Bill, 192
Lateef, Yusef, 142
*Latin American Suite* (Ellington), 73
Latin jazz, 126–28, 194
LaVerne, Andy, 194
Laws, Hubert, 182
Laziness, in melodies, 2
Ledbetter, Huddie "Leadbelly", 24
Lee, Peggy, 96, 98, 147
Length, of jungle-style compositions, 72
Leonard, Harlan, 78
Leslie Tone Cabinet, 137
"Lester Leaps In" (Basie), 82
*Let's Dance*, 85
Levey, Stan, 125
Levy, Hank, 118
Levy, Lou, 126
Lewis, Alonzo, 106
Lewis, George, 37, 167
Lewis, John, 116, 119, 120–22, 126, 154
Lewis, Mead Lux, 46, 47
Lewis, Ramsey, 139
*Liberian Suite* (Ellington), 73
Liebman, Dave, 176, 182, 184
*Light as a Feather* (Corea), 189
Lighthouse All Stars, 125
*Light Years* (Corea), 189
Lilt, rhythmic, 5
Lincoln, Abbie, 148
Lindsay, John, 60
Little, Booker, 138, 164
"Little Brown Jug" (Miller), 89
Little Jazz (Eldridge), 90
*Live at Redlands* (Kenton), 118
*Live Evil* (Davis), 160
"Livery Stable Blues" (ODJB), 40
Lloyd, Charles, 176
Lockwood, Didier, 193
Lomax, Alan, 24, 45
Lomax, John, 24
"Lonely Woman" (Silver), 133
Looping, 195
Los Angeles Junior Orchestra, 139
Los Angeles Neophonic Orchestra, 118
"Lotus Blossom" (Strayhorn), 70
Loud intensity levels, 8
Louis Armstrong and His Orchestra, 53
Lovano, Joe, 176, 193
"Love and Kisses", 145
"Lover Man" (Holiday), 145
"Lover Man" (Vaughan), 146, 147
"Lover" (Vaughan), 146
*Love Supreme* (Coltrane), 175
Low brass, 68
Lowe, Mundell, 169
Luis Russell Orchestra, 53
Lunceford, Jimmie, 85, 89, 96
Lunceford Orchestra, 96
*Lush Life* (Coltrane), 174
"Lush Life" (Strayhorn), 70
Lyons, Jimmy, 167
Lyrics
  bebop, 104
  blues, 24
  function of, 22
  swing era, 84

## M

Ma Rainy, 22, 25, 147
Machito, 127, 128
Magnarelli, Joe, 193
"Mahalia Jackson" (Ellington), 74
Mahavishnu Orchestra, 152, 181, 184
Maiden, Willie, 118
*Maiden Voyage* (Hancock), 187
"Maiden Voyage" (Hancock), 187
Maini, Joe, 126
Mainieri, Mike, 181
"Mainstem" (Ellington), 74
Major mode, 72
Malaby, Tony, 193
Male singers, 148
Malone, Russell, 193
"Mama's Got the Blues" (Smith), 25
Mambo, 127
Mangione, Chuck, 182
Manglesdorf, Albert, 167
Manhattan Transfer, 149
Mann, Herbie, 180, 182, 188
Manne, Shelly, 125, 126
Mannes College of Music, 169
Manone, Wingy, 60
*Man with the Horn* (Davis), 160
"Maple Leaf Rag" (Joplin), 28
Marable, Fate, 37, 38, 50
Maracas, 127
Marches, 28, 33
Marcus, Steve, 181
Mares, Paul, 36
"Margie" (Oliver), 89
Mariano, Charles, 142
"Marie", 91
Marie, Tania, 149
Marmarosa. Dodo, 114
Marr, Hank, 137
Marsalis, Branford, 95, 132, 176, 182, 193
Marsalis, Wynton, 132, 192, 193
Marsh, Warne, 116, 120, 126
Martin, Andy, 193
Martino, Pat, 193
Masada, 192
Masses, 72
Mastersounds, 137
Maupin, Bennie, 184
Mauteen, Taurus, 193
Mays, Lyle, 190

M-Base, 192
McBride, Christian, 193
McCall, Steve, 167
McCandless, Paul, 182
McCann, Les, 139
McDuff, Jack, 139
McFerrin, Bobby, 149
McGee, Howie, 114, 127
McKibbon, Al, 154
McKinney's Cotton Pickers, 90, 95, 96
McLaughlin, John, 159, 160, 180, 182, 184
McLean, Jackie, 132, 135, 137, 138, 142, 154
McNeeley, Jim, 194
McPartland, Dick, 59, 60
McPartland, Jimmy, 59, 60
McPherson, Charles, 138, 142
McRae, Carmen, 148
Measure, defined, 8
Medeski, Martin, and Wood, 192, 195
*Meditations* (Coltrane), 175
Mehldau, Brad, 194
"Melancholy Mood" (Silver), 133
Melodic repetition, 17
Melodic variation, vs. free improvisation, 4
Melodies
  bebop, 101, 104
  blues, 23
  cool style, 116
  Davis and, 159
  defined, 7
  early New Orleans jazz, 33
  in early New Orleans jazz, 34
  free jazz, 162
  hard bop, 130
  Miles Davis Quintet, 157
  ragtime, 27
  stride piano style, 43
  swing eighth-note pattern, 5
  swing era, 84
  work songs, 22
"Memphis Blues" (Handy), 24, 25
Mendes, Sergio, 128
Mercer, Johnny, 74
"Mercy, Mercy, Mercy" (Adderley), 136, 183
Merritt, Jymie, 139
Meter, 8, 116
Metheny, Pat, 182, 189–90, 193
*Metronome*, 94
Metronome All-Stars, 91
Mezzrow, Mezz, 60
*mf* symbols, 8
Micromoog synthesizers, 189
Middle passage, 18
Mike Manieri's White Elephant, 181
*Miles Ahead*, 155
*Miles Davis and the Modern Jazz Giants*, 154
Miles Davis fusion bands, 182–84
Miles Davis Nonet, 119, 123, 124
Miles Davis Quintet, 154, 157, 169, 173, 187
*Miles in the Sky* (Davis), 183
*Miles Smiles* (Davis), 157, 183
*Milestones*, 155
Miley, Bubber, 69, 71, 72, 91, 95
Milhaud, Darius, 123
Military band tradition, in early New Orleans jazz, 33
Miller, Glenn, 60, 85, 88, 89, 96, 97, 113, 119
Miller, Marcus, 182
Miller, Mulgrew, 194
Millinder, Lucky, 91
Mills, Florence, 147
Mingus, Charles, 39, 102, 110, 114, 139–42, 164, 167
"Mingus Fingers" (Mingus), 140
Minor mode, 72
Minstrel show, 21–22, 64
Mintzer, Bob, 193
Miraz, George, 193
"Misty" (Vaughan), 147
Mitchell, Blue, 132, 137, 138
Mitchell, George, 36
Mitchell, Red, 126
Mitchell, Roscoe, 166, 167
Mixed meters, 116
"Moanin'" (Mingus), 142
Mobley, Bill, 193
Mobley, Hank, 131, 132, 138, 155
Modal improvisation, 152, 156, 177
Modern Jazz Quartet, 110, 119, 120–22
Modern singers, 149
Modes, Davis and, 156
Mole, Miff, 55, 60, 97
Mondragon, Joe, 126
Monk, Thelonious, 92, 93, 101, 102, 109, 110, 111–12, 114, 130, 132, 135, 154, 173
Monroe, Clark, 100, 106, 109
Monterey Jazz Festival, 138
Monterose, J. R., 142
Montgomery, Buddy, 137
Montgomery, Monk, 137
Montgomery, Wes, 137–38, 139, 181, 194
Montuno section, 127
"The Mooche" (Ellington), 72
Mood, swing and, 5
Mood compositions, 72
"Mood Indigo" (Ellington), 72
Mood music, 159
Moody, James, 138, 148
"Moonlight Serenade" (Miller), 89
Moore, Brew, 127
Moore, Ralph, 193
Moreira, Airto, 189
Morgan, Lee, 132, 137, 138, 181
Morrell, Marty, 171
Morrow, George, 134–35, 139
Morton, Benny, 97
Morton, Jelly Roll, 33, 36, 37, 38–39, 41, 45, 63, 65
Moses, Bob, 181, 190
Moten, Bennie, 59, 78–79, 94
Moten, Buster, 80
"Moten Swing" (Moten), 79
Mother of the Blues (Rainey), 25
Motian, Paul, 167, 170, 171
Motown, 159, 179, 180
Mouzon, Alphonse, 182
Moye, Don, 166
*mp* symbols, 8
Mulligan, Gerry, 116, 117, 118, 119, 123–24, 125, 154
Multitrack recording, 2
Mundy, Jimmy, 97
Murphy, Mark, 148
Murphy, Spud, 97
Murray, David, 167
Murray, Sunny, 167
Music, 3, 7–13
Musical idiosyncracies, 12
Musical portraits, 74
Musical tag, in early New Orleans jazz, 35
Musicians
  bebop, 114
  hard bop, 138–39
  jazz-rock fusion, 182
Musso, Vido, 97
Mutes, 50
*My Favorite Things* (Coltrane), 175
*My Funny Valentine*, 157
"My Old Kentucky Home" (Foster), 22


# N


"Naima" (Coltrane), 175
Najee, 194
Naked City, 192
Nanton, "Tricky" Sam, 69, 71, 97, 113
Nash, Lewis, 193
National Association of Jazz Educators, 118
National Conservatory of Music, 62
Navarro, Fats, 108, 112–13, 114, 130, 134–35, 146, 154
*Nefertiti*, 157
"Nefertiti" (Shorter), 159
Neidlinger, Buell, 167
Nelson, Oliver, 137, 138, 164
Neoclassicism, 116

Neo-hardbop movement, 192
Nestico, Sammy, 82
Neumeister, Ed, 193
New Concepts of Artistry in Rhythm Orchestra, 118
*New Conversations* (Evans), 171
*New Jazz Conceptions* (Evans), 169
New Orleans, 18–19
New Orleans jazz, 2
New Orleans' music
- American attitude change, 40–41
- Creoles, 32
- early jazz, 32–35
- early jazz musicians, 35–39
- history, 31–32
- white jazz bands, 39–40

New Orleans Rhythm Kings (NORK), 36, 37, 40, 54, 59
New Orleans' style, vs. Chicago style, 58–59
*New Orleans Suite* (Ellington), 73
*Newport Jazz Festival Suite* (Ellington), 73
*New World a-Comin'* (Ellington), 73
New York, 58
New York Jazz Awards, 190
New York Philharmonic, 54
New York Voices, 149
"Nica's Dream" (Silver), 133
Nichols, Red, 55, 60, 88, 89
Niehaus, Lennie, 118, 120, 126
Nigeria, 17, 18
Nigerian tribe, 17
Nightclubs, 64, 77, 179
"A Night in Tunisia" (Gillespie), 109
1920s, as Jazz Age, 3, 41
Noble, Ray, 89
Nock, Mike, 182
*No Mystery* (Corea), 189
Nonjazz styles, 185
Nonmusical aspects, free jazz, 162
Nonsense syllables, scatting, 52
Nonsuggestion of bar lines, 120
Noodling, Beiderbecke, 54
Noone, Jimmie, 36, 37, 45
"Nostalgia in Times Square" (Mingus), 142
Notes, 1, 24
*Now He Sings, Now He Sobs* (Corea), 188
Nussbaum, Adam, 193
*The Nutcracker Suite* (Ellington), 73

## O

Oatts, Dick, 193
Oberlin Conservatory of Music, 62
Oboe, 9, 116, 125
O'Day, Anita, 98, 148
*Of Human Feelings* (Coleman), 164
Ogerman, Claus, 171
"Oh, Dem Golden Slippers" (Bland), 22
"Oh! Susanna" (Foster), 22
"Old Folks at Home" (Foster), 22
"Old Man Blues" (Ellington), 74
"Oleo" (Rollins), 136
Oliver, Joe "King", 35–36, 37, 38, 40, 41, 49, 50, 57, 59
Oliver, Sy, 85, 88, 89, 97, 192
Olympia Brass Band, 38
"One O'Clock Jump" (Basie), 80
Onward Brass Band, 36, 38
Oom-pah effect, 43
Open horn playing, 92
Opera, ragtime, 29
Orchestral textures, 119
Ore, John, 112
Organ, 183
Organists, 137, 139, 194
Original Creole Band, 41
"Original Dixie Jazz Band One-Step" (ODJB), 40
Original Dixieland Jazz Band (ODJB), 36, 40, 53, 54, 194
"Original Rags" (Joplin), 28
Ornamentation, in early New Orleans jazz, 33
*Ornette on Tenor* (Coleman), 164
Ornstein School of Music, 137
Ory, Kid, 25, 37, 41, 53, 139
Osby, Greg, 192, 193
Ostinato figures, 17
"Our Delight" (Dameron), 113
Overcommercialization, of big band swing, 99
Overdubbing, 171, 183, 185, 193

## P

Pace, Harry, 65
Pace-Handy Music Company, 65
Page, Oran "Hot Lips", 78, 88
Page, Walter, 78, 81, 97, 103, 185
*Paint the World* (Corea), 189
Palmieri, Eddie, 127, 128
Palomar Ballroom, 85
*Pangea* (Davis), 160
Paraphrase improvisation, 52, 59
*Paris Concert* (Jarrett), 188
"Parisian Thoroughfare" (Powell), 110
Parker, Charlie "Bird", 45, 95, 97, 101, 102, 105–09, 110, 114, 120, 124, 127, 130, 135, 136, 140, 146, 151, 152, 154, 174, 188, 196
Pascal, Hermeto, 128
Pass, Joe, 139
Passacaglias, 116
"Passion Flower" (Strayhorn), 70, 95
Pastorius, Jaco, 182, 185, 189
Patitucci, John, 182, 189–90, 193
Pat Metheny Group, 128, 182, 190
*The Pat Metheny Group* (Corea), 190
Patton, Charley, 24
Patton, John, 139
Paul Whiteman's Orchestra, 54
Payton, Nicholas, 193
"Peace Piece" (Evans), 156
"Peace" (Silver), 133
Peacock, Gary, 167, 188
Pedal point effect, 175
"Peggy's Blue Skylight" (Mingus), 142
Pendergast, Teddy, 77
Pentatonic scales, 16
Pepper, Art, 96, 118, 120, 126
Percussion instruments, 10–11, 15, 17, 192
Percussionists, Latin jazz, 128
"Perdido" (Vaughan), 147
Perez, Danilo, 194
Perez, Manual, 36, 50
Performance characteristics, of early New Orleans jazz, 34–35
Performer's art, jazz as, 4
Perkins, Bill, 126
Perry, Sascha, 194
Person, Houston, 139
Personal relationships, blues and, 23
Peterson, Oscar, 114
Petit, Buddy, 36, 37
Petrillo, James, 100
Pettiford, Oscar, 113, 114, 132, 146
Philadelphia Orchestra, 188
Philips, Flip, 127
Pianistic idiom, ragtime as, 27
Pianists
- bebop, 100, 103, 114
- Chicago style, 60
- cool style, 126
- free jazz, 167
- future, 194
- hard bop, 139
- Jazz Messengers, 132
- Latin jazz, 128
- Mingus's bands, 142
- swing era, 97

Piano, 11, 33, 34, 43–47, 59, 65, 84, 88, 109–12, 119, 125, 127, 130, 136, 138, 151, 152, 154, 156, 159, 161, 164, 165–66, 175, 187–88, 190
Pianoless quartet, 124
Pied Pipers, 89
Pierce, Nat, 97
"Pine Top's Boogie-Woogie" (Smith), 47
Pitch, 154
Pitch inflection, 16–17, 34

"Pithecanthropus Erectus" (Mingus), 141, 142
Pizzicato melodies, 74
Plagiarism, 2
Player pianos, 27
Pleasure, King, 148
Plunger mute, 69, 72, 74, 141, 157, 194
Pocket trumpet, 165
Polkas, 33
Pollack, Ben, 59, 60, 89, 91
Polyrhythm, 16
Ponty, Jon Luc, 182
"Poor Man's Blues" (Smith), 25
Pop music, 179
Pop singers, vs. jazz singers, 143
Popular songs, 33
*Porgy and Bess*, 155
*Porgy and Bess Revisited*, 92
Porter, Cole, 146
*Portrait of Jazz*, 171
Postbop idiom, 185
Potter, Chris, 193
Potter, Tommy, 106, 114, 135, 154
Powell, Bud, 45, 92, 103, 106, 109–10, 114, 132, 134–35, 140, 171, 188
Powell, Chris, 135
Powell, Mel, 97
Powell, Richie, 110, 134–35
Pozo, Chano, 109, 126
*pp* symbols, 8
"The Preacher" (Silver), 132
Pre-jazz blues singers, 147
"Prelude to a Kiss" (Ellington), 72
Pre-swing, 139
Priester, Julian, 167
Prima, Louis, 147
Primary timekeeper, bassists as, 103
Prime Time, 164, 181, 192
Primitive blues, 24
Prison songs, 22, 23
Procope, Russell, 97
Programmatic music, 139, 159
Progressive Jazz Orchestra, 118
Prohibition, 41, 83
*p* symbols, 8
Puente, Tito, 127, 128
Pullen, Don, 142, 167
Purim, Flora, 149, 189

## Q

Quadrilles, 33
Quality of a piece, 3
Quartal voicings, 176
Quebec, Ike, 139
*The Queens Suite* (Ellington), 73
*Quiet Nights*, 155
Quintet of the Hot Club of France, 104

## R

Ra, Sun, 165–66
Rabbit Foot Minstrels, 25
Rachmaninoff, 63
Radio, 2
Radio broadcasts, of Ellington, 69–70
Raeburn, Boyd, 116, 118
Ragging, in early New Orleans jazz, 33
Rags, 33
Ragtime
  African-American music and, 27–29
  big band swing and, 61
  influence on Kansas City style, 77
  vs. jazz, 34
  stride piano style and, 43
  vs. stride style, 43
"Ragtime Baby" (Stone), 28
Ragtime opera, 29
Rainy, Will "Pa", 25
Ramey, Gene, 106, 114
Ramsey Lewis Trio, 181
Raney, Jimmy, 114
Range, Armstrong and, 52
Rare groove, 195
Rattles, 15
Ravel, Maurice, 54, 55, 117, 171
Rawls, Lou, 96
Razaf, Andy, 44
Recompositions, 143
Recording format, 2
Recording strike, 100
Red Hot Peppers, 36, 37, 39, 45, 63
Red light district, New Orleans, 31
Red Norvo Trio, 140
Redman, Dewey, 167
Redman, Don, 25, 63, 65, 68, 84, 85, 95, 97
Redman, Joshua, 176, 193
Red Norvo Trio, 140
Reeves, Diane, 149
Rehak, Frank, 138
Reharmonization, 102
"Reincarnation of a Lovebird" (Mingus), 142
Reinhardt, Django, 93, 104
Release, 2, 5
Reliance Brass Band, 37, 38
*Reminiscing in Tempo* (Ellington), 73
"Reminiscing in Tempo" (Ellington), 73
Renaissance music, 120
Rent parties, 44
Repetition, 17
Research, 3
Return to Forever (band), 152, 181, 189
*Return to Forever* (Corea), 189
"Revelations" (Mingus), 142
Revivalism, 27
Revolution, through piece of music, 12
"Rhapsody in Blue" (Gershwin), 62
Rhumba beat, 126–27
Rhythm
  African, 16
  Armstrong and, 51
  big band style, 64
  Coltrane and, 177
  Davis and, 159
  defined, 4, 8
  hard bop, 130
  jazz combo, 59
  Kansas City style, 78
  Latin jazz, 127
  Miles Davis Quintet, 157
  as part of music, 1
  ragtime, 27
  smooth jazz, 194
  swing, 5
Rhythm and blues (R&B), 180
Rhythm and blues (R&B) jump bands, 129
Rhythmic lilt, 5
Rhythmic propulsion, 4
Rhythmic repetition, 17
Rhythm section, 33, 63, 64, 84, 101, 103–12, 120, 180
Rich, Buddy, 88, 97
Richards, Johnny, 118
Richmond, Dannie, 142
Ride cymbal, 110, 159
Ride rhythms, 37
Riff bands, 78
Riffs, 78
Riley, Ben, 112
Ring shouts, 32
Rivers, Sam, 167
Roach, Max, 93, 96, 106, 110, 113, 114, 126, 134–35, 139
Roberts, Charles "Luckyeth", 44
Roberts, Marcus, 194
Robinson, Bill, 74
"Rockin' in Rhythm" (Ellington), 73
"Rockit" (Hancock), 187
Rock music, 179
Rodgers, Richard, 146
Roditi, Claudio, 193
Rodney, Red, 114
Rodrigo, Joaquin, 155
Rogers, Shorty, 118, 125, 126
Roker, Mickey, 139
Roland, Gene, 118
Rollini, Adrian, 55
Rollins, Sonny, 114, 134–36, 138, 151, 154
*Romantic Warrior* (Corea), 189
Rondos, 116

"Room 608" (Silver), 133
Root, 7–8
Roppolo, Leon, 37
Rosenwinkel, Kurt, 193
"Rose Room" (Goodman), 104
Rosnes, Renee, 194
Rosolino, Frank, 114, 118, 125, 126, 138, 148
Ross, 148
"Round About Midnight" (Monk), 112
*Round Midnight*, 155
"Round Midnight" (Williams/Monk), 92
Rouse, Charlie, 112
Royal Roost Nonet, 116
Rubalcaba, Gonzalo, 128
Rubin, Vanessa, 149
"Ruby My Dear" (Monk), 112
Rudd, Roswell, 167
Rugolo, Pete, 118
Ruiz, Hilton, 128
Rumsey, Howard, 125, 126
Rushing, Jimmy, 78, 80, 97, 148
Russell, Curly, 114
Russell, George, 109
Russell, Luis, 37, 53
Russell, Pee Wee, 60
Russell, Ross, 106
Russo, William, 118

## S

Sabien, Randy, 193
Sacred concerts, 71
Salon groups, 33
Salsa, 126, 127, 188
"Salt Peanuts", 106
Samba, 18, 127, 128
Sampling, 195
Sampson, Edgar, 85, 90, 97
Sanborn, Dave, 182, 194
Sanchez, David, 128, 193
Sanchez, Pancho, 128
Sanders, Pharoah, 167, 176
Sandoval, Arturo, 128, 193
San Francisco Symphony, 188
Santamaria, Mongo, 128, 186, 188
"Sassy" (Vaughan), 147
"Satchel Mouth" (Armstrong nickname), 49
"Satin Doll" (Ellington/ Strayhorn), 74
Sauter, Eddie, 86, 97
Saxophone, 9, 58, 63, 64, 84, 90, 118, 146, 161, 176, 183, 188
Saxophone choir, 62
*Saxophone Colossus* (Rollins), 135
Saxophonists
  Chicago style, 60
  cool style, 117
  free jazz, 167
  Latin jazz, 128
Scales, 7, 16
Scatting, 52, 143, 145
Schuller, Gunther, 136
Schuur, Diane, 149
Scofield, John, 182, 184, 193
Scott, James, 29
Scott, Shirley, 139
Scott, Tom, 181, 182
Scriabin, Alexander, 171
Sea chanteys, 22
Second awakening, 27
Second Herd, 117
Self-expression, through music, 2
"Self-Portrait in Three Colors" (Mingus), 141
Sengalese, 18
Seven Steps to Heaven, 155, 157
Shakers, 15
*Shakespearean Suite (Such Sweet Thunder)* (Ellington), 73
Shank, Bud, 120, 125, 126
Shankar, Ravi, 181
*The Shape of Jazz to Come* (Coleman), 164
Shavers, Charlie, 91, 97
Shaw, Artie, 83, 87–88, 98
Shaw, Woody, 132
Shearing, George, 114, 126, 172
Sheets of sound, 174, 177, 184
Sheldon, Jack, 126
Shepp, Archie, 167, 176
Sheppard, Bob, 193
Shields, Larry, 37
"Shiny Stockings" (Basie), 82
Shorter, Wayne, 132, 152, 157–59, 176, 182, 184, 185
Shostakovich, Dmitri, 188
"The Sidewinder" (Morgan), 181
Siegelstein, Sandy, 154
*Silent Way* (Davis), 160
Silver, Horace, 131, 132–33, 136, 139, 151, 188
Simone, Nina, 148
Sims, Zoot, 117, 126
Sinatra, Frank, 83, 88, 91, 98, 147
Singers Unlimited, 149
Singleton, Zutty, 37
"Sister Sadie" (Silver), 132
Six-string electric bass, 189
*Sketches of Spain*, 155
Slagle, Steve, 193
Slave experience, 17–18
Slave music, 27, 128
Slide Five, 195
Sliding between notes, 24
Slim and Slam, 148
Sly and the Family Stone, 181
Smears, on trombone, 34
Smith, Bessie, 22, 25–26, 44, 58, 94, 145, 147
Smith, Buster, 97, 106
Smith, Carson, 126
Smith, Clarence "Pine Top", 47
Smith, Henry "Buster", 78, 97
Smith, Jabbo, 60
Smith, Jimmy, 137, 139
Smith, Joe, 25
Smith, Johnny, 126
Smith, Leo, 167
Smith, Mamie, 26, 44, 47, 65, 93, 147
Smith, Marvin "Smitty", 192, 193
Smith, Stuff, 60
Smith, Trixie, 26, 147
Smith, Willie "the Lion", 44, 80, 89, 96, 97
Smooth jazz, 194
Snare drum, 11, 34
"Snowy Morning Blues" (Johnson), 44
Social aspects, of bebop, 102–03
Social climate, jazz as reflection of, 2
Social importance, of jazz, 3
Sock cymbal, 37
Soft intensity levels, 8
Soft Machine, 180
Solfege, 24
"Solitude" (Ellington), 72
*Solo Concerts* (Jarrett), 188
"Solo Flight" (Christian), 137
Solo improvisation, 35, 58, 84
Soloists, 49–55, 130
Solos, 129–30
Solo section, 127
*Someday My Prince Will Come*, 155
*Something Else* (Coleman), 164
"Sometimes I'm Happy", 91
"Songbooks" (Fitzgerald), 146
"Song For My Father" (Silver), 133
"Song of India", 91
"Sophisticated Lady" (Ellington), 72
Soprano saxophone, 9, 10, 152, 175, 176, 183
*The Sorcerer*, 157
Soul jazz, 181, 194
*The Sound of Jazz*, 145
Sound organization, 1, 51–52
Sounds
  aesthetic experience and, 3
  of the blues, 23
  free jazz, 162
  as part of music, 1
Sousa, John Philip, 28
Southern Syncopated Orchestra, 38, 61, 62
"So What", 156
"Spain" (Corea), 189
Spanier, Muggsy, 60
Spasm bands, 18–19, 49
Speakeasies, 41, 57, 77, 83

Special Edition, 192
Speed, Chris, 193
Spirit, in swing, 5
Spirituals, 22, 23, 27, 32
Spivak, Charlie, 96
Spliced recordings, 183
Spyrogyra, 182
Stacy, Jess, 97
Stafford, Jo, 98, 147
Stan Kenton Orchestra, 117–18
Stark, Bobby, 90
Stark, John, 28–29
"State Street Special" (Yancey), 47
St. Cyr, Johnny, 38
*Steamin'*, 155
Steel bands, 18
Steely Dan, 182
Steig, Jeremy, 181
Steps Ahead, 182
Stereo recordings, 2
Stern, Mike, 184, 193
Steve Coleman and Five Elements, 192
Steve Marcus' Count's Rock Band, 181
Stewart, Bill, 193
Stewart, Rex, 92, 97
Stewart, Slam, 46, 114, 148
Stibel, Sol, 105
Stitt, Sonny, 108, 112, 113, 114, 138, 146, 174
"St. Louis Blues" (Handy), 25, 126
Stockhausen, Karl, 189
Stone, Fred, 28
Stone, Jess, 78
Stone, Sly, 180
Stop-time breaks, 35, 59
"Stormy Sea Blues" (Rainey), 25
*Stormy Weather*, 96
Story, Harry, 31
Storyville, 31, 45, 50
"Straight No Chaser" (Monk), 112
Strain, in marches, 28
"Strange Fruit" (Holiday), 145
Stravinsky, Igor, 117, 188
Strayhorn, Billy, 70, 71, 74, 97
Street cry, 23, 27
Stride piano, 43–47
Stride piano style, 43, 46, 82
String bass, 33, 34, 59, 74
String instruments, 10, 15, 33, 118
"St. Thomas" (Rollins), 136
Subdivision, defined, 9
Subdivision of the beat, by Parker, 107
*Such Sweet Thunder* (Ellington/Strayhorn), 70
Suites, 71, 72
*Suite Thursday* (Ellington), 73
Sullivan, Joe, 60
*Sun Bear Concerts* (Jarrett), 188
Superior Brass Band, 38
Swartz, Harvie, 193
Swing, 4–5
Swing eighth-note pattern, 5, 39, 63
Swing era
  alto saxophonists, 95–97
  history, 83–84
  important bands of, 85–90
  singers, 147
  style, 84–85
  tenor saxophonists, 92–95
  trumpet players, 90–92
Swingle Singers, 149
Symphonic jazz, 62, 63, 194
Symphonic style, 62
Syncopated melodies, 43
Syncopated music, 61
Syncopated rhythms, 5
Syncopation, 9, 17, 22, 27, 33
Syncretism, 18
Synthesizers, 180, 183, 185, 187


## T


Tailgate style, 34, 37
"Take Five" (Desmond), 123
Take Six, 149
"Take the 'A' Train" (Ellington/Strayhorn), 74
*Taking Off* (Hancock), 186
Tango rhythm, 126
Tape recordings, 2
Tate, Erskine, 60
*The Tattooed Bride* (Ellington), 73
Tatum, Art, 45–46, 100, 106, 120
Taylor, Art, 135, 139
Taylor, Billy, 114
Taylor, Cecil, 161, 164
Taylor, Eva, 147
Tchicai, John, 167
Teagarden, Jack, 25, 53, 60, 97, 100, 147
Technological advances, in music, 2
Teddy Hill Band, 108, 110
Teddy Hill Orchestra, 90
Tempo
  African music, 17
  bebop, 102
  Davis and, 154
  defined, 8
  free jazz, 162
  hard bop, 130
  of jungle style, 72
  swing, 5
  work songs, 22
"Tempus Fugit" (Powell), 110
"Tenderly" (Vaughan), 147
Tenor guitar, 137
Tenor saxophone, 9, 10, 64, 65, 80, 113, 117, 118, 120, 130, 131, 132, 134–36, 138, 151, 152, 154, 164–65, 166, 175, 182, 187, 189
Tenor saxophonists
  bebop, 100, 114
  cool style, 126
  future, 193
  hard bop, 138, 139
  Jazz Messengers, 132
  Mingus's bands, 142
  swing era, 92–95, 97
Tension, 2, 5
Terminal vibrato, 52
Territory bands, 77
Terry, Clark, 114, 148, 152, 154
Teschemacher, Frankie, 59, 60
Theater Booking Owners' Association (TOBA), 25
Theaters, 41, 64
"The Flaming Sword" (Ellington), 74
"The Jeep is Jumpin'" (Ellington/Hodges), 95
*The Köln Concert* (Jarrett), 188
Theme song, big bands, 84
"Them There Eyes" (Holiday), 145
"Things Ain't What They Used To Be" (Ellington), 95
Third stream music, 123, 139
The Thirteen Original Blue Devils, 93
"This Here" (Adderley), 136
Thomas, Joe, 89
Thompson, Lucky, 112, 114
Thornhill, Claude, 97, 116, 119
Threadgill, Henry, 167
*Three Sacred Concerts* (Ellington), 73
"Three to Get Ready", 123
"Tiger Rag" (Tatum), 46
Timbales, 127
Timbre, 8, 16, 75
*Time Out*, 123
Timmons, Bobby, 132, 136, 139
Tin Pan Alley, 3, 126, 147
Tio family, 35
Tizol, Juan, 127
Tjader, Cal, 188
TOBA theaters, 77
"Toby" (Moten), 79
Togo, 17
Tommy Dorsey Band, 88
Tommy Dorsey's Orchestra, 91
*Tomorrow is the Question* (Coleman), 164
Tom-tom drums, 11
Tonal manipulation, 16, 22, 23–24, 50
  African music, 17
  early New Orleans jazz, 34
  free jazz, 162
  by Oliver, 36

Tone color, 116, 154, 177
Tony WIlliams Lifetime, 152, 181, 184
Torme, Mel, 96, 148
Tough, Dave, 59, 60, 88, 97
Tower of Power, 182
Towner, Ralph, 182, 193
Trading fours, 13
Train compositions, 74
Trap set of drums, 11
*Treemonisha* (Joplin), 29
Triplet figure, 176
Tristano, Lennie, 116, 119, 120, 126, 161, 171
Trombone, 9, 33, 34, 63, 68, 69, 84, 89, 113, 118, 119, 139
Trombone glissandi, 34
Trombone players
- bebop, 114
- Chicago style, 60
- cool style, 126
- early New Orleans jazz, 37
- free jazz, 167
- future, 193
- hard bop, 138
- Mingus's bands, 142
- swing era, 97

Trumbauer, Frankie, 54, 55, 60, 80, 87, 94, 95
Trumpet, 9, 34, 59, 63, 65, 68, 69, 84, 88, 89, 90, 107–09, 112–13, 118, 119, 124, 130, 131, 134–35, 146, 162–64, 165, 186, 187, 192
Trumpeters
- bebop, 100, 114
- Chicago style, 60
- cool style, 126
- free jazz, 167
- fusion, 182
- future, 193
- hard bop, 138
- Jazz Messengers, 132
- Latin jazz, 128
- Mingus's bands, 142
- swing era, 90–92, 97

Tuba, 9, 33, 34, 59, 64, 70, 116, 119
Turner, Big Joe, 148
Turpin, Tom, 28
Turre, Steve, 193
Turrentine, Stanley, 137, 139
*Tutu* (Davis), 160
Tuxedo Brass Band, 38
Twelve-measure structure, of blues, 23
Twentieth-century classical music, 139
Tyner, McCoy, 175, 176, 180

## U

"Undecided" (Shavers), 91
*Unit Structures* (Taylor), 164
"Un Poco Loco" (Powell), 110
Upright bass, 10, 33, 139
Urban blues, 25, 26
Urbaniak, Michael, 182
US3, 195

## V

Valdez, Chucho, 128
Vaudeville, 22, 41, 64, 77, 80
Vaughan, Sarah, 45, 52, 96, 146–47, 148
Veal, Reginald, 193
"Vendome" (Modern Jazz Quartet), 121
Venuti, Joe, 60, 88
"Versaille" (Modern Jazz Quartet), 121
Vibraphone, 10, 63, 120, 121, 137, 189
Vibraphonist, 112
Vibrato, 63, 70, 80, 107, 152
- Armstrong and, 52
- bebop, 104
- cool style, 116

*Vienna Concert* (Jarrett), 188
Vinson, Eddie, 92
Viola, 10
Violin, 10, 33, 162–64, 182, 193
Violin players, 60
Vitous, Miroslav, 182, 184, 188
Vocal improvisation, 143
Vocalists, 49–55, 98, 128, 143–49, 189
Vocal jazz groups, 148–49
Voice, as instrument, 68, 75, 145, 146
Voicing, defined, 8
Voicing across sections, 68, 74
Volstead Act (1919), 77
Voodoo, 18
V.S.O.P. Quintet, 187

## W

Waldron, Mal, 142
Wall, Dan, 194
Waller, Fats (Thomas Wright), 44, 45–46, 80, 82
Walrath, Jack, 142
Walter Page and the Blue Devils, 78
Walton, Cedar, 132
"Waltz for Debbie" (Evans), 169
Wand, Hart, 24
"Warm Valley" (Ellington), 74
Washboard, 19
Washington, Dinah, 148
Washington, Grover, 182
Washtub basin, 19
"Watermelon Man" (Hancock), 186
Waters, Ethel, 26, 44, 65, 147
Watkins, Doug, 139
Watrous, Bill, 193
Watts, Jeff "Train", 193
Wa-wa pedal, 181, 183
Weather Report, 128, 152, 181, 184–85
Webb, Chick, 85, 89–90, 97, 127, 145
Webb, Speed, 90
Webster, Ben, 70, 71, 78, 93, 94, 97, 145
Webster, Freddy, 152, 154
Weckl, Dave, 182, 189
"Weepin' Woman Blues" (Rainey), 25
"Wellman Braud" (Ellington), 74
Wells, Dicky, 80, 82, 85, 96, 97
"Well You Needn't" (Monk), 112
Werner, Kenny, 194
*The Wes Montgomery Trio* (Montgomery), 138
Wess, Frank, 82
"West Coast Blues" (Montgomery), 138
West coast cool, 120
West Coast jazz, 115, 124. See also Cool style
"West End Blues" (Armstrong), 52
Western Africa, 17
Western European scales, 7
Weston, Paul, 97
Wettling, George, 60
"What a Wonderful World" (Armstrong), 53
"(What Did I Do To Be So) Black and Blue" (Waller/Razaf), 44
Wheeler, Kenny, 193
"When Lights Are Low" (Hodges), 96
White, Lenny, 182, 189
White Elephant, 181
Whiteman, Paul, 54, 62–63, 66, 88, 91, 119, 194
Whyte, Zack, 90
Wilcox, Ed, 85
Wiley, Lee, 147
Wilkins, Ernie, 82
Williams, Cootie (Charles Melvin), 69, 71, 91–92, 97
Williams, James, 132, 194
Williams, Joe, 148
Williams, Mary Lou, 46, 78, 85, 97
Williams, Richard, 142
Williams, Tony, 152, 155, 157–58, 180, 182, 183, 184, 187
Wilson, Cassandra, 149, 192
Wilson, Teddy, 45, 92, 94, 96, 97, 145
Winding, Kai, 113, 114, 118, 154
Witchcraft, 18
Wolverines, 54, 59
Wooding, Sam, 66
Woodman, Britt, 142
Woods, Phil, 138

Woodwind instruments, 9, 68, 118, 155, 166
Woody Herman Band, 117
"Woody 'n' You" (Gillespie), 109
Wordless vocals, 68, 75, 145
Word of Mouth Orchestra, 128
*Workin'*, 155
Workman, Reggie, 139
"Work Song" (Adderley), 136
Work songs, 15, 22, 23, 27, 32, 33
World music genre, 165
World Saxophone Quartet (WSQ), 166–67
World War II, 99–100
Writings, critical, 3

**X**

Xylophones, 15

**Y**

Yancey, Jimmy, 47
"Yancey's Stomp" (Yancey), 47
Yellowjackets, 128, 182
Yoruba tribe, 17, 18
Young, Larry, 139
Young, Lester, 22, 80, 82, 92, 93–94, 97, 100, 105, 107, 115, 116, 120, 132, 141, 145, 174, 188
Young, Trummy, 89, 97
Young, Willis, 93, 94

**Z**

Zawinul, Joe, 136, 159, 160, 180, 182, 183, 184, 185
Zorn, John, 192, 193

# JAZZ HISTORY OVERVIEW LISTENING LIST

This suggested listening list was selected from the archives of Rhapsody Music and can be found under the title "Jazz Overview List". These selections were chosen because they are most representative of different jazz genres and feature the most significant jazz innovators. Some of the selections are short and others are rather long. Instructors can use their own choices made from the list we have supplied or create their own required listening list. They can have students listen to an entire track or only a portion of it. Rhapsody contains many other selections that may be added or substituted for the ones we have selected. Students should be encouraged to go beyond the listening list and explore other similar recordings.

Instructions to access Jazz History Overview music playlist:

1. Create Rhapsody Account (see access card packaged with book)
2. Log on to HYPERLINK "http://www.kendallhunt.com/jazzhistoryoverview" www.kendallhunt.com/jazzhistoryoverview
3. Select Jazz Overview Playlist
4. Sign in to Rhapsody to listen to the entire playlist

## "O Berta, Berta" Leroy Miller and Group of Prisoners (Prison Work Song) Chapter 4

Recorded in the 1950s at the Parchman farm in Mississippi. "O Berta, Berta" is a work song performed in a loose call-and-response manner. A Mississippi prison work gang recorded it. The simple melody utilizes only three or four notes, but exhibits the essence of the blues by repeating the lowered (blue) 3rd scale degree. Notice the steady tempo and repetition of the words: the work performed reflects the tempo. Pay attention to how the tools hit the rocks on the 2nd and 4th beats of each measure. Also listen to the bent or blue notes that give it the sound of the blues. The singers perform the melody slightly behind the beat. All of the selections on the recording would be useful to hear because they contain the roots of jazz.

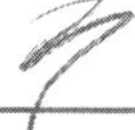

## Scott Joplin "Maple Leaf Rag" (Scott Joplin) 1916 Chapter 4

### Scott Joplin (piano roll)

One of the most famous ragtime pieces, "Maple Leaf Rag" was written by Scott Joplin in the 1890s and published by John Stark in 1899. This recording was made from a player piano roll made by Joplin himself in 1916. The multisection work is based on the formal construction of popular march music of the late nineteenth century. The highly syncopated rhythms and pentatonic melodies (five-note scale) are reminiscent of West African music. This is not jazz, but a style that jazz musicians adopted and transformed into jazz by changing the rhythms.

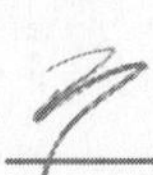

## Jelly Roll Morton "Maple Leaf Rag" (Scott Joplin) 1938 Chapter 4

Morton's recording transforms the rhythm of the original 1916 marchlike performance to one that swings with the easy lilt of the New Orleans style. This is from the famous 1938 Library of Congress Recordings. During this session Morton plays the piece in the older ragtime style, then says a few words and then plays it in the swinging "New Orleans" style. Jelly lightly embellishes the original melody and with these subtle changes turns the ragtime piece into jazz by the *manner in which he performs it*. The stiff syncopation of the early rag style is gone and replaced with one where beats 2 and 4 are emphasized and the eighth notes are swung in a triplet manner reminiscent of Louis Armstrong. Morton's rendition is clearly one of his many improvisations of Joplin's original version. Most likely each time Morton performed "Maple Leaf Rag," it was different.

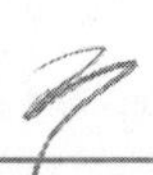

## Robert Johnson "Crossroad Blues" (Robert Johnson) 1937 Chapter 4

A great example of classic Mississippi Delta blues from the 1930s. Robert Johnson was a product of a long line of Delta bluesmen like Charley Patton, Willie Brown, and Son House. The song "Cross Road Blues" is both widely and loosely interpreted by many as a descriptive encounter of Johnson selling his soul to devil. It is based on the standard 12-bar blues, but Johnson takes some liberties by stretching each section turning the form into a 16-bar blues, while still retaining the I-IV-V chords of the standard progression. He utilizes call and response between his voice and the slide guitar notes creating a highly personal style dripping with all of the requisite elements of the blues. He recorded only 36 selections over a period of a few months between November 1936 and June 1937 in San Antonio, Texas.

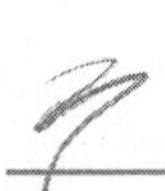

## Bessie Smith "St. Louis Blues" (W.C. Handy) 1925 Chapter 4

Bessie Smith, vocal; Louis Armstrong, cornet; Fred Longshaw, organ

Blues singer Bessie Smith is accompanied by cornetist Louis Armstrong, who performs in a call-and-response manner with her. Bessie was known as an urban or city blues singer. Her mentor was Ma Rainey. Bessie had a strong and distinctive voice and was one of the most popular singers of the 1920s. "St. Louis Blues" has an interesting formal structure. It is constructed as a 12-bar blues with an interlude in a minor key. Written by W.C. Handy, it is one of the most famous blues compositions ever written.

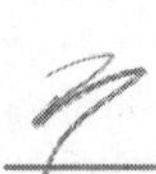

## Ma Rainey "Jelly Bean Blues" (Lina Arant/Ma Rainey) 1924 Chapter 4

Georgia Jazz Band (Ma Rainey vocals and members of the Fletcher Henderson Orchestra)

She was born Gertrude Pridgett in Columbus, Georgia in 1886. By the time she was fourteen, she was singing and dancing in local talent and minstrel shows where she began to incorporate her blues style of singing. She was known as "Queen" or "Mother" of the Blues and had an amazing ability to capture an audience with her profound lyrics and showiness. Her subject matter ranged from the pains of racial discrimination, sexual violence, mistreatment, and infidelity. "Jelly Bean Blues" is traditional 12-bar blues, but each 12-measure chorus has a different melody until the last two choruses, which remain the same. There is much instrumental interplay between Rainy and the members of her Georgia Band (all members of the Fletcher Henderson Orchestra). She ended up recording 100 songs between 1923 and 1928 on Paramount Records. During that time she was accompanied by many noted jazz musicians such as Louis Armstrong, Tommy Ladnier, Fletcher Henderson, and Coleman Hawkins.

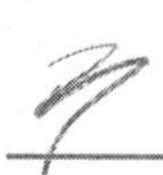

## James Reese Europe "Broadway Hit Medley" 1919 Chapter 4 & 9

This recording from April of 1919 was made upon Europe's triumphant return from France after World War I. The 369th Hellfighters Band, as they were called, was immensely popular in France and the United States. It is not a jazz band per se, but a concert/marching band that played ragtime influenced syncopated music that was the rage in New York and other large metropolitan cities. His orchestra played instrumental ragtime with a rhythmic vitality and excitement that made up for any technical shortcomings. Notice the "stiff" rhythms that lack the easy swing of the blues performers and musicians like Louis Armstrong. They recorded popular songs of the day, which included this Broadway medley, rags, blues, and traditional marches. You can hear stop time solos, some inflected notes and pitch bending, but nothing here is improvised.

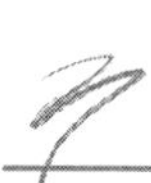

## Original Dixieland Jazz Band "Dixie Jass Band One-Step" (Nick LaRocca) 1917 Chapter 5

Tony Sbarbaro, drums; Eddie Edwards, trombone; Nick LaRocca, cornet; Larry Shields, clarinet; Henry Ragas, piano

"Dixie Jass Band One Step" became the first instrumental Jazz record ever released on February 26, 1917. Its success signaled the beginning of the Jazz Age which helped define the era called the "Roaring Twenties". This commercial band was an immediate success and performances included outrageous stage antics. Their music sounds *cartoonish* by today's standards and it is likely that not all New Orleans bands sounded like this one. The one-step was a popular dance of the period. This performance is full of stop time solos, collective improvisation, and exaggerated clarinet and trombone playing.

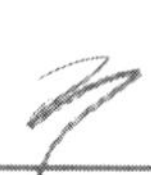

## King Oliver's Creole Jazz Band "Dippermouth Blues" (Joe Oliver) 1923 Chapter 5 & 7

Joe "King" Oliver, cornet; Louis Armstrong, cornet; Johnny Dodds, clarinet; Honore Dutrey, trombone; Lil Hardin, piano; Baby Dodds, drums; Bud Scott, banjo and vocal

Recorded in 1923 in Chicago by Oliver's band, "Dippermouth Blues" features a young Louis Armstrong playing 2$^{nd}$cornet to his mentor. It is named after Armstrong whose nickname was "Dippermouth." It is one of the earliest and most important recordings of an African-American jazz band. Much of this performance is in the older traditional New Orleans collectively improvised style. Listen near the end when Joe King Oliver steps aside (and yells "Oh play that thing") to allow his protégé Louis Armstrong to play a solo.

## Louis Armstrong and His Hot Five "Hotter Than That" (Lil Hardin) 1927 Chapter 7

Louis Armstrong, cornet and vocal; Kid Ory, trombone; Johnny Dodds, clarinet; Lil Armstrong, piano; Johnny St. Cyr, banjo; Lonnie Johnson, guitar

This recording features the great jazz and blues guitarist Lonnie Johnson. It shows a greater sense of form than many of the other recordings and features Armstrong's cornet playing and singing in addition to the call and response duet with Johnson's guitar. Contrast Armstrong's relaxed eighth notes to Dodds' stiff ragtime-like rhythm. Armstrong's phrasing on the cornet and scat singing are the same. The relaxed and easy swing of Armstrong and Johnson make the recording a success. Note the unusual rhythmic effect (3 vs. 2) of Armstrong's singing against Johnson's guitar accompaniment. This is one of the first recordings where Armstrong has an improviser (Johnson) of almost equal talent on his record.

| | |
|---|---|
| 00:00–00:08 | Collectively improvised introduction |
| 00:09–00:43 | ABAC form (8-bar sections): Armstrong plays the melody with rhythm section accompaniment |
| 00:44–01:18 | 2nd chorus: improvised clarinet solo by Johnny Dodds |
| 01:19–01:54 | 3rd chorus: Armstrong sings a "scat" solo with Lonnie Johnson's guitar accompaniment |
| 01:55–02:18 | 4th chorus: Armstrong and Johnson engage in a stop time trading of two bar phrases in a "call and response" manner; short solo piano interlude introduces the next section |
| 02:19–02:33 | Last chorus (AB) Improvised trombone solo by Kid Ory |
| 02:35–02:44 | Last chorus (A) Armstrong plays lead trumpet over a collectively improvised final section |
| 02:45–02:51 | Last chorus (C): Stop time; Armstrong improvises |
| 02:52–03:00 | Armstrong and Johnson engage in a "call and response" ending |

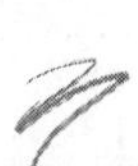

## Louis Armstrong and His Hot Five "West End Blues" (Oliver/Williams) 1928 Chapter 7

Louis Armstrong, vocal and trumpet; Johnny Strong, clarinet; Fred Robinson, trombone; Earl Hines, piano; Mancy Cara, banjo; Zutty Singleton, drums

"West End Blues" is one of Armstrong's most famous and important recordings. The opening trumpet introduction astounded jazz musicians, especially trumpet players. His phrasing, ease of playing, extension of the trumpet's range, and singing established his dominance as one of the most widely copied jazz musicians in the world. The stride pianist on the recording, Earl Hines, would soon become an influential and often copied musician as well.

## Louis Armstrong with Earl Hines "Weather Bird" (Joe Oliver) 1928 Chapter 7

Louis Armstrong, trumpet; Earl Hines, piano

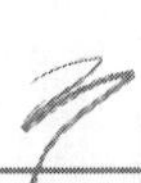

## Jelly Roll Morton's Red Hot Peppers "Black Bottom Stomp" (Morton) 1926 Chapter 5 & 8

Jelly Roll Morton, piano; George Mitchell, trumpet; Omer Simeon, clarinet; Kid Ory, trombone; Johnny St. Cyr, banjo; George Lindsay, bass; Andrew Hillaire, drums

Written by Jelly Roll Morton, "Black Bottom Stomp" was recorded in 1926 by his famous group, the Red Hot Peppers. It is a masterful arrangement done by the first important jazz composer and arranger. Notice how skillfully he combines different instruments to create interest in texture and color. He arranges for the band to alternate playing in 2/2 (march style) and 4/4 (swing style). The bassist also alternates between playing in 2 and 4: a modern concept that would not be common until the mid 1930s. The band was carefully rehearsed and their performances were highly polished. Morton was one of the first arranger/composers to find a balance between written and improvised music.

| | |
|---|---|
| 00:00–00:022 | ABB form (8-bar sections): Ensemble performs melody arrangement; listen to the precision of the instrumentalists as they are in sync with each other |
| 00:22–00:36 | 2nd chorus (BB—8-bar sections): Trumpet solo alternating with the ensemble using stop time breaks |
| 00:37–00:51 | 3rd chorus (BB): Improvised clarinet solo |
| 00:52–00:56 | Interlude (4 bars) |
| 00:56–01:01 | New Section (C—8 bars, D—12 bars): Ensemble—collective improvisation style with one stop time break |
| 01:02–01:14 | "Bell" tone stop time ensemble section |
| 01:15–01:32 | 2nd chorus (CD): Improvised clarinet solo with stop time breaks |
| 01:33–01:49 | 3rd chorus (CD): Improvised piano solo (stride style)—band drops out most likely so the piano can be clearly heard |
| 01:50–02:09 | 4th chorus (CD): Improvised muted trumpet solo with stop time breaks |
| 02:10–02:27 | 5th chorus (CD): Improvised banjo solo with stop time breaks |
| 02:28–02:47 | 6th chorus (CD): Ensemble collective improvisation section; drummer plays the cymbal during one stop time break |
| 02:48–3:05 | 7th chorus (CD): Last chorus has a stop time trombone solo (listen to him "smear" the sound using glissandi) |
| 03:05–03:13 | Tag |

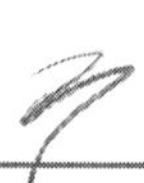

## Jelly Roll Morton's Red Hot Peppers "The Chant" (Mel Stitzel) 1926 Chapter 5 & 8

Jelly Roll Morton, piano; George Mitchell, trumpet; Omer Simeon, clarinet; Kid Ory, trombone; Johnny St. Cyr, banjo; George Lindsay, bass; Andrew Hillaire, drums

This Morton arrangement is full of many of his most often used signatures: short melodic phrases, unusual harmonic shifts, and utilization of many different thematic sections. This is like a mini-symphony, but lasts only three minutes. The opening phrase is unusually dissonant and very modern for its time. There is a banjo solo by St.Cyr, an excellent solo by clarinetist Omer Simeon, a solo by cornetist George Mitchell, and a short trombone solo from the inventor of the "tailgate" style, Kid Ory. All told this is a seamless work that flows from beginning to the end under the strict direction of Jelly Roll Morton.

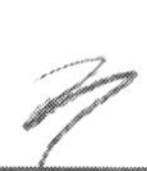

## Bix Beiderbeck Frankie Trumbauer and His Orchestra "River Boat Shuffle" (Hoagy Carmichael) 1927 Chapter 7

Bix Beiderbeck, cornet; Frank Trumbauer, C-melody sax; Bill Rank, trombone; Don Murray, clarinet; Irv Riskin, piano; Eddie Lang, guitar; Chauncey Morehouse, drums

This recording features one of Beiderbeck's best cornet solos on record. The piece starts out in the traditional collectively improvised style with Bix playing the lead line. The piece abounds in stop solos from all of the musicians. The guitarist is Eddie Lang—the only musician on this recording who could improvise on a level with Beiderbeck. Trombonist Bill Rank plays a number of good stop solos. Note clarinetist Don Murray's stiff "ragtime" style rhythm. Beiderbeck's lyrical solo is true improvisation on par with Louis Armstrong. Sadly, Beiderbeck's career was very short and one can only imagine how he might have developed. Listen to "Singin' the Blues" in the same collection and pay attention to saxophonist Frankie Trumbauer who was also ahead of his time in terms of sound and approach to playing.

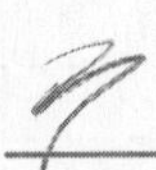

## James P. Johnson "Carolina Shout" (James P. Johnson) 1921 Chapter 6

James P. Johnson, piano

Listen to this live performance at Carnegie Hall as James P. Johnson shows why he was dubbed "The Father of Stride."

| | |
|---|---|
| 00:00–00:08 | 8-bar introduction starting in the upper register and then moving down the keyboard |
| 00:09–00:28 | 16-bar A section |
| 00:28–00:46 | 16-bar A section repeated but listen to the right hand improvisation based on the first A section melody |
| 00:47–01:04 | 16-bar B section: reminiscent of banjo chords |
| 01:04–01:21 | 16-bar C section |
| 01:21–01:37 | 16-bar D section – key changes to C major |
| 01:38–01:54 | 16-bar E section – key remains C major |
| 01:55–02:09 | 16-bar D section repeats but the right hand is improvising on first D section |
| 02:09–02:16 | Ending or Tag |

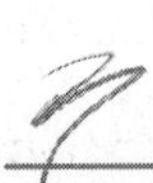

## Fats Waller "Handful of Keys" (Thomas Waller) 1929 Chapter 6

Waller was a master stride pianist. Listen to his steady left hand rhythm as he creates interesting melodies and impressive improvisations with his right hand.

| | |
|---|---|
| 00:00–00:08 | 8-bar "jumpy" introduction with right hand riffs |
| 00:09–00:37 | AABA form |
| 00:38–1:06 | 2nd chorus – melody is stated an octave higher (upper register of piano) |
| 1:07–1:10 | Short interlude similar to the introduction |
| 1:10–1:39 | New section (CDCE form) |
| 1:40–2:09 | Return to AABA form with ornamented melody |
| 2:10–2:43 | Last chorus (AABA); lots of improvisation on the melody including small breaks and "shouts" reminiscent of instrumental arrangements. |

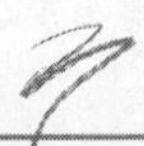

## Art Tatum "Tiger Rag" 1933 Chapter 6

Many jazz pianists have proclaimed Art Tatum to possibly be from another planet after hearing this amazing show of pyrotechnical display.

| | |
|---|---|
| 00:00–00:14 | Introduction with strange harmonic content that hint at French Impressionistic music. |
| 00:15–00:34 | AABA form |
| 00:35–00:40 | Interlude |
| 00:40–00:50 | CDCE form |
| 00:50–1:12 | Interlude with trills in the left hand and rhythmic chords in the right hand |
| 1:12–1:33 | FGFH form |
| 1:33–1:54 | FGFH form (2nd chorus) |
| 1:54–2:21 | FGFH form (3rd chorus) Impressive descending scale to end. |

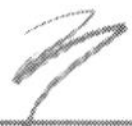

## Art Tatum "Willow Weep for Me" 1949 Chapter 6

Listen to how Tatum takes a simple popular song and gives it new harmonic content as well as numerous virtuosic flourishes.

## Mead "Lux" Lewis "Honky Tonk Train Blues" (Meade Lux Lewis) 1937 Chapter 6

Dubbed the "Father of Boogie Woogie," Lewis performed this song many times and in many different contexts including concert halls where one would expect to hear classical music. The typical 12-bar AAB form is used to present nine choruses. A new idea is introduced at the beginning of each chorus; however, the same refrain is used for the B section of every chorus. Lewis is truly amazing because he maintains a steady left hand rhythm while introducing cross rhythms with his right hand; in essence he is able to do what it normally takes two people to accomplish.

| | |
|---|---|
| 00:00–00:02 | Short introduction with tremolo chords |
| 00:03–00:18 | AAB form |
| 00:18–00:34 | AAB form (2nd chorus) |
| 00:34–00:50 | AAB form (3rd chorus) |
| 00:50–01:07 | AAB form (4th chorus) |
| 01:07–01:24 | AAB form (5th chorus) |
| 01:24–01:40 | AAB form (6th chorus) |
| 01:40–01:57 | AAB form (7th chorus) |
| 01:57–02:13 | AAB form (8th chorus) |
| 02:13–02:27 | AAB form (9th chorus) |
| 02:27–02:42 | Ending |

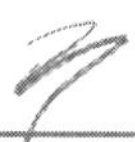

## Pete Johnson "Boogie Woogie" 1938 Chapter 6

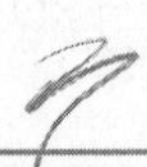

## Paul Whiteman Orchestra "Changes" 1927 (Walter Donaldson; arranged by Bill Challis)

(Listed under Bix Beiderbeck) Chapter 7 & 9

Dubbed the "King of Jazz" in the 1920s, Paul Whiteman led one of the most popular and successful commercial dance bands in the country. He hired the best arrangers and musicians of the period including the best known "hot" or jazz musicians including Bix Beiderbeck, Jack Teagarden, Frank Trumbauer, and Bunny Berigan. This bouncy piece features a string section, a scat singing vocal trio with Bing Crosby, full ensemble, and a short improvised solo by cornetist Bix Beiderbeck. Bill Challis arranged "Changes" making extensive use of the "Charleston" rhythm (you can hear it in many places). Whiteman wanted his music to be accessible and offered the public jazz "flavored" music while still featuring the best white jazz improvisers of the day.

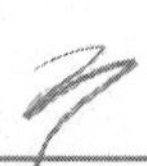

## Fletcher Henderson and His Orchestra "Copenhagen" (Charlie Davis; arranged by Don Redman) 1924 Chapter 9

This recording was made shortly after the Henderson Orchestra was hired to play at the famous Roseland Ballroom in New York City. He had just hired a young cornet player from Chicago by the name of Louis Armstrong. The Henderson Orchestra was typical of the New York orchestras, playing polite dance music from "doctored" stock arrangements. With the addition of Armstrong, Redman had more to work with and helped transform the group into a big jazz band. Redman's arrangement stresses the contrast between the saxes and brasses using clarinet trios and brass trios in call and response and pitting one section against the other. It is complex short work that features excellent section writing, contrast of timbre, texture and range, and an excellent solo by the exciting Louis Armstrong. The opening is written to sound like New Orleans collective improvisation, but it is all written out and flows seamlessly.

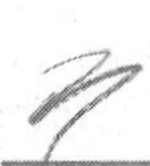

## Fletcher Henderson and His Orchestra "The Stampede" (Fletcher Henderson; arranged by Don Redman) 1926 Chapter 9

## Duke Ellington and His Orchestra "East St Louis Toodle-Oo" (Duke Ellington/Bubber Miley) 1927 Chapter 10

This is an excellent example of the Jungle Style that is always associated with Ellington. The piece is in reality a showcase for the talents of the trumpeter Bubber Miley. Miley's use of the plunger mute, his ability to growl into the horn and his excellent improvisational skills were the "secret" to Ellington's early success. Most "jungle" pieces are rather slow in tempo, feature growling trumpet solos or trombones, start in the minor mode and change to the major mode, then feature a series of solos, and end as they began. The second solo is performed by Harry Carney on baritone sax and the trombone solo is by "Tricky" Sam Nanton. This writing is not on the same level as Redman's work with Henderson, nor Bill Challis' work with Paul Whiteman, but it shows Ellington's resourcefulness by using the "colors" or voices he had in the orchestra. Ellington would remember things that worked well and they would often become part of his musical signature. This piece was recorded numerous times by Ellington and each time the arrangement was different, having been transformed by the composer himself or by the musicians that played the parts.

## Duke Ellington and His Orchestra "Dusk" (Duke Ellington) 1940 Chapter 10

"Dusk" is an excellent example of one of Ellington's mood compositions. After a short piano introduction, the wonderful yet haunting arrangement of the woodwinds with muted brass creates an image of the transitional period between day and night. Listen to the half-valve trumpet work of Rex Stewart (1:05–1:55); then a call and response between a trombone trio and the woodwinds (1:56–2:20); then an expressive solo is performed on a muted trombone by Lawrence Brown (2:50–3:04). "Dusk" concludes with the same unique combination of timbre and harmony as heard in the beginning. No other band was capable of producing such expressive effects.

## Duke Ellington and His Orchestra "Koko" (Duke Ellington) 1940 Chapter 10

Koko is one of the most revered Ellington compositions and arrangements. It came during one of Ellington's most prolific periods and features, perhaps, the greatest band that he ever assembled: the famous Blanton/ Webster band. This is one of his later "jungle style" pieces, but is not a vehicle for one soloist. The arrangement is flawless; it exhibits great organization and an overall sound that exhibits a sense of foreboding. Ellington's use of each band members' unique sound and improvisational style contributes to the success of the piece. It is a minor 12-bar blues. Soloists include the trombonist Tricky Sam Nanton and a rather dissonant and avant-garde solo from Duke, himself. Other outstanding performances include that of baritone saxophonist Harry Carney, trombonist Juan Tizol, and bassist Jimmy Blanton's strong, forceful playing is the anchor that keeps the piece moving forward.

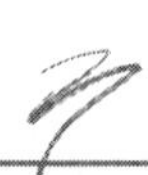

## Duke Ellington and His Orchestra "Cottontail" (Duke Ellington) 1940 Chapter 10

This composition is a contrafaction based upon Gershwin's "I Got Rhythm." It starts out as a small group piece with three horns playing the melody with the rhythm section. It quickly moves on to feature tenor saxophonist Ben Webster playing one his greatest solos ever recorded, short solos by Cootie Williams on trumpet, Harry Carney on baritone saxophone, Duke on piano, and one of the greatest saxophone section solis ever written. The brass section comes back playing a powerful call and response with the sax section and then rips into the final "B" section of the arrangement. The ensemble passages are beautifully written and executed with great precision. The band is tight and swings relentlessly pushed by Blanton on the bass. It is a tour de force for the entire orchestra.

## Duke Ellington and His Orchestra "Concerto for Cootie" (Duke Ellington) 1940 Chapter 10

Cootie Williams, trumpet (featured soloist)

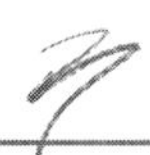

## Count Basie Orchestra "One O'clock Jump" (Count Basie, Eddie Durham) 1937 Chapter 11

This 12-measure blues is possibly the greatest "riff" arrangement from the Swing Era. A riff arrangement is a relatively simple concept whereby short chunks of melody are repeated by the trumpet section, trombone section, and sax section. Sections were pitted against each other building in tension until the end of the performance. Many times these "riff" arrangements were performed spontaneously by the musicians. Improvised solos carried greater importance in riff arrangements in contrast to the typical Swing Era big band performance that emphasized written arrangement over improvised solos. "One o'clock Jump" has been recorded over 100 times by many different groups. This performance begins with Basie playing two choruses on piano with the rhythm section.

| | |
|---|---|
| 00:00–00:10 | Rhythm section introduction |
| 00:11–00:26 | AAB form: 1st piano chorus played by Basie |
| 00:27–00:42 | 2nd piano chorus played by Basie |
| 00:43–00:59 | 3rd chorus features tenor saxophonist Herschel Evans playing a solo over a trumpet riff background |
| 1:00–1:15 | 4th chorus features trombonist Benny Morton playing a solo over sax riff background |
| 01:16–01:33 | 5th chorus features tenor saxophonist Lester Young playing a solo over a trumpet riff background |
| 01:34–01:49 | 6th chorus features Buck Clayton on trumpet soloing over a sax riff |
| 01:50–02:06 | 7th chorus features the rhythm section with Basie comping on the piano |
| 02:07–02:22 | 8th chorus features each section with distinctive riffs (saxes, trumpets, trombones) |
| 02:23–02:38 | 9th chorus—the saxes play a different riff over the trumpets and trombones |
| 02:29–end | 10th chorus—the sax riff changes, but the trumpet and trombone riff remains the same. |

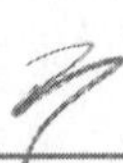

## Count Basie Orchestra "Doggin' Around" (Herschel Evans, Edgar Battle) 1938 Chapter 11

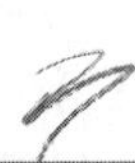

## Count Basie's Kansas City Seven "Lester Leaps In" (Young) 1939 Chapter 11 &12

Count Basie, piano; Buck Clayton, trumpet; Dickie Wells, trombone; Freddie Green, guitar; Walter Page, bass; Jo Jones, drums

A great example of the spontaneous riff style popular in Kansas City, this recording is a showcase for the great improvisational skills of tenor saxophonist Lester Young. Listen to his light, airy sound, slow vibrato and relaxed rhythmic manner in which he plays the notes. Young's playing would be a model for the next generation of bebop and cool saxophonists. Lester Young played long, improvised lines and tended to emphasize the upbeat, rather than the downbeat, as did many his contemporaries such as Coleman Hawkins.

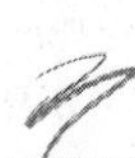

## Jimmie Lunceford and His Orchestra "Stratosphere" 1934 Chapter 12

"Stratosphere" is a complicated arrangement that borrows from classical repertoire and features precise execution and clarity of articulation. Notice that solos are not emphasized; rather the ensemble and arrangement are the highlights.

| | |
|---|---|
| 00:00–00:07 | Introduction |
| 00:08–00:37 | AABA form |
| 00:38–00:40 | Interlude (repeat of the introduction) |
| 00:41–01:07 | Next chorus; notice how the trumpets are slightly out of sync in the A sections. The B section features an alto saxophone solo played by Willie Smith. |
| 01:08–01:23 | Interlude with Classical devices including timpani drums |
| 01:24–01:57 | Last chorus |
| 01:58–02:17 | Dramatic ending with a clarinet glissando reminiscent of Gershwin's "Rhapsody in Blue" |

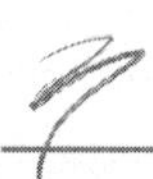

## Coleman Hawkins and His Orchestra "Body and Soul" (Green, Sauer, Heyman, Eyton) 1939 Chapter 12

Coleman Hawkins, tenor sax; Jackie Fields, Eustis Moore, alto saxes; Joe Guy, Jimmy Lindsay, trumpets; Earl Handy, trombone; Gene Rogers, piano; William Smith, bass; Arthur Herbert, drum

Coleman Hawkins is often referred to as the "father" of the jazz tenor sax with good reason. His career began in the early 1920s with singer Mamie Smith and later with the famous Fletcher Henderson Orchestra. This landmark recording showcases Hawkins advanced harmonic concepts and improvisational ability. Except for the opening 8 measures, the entire performance is an improvised solo based on the chord structure of the composition. His big sound was also the model for most tenor saxophonists of the era until Lester Young's sound became more desirable in the mid-1940s.

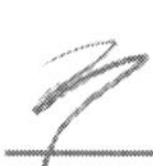

## Benny Goodman Orchestra "Down South Camp Meeting" (Fletcher Henderson) 1936 Chapter 12

Benny Goodman was a consummate clarinetist and bandleader. This arrangement was one of many purchased from Fletcher Henderson (Goodman eventually hired Henderson to write and arrange for his orchestra). It is typical of mid 1930s swing music: use of riffs and sectional writing. Goodman's band was known for its crisp precision and excellent soloists. This arrangement features Goodman prominently on clarinet and later pits section against section in typical call-and-response manner.

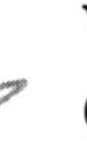

## Roy Eldridge and Benny Carter "I Can't Believe You're in Love With Me" (Jimmy McHugh, Clarence Gaskil) 1940 Chapter 12

Roy Eldridge, trumpet; Benny Carter, alto sax; Coleman Hawkins, tenor sax; Bernard Addison, guitar; John Kirby, bass; Sid Catlett, drums

This 1940 recording also features two giants of the saxophone, Coleman Hawkins, tenor sax and Benny Carter on alto sax. All three musicians play excellent solos. The track begins with Hawkins playing the melody with Eldridge and Carter answering in a collectively improvised manner. Hawkins plays the first improvised chorus then Eldridge follows with two clever choruses, which show his excellent technique and range. Benny Carter plays two choruses on alto sax and the last chorus is played in a collectively improvised manner with all three soloists playing. These soloists where among the best from the Swing Era and strongly influenced the next generation of beboppers.

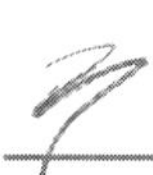

## Charlie Christian "Airmail Special" AKA "Good Enough to Keep" (Charlie Christian, Jimmy Mundy, Benny Goodman) 1941 Chapter 12 & 13

Benny Goodman Sextet: Benny Goodman, clarinet; Charlie Christian, guitar; Cootie Williams, trumpet; Artie Bernstein, bass; John Guarnieri, piano; George Auld, tenor sax

This simple riff composition, based on a 32-measure AABA form, provides a setting for some excellent solos. Charlie Christian's approach to improvisation was more advanced than his contemporaries and predates the bebop revolution of Charlie Parker and Dizzy Gillespie. The rhythm section style has been strongly influenced by the Count Basie rhythm section and tenor saxophonist Auld is a transitional figure between the swing style of Coleman Hawkins and the more modern bop style.

| | |
|---|---|
| 00:00–00:33 | AABA form: unison statement of a simple riff melody |
| 00:33–01:06 | 2nd chorus: Christian guitar solo (one chorus) with horn section background |
| 01:07–01:41 | 3rd chorus: Benny Goodman clarinet solo with riff background |
| 01:42–02:13 | 4th chorus: Cootie Williams plunger muted trumpet solo |
| 02:14–02:47 | 5th chorus: George Auld tenor sax solo with riff background |
| 02:48–end | 6th chorus: Ensemble riff with piano response |

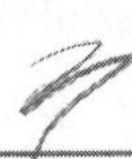

## Charlie Parker's Re-Boppers "KoKo" (Charlie Parker) 1945 Chapter 13

Charlie Parker, alto sax; Dizzy Gillespie, trumpet and piano; Curley Russell, bass; Max Roach, drums

This amazing improvisation by Parker is based upon the AABA composition "Cherokee." After a brief introduction that features Parker on sax and Gillespie on muted trumpet, Parker launches into two choruses that helped define modern jazz. The intro is typical of bop: fast, angular, jumpy, nervous sounding, and instrumentally conceived. Parker's solo represents the new shape of jazz. Parker's sound is dry with little vibrato; the antithesis of the typical sound of 1930s players of like Johnny Hodges and Benny Carter. He possessed extraordinary technique and great understanding of harmony. Many well established musicians of the 1920s and 1930s did not understand the new approach taken by Parker and Gillespie. Therefore, controversy swirled about these individuals in the mid to late 1940s.

| | |
|---|---|
| 00:00–00:25 | Introduction with sax, trumpet, and drums only |
| 00:25–01:15 | AABA form (each section is 16 bars): Parker's 1st solo chorus (B section is at 00:50) |
| 01:16–02:07 | Parker's 2nd solo chorus (B section is at 01:42) |
| 02:08–02:30 | 32 bar drum solo |
| 02:31–end | Ending—same as the introduction |

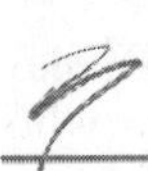

## Dizzy Gillespie's All-Star Quintet "Shaw 'Nuff" (Parker, Gillespie) 1945 Chapter 13

Dizzy Gillespie, trumpet; Charlie Parker, alto sax; Al Haig, piano; Sid Catlett, drums; Curley Russell, bass

## Charlie Parker's All-Stars "Parker's Mood" (Charlie Parker) 1948 Chapter 13

Charlie Parker, alto sax; John Lewis, piano; Curley Russell, bass; Max Roach, drums

This is a slow blues where Parker shows Kansas City roots. The blues were an integral part of his musical upbringing in Kansas City in the 1930s. Contrary to popular belief not all bop recordings were very fast—some were quite slow in tempo. He plays traditional blues with a modern flavor—the essential elements are there, but his musical language has evolved using modern vocabulary. He accents the upbeats, using very little vibrato, plays flurries of notes and other times leaves much space between his ideas. The melody is mostly improvised and the mood here for the most part is quite somber; appropriate for the blues. After the introduction Parker plays two choruses, followed by a chorus on piano by John Lewis, then Parker returns for one and then ends the recording with the same short melody he used for the introduction.

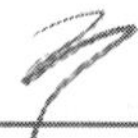

## Bud Powell "Tempus Fugit" 1949 Chapter 13

### Bud Powell, piano; Ray Brown, bass; Max Roach, drums

Bud Powell reveals himself as a significant composer and impressive pianist on this recording. His improvisation in choruses two through four features some of the best bebop lines of the 1940s influencing future generations of jazz pianists.

| | |
|---|---|
| 00:00–00:07 | 8-bar introduction |
| 00:07–00:33 | AABA form presented: bebop melody—contrasting B section |
| 00:34–00:38 | 6-bar interlude—last two bars are a stop time break to help launch Powell's solo improvisation |
| 00:39–01:04 | 2nd AABA chorus—improvised piano solo |
| 01:04–01:29 | 3rd chorus—piano solo continues |
| 01:29–01:53 | 4th chorus—piano solo continues |
| 01:53–02:18 | 5th chorus—AABA melody is restated but up an octave |
| 02:19–02:26 | Ending or tag |

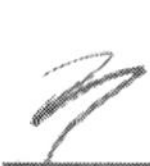

## Dizzy Gillespie "Manteca" (Dizzy Gillespie/Chano Pozo) 1947 Chapter 13 & 14

### Dizzy Gillespie Big Band

Dizzy Gillespie always loved the big band in contrast to many of his bebop contemporaries who felt confined by it. He was one of the first jazz musicians to utilize the sounds of bebop in a big band setting. Gillespie was enthralled by the sound of Afro-Cuban rhythms he heard in New York in the 1940s. In 1947, he heard Cuban percussionist and singer Chano Pozo and immediately hired him to perform in his big band. Manteca was cowritten by Pozo and Gillespie featuring Pozo on conga drum. Gillespie's success in blending jazz and Afro-Cuban music attracted the attention of other bandleaders who also hired Latin percussionists to augment their rhythm sections.

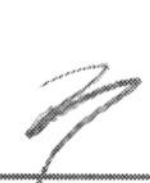

## Tadd Dameron Sextet "Lady Bird" (Tadd Dameron) 1948 Chapter 13

### Tadd Dameron, piano; Fats Navarro, trumpet; Wardell Gray, Allen Eager, tenor saxophones; Curley Russell, bass; Kenny Clarke, drums

Blue Note Records,

Tadd Dameron is one of the most important composers of the bebop era. Together with Thelonious Monk, he crafted an outstanding body of original compositions. He did not use contrafactions, but wrote entirely new material. Dameron began his career as a pianist and arranger in the 1930s and he later wrote for the Dizzy Gillespie Big Band. This recording features one of the most important trumpet players of the bebop era, Fats Navarro. Navarro was a few years younger than Gillespie and absorbed Dizzy's style and developed his own signature sound and approach. Narvarro was the first true bebop "baby" on the trumpet. Tenor saxophonists Allen Eager and Wardell Gray (2nd sax soloist) had absorbed Lester Young and Charlie Parker to play true bebop on the tenor saxophone. This 16-measure composition has an unusual harmonic structure and was quite a challenge to perform in the 1940s.

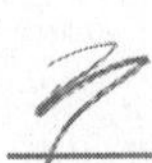

## Thelonious Monk Quartet "Misterioso" (Thelonious Monk) 1948 Chapter 13

Thelonious Monk, piano; Milt Jackson, vibraphone; John Simmons, bass; Shadow Wilson, drums

Blue Note Records
This is slow 12-measure blues with an angular melody based on the interval of a 6th . The tempo of composition initially appears to be medium until the vibraphone solo—at this time it becomes apparent that the real tempo is half of the opening statement of the melody. Although Monk is credited with being one of architects of bebop, his playing does not reflect the new style. His playing is full of dissonance, seemingly "wrong" notes, and an unusual approach to time and rhythm—this is the Monk style that so confused many critics of the 1940s and 1950s. This truth is that he was deliberate in his actions and his compositions are very complex.

| | |
|---|---|
| 00:00–00:11 | Piano introduction—Monk uses a minimum number of notes |
| 00:12–00:45 | AAB form: statement of the melody |
| 00:46–01:22 | 2nd chorus: improvised vibraphone solo by Milt Jackson |
| 01:23–01:58 | 3rd chorus: improvised piano solo by Thelonious Monk |
| 01:59–02:39 | 4th chorus: piano solo continues |
| 02:40–03:23 | 5th chorus: Milt Jackson states the melody and Shadow Wilson creates a double-time feel while Monk plays sporadic notes until he joins Jackson with the melody (03:03–03:23). At the very end, Monk uses a descending whole tone scale (one of his favorite devices) as a closing gesture. |

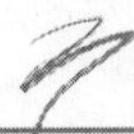

## Thelonious Monk Quintet "Criss Cross" 1951 Chapter 13

Thelonious Monk, piano; Sahib Shihab, also sax; Milt Jackson, vibraphone; Al McKibbon, bass; Art Blakey, drums

Blue Note Records
This is one of the most tricky and deceptive of Monk's compositions. It is full of surprises and his use of rhythmic displacement (disguising the 1st beat in the measure) makes it a challenge to play. The harmonies are unusual and often don't resolve in a traditional manner. It is a 32-measure AABA form, but difficult to distinguish because of the angular melody.

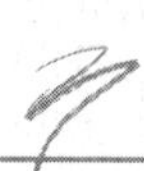

## Miles Davis and His Orchestra "Boplicity" (Cleo Henry, AKA Miles Davis) 1949 Chapter 14 & 17

Miles Davis, trumpet; Lee Konitz, alto sax; J.J. Johnson, trombone; Gerry Mulligan, baritone sax; John Lewis, piano; Nelson Boyd, bass; Kenny Clarke, drums; Bill Barber, tuba; Sandy Siegelstein, French horn; Gil Evans, arranger

*Birth of the Cool,* Capitol Records

This recording from the album, *Birth of the Cool,* is one of the most important recordings after the advent of bebop in the mid 1940s. This group, under the direction of Miles Davis was exploring sound, texture, and musical color through the arrangements of Gil Evans, Gerry Mulligan, John Carisi, and John Lewis. The popularity of the "cool" sound of the 1950s is the result of this group, although the title, *Birth of the Cool,* was not used until 1957. Gil Evans explores many traditional compositional techniques such as counterpoint and establishes an excellent balance between the written music (arrangement) and sections left open for musicians to improvise, much as Duke Ellington had done a generation earlier. This collaboration between Miles Davis and Gil Evans would be the first of many projects over the next ten years.

| | |
|---|---|
| 00:00–00:57 | AABA form: melody is stated by the nonet |
| 00:58–01:25 | 2nd chorus (only half-AA): improvised solo by Gerry Mulligan on baritone sax |
| 01:26–01:35 | Interlude arranged for the ensemble |
| 01:36–01:42 | Short improvised trumpet solo by Miles Davis |
| 01:43–01:59 | Ensemble section |
| 02:00–02:25 | Last chorus (AA): improvised trumpet solo by Miles Davis |
| 02:25–02:39 | Last chorus (B): improvised piano solo by John Lewis |
| 02:40–end | Last chorus (A): restatement of the melody heard at the beginning |

## Gerry Mulligan-Chet Baker Quartet "Line For Lyons" (Mulligan) 1953 Chapter 14

Gerry Mulligan, baritone sax; Chet Baker, trumpet); Carson Smith, bass; Chico Hamilton, bass

This group, which did not use a pianist, was one of the most popular in the early 1950s. Baritone saxophonist Mulligan and trumpeter Baker worked well together as a musical team. The relaxed manner in which they play was the epitome of the West Coast cool style. Without the piano, the texture of the group was rather transparent. Both Baker and Mulligan accompany each other and weave lyrical lines that complement each other. The drummer's role is much less interactive than in the bebop style. This composition uses a 32-measure AABA form.

| | |
|---|---|
| 00:00–00:46 | AABA form: melody is stated by baritone sax and trumpet |
| 00:47–01:10 | 2nd chorus (AA): improvised baritone solo by Gerry Mulligan |
| 01:11–01:34 | 2nd chorus (BA): improvised trumpet solo by Chet Baker with Mulligan playing harmony in the background |
| 01:35–01:59 | 3rd chorus (AA): Mulligan and Baker both improvise in a contrapuntal manner |
| 02:00–02:12 | 3rd chorus (B): last B section played as in the beginning |
| 02:12–02:21 | 3rd chorus (A): last A section played as in the beginning |
| 02:22–02:32 | Short tag |

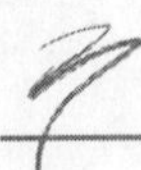

## Miles Davis with Gil Evans Orchestra "Summertime" (George Gershwin) 1958 Chapter 14 & 17

Miles Davis (trumpet); Gil Evans (arranger/conductor)

*Miles Davis/Gil Evans Porgy and Bess,* Columbia Records
Miles Davis and Gil Evans worked together on the *Birth of the Cool* sessions in 1949 and 1950. In the late 1950s the two collaborated on three more recordings. This recording is from the album *Porgy and Bess.* The arrangements feature a large jazz orchestra with extended instrumentation and they are often referred to as "third stream." There are elements of orchestral texture and sensibility. Davis is the only soloist throughout the entire record. His harmony-muted trumpet sound is haunting as are the lyrical solos he plays. Evans borrows from Jelly Roll Morton and Duke Ellington in the manner in which he blends written music with Davis's improvisations finding a perfect balance between the two.

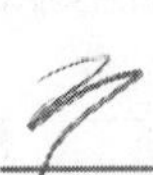

## Modern Jazz Quartet "Django" (John Lewis) 1960 Chapter 14

Milt Jackson, vibraphone; John Lewis, piano; Percy Heath, bass; Connie Kay, drums

*Modern Jazz Quartet European Concert,* Atlantic Records
This composition shows how John Lewis was influenced by European music in its construction. The piece starts out slowly with a quasi "classical" sound. It picks up speed and moves on to a swing feel. The solo part of the composition is broken into four separate sections (AABCD form) and there is also a short interlude between the two soloists. Each section has a distinctive feel that is reflected in the subtle changes in the rhythm section.

| | |
|---|---|
| 00:00–00:37 | Introduction, played by vibraphone, begins slowly but then accelerates to a medium swing tempo |
| 00:38–00:54 | AA (each A section is 6 bars long): improvised vibraphone solo begins—bassist plays in "2" and the drummer uses brushes |
| 00:54–01:03 | B (8 bars): vibraphone solo continues; bass establishes a pedal tone; drummer uses sticks |
| 01:04–01:10 | C (4 bars): vibraphone solo continues; bass returns to playing in "2" |
| 01:10–01:21 | D (8 bars): vibraphone solo continues; blues influence; bass plays a boogie-woogie repetitive pattern; drummer plays a shuffle rhythm |
| 01:22–02:04 | 2nd chorus: vibraphone continues to improvise |
| 02:05–02:48 | 3rd chorus: vibraphone continues to improvise |
| 02:49–02:54 | Interlude |
| 02:55–03:40 | 4th chorus: improvised piano solo |
| 03:41–04:31 | 5th chorus: piano solo continues but at 03:41 a gradual slowing of the beat (ritardando) occurs leading back into the slow introduction which will now serve as an ending. |
| 04:32–05:11 | Slow introduction used as an ending |
| 05:12–05:32 | Vibraphone and piano cadenza |

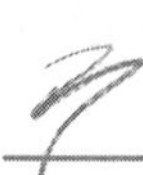

## Dave Brubeck Quartet "Take Five" (Paul Desmond) 1959 Chapter 14

Dave Brubeck, piano; Joe Morrello, drums; Paul Desmond, alto sax; Eugene Wright, bass

*Time Out,* Columbia Records
The Dave Brubeck Quartet achieved national recognition for this daring composition challenging people to dance to a beat arranged in groups of five rather than the usual four.

| | |
|---|---|
| 00:00–00:07 | 4-bar drum introduction: Joe Morrello establishes the unusual 5/4 time signature |
| 00:07–00:20 | Piano joins in with a 5/4 vamp (repetitive harmonic pattern) |
| 00:20–01:04 | ABA form (8-bar sections): alto sax states the melody |
| 01:04–01:50 | Improvised alto sax solo by Paul Desmond over the opening vamp; Desmond's style is the essence of cool-minimum notes, smooth tone, soft dynamic |
| 01:50–04:21 | Improvised drum solo over the opening vamp; Morrello shows he can create interesting rhythms while still keeping track of the 5/4 time signature. |
| 04:21–05:01 | ABA form: melody is restated as in the beginning |
| 05:02–05:24 | Ending or tag |

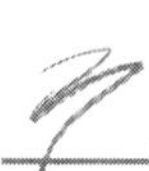

## Dave Brubeck Quartet "Blue Rondo a la Turk" (Dave Brubeck) 1959 Chapter 14

Dave Brubeck, piano; Joe Morrello, drums; Paul Desmond, alto sax; Eugene Wright, bass

*Time Out,* Columbia Records

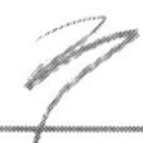

## Tito Puente "Mambo Gozon"ca. 1960 Chapter 14

Tito Puente, bandleader, timbales

*Lo Mejor de lo Mejor,* U.S. Latin Records
Tito Puente was known as the "El Rey del Timbal," one of the greatest Latin bandleaders and percussionists. He was able to bridge the gap between Latin salsa and American jazz. He was very popular with both American and Latino audiences. His band, together with those of Machito and Tito Rodriguez, helped to usher in the mambo craze of the 1950s, which led directly to the popularity of the salsa style, especially popular from the mid 1970s to present. Puente often hired the best American jazz musicians for his recordings.

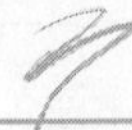

## Eddie Palmieri "Revolt/La Libertad Logico" 1971 Chapter 14

Eddie Palmieri, bandleader, piano

*Vamonos Pal' Monte,* Fania/Emusica Records
Palmieri is a bandleader, composer and pianist. Raised in New York City of Puerto Rican and Italian ancestry, his bands combine jazz improvisation and harmonic sophistication with Afro-Cuban rhythms. He is a well respected pianist who shows the influence of McCoy Tyner. *LA LIBERTAD LOGICO* was also famous as a battle cry for Latino empowerment and equality.

## Jerry Gonzalez "Evidence" (Thelonious Monk) 1979 Chapter 14

Jerry Gonzalez, percussion , trumpet; Hilton Ruiz, piano; Mario Rivera, tenor sax; Nicky Marrero, timbales; Andy Gonzalez, bass; Edgardo Miranda, guitar; Steve Turre, trombone; Don Alias, drums; Frank Rodriguez, percussion

*Ya Yo Me Cure,* Sunnyside Records
This recording is an excellent example of a jazz standard interpreted in a Latin jazz style. Gonzales is equally at home playing jazz standards as well as Afro-Cuban music. Gonzalez is able to fuse African-based rhythms with jazz elements without compromising the essence of either style.

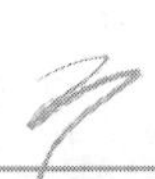

## The Jazz Messengers "The Preacher" (Horace Silver) 1955 Chapter 15

Horace Silver, piano; Art Blakey, drums; Kenny Dorham, trumpet; Hank Mobley, tenor sax; Doug Watkins, bass

*Horace Silver and the Jazz Messengers,* Blue Note Records
This composition by pianist Horace Silver is typical of many of his catchy, bluesy, gospel inflected melodies. It is a short piece: only 16 measures long; the form is perhaps best conceived as four different sections each 4 measures long: ABCD. However, A, B, and C all begin the same but each has a slightly different ending. Silver harmonizes the trumpet and tenor sax on the melody and later writes a riff for them to play behind his piano solo. The original Jazz Messengers featured Horace and drummer Art Blakey. Shortly after this record was made, Horace left to form his own quintet.

| | |
|---|---|
| 00:00–00:22 | 1st chorus: trumpet and tenor sax state the melody in harmony with each other |
| 00:23–00:44 | 2nd chorus: restatement of the melody |
| 00:45–01:05 | 3rd chorus: improvised trumpet solo |
| 01:06–01:26 | 4th chorus: trumpet solo continues |
| 01:27–01:47 | 5th chorus: improvised tenor sax solo |
| 01:48–02:09 | 6th chorus: tenor sax solo continues |
| 02:10–02:29 | 7th chorus: improvised piano solo |
| 02:30–02:50 | 8th chorus: piano solo continues |
| 02:51–03:10 | 9th chorus: piano solo continues with background riffs played by the trumpet and tenor sax |

| | |
|---|---|
| 03:11–03:30 | 10th chorus: piano solo continues with background riffs played by the trumpet and tenor sax |
| 03:31–03:52 | 11th chorus: melody is stated as in the beginning |
| 03:53–04:18 | 12th chorus: restatement of the melody |

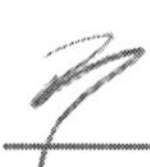

## Art Blakey and the Jazz Messengers "Moanin'" (Bobby Timmons) 1958 Chapter 15

Art Blakey, drums; Bobby Timmons, piano; Lee Morgan, trumpet; Benny Golson, tenor sax; Jymie Merritt, bass

*Moanin',* Blue Note Records
Art Blakey's Jazz Messengers was the epitome of the 1950s hard bop band. The band featured some of the best hard bop musicians and helped to establish the "Blue Note" sound. The musicians, especially trumpet players, who played in the band make up a "whose-who" list of jazz greats from the 1950s through the 1980s. *Moanin'* is a 32-measure AABA piece written in the "gospel jazz" style by pianist Bobby Timmons. The melody is simple, catchy, and brings to mind the sound of the blues.

| | |
|---|---|
| 00:00–00:14 | AABA form (A): piano plays the melody as the trumpet and tenor sax respond "A-men" |
| 00:15–00:30 | AABA form (A): trumpet and tenor sax state the melody as the piano responds "A-men" |
| 00:31–00:43 | AABA form (B): trumpet and tenor sax state the melody |
| 00:44–00:59 | AABA form (A): piano plays the melody as the trumpet and tenor sax respond "A-men" |
| 00:57–00:59 | Art Blakey plays a press roll on the snare drum (one of his trademarks) introducing the first soloist. |
| 01:00–02:00 | 2nd chorus: improvised trumpet solo by Lee Morgan |
| 02:01–03:03 | 3rd chorus: trumpet solo continues |
| 03:04–04:01 | 4th chorus: improvised tenor sax solo by Benny Golson |
| 04:02–05:02 | 5th chorus: tenor sax solo continues |
| 05:02–06:02 | 6th chorus: improvised piano solo by Bobby Timmons |
| 06:02–07:01 | 7th chorus: piano solo continues |
| 07:01–07:58 | 8th chorus: improvised bass solo |
| 07:58–08:56 | 9th chorus: melody is restated as in the beginning |
| 08:56–09:35 | Ending: B section phrase is repeated three times with a piano cadenza at the very end |

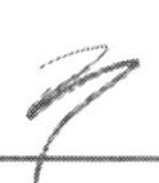

## Clifford Brown-Max Roach Quintet "What Is This Thing Called Love" (Cole Porter) 1956 Chapter 15

Clifford Brown, trumpet; Max Roach, drums; Sonny Rollins, tenor sax; Richie Powell, piano; George Morrow, bass

*At Basin Street,* Emarcy Records
This group epitomized hard bop of the mid-1950s. The recording begins with the trumpet player and saxophonist improvising over an Afro-Cuban groove. It uses a 32-measure AABA form performed at a very fast tempo. Browns' trumpet solo is the essence of hard bop trumpet playing and it was the most widely emulated of the 1950s. Rollins is also an important hard bop tenor saxophonist.

By far the most creative soloists are Brown, Rollins, and Roach. The pianist Richie Powell and bassist George Morrow are excellent supporting musicians, but not necessarily outstanding soloists.

| | |
|---|---|
| 00:00–00:57 | Introduction—trumpet and tenor sax play over an Afro-Cuban style rhythm; Clifford Brown dominates the musical conversation |
| 00:58–01:25 | AABA form: statement of the melody; Brown plays the A sections; Sonny Rollins plays the B section |
| 01:26–01:53 | 2nd chorus: improvised trumpet solo |
| 01:53–02:20 | 3rd chorus: trumpet solo continues |
| 02:21–02:47 | 4th chorus: improvised tenor sax solo |
| 02:48–03:14 | 5th chorus: tenor sax solo continues |
| 03:15–03:40 | 6th chorus: improvised piano solo |
| 03:41–04:07 | 7th chorus: piano solo continues |
| 04:08–04:34 | 8th chorus: improvised bass solo |
| 04:35–05:01 | 9th chorus: new melody played by the trumpet and tenor in the A sections only, B section is a bass solo |
| 05:02–05:25 | 10th chorus: improvised drum solo |
| 05:26–05:48 | 11th chorus: drum solo continue |
| 05:49–06:14 | 12th chorus: trumpet and tenor sax trade 8 bars each of the form |
| 06:15–06:40 | 13th chorus: trumpet and tenor sax trade 4 bars each of the form |
| 06:41–07:05 | 14th chorus: a new melody is used for the first two A sections; B section is a drum solo; the last A section is the original melody played in the high register by the trumpet |
| 07:06–07:33 | The introduction serves as an ending |

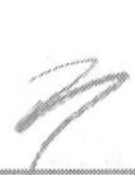

## Charles Mingus "Better Get Hit in Yo' Soul" (Charles Mingus) 1959 Chapter 15

Charles Mingus, bass; John Handy, Booker Ervin, Shafi Hadi, saxophones; Willie Dennis, Jimmy Knepper, trombones; Horace Parlan, piano; Danny Richmond, drums

*Mingus AhUm*, Columbia Records
From the album *Mingus Ah Um*, this selection showcases Mingus's blues and gospel roots in his music. It begins with Mingus playing a short bass solo and then moves into a romping 6/8 meter. The composition is in the AABA form, but the solos are based on the 12-bar blues. Listen to horn backgrounds played behind the first sax solo and the hard driving piano solo by Horace Parlan. The handclapping behind the second tenor solo is reminiscent of black church music. Typical of much Mingus' music, this piece is rough edged, loose and has a great deal of spontaneity.

| | |
|---|---|
| 00:00–00:016 | Bass introduction with piano and trombone riffs |
| 00:16–01:09 | AABA form (A=10 bars, B=8 bars): ensemble states a gospel-like melody |
| 01:09–01:25 | 12-bar blues form: improvised tenor sax solo |
| 01:25–01:41 | 2nd blues chorus: tenor sax solo continues with horn backgrounds |
| 01:42–01:58 | 3rd blues chorus: tenor sax solo continues (backgrounds stop) |
| 01:58–02:14 | 4th blues chorus: piano vamp (repetitive right hand pattern—gospel influenced "funk" style) |

| | |
|---|---|
| 02:15–02:30 | 5th blues chorus: piano vamp continues with horn backgrounds |
| 02:30–02:46 | 6th blues chorus: piano vamp continues; tenor "moans" in the background |
| 02:46–03:02 | 7th blues chorus: piano vamp continues |
| 03:02–03:18 | 8th blues chorus: new riff is introduced by the ensemble |
| 03:19–03:34 | 9th blues chorus: piano vamp continues |
| 03:34–03:50 | 10th blues chorus: band stops; improvised tenor sax solo accompanied by a 2-measure hand clapping pattern on beats 2, 5 of the first bar and 2, 3 and 5 of the second bar |
| 03:51–04:06 | 11th blues chorus: tenor sax solo continues with the hand clapping |
| 04:06–04:22 | 12th blues chorus: tenor sax solo continues with the band joining in |
| 04:22–04:37 | 13th blues chorus: tenor sax solo continues |
| 04:38–04:52 | 14th blues chorus: improvised drum solo |
| 04:53–05:09 | 15th blues chorus: band plays background riff |
| 05:09–05:25 | 16th blues chorus: band continues with background riff with tenor sax "moans" |
| 05:25–05:40 | 17th blues chorus: improvised drum solo |
| 05:40–05:56 | 18th blues chorus: more background riff |
| 05:57–06:11 | 19th blues chorus: improvised drum solo |
| 06:11–07:02 | Opening AABA melody is restated |
| 07:02–07:20 | Ending: listen for the "A-men" gospel influence |

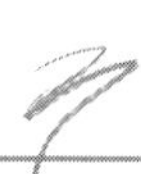

## Cannonball Adderley Quintet "This Here" (Bobby Timmons) 1960 Chapter 15

Julian (Cannonball) Adderley, alto sax; Nat Adderley, cornet; Bobby Timmons, piano; Louis Hayes, drums; Sam Jones, bass

*Cannonball Adderley Quintet Live in San Francisco,*
Riverside Records
Cannonball was a great storyteller. Listen to his opening monologue about the "roots of church music." Adderley's music was steeped in the gospel funk of hard bop. This piece, written by Bobby Timmons, is in 3/4 time. Each solo chorus begins with the piano and bass playing a repetitive figure and later moving to the traditional walking bass and drum ride figures. The form can be perceived as a 16-bar A section followed by a 16-bar B section; thus AB (although there is an extra 4 bars after each AB when the melody is played; however, not for the solos)

| | |
|---|---|
| 00:00–00:58 | Cannonball Adderley gives an explanation of the composition they are about to perform. |
| 00:59–01:21 | Introduction: Bobby Timmons plays a repetitive pattern; soon after he is joined by the bass and drums |
| 01:22–02:00 | AB form (4-bar extension): alto sax and cornet play the melody |
| 02:01–02:37 | AB form (4-bar extension): melody is restated |
| 02:38–05:24 | 3rd-7th choruses: improvised alto sax solo |
| 05:25–07:35 | 8th-11th choruses: improvised cornet solo |
| 07:36–08:07 | 12th-13th chorus: improvised piano solo |

| | |
|---|---|
| 08:08–09:13 | 14th-15th choruses: piano solo continues with background figures by the horns |
| 09:14–10:54 | 16th-17th choruses: piano solo continues |
| 10:55–11:30 | 18th chorus: melody is stated as in the beginning |
| 11:31–12:11 | 19th chorus: melody is restated |
| 12:12–12:29 | Fade out ending |

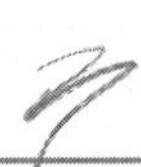

## Billie Holiday "Strange Fruit" (Abel Meeropol) 1939 Chapter 16

An early protest song against racial violence, it became a trademark for Holiday throughout the remainder of her career.

| | |
|---|---|
| 00:00–00:29 | A somber introduction more reminiscent of a funeral dirge arranged for a small combo. |
| 00:29–01:09 | The introduction continues with solo piano. |
| 01:10–3:01 | Holiday finally enters with the moving lyrics originally written by Abel Meeropol. Listen to how Holiday uses her vocal ability to achieve a maximum dramatic effect. |

## Billie Holiday "God Bless the Child" (Billie Holiday/ Arthur Herzog, Jr). 1941 Chapter 16

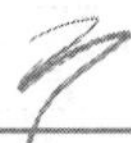

## Sarah Vaughan "Shulie a Bop" 1954 Chapter 16

John Malachai, piano; Joe Benjamin, bass; Roy Haynes, drums, Sarah Vaughan, vocals

As an accomplished jazz pianist, Sarah Vaughan used her instrumental skills to create improvised scat solos. Her remarkable voice had very few limitations. Listen to the wide range and the varied tonal qualities she uses in this short selection.

| | |
|---|---|
| 00:00–00:04 | Four bar piano/bass/drums introduction |
| 00:05–00:26 | 1st chorus: Vaughan scats |
| 00:26–00:47 | 2nd chorus: Vaughan quotes Georges Bizet's opera "Carmen" at the opening of the second chorus |
| 00:48–01:09 | 3rd chorus: Piano solo by John Malachai |
| 01:10–01:29 | 4th chorus: Bass solo by Joe Benjamin |
| 01:30–01:50 | 5th chorus: Drum solo by Roy Haynes |
| 01:51–02:10 | 6th chorus: Vaughan scats |
| 02:11–02:42 | 7th chorus; Vaughan scats adding a spontaneous ending |

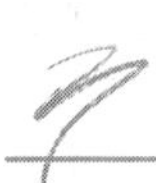

## Ella Fitzgerald "Mack the Knife" (Kurt Weill/Bertolt Brecht) 1960 Chapter 16

Paul Smith, piano; Wilfred Middlebrooks, bass, Jim Hall, guitar; Gus Johnson, drums

| | |
|---|---|
| 00:00–00:29 | Introduction with the band playing a vamp while Ella speaks to the audience; notice Ella mentions she is worried about remembering all the words. She knows she will have to remember each verse (different lyrics sung to each chorus). Listen as the key center of each chorus will move up one half step. |
| 00:29–01:49 | Ella sings the first two choruses; however, notice that her timing indicates the words are coming into her head at the last moment. |
| 01:50–03:12 | The remaining choruses are totally improvised because Ella no longer can remember the words. Therefore, she must rely on her quick wit and scatting ability to make it through the rest of the song. |
| 03:13–03:39 | In this chorus Ella's vocal quality imitates the singing of Louis Armstrong with whom she had performed many times in the 1950s. |
| 03:40–04:31 | Ella continues to improvise lyrics for the remainder of the song. |
| 04:32–04:48 | Tag |

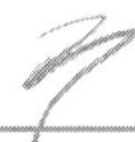

## Miles Davis "Four" (Miles Davis) 1956 Chapter 17

Miles Davis, trumpet; John Coltrane, tenor sax; Red Garland, piano; Philly Joe Jones, drums; Paul Chambers, bass

*Workin,* Prestige Records

| | |
|---|---|
| 00:00–00:11 | Introduction: drum solo |
| 00:12–00:46 | ABAC form (8 bar sections): melody is played by trumpet and tenor sax |
| 00:47–02:42 | 2nd-4th choruses: improvised solo by Miles Davis |
| 02:43–04:34 | 5th-7th choruses: improvised solo by John Coltrane |
| 04:35–05:51 | 8th-9th choruses: improvised piano solo by Red Garland |
| 05:52–06:29 | 10th chorus: Miles trades 4-bar phrases with Philly Joe Jones |
| 06:30–07:07 | 11th chorus: the melody is restate as in the beginning |
| 07:08–07:16 | Tag |

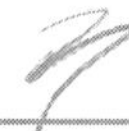

## Miles Davis "So What" (Miles Davis) 1959 Chapter 17

Miles Davis, trumpet; John Coltrane, tenor sax; Cannonball Adderley, alto sax; Paul Chambers, bass; Jimmy Cobb, drums; Bill Evans, piano

*Kind of Blue,* Columbia Records

This 32-measure AABA composition helped move jazz to another level. Miles Davis was looking for a new type of improvisational vehicle that was the antithesis of the typical bop derived music that was so prevalent. "So What" with its use of only two chords, ushered in a new approach to jazz: modal jazz. The presence of Bill Evans and John Coltrane added to the success of the recording because they were both interested in this new approach. It is interesting to note how each soloist chooses to approach this new type of composition.

| | |
|---|---|
| 00:00–00:31 | Bass and piano play a slow out of tempo intro—parts of it are in unison |
| 00:32–00:48 | Bassist plays melody on A section with piano answering |
| 00:49–01:01 | Bassist continues to play 2nd A with horns answering |
| 01:02–01:16 | B section continues with bassist playing melody |
| 01:17–01:30 | Last A section continues |
| 01:31–02:27 | 1st chorus: improvised trumpet solo by Miles Davis |
| 02:28–03:24 | 2nd chorus: trumpet solo continues |
| 03:25–04:19 | 3rd chorus: improvised tenor sax solo by John Coltrane |
| 04:20–05:16 | 4th chorus: tenor sax solo continues |
| 05:17–06:10 | 5th chorus: improvised alto solo by Cannonball Adderley |
| 06:11–07:04 | 6th chorus: alto solo continues |
| 07:05–08:02 | 7th chorus: improvised piano solo by Bill Evans with horns playing background riff |
| 08:03–08:58 | Melody is returns without the bass playing as in the beginning, but comes in 8 measures later with repeated melody to the end. |
| 08:59–09:35 | End of the form—the horns drop out and bass and piano play the repeated figure to the end |

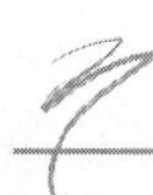

## Miles Davis "Freedom Jazz Dance" (Eddie Harris) 1966 Chapter 17

Miles Davis, trumpet; Wayne Shorter, tenor sax; Tony Williams, drums; Herbie Hancock, piano; Ron Carter, bass

*Miles Smiles,* Columbia Records
Listen carefully to the way Tony Williams plays the cymbals with his hi hat snapping on all four beat in the measure and Ron Carter playing funk inspired bass lines. This recording show that Davis, again, was not afraid to move away from traditional swing inspired jazz. Here we have Miles Davis playing "free jazz"—no preset harmonies.

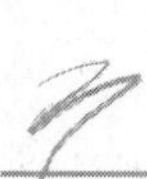

## Miles Davis "Miles Runs the Voodoo Down" (Miles Davis) 1969 Chapter 17 & 21

Miles Davis, trumpet; John McLaughlin, guitar; Bennie Maupin, bass clarinet, Wayne Shorter, soprano sax; Chick Corea, electric piano; Joe Zawinul, electric piano; Dave Holland, bass; Jack DeJohnette, drums; Don Alias, percussion; Jim Riley, percussion

*Bitches Brew,* Columbia Records
During this period Miles did not have a set group: The participants were drawn from a pool of musicians familiar with his new work. This recording was culled from many hours of "jamming" in the recording studio and was spliced together long after the musicians had left. This is not a song, per se, but a series of musical ideas executed. There is no formal structure or clear cut choruses; the musicians rely on intuition and cues from Miles. They are more concerned with improvisation based on mood, texture, rhythmic groove, and color rather than on traditional chord progressions.

| | |
|---|---|
| 00:00–00:33 | Introduction: drums and bass; later guitar is added; then bass clarinet |
| 00:34–04:16 | Miles enters with a loosely structured melody; followed by an improvisation |
| 04:17–06:13 | Improvised guitar solo by John McLaughlin; listen to his rock-influenced style |
| 06:14–08:01 | Improvised soprano sax solo by Wayne Shorter |
| 08:02–10:41 | Improvised electric keyboard solo by either Chick Corea or Joe Zawinul |
| 10:42–13:36 | Miles continues with his improvisation |
| 13:37–14:01 | Rhythm section continues without Miles until the end |

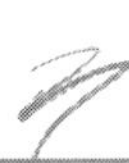

## Ornette Coleman "Congeniality" (Ornette Coleman) 1959 Chapter 18

Ornette Coleman, alto sax; Don Cherry, trumpet; Charlie Haden, bass; Billy Higgins, drums

*The Shape of Jazz to Come,* Atlantic Records

## Ornette Coleman "Lonely Woman" (Ornette Coleman)1959 Chapter 18

Ornette Coleman, alto sax; Don Cherry, trumpet; Charlie Haden, bass; Billy Higgins, drums

*The Shape of Jazz to Come,* Atlantic Records

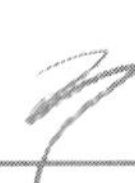

## Ornette Coleman "Change of the Century" (Ornette Coleman) 1960 Chapter 18

Ornette Coleman, alto sax; Don Cherry, trumpet; Charlie Haden, bass; Billy Higgins, drums

*Change of the Century,* Atlantic Records

By the time of this recording, Ornette Coleman and his Quartet were confident they were pioneering an approach to jazz that was the most significant of the twentieth century. Listen for the absence of harmony and a complete emphasis on melody. In addition, the role of the bass player is no longer relegated to simply walking bass lines. An uninterrupted, steady beat is very much in question as well.

| | |
|---|---|
| 00:00-00:28 | AABA melody presented—the notes are played at an extremely fast pace making the melody difficult to process. |
| 00:28-02:29 | Improvised alto sax solo—the AABA form no longer serves as the basis—both form and steady time are abandoned. Charlie Haden sometimes uses the bow; at other times he walks a fast line. |
| 02:30-4:10 | Improvised trumpet solo |
| 04:11-04:40 | AABA melody is restated |

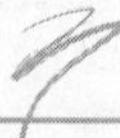

## Cecil Taylor "Tales (8 Wisps)" (Cecil Taylor) 1966 Chapter 18

Cecil Taylor, piano; Henry Grimes, bass; Alan Silva, bass; Andrew Cyrille, drums

*Unit Structures,* Blue Note Records
This recording demonstrates nontraditional ways of playing an instrument. Taylor's approach to the piano is percussive at times; he will not only use his fingers but also his fists and elbows. Henry Grimes bows the bass in the uppermost register or plucks the strings below the bridge. Andrew Cyrille uses the drums to create texture rather than steady rhythms. Cecil Taylor's music can be shocking to those who are not open to new and different ideas. However, he had a liberating effect on many jazz musicians of the 1960s.

## Eric Dolphy "Hat and Beard" (Eric Dolphy) 1964 Chapter 18

Eric Dolphy, alto sax; Freddie Hubbard, trumpet; Bobby Hutcherson, vibraphone; Richard Davis, bass; Tony Williams, drums

*Out to Lunch,* Blue Note Records

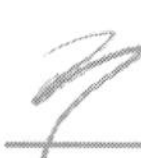

## Bill Evans "Autumn Leaves" (Joseph Kosma) 1960 Chapter 19

Bill Evans, piano; Scott LaFaro, bass; Paul Motian, drums

*Portrait in Jazz,* Riverside Records
This recording is definitive by virtue of the obvious exchange of ideas occurring especially during the first three choruses. It's as though the three musicians are having a musical conversation. Although the casual listener might think the 2nd and 3rd chorus ignore the tune's structure, all three players have an equal exchange of ideas (conversation-like) while maintaining strict adherence to the structure.

| | |
|---|---|
| 00:00–00:08 | Introduction |
| 00:08–00:47 | AABC form—LaFaro plays small melodic ideas in the first two A sections; then walks a more typical bass line in the B section (00:28—the C section ends with a stop time break in the last two bars to launch an 8 bar bass solo. |
| 00:47–01:24 | 2nd chorus: 8-bar bass solo; then piano enters at the 2nd A section (00:56); then drums enter at the B section (01:06). All exchange ideas (have a musical conversation). |
| 01:25–02:02 | 3rd chorus: the "musical conversation" continues |
| 02:02–02:39 | 4th chorus: Paul Motian changes from brushes to drum sticks and the trio plays in a more normal fashion (bass walks; drums play time; piano improvises a solo). |
| 02:40–03:16 | 5th chorus: piano solo continues |
| 03:17–03:53 | 6th chorus: piano solo continues |
| 03:54–04:30 | 7th chorus: piano solo continues |

| | |
|---|---|
| 04:31–05:07 | 8th chorus: The trio returns to the exchange of ideas as in the 2nd and 3rd chorus; drums drop out at the B section: then piano drops out at the C section leaving a bass solo; thus the trio reverses the order of entry in the 2nd chorus. |
| 05:08–05:45 | 9th chorus: restatement of the melody |
| 05:46–05:59 | Tag or ending |

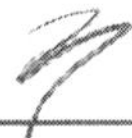

## Bill Evans "Waltz for Debbie" (Bill Evans) 1961 Chapter 19

Bill Evans, piano; Scott LaFaro, bass; Paul Motian, drums

*Live at the Village Vanguard,* Riverside Records

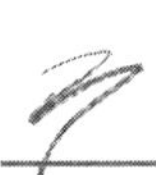

## Bill Evans "Nobody Else But Me" (Jerome Kern) 1978 Chapter 19

Bill Evans, acoustic piano and electric piano

*New Conversations, Warner Brothers*

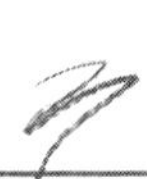

## John Coltrane "Giant Steps" (John Coltrane) 1959 Chapter 20

John Coltrane, tenor sax; Tommy Flanagan, piano; Art Taylor, drums; Paul Chambers, bass

*Giant Steps,* Atlantic Records

"Giant Steps" is the epitome of complex hard bop composition. It is a short 16-measure work best conceived as an 8-bar A section followed by an 8-bar B section; however, the harmony moves so quickly that it is one of the most challenging jazz compositions ever written and has become a "test" piece for jazz musicians worldwide. Coltrane was infatuated with devising new and unusual chord progressions and had been working on this particular progression for months, consequently when he recorded "Giant Steps" he was very comfortable improvising over the form. The pianist, Tommy Flanagan, was not so familiar with this challenging composition—he had great difficulty playing through the progression and eventually gives up in the middle of his solo, before Coltrane comes back in for two more choruses. Coltrane's improvisation uses digital patterns based upon specific notes in each chord (1-2-3-5). Coltrane also used this particular harmonic formula on a number of compositions in the late 1950s and early 1960s.

| | |
|---|---|
| 00:00–00:26 | 1st and 2nd choruses: Coltrane plays the melody |
| 00:27–02:53 | 3rd-13th choruses: improvised tenor sax solo |
| 02:53–03:44 | 14th-17th choruses: improvised piano solo by Tommy Flanagan |
| 03:44–04:09 | 18th-19th choruses: more tenor sax improvisation |
| 04:10–04:35 | 20th-21st choruses: melody is restated |
| 04:35–04:46 | Ending: tenor sax cadenza |

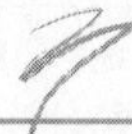

## John Coltrane "Naima" (John Coltrane) 1959 Chapter 20

John Coltrane, tenor sax; Wynton Kelly, piano; Jimmy Cobb, drums; Paul Chambers, bass

*Giant Steps,* Atlantic Records
"Naima" is one of Coltrane's most famous compositions from the album *Giant Steps*. It is a 32-measure AABA form ballad. The harmonies move slowly and the performance features a technique performed by the bassist referred to as pedal point. Listen carefully to the bassist and you will hear that he keeps repeating the same note over and over while the harmonies change above it. This technique will play an important role in many of Coltrane's compositions and performances post-1960. It gives the music a "floating" quality. The only improvised solo is from the pianist, Wynton Kelly. Coltrane would later record this composition numerous times.

| | |
|---|---|
| 00:00–01:22 | AABA form (8-bar sections): Coltrane states the melody |
| 01:23–02:47 | 2nd chorus: improvised piano solo by Wynton Kelly |
| 02:48–03:38 | 3rd chorus (only BA): Coltrane states the melody starting from the B section |
| 03:39–04:23 | Ending: the last phrase is repeated three times followed by a concluding phrase. |

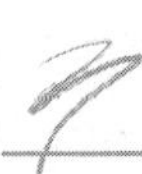

## John Coltrane "My Favorite Things" (Richard Rogers) 1960 Chapter 20

John Coltrane, soprano sax; Jimmy Garrison, bass; Elvin Jones, drums; McCoy Tyner, piano

*My Favorite Things,* Atlantic Records
This is an important album as well as a major turning point for Coltrane's music. This album introduced his new quartet, and on this particular track, a new approach to playing. At over 13 minutes in length "My Favorite Things" was one of the first long tracks released on an album. The 3/4 meter, modal nature (alternating between the dorian and ionian modes), and pedal bass figures ushered in a new era for Coltrane. Much of his music post-1960 featured this swaying hypnotic-like feel with long experimental improvisations. This music, together with Ornette Coleman's music, initiated a departure from structured choruses for improvisation, bebop style melodies, and strict adherence to present harmonies.

| | |
|---|---|
| 00:00–00:18 | Rhythm section introduction: Listen to McCoy Tyner's drone in the bass register followed by modal piano voicings. |
| 00:19–02:20 | Coltrane states the melody on soprano sax—he is not afraid to ornament the melody. Unlike the original version by Rodgers and Hammerstein, interludes are included between phrases and some of the original melody is not present. |
| 02:20–07:01 | Improvised piano solo by McCoy Tyner; it is an unusual jazz solo for the time since he mostly plays harmony and only plays melody when he wants to move between minor and major tonalities. This solo uses much repetition creating an almost meditative effect. |
| 07:02–07:27 | Coltrane returns with a shortened statement of the melody. |
| 07:28–12:16 | Improvised soprano sax solo; Coltrane also uses a short phrase of the melody (09:43) to initiate a change from minor to major tonality. |
| 12:17–12:54 | The melody is restated beginning with major tonality; this time the rest of the original song is included. |
| 12:55–13:45 | Coltrane improvises to the end. |

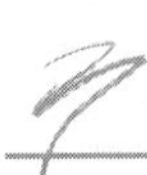

## John Coltrane "Acknowledgment" (John Coltrane) 1965 Chapter 20

John Coltrane, tenor sax; Jimmy Garrison, bass; Elvin Jones, drums; McCoy Tyner, piano

*A Love Supreme,* Impulse Records
As Coltrane performed in the mid 1960s his music began to take on more spiritual or perhaps meditative qualities. The result was his suite entitled *A Love Supreme.* "Acknowledgement" is the first part of the four-part suite. This movement is not a highly structured work and reflects his interest in free form playing. There are unifying factors, but this is not a 32-measure AABA form. Coltrane improvises on a theme until he has exhausted his ideas. In a live performance he might have improvised for 30 minutes or more.

| | |
|---|---|
| 00:00–00:31 | Introduction: Coltrane improvises over one basic harmony; time is suspended-there is no steady beat |
| 00:32–01:03 | The main theme (4-note motive) is stated by Jimmy Garrison; Elvin Jones plays an Afro-Cuban style rhythm; McCoy Tyner comps using quartal voicings (based on the interval of a 4th) |
| 01:04–04:39 | Coltrane enters on tenor sax with his own them and then moves into an improvisation based on his theme. |
| 04:40–04:53 | Coltrane winds down his solo |
| 04:54–06:04 | Coltrane plays the 4-note motive—alternating between the high and low registers |
| 06:05–06:42 | Coltrane sings (or chants) the 4-note motive to the words "a love supreme" |
| 06:42–07:19 | Vocal ends and the rhythm section gradually reduces the intensity level |
| 07:20–07:43 | Ending: Jimmy Garrison improvises on the 4-note motive by himself |

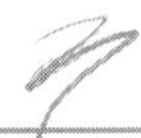

## Chick Corea "Spain" (Chick Corea) 1972 Chapter 21

Chick Corea, piano; Flora Purim, vocals: Joe Farrell, flute; Stanley Clarke, bass; Airto Moreira, percussion

*Light as a Feather,* Polydor Records
Although Miles Davis had already been using electric piano in his fusion bands of the late 1960s, this recording established it as a standard instrument that could hold its own with its acoustic counterpart as well as any other jazz instrument capable of producing convincing solos. In addition, *Spain* became another important example of the integration occurring between jazz and Latin styles of music.

| | |
|---|---|
| 00:00–01:14 | Slow introduction: taken from Gil Evans/Miles Davis *Sketches of Spain* (an arrangement of Rodrigo's *Concerto for Guitar and Orchestra*)—electric piano and bass played with a bow. |
| 01:15–01:42 | Interlude: this section will serve to separate the main melody from either the introduction or the improvised solos—listen to the timbre created by the combined electric piano and flute along with wordless vocals. |
| 01:43–02:08 | Interlude is repeated. |
| 02:08–02:29 | ABC form—24-bar melody arranged in 8-bar sections, no section is repeated. |
| 02:30–02:46 | Interlude |

| | |
|---|---|
| 02:47–04:32 | Improvised flute solo for 5 choruses (3rd chorus— 03:08, 4th chorus – 03:29, 5th chorus—03:50, 6th chorus—04:11) |
| 04:32–04:53 | 7th chorus—ABC melody |
| 05:54–05:11 | Interlude |
| 05:11–06:57 | Improvised solo for 5 choruses (9th chorus— 05:32, 10th chorus—05:53, 11th chorus—06:14, 12th chorus—06:35) |
| 06:57–07:17 | 13th chorus—ABC melody |
| 07:18–07:34 | Interlude |
| 07:35–08:35 | Improvised bass solo for 3 choruses (15th chorus— 07:55, 16th chorus—08:16) |
| 08:36–08:57 | 17th chorus—ABC melody |
| 08:58–08:29 | Interlude |
| 08:30–09:50 | Ending |

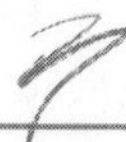

## Chick Corea "The Magician" (Chick Corea) 1976 Chapter 21

Chick Corea, piano; Al Demiola, guitar; Stanley Clarke, bass; Lenny White, drums

*Romantic Warrior,* Columbia Records

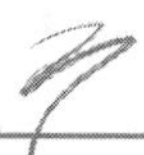

## Chick Corea "Gotta Match" (Chick Corea) 1986 Chapter 21

Chick Corea, piano; John Patitucci, bass; Dave Weckl, drums

*The Electric Band,* GRP Records

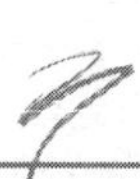

## Herbie Hancock "Maiden Voyage" (Herbie Hancock) 1965 Chapter 21

Herbie Hancock, piano; Freddie Hubbard, trumpet; George Coleman, tenor sax; Ron Carter, bass; Tony Williams, drums

*Maiden Voyage,* Blue Note Records

This is one of the best examples of modal jazz from the mid 1960s. This was Mile Davis's rhythm section without Miles. "Maiden Voyage" has become a jazz standard and is easily one of the most recognizable Hancock compositions. It is a 32-measure AABA form. The rhythm section does not play in a traditional swing style, but relies on even eighth notes. Pay close attention to Tony Williams' use of the cymbals in the recording and the way Hancock accompanies the soloists.

| | |
|---|---|
| 00:00–00:15 | Introduction |
| 00:16–01:19 | AABA form: melody played by trumpet and tenor sax; the drummer concentrates his time on the cymbals and the bassist plays a repetitive figure throughout the performance. Hancock plays colorful voicings on the piano to help create a "mood." |
| 01:20–02:22 | Tenor sax solo chorus |

| | |
|---|---|
| 02:23–04:23 | Two trumpet solo choruses |
| 04:24–05:23 | 1st piano solo chorus |
| 05:24–06:22 | 2nd piano solo chorus |
| 06:23–07:25 | The melody returns as in the beginning |
| 07:26–end | Ending: Freddie Hubbard trills a note and fades out |

## Herbie Hancock "Chameleon" (Herbie Hancock) 1974 Chapter 21

Herbie Hancock, keyboards; Bennie Maupin, tenor sax; Paul Jackson, bass; Harvey Mason, drums

*Headhunters,* Columbia Records
"Chameleon" is from one of Hancock's best selling albums. It shows the influence of pop/funk dance rhythms. Hancock, as well as Miles Davis, was well aware of changes in African-American popular music and this track shows the influence of Sly (and the Family) Stone. Hancock is a master of the use of keyboard synthesizers and uses them to create thick textures and great musical color. This track was a very successful crossover hit played on jazz as well as popular music radio stations.

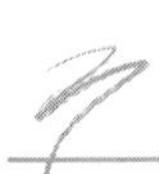

## Weather Report "Surucucu" (Wayne Shorter) 1972 Chapter 21

Jo Zawinul, keyboards; Wayne Shorter, soprano sax; Miroslav Vitous, electric bass; Eric Gravatt, drums; Don Um Romao, percussion

*I Sing the Body Electric,* Columbia Records
Weather Report was the most original and innovative of the 1970s fusion bands. This recording features the percussionist prominently. Romao uses a wide variety of percussion instruments, whistles, wooden flutes, and his voice to create a complex texture of sound and rhythm. Zawinul's masterful use of electronic keyboards creates another level of percussive texture and color. The line between solo and accompaniment is not clear and the performance is truly collective. The piece is broken into several sections and does not adhere to strict formal structure the way bebop did. It was recorded live at a concert in Tokyo, Japan.

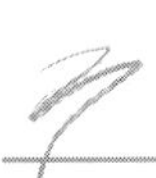

## Weather Report "Havona" (Jaco Pastorius) 1977 Chapter 21

Jo Zawinul, keyboards; Wayne Shorter, soprano sax; Jaco Pastorius, electric bass; Alex Acuna, drums

*Heavy Weather,* Columbia Records

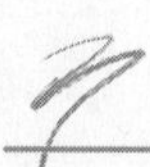

## Jaco Pastorius "Portrait of Tracy" 1976 (Jaco Pastorius) Chapter 21

Jaco Pastorius, electric bass

*Jaco Pastorius,* Epic Records
This recording is a bass solo performed on a fretless electric bass. Jaco uses harmonics and his incredible ability to generate clean and pure double stops in this appealing song he composed. In fact, it was so attractive that twenty-four years later, it hit the top 40 charts when SWV (Sisters With Voices) used it as the basis for their hit song "Rain." No one else has made such an impact on the bass.

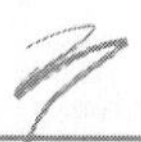

## Keith Jarrett "Margot" 1967 (Keith Jarrett) Chapter 21

Keith Jarrett, piano; Charlie Haden, bass; Paul Motian, drums

*Life Between the Exit Signs,* Atlantic Records
This recording demonstrates Jarrett as a master pianist and improviser. He truly has no technical limitations and can immediately react to his drummer and bassist in the "Bill Evans 1960s Trio" manner of an exchange of ideas between each member of a trio. Jarrett's sense of touch and color betray both his jazz and classical background.

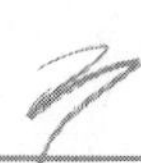

## Pat Metheny "Third Wind" (Pat Metheny) 1987 Chapter 21

Pat Metheny, acoustic and electric guitars, guitar synthesizers; Lyle Mays, keyboards; Steve Rodby, acoustic and electric bass; Paul Wertico, drums; Armando Marcal, percussion, voice

*Still Life (talking),* Nonesuch Records

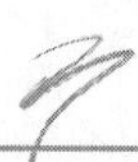

## Michael Brecker "Nothing Personal" (Don Grolnick) 1987 Chapter 21 & 22

Michael Brecker, tenor sax; Kenny Kirkland, piano; Pat Metheny, guitar; Charlie Haden, bass; Jack DeJohnette, drums

*Michael Brecker,* Impulse Records
This recording is a highlight performance by one of the most important post–John Coltrane tenor saxophone stylists since 1970. Brecker's sound and approach to playing functions as a model for other saxophonists of the late twentieth and early twenty-first centuries.

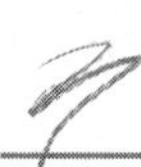

## Dave Douglas "Red Emma" (Dave Douglas) 1997 Chapter 22

Dave Douglas, trumpet; Brad Shepik, guitar; Jim Black, drums

*Tiny Bell Trio,* Songlines Recordings
Trumpeter and composer Dave Douglas is one of the most inventive musicians in music today. His music spans many genres and he is capable of playing and writing in almost any idiom. The Tiny Bell Trio is one of the groups he directs and plays with. The music here is of a distinctly eastern European flavor and is reminiscent of klezmer music. It may be due to his long association with saxophonist and composer John Zorn. His music is more typical of the twenty-first century "jazz" musician who borrows sounds from other idioms and cultures, and blends them into new and fresh music.

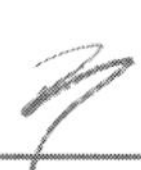

## Groove Collective "Jay Wrestles the Bari Constrictor, Part 2/Nightwaves" 1996 Chapter 22

*We the People,* Impulse Records
This ten-member group led by Josh Roseman blends, funk, free, new age, soul, Caribbean music, and many other styles in an original and energetic manner. This multisection piece shows the depth and diversity of the group and makes the recording feel like a jam session.

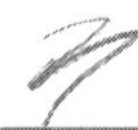

## Us3 "Cantaloop" (Flip Fantasia) 1993 Chapter 22

Geoff Wilkinson, producer

*Hand on the Torch,* Blue Note Records-Parlaphone
"Cantaloop" is a good example of blending jazz with rap, sampling, digital looping, and acid jazz to produce an altogether unique sound. It is based on Herbie Hancock's composition, "Cantaloupe Island," recorded on Blue Note Records in the mid 1960s. By having jazz musicians play over Hancock's tracks, they acknowledged the past and looked to the future. This track was a big hit in dance clubs all over the world in the mid 1990s.